'The over-Turner', sneered a facetious academic critic of the day – right for the wrong reasons. For his younger contemporaries accepted Turner as a technical revolutionary, as a prophetic visionary. Certainly he anticipated much in twentieth century painting, from impressionism to abstract colour experimentation. And his fans have admired, ever since, most of the right works for most of the right reasons.

'Odd then, that old J.M.W.T. has been so ill-served by biographers and, until lately, by critics. In his new critical biography Mr. Jack Lindsay – having first marinaded himself in all the arts of the period, as is his wont – does some salutary overturning of primary sources before emerging with a lively and credible full-length portrait'

The Observer

A Critical Biography by

Jack Lindsay

Turner

His Life and Work

A PANTHER BOOK

GRANADA

London Toronto Sydney New York

Published by Granada Publishing Limited in 1973
Reprinted 1975, 1981

ISBN 0 586 03852 3

First published in Great Britain by
Adams and Dart Ltd, and in the USA
by New York Graphic Society 1966
Copyright © 1966 Jack Lindsay

Granada Publishing Limited
Frogmore, St Albans, Herts AL2 2NF
and
36 Golden Square, London W1R 4AH
866 United Nations Plaza, New York, NY 10017, USA
117 York Street, Sydney, NSW 2000, Australia
100 Skyway Avenue, Rexdale, Ontario, M9W 3A6, Canada
61 Beach Road, Auckland, New Zealand

Printed and bound in Great Britain by
Cox & Wyman Ltd, Reading
Set in Monotype Times

Granada ®
Granada Publishing ®

Contents

List of Illustrations   6
Foreword   7
1 Childhood and Early Youth   11
2 Apprentice Years   26
3 Associate of the Royal Academy   40
4 The World of Art   57
5 The World of Poetry   72
6 Academician   88
7 Cataclysm and the Earthly Paradise   110
8 Pause and Renewed Stress   127
9 Hannibal Crosses the Alps   146
10 Personal Crisis   161
11 Politics and Symbolism   177
12 Gathering Strength   191
13 Italian Light   207
14 The Fires of Colour   224
15 The Sea of Blood   239
16 The 'Forties   252
17 The Theory of Colour   271
18 Last Days   283
Notes   291
Appendices   345
1 Opinions on Wilson   345
2 Akenside, Thomson, and the Earthly Paradise   348
3 Turner and the Industrial Scene   350
4 Turner and his Fellow Artists   351
5 Varnishing Days   353
6 Turner and his Art   355
7 Engravings   356
8 Turner and Money   362
9 Letter of Evelina Dupuis   363
Bibliography   367
Index   375

List of Illustrations

J. M. W. Turner, after a drawing by George Dance dated 31 March 1800

Sandycombe Lodge, Twickenham, engraving after W. Havell

Frosty Morning exhibited 1813

Nude study. Watercolour, c. 1811

Turner varnishing a picture at the Royal Academy, after the painting by T. Fearnley

Lovers in moonlight (East Cowes Castle), 1821. Crayon and white chalk

Old man and children. Pen and ink

Sketchbook study for *Crossing the Brook*. Ink and wash

FOREWORD

THIS book originated from a study of Turner's verses and a realization that in them lay many essential clues to his development and his views on life and art. I put forward some ideas on this subject in an essay in *Life and Letters* as far back as 1947; and this essay I may claim as pioneering in the modern understanding of Turner. It was followed by Ann L. Livermore's valuable essay on the relation of Turner and Thomson in 1957. In the past few years there has been work by J. Ziff and J. Gage; and at the same time a deepening in the general appreciation of Turner's art by such writers as Rothenstein and Butlin, Clare, Kenneth Clark, A. Stokes, Kitson, and others. A collection of Turner's verse has been edited by myself under the title of *The Sunset Ship* (Scorpion Press, 1966).

It was while working on the verses and going systematically through the sketchbooks that I realized what a far-reaching key to Turner's mind had been lying unused in full view of scholars and critics; and I set about the composition of the present book. Some while back C. Lewis Hind observed, "The Turner sketch-books are as valuable in their way as, say, a discovery of diaries kept by Shakespeare from the day he first left Stratford to the hour he returned home full of honour and wisdom." There was far more truth in his words than he meant. For he was thinking mainly of the way in which the sketchbooks help us to see how Turner worked from rough sketches into finished pictures; but with their scribbles in prose and verse they also afford us precious glimpses of his deepest reactions in thought and emotion, as well as showing us many of his experimental activities. This book is the first to make anything like a thorough use of their revelations.

It is generally agreed that Turner has been unfortunate in his biographers, "Astonishing as it is," observed Sir John Rothenstein, "there is to this day not even a biography of him that is both reliable and organized as a readable Life." There are only three works that need mentioning: those of Thornbury, Falk, and Finberg. Thornbury's *Life* of 1862 has the sad distinction of a claim to being the most confused, haphazard, and slovenly work of biography in our language. While it does include some reminiscences of much interest, such as those of Trimmer or Mayall, Thornbury himself contributes nothing but misunderstanding and disorder. A writer in the *Times Literary Supplement* in July 1963 remarked, "Later biographers no longer had access to the sources from which he drew, and misused, information. They were in the predicament of being forced to refer to him and unable to trust him. Conscientiously the poet and critic William Cosmo Monkhouse set about the task in the 1890s of 'reducing the known facts about Turner to something like order', though the little book he produced was still overshadowed, as others have been, by the purple cloud of Ruskin's prose and Thornbury's dismal and tainted smog." In 1938 Falk published his pedestrian work, which remained throughout on a trivial journalistic level. The reason for referring to it here lies in the fact that it collected some useful information about Sarah Danby and Mrs. Booth, and clearly differentiated between Sarah and Hannah Danby. One of the causes of the biographers' distaste for Turner's personal life derived from their confusion between the two women, Hannah (at least in her last years) being described as a strange musty hag. (Even Greig in his edition of Farington's *Diary* falls into this confusion.)

An error, however, into which Falk himself was led by taking Thornbury at his face-value may be noted here. He built up a plausible case for the existence of an illegitimate son, Hugh Danby, borne by Sarah. The only definite evidence for Hugh came from Thornbury's version of the Chancery decision (ii, 294). The suit is there cited as being carried on by Henry Scott Trimmer and the other executors against Hugh Danby and the various relations of Turner who contested the will. Certainly a Hugh Danby who did not appear in the will or codicils, yet was admitted to such a prominent position in the decision, would seem to have had an important kinship claim. However, the original document in the Public Records Office shows that "Hugh" was an error in transcription by Thornbury. The person named was the housekeeper Hannah, who had various claims on Turner's estate. Thornbury had had his eye caught by the Hugh in Munro's name among the executors, and thus carelessly made the mistake on which Falk built his suppositions.

Finally in 1939 Finberg produced his massive volume, but in his reaction against Thornbury he kept almost entirely to the definite external facts of Turner's artistic career. "To start again, without prepossessions and prejudgements, as if 'embarking on a voyage of discovery', was the aim of the late A. J. Finberg", wrote the critic cited above. "He devoted himself to bringing together all the facts that could yet be obtained in the form of a monumental 'Chronicle-biography'. As a scholarly researcher, compiler and chronicler, Finberg did an excellent job. His *Life of Turner* is the one reliable source-book we have. In his reaction, however, against eloquence and error, he also excluded any pretension to literary art . . . Finberg left the evidence to speak for itself. Yet evidence never does so entirely; otherwise there would be no need for advocates."

But he also halted his voyage of discovery sharply at the outer edge of anything connected with Turner's personal life. Even if the Danbys and Mrs. Booth had played only a domestic role, they were closely bound up with Turner over large periods of his life; yet Finberg disposes of them in a few lines Because of his aversion from them he runs into errors even in those sparse passages. He could not bear to examine at all the evidence about Turner's Chelsea years, mentioned an unreliable statement by Leopold Martin but ignored Turner's visit to Etty in September 1846 and the Chelsea rate-books. Unable to escape Farington's comment on Sarah's living with Turner in 1809, he wrote, "She remained in Turner's employ as housekeeper for the remainder of his life, and her children came to be regarded by the gossips as Turner's offspring . . . There is no evidence to suggest that Mrs. Danby was anything more than a housekeeper." But there is no evidence to suggest she was ever his housekeeper at all. The first sentence in Finberg's comment could only have been written if he confused Sarah with Hannah; his index even suggests that she was at Turner's funeral. He does not mention that her children consisted of three girls, daughters of John Danby, whom Turner never mentioned in his Will or codicils, and two, who were not John Danby's, and to whom he made bequests –

one of them herself claiming to be Turner's daughter: a claim implicitly accepted in the Chancery action after his death. Finberg even cut Turner's letters to Holworthy when he thought they grew a little too warm on the subject of women.

It is unpleasant to be forced to make these comments on a man to whom every writer on Turner must owe a great debt and who certainly provided in general the firm structure which is quite lacking in Thornbury's quagmire. The debt that this book owes him will be apparent in the Notes; but no one has ever claimed that his work is a satisfactory biography.

JACK LINDSAY

I should like to thank the following for their help: the Keeper of the Print Department, British Museum; Martin Butlin of the Tate Gallery; C. W. M. Turner of Frognal, Hampstead; the Essex County Librarian; W. R. Maidment, Librarian for Highgate; C. Edwards, Librarian for Chelsea; Ann L. Livermore; Prof. J. Ziff; Dr. R. D. Gray (for his paper on Turner and Goethe); C. L. Robertson of the Foreign Office Library; and R. F. Drewery of the Kingston-upon-Hull Public Library.

Chapter One

Childhood and Early Youth

On 27 August 1773 William Turner and Mary Marshall were married by the curate in St. Paul's Church, Covent Garden. William was 28 years old, and Mary 34. The pair seem to have been in a hurry; for earlier that month a special licence had been obtained and William was a thrifty fellow who did not like unnecessary expenses. A barber, he had come to London from South Molton in Devon, where he had been born on 29 June 1745. We can trace the line back to John Turner, saddler, of South Molton, who in 1739 married Rebecca Knight and died in early 1765. His will of 1760 shows that he did not own much wealth; he left his eldest son "all my working tools and my best suit of cloathes and my best hatt and wig"; William, the second son, got a white coat; and all five sons and two daughters were bequeathed a guinea each on reaching the age of 21; the rest of his "goods and chattels and money" (value not stated) went to his wife, who survived him by thirty-seven years.

Mary's father was William Marshall, who had married Sarah, daughter of Joseph Mallord, citizen and butcher of St. Mary, Islington. In his will Marshall is described as salesman of the same district. He had four children: a boy, Joseph Mallord William, who became a butcher at Brentford, and three girls, of whom the eldest married a curate. Mary was the second daughter, with a younger sister Ann.

The Marshall family were thus superior in social status to the Turners; and perhaps the haste of Mary's marriage came from some opposition on their part. She was already 34 and may well have considered William Turner her last chance. Joseph Mallord on his death left several houses, including four at Wapping, with some land, to his wife: directing that, on her death, they were to go to his daughter Sarah and then to her son, the butcher. On the latter's death they were to be divided among the testator's three granddaughters, one of whom was our Mary. So, when the butcher died in 1820 Mary's son inherited his mother's share.

Her pride in her family can be read in the names given to her son, born on 23 April 1775, St. George's Day: Joseph Mallord William Turner. The place of birth was 21 Maiden Lane, Covent Garden, where William had become joint-tenant with Elizabeth Hawkes in June 1773, though the premises were rated as a single property. In 1774 the building was divided, the woman being responsible for No. 20 and William for 21: except for the basement, which from about 1730 had been used as a tavern, *The Cider-cellar*. A tract, *Adventures underground*, of 1750, has some account of this odd "midnight concert-room", which has remained famous as the haunt of the scholar Richard Porson. Timbs writes: "We remember the place not many years after Porson's death [in 1808] when it was, as its name implies, in the basement, to which you descended by a ladder to the concert-room, which, in another house, would have been the kitchen, or the cellar; and the fittings of the place were rude and rough."[1]

No. 21 also held an auction-room which a previous tenant had let to the Free Society of Artists for their annual shows in 1775 and 1776; and in 1769 an offshoot, the Incorporated Society of Artists, had hired "Moreing's late Auction Room" for their school of painting, drawing, and modelling. For three years they had their classes there, lectures on anatomy and the "nature and properties of Color", and meetings of directors or fellows. Among the young artists who attended were Romney, Wheatley, H. Walton, Ozias Humphrey, and Farington. Then the Society got into money troubles, and the easels, casts, and other paraphernalia had been removed a little over six months before the Turners took the house over. At this time Covent Garden was a fashionable quarter, known for its perruquiers or hairdressers, its dealers in articles of dress and personal adornment; in shopping hours the streets were crowded with carriages. Perruquiers were thick in Tavistock Street and Henrietta Street, but also in Maiden Lane. There stood the sign of *The White Perruque*, at which Voltaire once lodged. William Turner seems to have been a capable barber, who dressed wigs, shaved beards, and waited on gentlemen of the Garden at their own houses.

On Lady Day 1776 his name is not found among the Lane's ratepayers; but the family cannot have moved far. A daughter Mary Ann, born in 1778, was christened on 6 September at the same church of Covent Garden as her brother had been. She died in her eighth year, when the latter would have been almost 11, and was buried in church on 20 March 1786. The register described her as "from St. Martin in the Fields".

The children had had ample time to come to know one another; and the death must have affected the boy. He was sent (we learn from E. Bell, an engraver) to his uncle at Brentford "in consequence of a fit of illness". Whether the illness was his own or his sister's is not made clear; but his parents were evidently afraid for his health. His butcher uncle lived on the north side of Brentford market-place, next to an old inn, *The White Horse*.²

The boy attended the Free School as a day-boarder. The master was John White, and the school of some fifty boys and ten girls stood in the High Street. Turner must have kept pleasant memories; for later he used to like visiting Trimmer at Heston, "not merely for the fishing and fresh air, but because Mr. Trimmer was an old friend and a lover of art, and because he was close to his old school at Brentford Butts, now a public-house, exactly opposite the Three Pigeons". Trimmer's son tells how "in his way to and from that seat of learning, he amused himself by drawing with a piece of chalk on the walls the figures of cocks and hens. I have authority for this anecdote; it was told by Turner himself to my father".³ He is said to have coloured plates, some seventy, at twopence each, in Boswell's *Antiquities of England and Wales*, for a distillery foreman.⁴

How long the boy Turner stayed at Brentford we do not know; Thornbury says about a year. But this period in a country town, set on a river, was certainly of great importance in his development. He came to know the reaches of the upper Thames in the neighbourhood, walked about Putney

and Twickenham, and stared across serene and spacious
meadowland, paddock or park, with tree clumps and stately
mansion entries, the chestnut avenue of Bushey Park, the iron
gates and carved pillars, the terraces of Hampton Court;
reedy shores with swans and green nooks, the river in its
many moods, reflecting cattle and summer elms. When he
came to build a house of his own he chose Twickenham for
the setting.

Against this rich and quiet country scene we must set the
rowdy townscape in which the boy had grown up. Ruskin has
described incomparably well the impact of London: Turner's
"foregrounds had always a succulent cluster or two of green-
grocery at the corners. Enchanted oranges gleam in Covent
Garden of the Hesperides; and great ships go to pieces in
order to scatter chests of them on the waves. That mist of
early sunbeams in the London dawn crosses, many and many
a time, the clearness of Italian air; and by Thames' shore,
with its stranded barges and glidings of red sail, dearer to us
than Lucerne lake or Venetian lagoon, – by Thames' shore
we will die." Turner was never afraid of bringing dingy odd-
ments into his works, "smoke, soot, dust, and dusty texture;
old sides of boots, weedy roadside vegetation, dunghills,
straw-yards, and all the spillings and strains of every common
labour. And more than this, he could not only endure, but
enjoyed and looked for *litter*, like Covent Garden wreck
after the market. His pictures are often full of it, from side to
side; his foregrounds differ from all others in the natural way
the things have of lying about in them. Even his richest
vegetation, in ideal work, is confused; and he delights in
shingle, *débris*, and heaps of fallen stone. The last words he
ever spoke to me about a picture were in gentle exultation
about his St. Gothard: 'That litter of stones which I en-
deavoured to represent.' "

From his London life he gained his insight into the changes
steadily coming over the world into which he had been born.
Unlike country-bred Reynolds and Gainsborough, with their
ingrained respect for the squire and his values, he "perceived
the younger squire in other aspects about his lane, occurring
prominently in its night-scenery, as a dark figure, or as one of
two, against the moonlight" – that is, drunken or whoring.
"He saw also the working of city-commerce, from endless

warehouses, towering over Thames, to the back shop in the lane, with its stale herrings – highly interesting, these last; one of his father's best friends, whom he afterwards visited affectionately at Bristol, being a fishmonger and glue-boiler; which gives us a friendly turn of mind towards herring-fishing, whaling, Calais poissardes, and many other of our choicest subjects in after life; all this being connected with that mysterious forest below London bridge on one side; – and on the other, with those masses of human power and national wealth which weigh upon us, at Covent Garden here, with strange compression, and crush us into narrow Handcourt. 'That mysterious forest below London Bridge' – better for the boy than wood of pine or grove of myrtle. How he must have tormented the watermen, beseeching them to let him crouch anywhere in their bows, quiet as a log, so that only he might get floated down there among the ships, and by the ships, and under the ships, staring and clambering; – these the only quite beautiful thing in all the world, except the sky; but these, when the sun is on their sails, filling or falling, endlessly disordered by sway of tide and stress of anchorage, beautiful unspeakably; which ships also are inhabited by glorious creatures – redfaced sailors, with pipes, appearing over the gunwales, true knights, over their castle parapets – the most angelic beings in the whole compass of the London world."[5]

Clearly from these early years came his deep passion for seacraft and all things of the sea, which did so much in determining the whole direction of his art. Thornbury tells us: "Mr. Trimmer and Turner were one day looking over some prints. 'This,' said Turner, with emotion, taking up a particular one, 'made me a painter.' It was a green mezzotinto, a Vandervelde – an upright; a single vessel running before the wind and bearing up bravely against the waves."[6] Turner may have made this generous tribute; but the Van der Velde picture could only have crystallized an emotional and aesthetic response slowly and deeply bred in him by the London waterside with its yellow and madder sails, its green and vermilion dragonfly boats, its deep-sea sailors with their rumours and tales of ships sailing all over the world and daring a thousand storms. The boy watched the tide racing through the massive bridge and all the varied craft that came into the wharves and moorings, on the northern side or among the rickety sheds

and boathouses over at Lambeth. Many years later he compared pictures and ships in a letter. The Royal Academy show
is closing "and the Spanish Fleet (*alias* pictures) will be
removed from their present moorings to be scattered W + E

$$\begin{array}{c} N \\ W + E \\ S \end{array}$$

like the Armada". So he fears that he himself "may be driven
before the wind with his passport" off to Switzerland.[7]

On the Lambeth side another young boy, born in the same
year as Turner, was also observing the London world. Tom
Girtin was the son of a Southwark brushmaker; and till his
father's death in 1783 he roamed about by the riverside and
the ancient buildings that Turner also knew: the Gothic ruin
of St. Saviour, where Girtin was baptized, and the broken
walls of the Priory of St. Mary Overy – though in other parts
old Southwark had given way to the boilers and vats of
Thrale's Brewery. Girtin said that he based his method of
depicting ruined masonry on his later study of the old Savoy
Palace (swept away for the approach to Waterloo Bridge);
and the first drawing that Turner exhibited at the Royal
Academy was his LAMBETH PALACE of 1790, a view of the
Lollard's Tower with old Westminster Bridge.[8]

We can learn much of Turner's own childhood from the
way in which he depicted children and their activities. They
occur often in his sketches and paintings; and, taken together,
they present a consistent and deeply felt view of childhood's
world, which is quite unlike that to be found in the work of
any other artist of the period. We see nothing here of the
prettification and idealization that rule in Reynolds, Gainsborough, and scores of less-talented artists. Even Morland,
close to common life in certain respects, depicted children
ideally sleek and cosy. With Turner, however, it has been well
observed that there is "a needle-sharpness about many of his
tiny sketches showing that 'old-fashioned look' of boys and
girls prematurely experienced in the ways of the world, as he
intends to show them, shrewd, capable, alert. His children
grow up in a world of values of which their aristocratic cousins
in oil have no knowledge at all, but it is a child's whole
universe, with a sense of proportion all its own. They are not
rosy-cheeked cherubs, with dimpling hands and dreamy eyes,
except on one or two occasions, when he draws them in ink"

(imitating Old Masters). In 1802, in the Louvre, he criticized Domenichino's *Virgin and Child*. "The characters are poor", the Child is "without grace or meekness or sensibility", the Mother is "rather inanimate and listless, and attempts attention and adoration of his supposed sagacity". He considered the woman who in Poussin's *Deluge* holds up her child to be "unworthy the mind of Poussin, she is as unconcerned as the man floating with a small piece of board". When he tried himself to depict the infant Jesus he produced a well-built child lying on his back and kicking out his legs as well as flexing the muscles of his arms; the face shows the same precocious intelligence as the other child studies.[9]

In some lines of 1810 he described the village school:

> Close to the millrace stands the school,
> To urchin dreadful, on the dunce's stool
> Behold him placed behind the chair
> In doleful guise twisting his yellow hair
> While the grey matron tells him not to look
> At passers by thro' doorway, but his book.[10]

An early sketch shows an oldish man reading to a group of children, crowded round him, who listen with sharp intent faces.[11]

We see similar children engaged in all sorts of labour. They harvest, glean, pull a plough, drive cattle, do shepherding tasks, feed hens, gather straw or sticks, load carts, mind babies, attend to fires, draw water, fill kettles, water horses at ponds, open tollgates. They go along with drivers, learn to hold the reins and flick a whip; and both in England and on the Continent they are yoked to twigcarts. Ships have their boy drummers and other youngsters in the crew. At harvest-home children are among the farmers and womenfolk who surround the agents at a table. In a cottage interior, which Turner drew in his teens, we see three children before a fire, the girls playing with a cat while the boy kneels and breaks twigs across his knees.

Children picking up Horse Dung, gathering Weeds. Driving asses with coals. Milk carriers to Manchester. Yorkshire with Barrels. Pigs, Geese, Asses, Browsing upon Thistles. Asses going to Coal Pits [a sketchsheet, 1807–9].
    Men shovelling away Snow from the Carriage – Women and

Children hugging – The sky pink – the light and the cast shadows rather warm – Trees all covered with the snow – the Trees in the distance and the Wood getting darker [another, 1819].[12]

These jottings typically show Turner's interest in scenes of work, and the way in which children are thoroughly involved with such scenes. At the same time the child's absorption in play is stressed: "Wood – Corn – Childn at Play" runs an inscription to a drawing of landscape with what seems a ruined abbey, of about 1816. Ruskin comments:

Look at the girl putting her bonnet on the dog in the foreground of "Richmond, Yorkshire"; the juvenile tricks of the "Marine Dabblers" of the *Liber Studiorum*; the boys scrambling after their kites in the "Woods of the Greta and Buckfastleigh"; and the notable and most pathetic drawing of the "Kirkby Lonsdale Churchyard", with the schoolboys making a fortress of their larger books on the tombstone to bombard with the more projectile volumes.[13]

We see hoops, especially the plebeian iron ones, by the Thames reaches as well as in Germany and France. But games of wind and water are what specially fascinate the artist. Kites are common: in coastal scenes where a strong wind blows, on Richmond Hill, in Scotland and Wales, as well as on the Rhine or the Bay of Naples. In that Bay he records: "Boy flying kite. Some without Coats. Children drawing each other in (square-shaped diagram) Basket covered with vine-leaves." In an Oxford drawing he was particular about the way in which a kite was engraved; at Stonyhurst boys fly kites as well as sail boats on the lake. About 1815–16 we meet "Children playing with Water Hellebore as Umbrellas".[14]

Seaside games appear in prints like those dealing with Juvenile Tricks, Marine Dabblers, Young Anglers, or such a painting as THE NEW MOON; or I'VE LOST MY BOAT; YOU SHAN'T HAVE YOUR HOOP. (1840). In river sketches we find, "Boys naked, fishing", "Boy with fishing rod", "Boys splash at fish".[15] Children play at a weir. A sketchbook of about 1823–4 has several incidents: "Children fishing with clothes tucked up. Love instead of fishing – Blue apron. Water cart. Children digging a Sand-heap." The same book has many drawings of the Thames-side in London: "Wapping. Mud Larks. Green Pie. Scotch Wharf."[16] There is a "Boy dabbling" in the bay a

Scarborough; and in the last sketchbook of all we see children playing on the sea-shore, apparently at Margate. Turner writes, "The lost vessel."[17]

The image of a boy launching a toy boat was so important to Turner that we may assume it held childhood memories. In a sketch we meet "Boys with a dish floating for a Boat." In a poem, written while fishing at Purley about 1809 amid rain, he ends:

> The daring boy, thus Britain early race
> To feel the heaviest drop his face
> Or heedless of the storm or his abode
> Launches his paper boat across the road
> Where the deep gullies which his fathers cart
> Made in their progress to the mart
> Full to the brim deluged by the rain
> They prove to him a channel to the main
> Guiding his vessel down the stream
> The pangs of hunger vanish like a dream.[18]

The first confused line seems to link the boy with the typical early British adventurer; the following lines make the paper boat symbolic of the processes that have turned Britain into the greatest sea power of the world – the ruts of the cart rolling to the little local market serving as the channel to the distant sea routes of world trade. (The clumsiness of Turner's diction must not be used as an excuse for denying the complexity of his thought, above all the richness of his sense of symbolic correspondences.) In 1811 he describes in his Western Itinerary "the little native wading in the stream" with his toy boat made of sticks, and breaks off with the cry that such brave exploits end by begetting "the great Demagogues that tyrannies on earth".[19] The "small beginnings" end in war. In the strange poem on the Argo written about the same time the account of a splendid launching ends abruptly with the grotesque image of a child wrecking a vessel that does not come up to expectations.

> Rage disappointments fired his breast distrest
> He plunged her into Thames breast
> You shall no longer loose your prize
> She is good for nothing damn her eyes.[20]

We shall have more to say of these developments of the image later; here it is enough to note its great emotional significance for Turner.

Robert, son of the artist Leslie, described a meeting at Petworth in 1834. He pleasantly evokes Turner the fisherman, the haunter of watersides, who still liked making little boats. Robert was 8 at the time. One September evening when the sun had set beyond the lake, he and his father saw a solitary man "pacing to and fro, watching five or six lines or trimmers, that floated outside the water lilies near the bank."

"There," said my father, "is Mr Turner the great sea painter." He was smoking a cigar, and on the grass, near him, lay a fine pike. As we came up, another fish had just taken one of the baits, but, by some mischance, the line got foul of a stump or tree root in the water, and Turner was excited and very fussy in his efforts to clear it, knotting together bits of twine, with a large stone at the end, which he threw over the line several times with no effect. "He did not care," he said, "so much about losing the fish as his tackle." My father hacked off a long slender branch of a tree and tried to poke the line clear. This also failed, and Turner told him that nothing but a boat would enable him to get his line. Now it chanced that, the very day before, Chantrey, the sculptor, had been trolling for jack, rowed about by a man in a boat nearly all day; and my father, thinking it hard that Turner should lose his fish and a valuable line, started across the park to a keeper's cottage, where the key of the boat-house was kept. When he returned, and while waiting for the boat, Turner became quite chatty, rigging me up a little ship, cut out of a chip, sticking masts into it, and making her sails from a leaf or two torn from a small sketch-book in which I recollect seeing a memorandum in colour that he had made of the sky and sunset. The ship was hardly ready for sea before the man and boat came lumbering up to the bank, and Turner was busy directing and helping him to recover the line, and, if possible, the fish. This, however, escaped in the confusion. When the line was got in, my father gave the man a couple of shillings for bringing the boat; while Turner, remarking that it was no use fishing any more after the water had been so much disturbed, reeled up his other lines, and slipping a finger through the pike's gills, walked off with us toward Petworth House. Walking behind, admiring the great fish, I noticed as Turner carried it how the little tail dragged on the grass, while his own coat-tails were but little further from the ground; also that a roll of sketches, which I picked up, fell from a pocket in one of those coat-tails, and Turner, after letting my father have a peep at them, tied the bundle up tightly with a bit of the sacred line. I think he had taken some twine off this bundle of sketches when making his stone rocket apparatus, and that this led to the roll working out of his pocket. My father knew little about fishing or fishing-tackle, and asked Turner as a matter of curiosity, what the line he had nearly lost was worth. Turner answered that it was an expensive one, worth quite half a crown.[21]

This glimpse of Turner when he was nearly 60, with his small stature and his thrifty habits, is not irrelevant to our effort to get inside his childhood. The fascination with water and boats, and the carefulness over money, were aspects of his character that had roots in his early years and never left him. In his last sketchbook we noted children on the seashore "The lost Vessel". His love of play and his concern about money both chime in with the picture provided by his art of the harsh toilsome life of the children of the labouring classes, in whom an ingrained sense of hardship and the unslackening threat of hunger and penury do not destroy a playful delight in the direct and simple pleasures within their grasp. Further, the account brings out the sympathetic enjoyment which Turner always found in the company of children.

Indeed, apart from a handful of persons with whom he felt at ease, he was perhaps throughout his life happiest among children, able to relax and put aside the problems which the adult world raised for him. Making a sketch of a little girl running, he could not resist writing at the side, "My dear". Clara Wells wrote, "Of all the light-hearted, merry creatures I ever knew, Turner was the most so; the laughter and fun in our cottage was inconceivable, particularly with the juvenile members of the family. I remember one day coming in after a walk, and when the servant opened the door the uproar was so great that I asked the servant what was the matter. 'Oh, it's only the young ladies (my sisters) playing with the young gentleman (Turner), Ma'am.' When I went into the sitting-room, he was seated on the ground, and the children were winding his ridiculous long cravat round his neck; he said, 'See here, Clara, what these children are about'."[22]

He was probably then in his early twenties; but his way of dropping before children all the defences he painfully built up against the rest of the world was maintained throughout his days. Thornbury tells us of his middle age, "Mr. Trimmer's sons, who are still living, remember Turner as an ugly, slovenly old man, with rather a pig-like face; in fact, must I confess it? something of a 'guy'; and describe how he made them laugh, and how pleasant and sociable he was. They recollect him mixing some sort of paste with his umbrella, and their mother, on one occasion, in fun, carrying off one of his sketches against his will, for he was not of the 'give-away family' by any means." (He needed his sketches for work purposes.) Young Trimmer adds, "When a child, I have been out fly-fishing with him on the Thames; he insisted on my taking the fish, which he strung on some grass through the gills, and seemed to take more pleasure in giving me the fish than in taking them. These little incidents mark character. He threw a fly in first-rate style, and it bespeaks the sportsman whenever the rod is introduced into his pictures."[23]

In yet later years the son of his friend Fawkes remarked, "When Turner was so much here in my father's lifetime, I was but a boy, and not of an age to appreciate or interest myself in the workings of his mind or pencil; my recollection of him in those days refers to the fun, frolic, and shooting we enjoyed together, and which, whatever may be said by others of his temper and disposition, have proved to me that he was in his hours of distraction from his professional labours, as kindly-minded a man and as capable of enjoyment and fun of all kinds as any that I have ever known." Turner never liked being overlooked as he worked, and no one at Farnley had ever seen him paint, but

one morning at breakfast Fawkes said to him, "I want you to make me a drawing of the ordinary dimensions that will give some idea of the size of a man of war." The idea hit Turner's fancy, for with a chuckle he said aside to Walter Fawkes' eldest son [Francis Hawksworth], then a boy of about 15, "Come along Hawkey and we will see what we can do for Papa", and the boy sat by his side the whole morning and witnessed the evolution of THE FIRST RATE TAKING IN STORES. His description of the way Turner went to work was very extraordinary; he began by pouring wet paint onto the paper till it was saturated, he tore, he scratched, he scrubbed at it in a kind of frenzy and the whole thing was chaos – but gradually and as if by magic the lovely ship, with all its exquisite minutae came into being and by luncheon time the drawing was taken down in triumph.[24]

Both Turner's parents had important effects on his development. William Turner lived on till 1829, when he died at the age of 82, a tough, sprightly, and earthy character, with a native intelligence which had been little refined but which enabled him to grasp something of the unusual person he had begotten. His relations with his son seem to have been throughout very close and very friendly. F. E. Trimmer, who knew him after his retirement, thus described him: "He was about the height of his son, a head below the average standard, spare and muscular, with small blue eyes, parrot nose, projecting chin, fresh complexion, an index of health, which he apparently enjoyed to the full. He was a chatty old fellow, and talked fast; but from speaking through his nose, his words had a peculiar transatlantic twang. He was more cheerful than his son, and had always a smile on his face. When at Sandycomb Lodge, he was to be seen daily at work in his garden, like another Laertes, except on the Tuesday, which was Brentford market day, when he was often to be seen trudging home with his weekly provisions in a blue handkerchief, where I have often met him, and asking him after Turner, had answer, 'Painting a picture of the battle of Trafalgar.'" Thornbury adds, "He had a habit of nervously jumping up on his toes every two or three minutes, which rather astonished strangers."[25] He also states that William used to claim he had given his son "a good eddycation", and Alaric Watts declares that Turner had been taught to read by his father, but otherwise was "entirely self-educated". The fact seems that from early years William had high hopes of his son and did his humble best to help him to develop in his own way. Turner himself said that "Dad never praised me for anything but saving a halfpenny".[26]

Two letters have been preserved, which show that William was not very literate. They were written to a nephew in Devon about the visits he paid to London. William liked to keep as much contact with his family as circumstances allowed; but his son had little interest in the other Turners. The first letter, of 1 September 1812, is rather irregular in script:

Dear Nephew I did not have your letter till the 25 was in Queen Ann street 10 Days Return here the Day you wrote your letter I came to town yesterday but Could not Return as it is so far your Uncle I and Wife was very well yesterday I have not heard some time since that Brother Price wife was dead Jonathan sent to Joshua saying nothing would give him more pleasure for to se all his Brothers. But at one time as he thought you would be their as to Mathews the[y] are Brush maker not Merchants I went to Cartwright and Co in Hatten gardens 22 the[y] said that the[y] might be 30 next week I am glad you are all well as we are Ditto I remain yours W. Turner.

On 22 May 1821 he wrote from Twickenham in a better hand:

Dear Nephew I cannot come to London haveing so short notice I have seen the Coach this morning and I find that th[ey] Change Horses at the Kings Arms Hounslow the Coachman Comes Every Day but Sundays on Friday I will be at the Kings Arms Ready to see please God I am till then yours W. Turner.

if you dont on Friday send me word I only Read yours Last Night[27]

Trimmer got from Hannah Danby, Turner's later house-keeper, an account of the mother, which Thornbury thus retails: "She was a native of Islington, but at Turner's decease they had not succeeded in finding an entry of her baptism. There is an unfinished portrait of her by her son, one of his first attempts." Thornbury thought it a poor work. "It is not wanting in force or decision of touch, but the drawing is defective. There is a strong likeness to Turner about the nose and eyes. Her eyes are blue, lighter than his, her nose aquiline, and she has a slight fall in the nether lip. Her hair is well frizzed – for which she might well have been indebted to her husband's professional skill – and is surmounted by a cap with large flappers. She stands erect, and looks masculine, not to say fierce; report proclaims her to have been a person of ungovernable temper, and to have led her husband a sad life. In stature, like her son, she was below the average height." Trimmer remarks that he never saw her, never heard Turner mention her, nor ever heard of anyone who had seen her; and Thornbury adds that Turner "fiercely resented any allusion to his mother's family in after life". The portrait is lost; but we have a sketch in a 1794 notebook, which shows an elderly woman asleep in a chair, with a mop cap, and which may be taken as a sketch of Mary Turner in one of her quiet moments[28].

Her furious rages, which led to insanity, had a profound

effect on her son. All the evidence suggests that he felt an intense sympathy with his father in the distracted and difficult household, and that the shared sufferings of the years in Maiden Lane set the seal on the close though inarticulate friendship that grew up between them. The anguish of the wretchedly riven home left an indelible impression on Turner, as it could not fail to do, and determined many of his deepest emotional patterns.

Chapter Two

Apprentice Years (1787-96)

TURNER had no definite art training. Dayes, writing some time before 1805, summed him up, "Highly to the credit of this artist, he is indebted principally to his own exertions for the abilities which he possesses as a painter, and for the respectable position that he holds in society. He may be considered as a striking instance of how much may be gained by industry, if accompanied with temperance, even without the assistance of a master. The way he acquired his professional powers, was by borrowing, where he could, a drawing or a picture or by making a sketch of any one in the Exhibition early in the morning, and finishing it at home. By such practices and by a patient perseverance, he has overcome all the difficulties of the art; so that the fine taste and colour which his drawings possess, are scarcely to be found in any other, and are accompanied with a firm broad chairo-oscuro, and a light and elegant touch."[1] Though he had various masters for short periods, what Dayes says is substantially true. He picked up hints where he could, and taught himself. (Probably Dayes had lent him some of his own drawings with their careful draughtsmanship meekly tinted with thin washes.)

The earliest drawing dated with certainty is a copy of an engraving of an Oxford view, signed "W. Turner, 1787": when he was 12 years old. He lacked a sure grasp of perspective, but was already not without facility; he had clearly been drawing for some time.[2] The first known studies from nature are in a small sketchbook of twenty pages, labelled Oxford, though it mainly deals with the neighbourhood. No doubt he had been staying at Sunningwell, where his uncle, retiring from his butcher's shop, had a house.[3] The year was probably 1789. He was also drawing views of London and had begun working for money. His father hung the drawings round the door of his shop, marked at prices from two to three shillings. One, "bought from the hairdresser's window" is described as imitating Sandby.[4] We can safely say that in 1789 Turner was accepted by the family as destined to be an artist. His father told Stothard, as he was cutting his hair, "My son is going to be a painter."[5]

By 1790, and probably earlier, the Turners were back in Maiden Lane, now at No 26, opposite *The Cider-cellar*.[6] Thornbury describes the house, which he took to be Turner's birthplace: "The old barber's shop was on the ground floor, entered by a little dark door on the left side of Hand Court. The window was a long, low one; the stairs were narrow, steep, and winding; the rooms low, dark, and small, but square and cosy, however dirty and confined they may have been. Turner's bedroom, where he generally painted, looked into the lane, and was commanded by the opposite window. The house to which he afterwards removed, for more quiet and room, I suppose, is at the end of Hand Court, and is on a larger scale, with two windows in front, but it must have been rather dark, though less noisy than his father's house." As for the Court, "it was a sort of gloomy horizontal tunnel, with a low archway and prison-like iron gate of its own, and you had to stand a good minute in the dim light of the archway before you could see the coffin-lid door to the left that in the days of Garrick opened into a small hairdresser's shop". Watts (on the authority of Duroversay) says that William Turner lived most of his time in the cellar or basement. No doubt the kitchen was there.

Thornbury tells us that after his return from Brentford Turner was sent to a floral drawing-master, Palice, in Soho; before 1788 he went on to Thomas Malton in Long Acre to learn perspective; in 1788 he went to a Margate school kept by Coleman; and some time before 1789 he attended Sandby's school in St. Martin's Lane, and worked under Thomas Hardwick for training as an architect. This account probably pieces together several bits of hearsay. Malton was not in Long Acre till May 1796.

However, Turner may well have had brief links with various masters. A water-colour of Isleworth Church, based on a sketch in the Oxford notebook, was made for Hardwick, who, son of a mason and builder, lived and worked at New Brentford. And at least two other drawings were made for him about the same time, one of them dealing with the old church at Wanstead replaced in 1790 by one that Hardwick himself built. Further, Farington says that Turner did for a while study under Malton, a capable teacher, whose influence showed for a couple of years in his pupil's work. Thornbury, however, embroiders the relationship with a pathetic tale of Malton at first rejecting Turner as hopelessly bad, then at last relenting. To this fabrication he adds that Turner used to say, "But my real master, you know, was Tom Malton of Long Acre." Later, in preparing his perspective lectures Turner drew on Malton's book on the subject.[7]

By 1789 Turner was becoming known to several artists as a talented lad. A clergyman, Robert Nixon, noticed the drawings round the shop and took Turner to J. F. Rigaud, who, according to the latter's son, "greatly encouraged him, introduced him to the Royal Academy as a student, and was the first friend he had among the Royal Academicians". Mauritius Lowe, a dissolute artist, is also said to have taken him up. Anyhow, late in the year, Turner was entered as a student. On 11 December, with Reynolds in the chair, drawings made from casts in the Academy's school by six probationers were shown by the Keeper and were approved. Turner's name, perhaps by chance, came first on the list. Registers show that he worked on regularly till October 1793, making studies in chalk and stump from casts in what was called the Plaister Academy.[8]

Girtin was apprenticed to Edward Dayes, an unstable character; and tales were later told of his objection to being kept at colouring prints, with a resulting quarrel that landed him in Bridewell. It has further been suggested that Dr. Monro as deputy-physician there rescued him. However, there is no proof of the whole story; we see Dayes' work continuing to have a strong effect on both Girtin and Turner in 1792–4. There was possibly a further connexion with

John Raphael Smith, then about 40 years old, a friend of
Morland and a gallant of the ladies, who had begun as a
linen-draper at Derby but had become a skilful mezzotinter,
producing plates from the paintings of beauties by Reynolds,
Gainsborough, Romney. Smith also drew and painted,
dealt in prints and published them, at his place in King Street,
close to Maiden Lane. (Girtin's sketchbook of 1800 has a
pen-and-ink, *J. R. Smith waiting for the Mail Coach*.) Girtin
may have coloured prints for Smith as part of his work under
Dayes; we are told that he disposed of his own drawings
through Jack Harris, frame-maker and boon-companion
of Smith. Turner too possibly coloured prints for Smith;
and he and Girtin may have thus become acquainted. In any
event, two such eager and ambitious lads, working in much
the same environment, would certainly have come up against
one another at establishments such as those of Dayes, Smith,
or Harris. Smith's fine gradations of light and shade would
have interested them. According to a self-portrait in pencil
Girtin had a nose as aquiline and prominent as Turner's,
strongly marked brows, slightly protruding upper lip, and
determined chin; he looks a little dishevelled. (Dance's
portrait is, however, more restrained.) A verse-reference
of December 1789 to his cropped "Brutus head" suggests that
he wore his hair in the defiant style expressing democratic or
revolutionary sympathies.

Turner always held Reynolds in high respect; and we may
assume that he was present when Reynolds delivered his last
Discourse on 10 December 1790, when the floor of the Great
Room at Somerset House threatened to collapse. He had two
water-colours hung at the exhibition of 1791. During the
vacation he seems to have gone to Bristol and Malmesbury.
He visited his father's old friend, John Narraway, fellmonger
and gluemaker, who was living prosperously in Broadmead,
Bristol. One of the nieces says that he was nicknamed the
Prince of the Rocks, he spent so much time on the cliffs over
the River Avon. Though he found it hard to handle such a
subject, his design of the river glimpsed from the heights
below Clifton has fresh boldness.[9]

He was back in the Plaister Academy when it opened on
10 January 1792. Four days later the Pantheon in Oxford
Street caught fire and was gutted by daybreak. Turner was

soon on the spot and sketched the building from both inside
and outside, showing already his keen interest in a moment
of elemental violence. Excited spectators throng road and
pavement; the hand-engine in the front is carefully observed;
antique casts supply some of the gestures for the firemen,
but there are touches of original vision in the odd shapes
into which water dripping from cornices and mouldings has
frozen. Despite conventionality there is a sort of brisk energy,
an ardent rush into a scene of dangerous movement. His
characteristic attitudes, as with the Avon view, are already
showing through.[10]

He exhibited drawings of the Pantheon and of Malmesbury,
and went off again to Wales, first to the Narraways, then on to
Chepstow and other sites, and returned via Hereford and
Oxford. In June he graduated to the life class. July seems to
have been spent on another tour. In August he attended
the class only five times; he may have been in Kent. Then when
the school reopened in October he drew regularly till 20 December – and then after the reopening on 10 January 1793 he
was present nearly every evening till the closure for the
Exhibition. On 27 March he was awarded the Greater
Landscape Pallet for "landscape drawing in Class 190" by the
Society of Artists; and in April, with three other prize-winners,
gave proof of his abilities in the Society's rooms.[11] Among his
three drawings in the Academy were an Avon view and the
RISING SQUALL, HOTWELLS, in which his interest in ships
and storm shows itself.[12] He made a summer tour to Hereford.
Back in London, he twice attended the life class in August,
then went on a tour of Kent and Sussex, accompanied by the
engraver Bell. About this time he began to supply publishers
with drawings to be engraved: a practice that continued
throughout his life.[13]

He was thus too busy to attend classes in early 1794.
He exhibited five water-colours and at last drew newspaper
notice. The *Morning Post* said: "The young artist should
beware of contemporary imitations. This present effort evinces
an eye for nature, which should scorn to look to any other
source." Turner was now beginning to master the topographical tradition. He made a tour of the Midlands; and his
eight works on show in April 1795 increased his growing
reputation. There was no sign of a new vision, but the range of

themes suggested his eager force. Many minor influences had
been absorbed without overwhelming him.[14] He showed a keen
interest in scenes of action as well as in mere topographical
verisimilitude. His sketchbooks more than his finished works
reveal the turmoil of his mind, with their intermingling of
pastoral scenes with storm and wreck, windmills, cottage
interiors, watermills, merry-go-rounds, foundries, a donkey in
a water-cart, pigs being shipped, men ploughing, showmen's
vans and stalls, an upturned cart, sailors thrown on rocks,
cats, fishwives. Already he was moving beyond the topographical systems.

The habit of sketching tours was to stay with him all his life.
"Turner at this time", says Lovell Reeve, "was a short,
sturdy, sailor-like youth, endowed with a vigorous constitution, and inured to hard beds and simple fare. There could not
be better qualifications for the pedestrian sketching tours that
he now commenced. He often walked twenty-five miles a day,
with his baggage tied up in a handkerchief swinging on the
end of a stick; rapidly sketching all the good places of composition he met; making quick pencil-notes in his pocket-book,
and photographing into his mind legions of transitory effects
of cloud and sky with the aid of a stupendously retentive and
minute memory." On an Oxford tour, probably of 1793, the
journey "was made on foot in the company of a poor artist
named Cook, who afterwards turned stone-mason. Cook's
feet got sore, and I believe he was soon left behind by the
indefatigable Turner. As for sleeping, the thrifty lad, careful
never to affect prematurely the style of the fine gentleman,
rested in any humble village public-house whereat he could
obtain shelter." His orderliness is shown by the lists he
compiled of places to be visited, with information about them
and notes on intervening distances. "On one of his tours
Turner is reported to have subsisted for four or five days on a
guinea. He once told a friend that in some of his early rambles
the price of the drawing – thirty pounds – did not pay for the
expenses; whereupon he took to a broader, quicker style.
Travelling for Mr. Cadell it is reported that he declined to
saddle the publisher with the expenses of a post chaise, but
took the ordinary mail coach." An item in an expense list –
"Boxing Harry, 2s. 6d." – excited interest; it was a slang
term for making a single meal do for two.[15]

He made two tours in the summer of 1795: in South Wales and the Isle of Wight. More and more he turned to the world of man's labour, especially when connected with the sea; and he had come to love the coast, its varying rocks and levels. As yet he could not master the movement of water that so fascinated him, though at moments he caught something of what he wanted. But all the while his facility and his power of observation grew. (Entries in notebooks show that commissions were coming in; he seems to cite four guineas as the price for two drawings.) On this tour he drew nine mills and two kilns not cited in the itinerary which he (or more probably someone else) made up in London before he left. The interest in such sites, deep rooted in Turner's own nature, was encouraged by the Picturesque aesthetic – though, more widely, the taste for work-places can be traced back through Paul Sandby to the Dutch painters of the seventeenth century. Turner had no doubt seen at Dr. Monro's the drawings by Loutherbourg and J. Laporte which deal with similar material; and it is significant that when Monro's works of art were later sold he bought the Loutherbourgs.[16]

From October on to March 1796 he seems to have been occupied with finishing off works. With Thomas Girtin he spent many evenings from 6 to 10 p.m. at Dr. Monro's house in the Adelphi Terrace, while also attending the life class.[17] In 1796 he showed ten drawings, mainly architectural, though one depicted Wolverhampton Fair. Church interiors were done with much detail, but also with a growing sense of lofty space and diffused light. Farington noted, on 2 April, of the exhibits, "they are very ingenious, but it is a manner'd harmony which he obtains".

But now he at last launched himself into oils, with a night piece, FISHERMEN AT SEA. Bell, who had gone sketching with him on the Thames, tells how he was there "in the little room in Maiden-lane, when Turner made his first attempt in oil, from a sketch in crayon, of a sunset on the Thames, near the Red House, Battersea". This sketch had been made the previous day, when both Bell and Turner, in a boat, had been nearly set fast in the mud by the tide leaving them stuck some distance from the shore. It was with great difficulty they eventually got afloat, so heedless had the enthusiasts been of either tide or time. Bell also mentions that "Turner's first oil of any size or consequence was a view of flustered and scurrying fishing-boats in a gale of wind off the Needles, which General Stewart bought for £10".[18]

Turner had at last gained some control over the movement of water, the complex tensions and the unity of its flow, which were to be central concerns of his art till the end. Critics liked the night piece and John Williams (alias Anthony Pasquin) recognized an original mind: "The boats are buoyant and swim well, and the undulation of the element is admirably deceiving." Turner was still sufficiently inside the period's system of values for his development to be generally acceptable.[19]

In 1796 he does not seem to have travelled much, though he may have been on the south coast (at Brighton). He was now 21 and perhaps had become run down through overwork or the strains at home. His work seems to halt for a while, whereas we would expect a strong effort to build on the successes of 1795. Thornbury, in one of his inflated passages, describes an unhappy love-affair at Margate, which about this time blighted Turner's youth and indeed his whole life. While we may reject Thornbury's sentimental inventions, we must not be so irritated by them as to deny the likelihood of a love-affair, and one that went wrong, in Turner's life at this juncture. A drawing of Margate made in 1792 is the first proof of a connexion with the place, but Thornbury states that Turner had been at school there and fell in love with the sister of a schoolfellow with whose family he became friendly. He "sighed, wrote verses, blushed, doubted certainties, and was certain about love-tokens that to any sane person were more than doubtful", and so on. Then "one eventful hour in the summer dusk he dares to ask the question; he hears the whispered, bashful, 'yes', his soul soars up again to the seventh heaven, and there joy crowns it". Thornbury vaguely gives the date as 1796. The lovers parted. Turner promised to write often, but no letter arrived and the girl was unhappy with a harsh stepmother. After two years she gave up hope and accepted another suitor; but within a week of the marriage day Turner turned up, "frantic at hearing what had occurred". Despite the lack of answers, he had kept on writing, but the stepmother had intercepted the letters. Now he begged the girl to marry him after all. She refused, "and Turner left in bitter

grief, declaring that he would never marry, and that his life
henceforth was hopeless and blighted". The marriage, with
his curse on it, was miserable; and Turner himself "gradually
began to change – not into a misanthrope, for that he never
was – but into the self-concentrated, reserved money-maker".[20]

The tale may have been devised as a desperate effort by
Thornbury to impose some sense on Turner's character,
which completely baffled him. Still, he may have built this
fantasy on some slight hint he got in collecting his material.
An ardent youth like Turner might well have had an unfortunate love-affair; but such an experience in itself would
not have warped so strong a person. His failure to marry had
other reasons behind it, for which we must look mainly to his
mother, whose insanity had been growing worse through these
years. With such a domestic background Turner may well
have been afraid of throwing in his lot with a woman. But a
setback in youth could have potently contributed to his fears
and doubts, the lack of personal self-confidence which we find
was afflicting him at this period and which left its trace in his
whole later demeanour.

R. C. Leslie provides some slight confirmation of an unhappy love-affair at Margate. At Deal he lived next door to
Mrs. Cato, who had been Miss White. Of her and her friend
he writes:

They belonged to that extinct nerveless race of women who liked
and encouraged barrel-organ grinders, so that for an hour or so
every day of our stay at Deal, the rugged roar of the surf was
mingled or softened by popular airs of the period. I was also much
interested to find that, as natives of Margate, they knew of J. M. W.
Turner as a young man, when he used to visit friends of theirs
there, to see a young lady to whom he was then engaged to be married. The old ladies took no interest in Turner the artist and spoke
of him only as a poor delicate youth, who was not expected to
live long, and said that the young lady's relations wished the engagement broken off on that account.

Mrs. Cato does not seem a very reliable witness, but Leslie
accepts her story.

No doubt Turner in fact had much charm – of the sort that
came out when he was at ease, as in the account by Clara Wells.
Thornbury refers to his large features, not unjewish-looking,
handsome, with clear grey-blue eyes and arched brows,

and to his negligence in dress.[21] As we have seen, he was quite
small in build, and later grew heavy and stocky. A small oval
self portrait in water-colour was given to the Narraways;
a niece, Ann Dart, thought Turner drew it when "about
eighteen years old". It suggests a short youth, compact in
build, with vigilant eyes, prominent nose, firmly closed lips,
lots of longish hair falling untidily over his shoulders; the
cravat is loosely tied and the striped coat and waistcoat
do not seem a good fit. No doubt he was used to buying cheap
ready-made clothing, a habit that seems to have stayed with
him. Another portrait, this time in oils, has the appearance
of having been made a year or two later. The features have
filled out; there is a sensuous look about the full lips; the
eyes are grey-blue under the brown hair; and the clothes are
somewhat smarter. Turner seems to be trying to make more
of himself.[22]

Ruskin, seeing this work many years later, recognized in it
"entirely the germ and virtually capable contents of the man".
And on 30 May 1860 Ann Dart was persuaded to write down
her memories for him. Turner, she said, was "not like young
people in general, he was singular and very silent, seemed
exclusively devoted to his drawing, would not go into society,
did not like 'plays', and though my uncle and cousins were
very fond of music, he would take no part, and had for music
no talent. When asked to make the portrait you have purchased he said it was no use drawing such a little figure as mine,
it will do my drawings an injury, people will say such a little
fellow as this can never draw. When the portrait was given to
us it was long hung in the stairs, my cousin saying he would
not have the little rip hung in the drawing-room. He had no
facility for friendship, and though so often entertained by my
uncle he would never write him a letter, at which my uncle was
very vexed. My uncle indeed thought Turner somewhat
mean and ungrateful." Yet, "he would do anything my uncle
or cousins would ask him in the way of taking sketches in the
neighbourhood", and "he gave us many of these drawings
which we have since given away". She admits that though he
was difficult to understand and would talk little, people could
not help liking him, "because he was so good humoured".
She says that "he was in my uncle's house as one of the family,
did not make himself otherwise than pleasant but cared little

about any subject except his drawing, and did not concern himself with anything in the house or business". She adds, "Turner during his visit would sometimes go out sketching before breakfast, and sometimes before or after dinner", and "he was not particular about the time of returning to his meals".

Further in her invaluable though undiscerning account she describes him "as a plain uninteresting youth both in manners and appearance, he was very careless and slovenly in his dress, not particular what was the colour of his coat or clothes, and was anything but a nice looking young man. In the year 1800 he was a fortnight at my uncle's, with whom I was then visiting, and I speak from my recollection, seeing him continually at meals and other times. He would talk of nothing but his drawings, and of the places to which he would go for sketching. He seemed an uneducated youth, desirous of nothing but improvement in his art. He was very difficult to understand, he would talk so little." And she repeats, "He was sedate and steady, he did not in the evenings go out except with our family, and mostly we staid at home, and Turner would sit quietly apparently thinking, not occupied in drawing or reading. He was not at table polite, he would be helped, sit and lounge about, caring little for anyone but himself." She concludes, "Turner went from my uncle's house on a sketching tour in North [altered from South] Wales. My uncle gave him a pony, and lent him a saddle, bridle and cloak, but these he never returned. My uncle used to exclaim what an ungrateful little scoundrel, and with this incident the intercourse between Turner and our family terminated, though his father visited us three or four times afterwards between 1800 and 1822."[23]

She was writing in 1860 from memory, and her date 1800 must be taken as a rough guess. Her account summarizes what the Narraways said among themselves on the odd guest; and the last occasion on which Turner visited them was certainly 1798, when the episode of the pony occurred. (We can only conclude that there was some misunderstanding about the loans; for Turner was scrupulous in such matters.) The preoccupied mood that Ann Dart described was derived from more than a young man's absorption in his art. It revealed an acute sense of anxiety, in which nothing but the

complete surrender to an engrossing activity could provide
any release or palliation. And we see something more than
shyness; there is a painful sense of personal inadequacy. The
feeling of being physically unimpressive and even ridiculous
must have been intensified by his shame and misery about
his mother. His love of art was reinforced by a relentless
pressure of nervous suffering; and we touch on one aspect
of the mechanism that made him such an indefatigable worker
all his life. We cannot reduce his artistic activity to the
revulsions driven in on him through his home life; but at the
same time we cannot ignore the effect of those revulsions.
They now constituted a dynamic part of his inner struggle.
As always in the case of a richly creative sensibility, the
personal pangs and agonies were drawn into a continually
wider sphere of reference. There they had their role of intensifying responses and attitudes without reducing them to the
narrowly personal sphere. Turner's attitudes to art and society
were deeply and pervasively tinged by emotions born from his
home experience, but universalized in the process of their
development and expansion. How this worked out is the story
we have to tell.

The gaucherie and sense of isolation which his experiences
begot in him had the effect of making him find ever more
difficult and unpalatable the normal ways whereby men adapt
themselves to conventional requirements; and his resistance
to social pressures facilitated his building-up of resistance
to the ruling criteria of art criticism. His conviction that he
was ridiculously small and unlikeable inevitably strengthened
people's awareness of what oddities there were in his appearance and manners. He thus had no trouble in finding what
seemed verifications of his sense of personal difference and
peculiarity. For instance, it must have been with a shock at
once bitter and exultant that in 1805 he read in Dayes's
Works the sentence following the passage already cited:
"The man must be loved for his works; for his person is not
striking, nor his conversation brilliant." Such a depreciation
would wound keenly, yet would have an effect of confirming
Turner in the belief that he had chosen the right course in
turning painfully away from easy satisfaction to the practice
of art and communion with nature as his sole effective com-
pensation for the deprivations and deficiencies that seemed to

be his lot. (His father's nervous trick of jumping on to his toes suggests that he, too, was keenly self-conscious about his short stature.)

The picture given by Ann Dart must be supplemented with that by Clara Wells. Her father, W. F. Wells, water-colour painter and teacher, though some thirteen years older than Turner, had become a close friend of his; indeed, he seems the only person to whom Turner took something of a filial attitude. Clara, his daughter, tells us that their house was in Turner's early years "a haven of rest from many domestic trials too sacred to touch upon" – that is, from his mother's outbursts and violences. "Turner loved my father with a son's affection; to me he was an elder brother." She adds that he "in very early life, was a constant and almost daily visitor at my father's house, whom he regarded as an able counsellor in difficulties. He usually spent three or four evenings in every week at our fireside, and though very much more than half a century has elapsed, I can still vividly recall to mind my dear father and Turner sketching or drawing by the light of an Argand lamp, whilst my mother was plying her needle, and I, then a young girl, used to read aloud some useful or entertaining work." She says, "There was more hidden good and worth in his character than the world could imagine; he had a tender, affectionate heart, such as few possess." His faults have been published to the world, but "his many virtues are known only to a very few." Further, "let it not be thought that Turner's heart was closed to the many appeals to his benevolence which came before him. I know he gave ungrudgingly, but he was no boaster of good deeds. Another trait of character, which ought to be named, is the liberality with which he viewed the works of other artists; if he could not speak a word of praise, he carefully abstained from giving any opinion. I never heard him utter a syllable of dispraise of any artist. Though thoroughly modest and unpretending, yet he had a full appreciation of his own merits, and no one so much enjoyed his exquisite pictures as he did himself; it was a matter of real sorrow to him to part with any favourite picture, and on more than one occasion, when he had been looking graver than usual, and I have asked if anything vexed him, he has said, 'No, only I've been sending some of my *children* away to-day.'"[14]

The latter of these comments refer to Turner's life as a whole. Clara, later Mrs. Wheeler, knew him well till the end. But the account of his coming to the Wells house for refuge, can only refer to the later 1790s. There alone he could relax, whereas with other people such as the Narraways he was amiable but apart, and felt his sense of difference and personal insignificance driven in upon him.

Chapter Three

Associate of the Royal Academy (1797-9)

ABOUT this time Turner and Girtin were making drawings for Dr. Monro.[1] It used to be said that in order to help in training the young pair he paid them to copy water-colours by J. R. Cozens under his supervision.[2] In fact, his house was a sort of work club. Farington, under 30 December 1794, notes, "Dr. Monro's house is like an Academy in an evening. He has young men employed in tracing outlines made by his friends, etc. – Henderson, Hearne, etc., lend him their outlines for this purpose." When Cozens broke down he had come under the care of Monro who was physician to Bethlehem Hospital and who thus gained his sketchbooks.[3] Monro had been a pupil of the landscapist J. Laporte, and had gone sketching with Gainsborough. He had a country house at Fetcham, Surrey, and later at Bushey, Herts. At the Adelphi he had a large collection of paintings and drawings by Rembrandt, Claude, Wilson, Canaletto, Morland, Gainsborough, and by Sandby and other water-colourists, including Cozens and Hearne. His carriage had a rack for a portfolio of drawings as Sir George Beaumont's had for the small Claude painting, *Narcissus and Echo*. Turner gained much from his connexion with Monro, though perhaps he ended by feeling that the facility he acquired was threatening to impose on his drawing certain imitative stereotypes. Or he may have thought that the employment was below his growing dignity as an artist. He gave up the work, for which he had been paid half a crown and supper each evening. (Three-and-six was the sum he mentioned to Farington, insisting that Monro had been "a material friend to him". His father, however, grumbled at the pay.)[4]

A sketch, probably by Monro himself, shows Turner at work. A young man with ruffled hair, beakish nose, is drawing intently by candlelight at a sort of double desk or easel. Mrs. Monro disliked the hard-up young artists, who were too taken up by their studies to be elegantly mannered; when they came she shut herself up in her room[5] Through these evenings Turner became fully acquainted with Girtin, whose quick adventurous mind was of great value to him at this phase of his development. On the other hand, the connexion of Monro with Bethlehem Hospital, to which soon Mrs. Turner was to go, and in particular his tending of J. R. Cozens, who after his breakdown died in the Hospital in 1797 – about the time when Turner gave up working at the Adelphi – must have set up a certain strain. Instead of wholly escaping from the atmosphere of home, as he did with Wells, Turner at times could not but have been painfully reminded of the things he most wanted to forget.

The pictures he exhibited in 1797 were generally liked. Pasquin again approved, especially "as all our marine painters have too servilely followed the steps of each other, given us pictures more like japanned tea-boards, with ships and boats on a smooth and glossy surface, than adequate representations of that inconstant, boisterous and ever-changing element". *The Times* recognized the link of his picture of sunset, ominous of storm, with the poetic tradition of Falconer's *Shipwreck*, and declared, "we never beheld a piece of the kind possessing more imagination or exciting more awe and sympathy in the spectators".[6] Even more striking was the recognition of Turner's originality by Thomas Greene of Ipswich, a man of literary interests, who wrote in his diary:

June 2, 1797. Visited the Royal Exhibition. Particularly struck with a sea view by Turner – fishing vessels coming in, with a heavy swell, in apprehension of tempest gathering in the distance, and casting, as it advances, a night of shade; while a parting glow is spread with fine effect upon the shore. The whole composition, bold in design, and masterly in execution. I am entirely unacquainted with the artist; but if he proceeds as he has begun, he cannot fail to become the first in his department.[7]

Among the water-colours THE TRANSEPT OF EWENNY PRIORY
shows well what Ruskin called his use of litter. Here the litter
of pigs, poultry, farm tools, the woman and child, form a
contrast with the large empty space of ancient gloom, and
link with the sunlight bursting in through the doorway.

In the summer, probably late June, Turner made a wide
tour of the north that took him through Leeds, Durham,
Berwick, along the Tweed, over into the Lake Country, and
down into Lancaster. His style of recording now shows more
breadth, a sense of distance. We see the influence of Girtin,
though Turner tends to stronger contrasts of light and
shadow. Girtin had made various technical innovations, such
as the use of absorbent off-white cartridge paper; he gave up
the old monochrome underpainting and tried a richer handling
with broad washes sometimes offset by dark blots; above all
he sought for depth in water-colour. Pye, writing of some
drawings made for Henderson in or before 1793, says,
"They are like Malton's in form and perspective; but in
nothing else. They are invested with new effects, being
composed alike of colour and *clair-obscur*."[8]

In the drawings of the northern tour we see Turner, as ever,
interested in scenes of work – a woman lunching at a gravel pit,
men with a windlass hauling a fishing-boat out of surf,
or taking on sail in a boat. However, despite the rapid development through which he was going, his fellow artists tried to
see in him a clever fellow without any drive. Hoppner, on
5 January 1798, is recorded by Farington as saying that he was
"a timid man afraid to venture".

While waiting to hear how his pictures were going to be
hung, Turner went on a short visit to the Rev. Robert Nixon
at Foots Cray, Kent, arriving late on an April afternoon.
Stephen Rigaud was there, two years his junior, and later
recalled the event. (Nixon had introduced Turner to the elder
Rigaud, who helped him into the Academy school.) "Mr.
Nixon was also a pupil of Turner's in landscape painting,
and of mine in figures." The trio agreed to go on a picnic
sketching tour for three days on Monday. "The next day
being Sunday, I accompanied our mutual friend to the parish
church close by, which stood almost concealed by tall majestic
trees, a sweet secluded spot, whose solemn stillness seemed to
invite the soul to meditation and to God. As for Turner it had

no such attraction. He worshipped nature with all her beauties; but forgot God his Creator and disregarded all the gracious invitation of the Gospel. On our return from church we were grieved and hurt to find him shut in the little study, absorbed in his favourite pursuit, diligently painting in water-colours." Throughout his life Turner maintained this total lack of interest in religion, as if it were something so unimportant that he need not even indicate his blank unconcern.

Next day, after an early breakfast, they set out. "It was a lovely day, and the scenery most delightful. After having taken many a sketch and walked many a mile, we were glad at length to seek for a little rest and refreshment at an inn. Some chops and steaks were soon set before us, which we ate with the keen relish of appetite, and our worthy friend the Clergyman, who presided at our table, proposed we should call for some wine, to which I made no objection, but Turner, though he could take his glass very cheerfully at his friend's house, now hung his head, saying – 'No, I can't stand that.' Mr. Nixon was too polite to press the matter further, as it was a pic-nic concern; so giving me a very significant look, we did without the wine. I mention this anecdote to show how early and to what an extent the love of money as a ruling passion already displayed itself in him, and tarnished the character of his incipient genius; for I have no hesitation in saying that at that time he was the richest man of the three; Mr. Nixon having then but a very small Curacy, and I having little more than the pocket money allowed me by my Father, whilst Turner had already laid up something in the funds, and for which my good friend Mr. Nixon was one of the Trustees whilst he was still under age. This little incident, though calculated to throw a chilly influence over the cordiality of our sketching party, could not prevent our greatly enjoying the remaining part of our beautiful tour, particularly the river scenery on the banks of the Medway as far as Aylesford; and the end of the third day we returned to the quiet rural parsonage of Foots Cray, very much delighted with our excursion."[9]

Rigaud here reflects the sort of misconception that early grew up round Turner and thickened in the later years. As well as being godless, the fellow was no gentleman, mean

and self-regarding. But at no time was the love of money
a ruling passion with Turner. Doubtless his remark at the inn
arose out of a mixture of frugality with a dislike of drinking
wine when he wanted to go on sketching with a fresh mind.
As for meanness, a note on the inside of a sketchbook cover,
probably of 1795, mentions, "Lent Mr. Nixon 2. 12. 6."
We may add that Nixon must have broken Turner's confidence; for Rigaud could not have known about the funds
unless Nixon had told him. This year 1798 was a very difficult
one for artists. Raimbach, the engraver, who had joined the
Academy in the previous autumn, says in his *Memoirs* that
the grave state of national affairs took everyone's thoughts
away from the arts. "Everything connected with them was at
the lowest ebb." Only the fashionable portraitists were doing
well; Reinagle and Wheatley were granted aid by the R.A.
Council.[10]

The private view at the Royal Academy was on Friday. On
Sunday Farington found Turner there "touching on his pictures – seemed modest and sensible". On the 27th he breakfasted with Beaumont. "West was full of Turner's drawings.
He thinks them manner'd – also Girtin's. Likes my small pictures." Not long after we find Opie impressed by Turner's
works. "He thought him a strong mannerist." Of the oils,
DUNSTANBURGH rightly made the critic of *St. James Chronicle*
think of Wilson on account of the breadth of treatment. Turner was also taking over from Wilson an interest in bright
yellows, pinks, blues. Indeed, helped by Wilson and drawing
to some extent on the modish Picturesque, he was breaking
through into a personal control of the oil medium.[11] The
movement and diffusion of a luminous atmosphere around the
mountain forms is linked with light centralization and aided
by compositional devices of looking from above into the distance or lifting up the foreground. Subtle gradation of tone
appears, and Turner's own character is to be noted in the
stress on dramatic aspects of weather. The influence of Salvator Rosa and Poussin is also to be felt, mingling with that
of Wilson. In BUTTERMERE the touches of white prelude the
way in which he is to drive up the colour key.[12]

After visiting Malmesbury to do some commissioned drawings, he went on to Bristol. Miss Narraway gave him a recipe
for making a herbal ointment to use on cuts, and he was lent

the pony which he was expected to return, but did not. He seems to have been feeling more cheerful, to judge by the glees and the songs by Charles Dibdin that he wrote down.[13] Then he made an extensive tour of North Wales, in which a main aim was to see country hallowed through its connexion with Wilson. As late as 1847 he wrote to a friend sketching in Wales near Haverfordwest, "known by being the seat of Esquire Johns a fine place well wooded and he employ'd Stothard to paint the same so think you will find some pictures by him there. I do not think you [could] have hit upon a more desirable spot for your pencil and hope you may feel – just what I felt in the days of my youth when I was in search of Richard Wilson's birthplace."

On 26 September he called on Farington. "He had been in South and North Wales this summer – alone and on horseback – one clear day and Snowdon appeared green and unpicturesque to the top." (Note the adjective showing that he is still to some extent thinking in terms of the Picturesque.) "I mentioned election of Associates and told him He should have my vote. He expressed himself modestly for my good opinion." Farington, a feeble artist who wanted to be the power inside the R.A., had already noted that Lawrence was friendly towards Turner, and, in a lesser degree, so was Hamilton. Turner had entered as a candidate, though he was only 23 and a by-law, passed two years before, laid down 24 as the age of those eligible.

On 24 October, Turner, who well knew how important it was to conciliate Farington, again called, after visiting Lord Yarborough's estate to make three drawings for the Mausoleum designed by Wyatt. He "had promises of votes from Bacon, Nollekens, Bourgeois, Gilpin, Stothard, etc., to be an Associate. I told him I saw no necessity for further application. I thought his chance so certain that I would wait the event, which He said He would do. He talked to me about his present situation. He said that by continuing to reside at his Father's he benefited him and his Mother; but he thought he might derive more advantages from placing himself in a more respectable situation. He said, He got more commissions at present that he could execute and got more money than He expended. The advice I gave him was to continue in his present situation till He had laid aside a few hundred pounds,

and He then might with confidence, and without uneasy apprehension place himself in a situation more suitable to the rank
He bears in the Art." Later in the same day, it seems, "I afterwards called upon him at his Father's a Hair Dresser, in
Hand-Court, Maiden Lane. – The apartments to be sure,
small and ill calculated for a painter. He shewed me two Books
filled with studies from nature – several of them tinted on the
spot, which He found, He said, were much the most valuable
to him.[14] He requested me to fix upon my subject which I preferred in his books, and begged to make a drawing or picture
of it for me. I told him I had not the least claim to such a
present from Him, but on his pressing it I said I would take
another opportunity of looking over his books and avail myself of his offer. Hoppner, He said, had chosen a subject at
Durham. Hoppner, He told me had remarked to him that his
pictures tended too much *to the brown* and that in consequence
of that observation, He had been attending to nature in order
to be able to correct it."

Turner had certainly a fair sum already laid by, but was
reticent about such matters. His guarded remarks to Farington, the only known ones in which he mentioned his mother,
suggest that he was still staying at home in order to help his
father, not only financially. On Monday he again called on
Farington, anxious about the election which was to take place
that evening. Out of twenty-four candidates, however, Shee
and Rossi were chosen, with Turner certainly third; he got
into the second ballot. Next day he called on Farington to
thank him for his aid. Next Sunday, dining at Hoppner's,
Farington found Turner and Girtin there.[15]

Early this year an event occurred which had important
consequences for Turner. On 16 May the glee composer John
Danby suddenly died. It seems certain that Turner already
knew the family. Otherwise the speed with which he made
Danby's widow his mistress is hard to explain. Danby, apparently of Yorkshire, had written songs for the musical perfor-
mances at Vauxhall and Ranelagh. He then lived at 8 Gilbert's
Buildings, Lambeth, but later moved to 26 Henrietta Street,
close to Maiden Lane. Presumably it was about this time that
Turner met him. Girtin, who resided for a while in the same
street, may have been the intermediary – or A. W. Callcott, who
was soon to be a disciple and friend of Turner, and who must

have known the musical world well, being the younger brother of J. W. Callcott. The latter and Danby were probably the best and most popular of the period's glee composers. Danby, whose songs were rather in the lush pastoral style, was also organist of the Spanish Embassy's chapel near Manchester Square, for which he wrote masses, motets, and magnificats. He was a Catholic; and in his last years he lost the use of his limbs, contracting some kind of arthritis, it was said, through sleeping in a damp bed. He had married a young woman, Sarah, who seems to have been an actress or singer, and who bore him four children. A concert for his benefit was held in Willis' Rooms, St. James's; but after the excitement, on his return home, he died at half past eleven that night at 46 Upper John Street, Fitzroy Square.[16]

The position of Danby is of interest to us; for it is almost the only way open to us for assessing the character and social status of Sarah, who, however obscurely, played an extremely important part in Turner's emotional life for many crucial years. The period was the great one for glees (1750–1830), following that of catches and preceding that of part-singing; in glees the highest parts were for adult male altos singing in falsetto: an English speciality. Two of Danby's best-liked glees were *Awake, Eolian Lyre*, and *Fair Flora decks the Flow'ry Ground*. His widow, left in difficult circumstances, published a posthumous collection of his compositions in 1798. We may conjecture that it was while helping and consoling her Turner fell in love and persuaded her to become his mistress. She bore him two girls; and the liaison must have begun not long after Danby's death. Danby himself was only 41 when he died, and Sarah seems to have been much younger, probably about Turner's own age. There is no reason to think that the wife of a man like John Danby would be anything but handsome, intelligent, and well educated. The sole remnant of her is a firm signature in the copy of the posthumous glees belonging to the Madrigal Society; she may well have had a hand in editing the book. Since almost all writers on Turner have confused her with her niece Hannah, whom she later introduced into the Turner household and who in her final years was dwarfish and repulsive, they have done their best to shuffle her off the biographical scene with a few words of disgust. Thus Hamerton wrote:

We all know the pictures of Titian and his mistress, and his portraits of her, yet nobody talks of the immorality of Titian; but Turner's domestic arrangements with Mrs. Danby and Mrs. Booth give more acute pain to our sense of propriety because they seem more degrading. We all make distinctions of this kind, and we cannot help it. Lord Byron's *liaison* with the elegant and accomplished young Countess Guiccioli shocks us less than his intimacy with the vulgar Venetian woman who preceded her. In Turner's conduct in this respect there were two offences, one against morality and the other against good taste.

But there is every probability that Sarah Danby was more than elegant and accomplished enough to avoid shocking Hamerton.

A Mr. Danby and Eustace Danby appear in the list of subscribers to the posthumous glees; and we may assume these to have been relations of her husband. Perhaps they helped in bringing up the four children that she bore to him; we find one of the girls, Caroline Melissa, marrying H. G. Nixon, organist of St. George's Cathedral,[17] London, so that the musical connexions must have been kept up. It seems significant also that Turner, whom the Narraways had thought to dislike music, became very interested in it round this period. A sketchbook of 1798, dealing with his Welsh tour, has the Dibdin songs already mentioned, as well as the words of two songs of a glee type. One tells of a wayworn traveller "wandring drearily and sad unraveller of the Mazes toward the Mountain top"; the other is a long-song, "Tell me Babbling Echo why". The slight confusion of constructions in the first is probably the result of Turner writing the words down from memory; and there is no doubt the same explanation for a doublet in the second stanza of the other:

> Bold intruder Night and Day
> Busy telltale hence away
> Me and my care in silence leave
> Come not near me while I grieve.[18]

"Telltale" has "censor" written over it: which with its lack of relevance seems a correction by Turner himself. "Censor" is an odd term for the Babbling Echo, and seems to reflect Turner's own fears of betraying echoes that he would prefer to be censored.

Why did he never marry Sarah Danby? We are reduced to

conjecture, but it seems likely that the barriers were, at least in the beginning, all on his side. If Sarah succumbed to the extent of bearing him two children, it is unlikely that she would have refused the security which marriage would have given her. We can only suppose that the deep-rooted sense of caution which Turner had developed was strong enough to suppress any wishes he had for an open and settled relationship. About this time his mother's madness was coming to a head. The fear and the mistrust of women that marked his life had their plainest source in the anguished spectacle of his tormented father. At all costs he did not want to let himself in for such a dilemma; yet he was clearly driven by a strong sensuality. Perhaps he began with Sarah an experimental liaison that was meant to be a trial of them both: to find out if they were suited for one another and if close contacts would reveal the violent conflicts which he had seen at home. But a trial under such circumstances was not likely to succeed. The elements of doubt and suspicions that begot it would tend to create a tension, a watchful unhappiness, that would defeat the better hopes. Turner could not but make a difficult partner in any married relationship with his distracted work obsession, his suspicions of women, his anxious need to build up a stable system of finance in a world where he saw only instability. We cannot tell if Sarah on her side brought in further difficulties and problems. In her own worried uncertainty, with her four Danby infants, to whom were soon added two more children, illegitimate, she may well have shown strain and bad temper.

We have ample evidence that Turner, later on, was capable of extreme generosity; we must not accept the legend of grasping miserliness. But we must recognize that the fear inculcated by his harried home had brought about an intense mixture of frugality, self-discipline verging on asceticism, and money-saving as a weapon against a fickle and treacherous world. Many of the finest qualities of his nature became inextricably entangled with the fears, often harsh and irrational, which had gathered round the question of money. A proud woman may well have found intolerable the conditions with which he hedged her round in money matters. With his extreme care in leaving no clues as to his sexual life, he seems to have made only a single reference to payments to her: "Mrs. D 4–4" (4 guineas) in a notebook of 1809–11.[19]

In 1799 Turner's work showed a steady advance. He exhibited seven water-colours and four oils. The *True Briton* recognized the classic quality he was achieving in oils: HARLECH CASTLE "combines the style of Claude and of our own excellent Wilson, yet wears an aspect of originality that shows the painter looks at Nature with his own eyes".[20] Green of Ipswich

was again struck and delighted with Turner's Landscapes: particularly with fishermen in an evening – a calm before a storm, which all nature attests is preparing, and seems in death-like stillness to await: and Caernarvon Castle, the sun setting in gorgeous splendour behind its shadowy towers:– the latter in water colours; to which he has given a depth and force of tone, which I had never before conceived attainable with such untoward implements. Turner's views are not mere ordinary transcripts of nature: he always throws some peculiar and striking *character* into the scene he represents.[21]

While on one side he was moving towards Wilson, on another side he was moving away. We can see this movement if we compare his KILGARRAN CASTLE with the painting by Wilson of the same subject (almost certainly unknown to him). In Wilson's picture, cold in tone and presumably early, there is a single strong progression into the distance along the converging banks of the river, which do not meet; in Turner's painting of this year the banks come together, as they do in three water-colours and a pencil-drawing, making variously angled Vs. His work represented "hazy sunrise, previous to a sultry day", and the light was drawn down into the large cleft, of which the V-shape was repeated upside down in reflections on the water. The effect is of a rhythmic movement of planes into the luminous cleft, which balances the bright sky on the left and light-misted ruins on the right – something of a swinging-round of vanes. Turner thus shows a new and characteristic dynamic element, though it is still embryonic.[22] His liking for a correspondence of forms, especially of earth and sky in water, is also already apparent. To take a late example: in CAMPO SANTO, VENICE (1842), the white butterfly-winged sails of a boat, projecting into the sky, are reflected in the water, where the drawn-out image is the main of several verticals that draw our eyes up into the light.

This year Turner also showed his BATTLE OF THE NILE, a popular theme, since there were three other attempts at it (by Pocock and Cleveley). He had begun to think of grand historical canvases; and with his love of ships and the sea it was natural that his first such work dealt with an event of the naval war going on at the moment. This year had seen a new magazine *Naval Chronicle*, which began with a series of essays on the Picturesqueness of Marine Scenery, aimed at stirring sailors to study the ocean and deepen their religious awe; the essayist had been roused to write by the reply of an "eminent Painter" to complaints about the uniformity of the sea.[23] The essays were further aimed at painters themselves, who were bidden to note and define the striated saltfoam of the wake (as Turner was soon to do in works like CALAIS PIER and SHIPWRECK) and to give up the use of barrels and floating spars to bear their signatures.[24] In his efforts to make his descriptions more vivid the writer cited such poets as Thomson and Mallet. The *Naval Chronicle* went on to draw up a catalogue of *Marine Designs, Naval Portraits &c in the Exhibition at the Royal Academy*, declaring that Marine Painting was still in its infancy in Britain, "cramped, and greatly confined to portraits of particular ships, or correct representations of particular actions, which forbid the artist from indulging in the fine rolling phrenxy of imagination".[25] William Gilpin, indeed, in his *Observations*, published a few months before the battle of 1 August 1798, had stated that a conflagration by night "presents us with the justest ideas of the great principles of light and shade", and that "the burning of ships is productive of greater ideas, and more picturesque circumstances than the burning of houses". Van der Velde's attempt to depict the Armada had the misfortune of having to deal with a number of fires, "which can never have so good an effect as one".[26] Turner could not have read the *Naval Chronicle* before he painted his picture, though he may well have read Gilpin; but his use of the theme of the *Orient*'s explosion shows how closely certain of his ideas fitted in with contemporary trends. What he did was to carry these trends to more fully logical conclusions and to give them a new depth by his personal interpretation.

A sketchbook of 1798 shows how his mind was turning to large themes. One sketch seems to have been made for a picture on a Plague of Egypt. A design of an army on mountains gazing at a distant land probably represents Hannibal on the Alps before the descent into Italy. A third sketch shows Roman soldiers climbing.[27]

The enlargement of his interests is further shown by the way in which he was trying to learn French, and was now putting verse quotations under his pictures: passages from Milton (twice), Thomson, Mallet, Langthorne. He used Milton to mythologize or deepen the significance of his battle scene. He must have long been reading several poets, especially Thomson; but it was now that he saw how his poetic and artistic interests converged and formed a unity.[28]

About this time Lord Elgin was looking for an artist to draw antiquities at Athens. West, it seems, recommended Turner; but luckily Elgin had an aristocratically low opinion of artists as mere craftsmen and offered only a pittance of a salary. Girtin, too, was asked to go; his work was to include assistance to Lady Elgin in decorating fire-screens and the like; he promptly refused. Robert Smirke also was too expensive for Elgin. If Turner had gone, the whole course of development night have been changed.[29]

In the spring of this year an important artistic event occurred. Two Claudes, brought to England from Italy, were privately shown in Lincoln's Inn Fields: The *Sacrifice to Apollo* and *The Landing of Aeneas*. Beckford soon bought them, and at his house in Grosvenor Square, on 8 May, Turner told Farington that "he was both pleased and unhappy while he viewed" the *Sacrifice*; "it seemed to be beyond the power of imitation".[30] Next day Farington again found him there, as well as Girtin and Constable. In those days, with no public galleries and almost all important pictures closed away in rich mansions, a chance to look at works like these Claudes was eagerly snatched at by painters. An effect of the French Revolution, and of subsequent events such as the invasion of Italy, highly useful to English art, was the dispersal of large numbers of art-works, many of which reached England. T. M. Slade had managed to buy the Flemish, Dutch, and German pictures from the Orleans collection and smuggle them out of Paris; they were exhibited in London in the spring of 1793. Now works were coming in from Italy, often bought up by English artists in Rome and carried to England in the teeth of French privateers and Algerian corsairs. The Altieri Claudes had been acquired by Fagan and Grignion, who took them along refugee-crowded roads from Rome to Naples in a wagon, then into a polacca. Shut in a cabin with thirty or forty other fugitives, the artist-dealers reached Palermo in a bad storm. Grignion, painting Nelson's portrait, was able to raise the subject; and Nelson at once wrote an order to the Governor of Gibraltar asking for a convoy to protect the *Tigre*, a small armed vessel in which the paintings were dispatched. After being chased by several enemy ships, the *Tigre* reached Falmouth, where the Claudes were almost lost through the lack of any consignment note. Auctioned, they were bought back for a small sum and brought to London.[31] West in an address in 1801 at the R.A. referred to the difficulties of young artists in seeing good paintings; *The Times* took up the theme; and Angerstein and other collectors made some response, but it was to be many years before artists and public had easy access to galleries of fine pictures.[32]

Turner was now once more hoping to become an Associate. On 27 May he called on Farington, who told him he would certainly be elected if he put his name down. "He expressed himself anxious to be a member of the Academy." He had been paid forty guineas, more than he asked, by Angerstein for a drawing; Beckford had written from Portugal to ask him to go to Fonthill, "but he does not know what the commission is to be. He is also to make views of Salisbury Cathedral for Sir Richard Hoare." He had thus for the moment won over the connoisseurs.[33]

Calling again on 6 July, he was given further reassurance. "He talked to me of removing from his father's house in Hand Court, Maiden Lane. I advised him to take lodgings at first and not to encumber himself with a House. Smirke and I, on our way to the Academy, drank Tea with him and looked over his sketch books. He said he had 60 drawings bespoke by different persons." They again on the 8th visited Hand Court to choose subjects to be drawn for them (as gifts, one assumes). Stimulated by the sketches of South Wales, Farington decided to make a tour there himself. On Sunday the 21st, in the morning, Turner came with directions for the tour; and later that day Farington went to see Hoppner at Fulham, with his wife Susan, the Opies, and Fuseli, and found Sawrey Gilpin there. As the weather was fine, they dined on the grass,

as they'd done on the 7th; then they "walked out on the
bank adjoining the Bishop of London's garden, and were
delighted with the Landscape scenery. Turner came to tea.
He told me he had no systematic process for making drawings.
He avoids any particular mode so that he may not fall into a
manner. By washing and occasionally rubbing out, he at last
expresses in some degree the idea in his mind." They left
Fulham at half past eight.

The term "mannerist" was used at this time to denote any
artist who had a recognizable style imposed on his material –
the ideal being stated as a pure transcription of nature in which
no distinctive effects of style stood out. Thus Virtue had used
the term mannerist for Jervas, whose portraits were "like
fan-painting" with no blood in them. Wedgwood, describing
an artist who gives all his heads "a Family likeness", calls him
"a strong mannerist". And Dayes thus sets out the position:

The word manner may be applied to color, light and shade, and
pencilling. It is expressive of certain peculiar marks that invariably
characterise the works of each individual, as in some a blue-
ness in the coloring prevails, in others a grey or yellow, while
others are distinguished by a harshness in the shadows; in one
the pencilling is round; in another, square or forked. So far is a new
manner from being a mark of genius, as some assert, that, could
perfection in painting ever be attained, it would be unaccompanied
by any peculiarity whatever.[34]

It is hard to think that he did not have in mind there a rebuke
for Girtin, and perhaps Turner, too. He cites Reynolds:
"Peculiar marks I hold to be generally, if not always defects,
however difficult it may be wholly to escape them."[35]

Turner was doubtless aware that he was being called a
mannerist, and was himself keen not to fall into easy tricks.
However, in his mouth the term truth-to-nature had a wholly
different meaning than in Dayes's.

Orders were keeping him busy. He worked for three weeks
at Fonthill, then went to draw in Lancashire for a publisher,
and turned off for North Wales. On 14 and 17 October he was
once more drawing in the life class. On the 13th he had asked
Farington's opinion of lodgings in George Street, Hanover
Square. "I thought it a very good situation. He told me that
he first taught drawing at 5 shillings an hour, and never had
more than 7s. 6d. His last practice was to make a drawing in

the presence of his pupil and leave it for him to imitate."
On the 30th he told how he had been "in Kent painting from
Beech trees." (He must have been visiting Wells at Knockholt;
and his emphasis on the beeches suggests an anti-picturesque
attitude; for Gilpin and Price had denounced that tree at
length.)[36] "Very anxious about the election. Has heard that
Sandby and others are for Woodforde. I told him he had no
reason to fear. He has looked at lodgings in Harley St. which
he may have at about £50 or £55 a year, and asked my opinion
of the situation. I said if the lodgings were desirable, the
situation is very respectable and central enough." (Though
Turner no doubt thought it useful to get·the advice of so
worldly-wise a person on his lodgings, one feels that he is
genuinely agitated about the question; the wrench of leaving
his home, whatever the difficulties there, must have been
extreme.) On 4 November, Turner called again, to say that
"an attempt would be made to add to the number of Associates more than had been voted". The list held the names of
sixteen painters, three architects.

An argument had arisen about rescinding a resolution that
only four vacancies should be filled. The aim seems to have
been to embarrass West; but Turner was affected because
some of his supporters were among the recalcitrants who, after
proposing the cancellation of the year's elections, now refused
to vote. Still, though West voted against him, he was easily
elected. Next day, 5 November, he called on Farington to
thank him, and lost no time in joining the Academy Club;
for he attended the dinner there on the 8th, as also on the
22nd, and on 6 December.

He also took the plunge and rented the rooms in Harley
Street. On 16 November he had called again on Farington.
"He reprobated the mechanically systematic process practised
by [John or Warwick] Smith and from him so generally
diffused. He thinks it can produce nothing but manner or
sameness. The practice of [blank] is still more vicious. Turner
has no settled process but drives the colours about till he has
expressed the idea in his mind. J. Serres is to have the use
of a parlour and a room on the 2nd floor in the House in which
Turner lodges in Harley St., which he much objects to as it
may subject him to interruption. Serres to use these rooms
from Ten in the forenoon till 3 or 4 in the afternoon, when the

Rev. Mr. Hardcastle is to have the use of them, he being the
Landlord. Serres' wife etc. are in other lodgings where his
family concerns are carried on."

J. T. Serres had followed his father, Dominic Serres,
a Gascon, as marine painter to the King in 1793; he also
became marine draughtsman to the Admiralty – in which role
he at times made sketches of the enemy's coast, being provided
with a ship for the purpose, at a salary of £100 a month.
Though a mediocre painter he thus shared with Turner an
interest in the sea. No doubt what Turner feared was his wife
Olivia. While under age she had fallen in love with Serres,
who was her drawing-master. She exhibited landscapes herself
in the Royal Academy in 1794 and 1804–8, and in the British
Institution in 1806. She was, however, a violent character,
who ruined Serres with her extravagances, and who developed
delusions of being a princess, the daughter of the Duke of
Cumberland, who was George III's brother.[37] Hence Turner's
remark that she was living elsewhere (81 Wimpole Street)
and hence no doubt his fears of having Serres in the same house
at all. During his residence at Harley Street he must have
continually heard the latest tales of Mrs. Serres's goings-on,
and these would not have helped in his relations with Sarah
Danby. They could hardly have failed to increase his fears and
suspicions of wives, coming at this crucial moment in his
development. Sarah seems to have continued as a subtenant
at 46 Upper John Street, not very far away.

On the last day of 1799 Turner attended a council meeting
of the Royal Academy and was given his diploma.

Chapter Four

The World of Art

TURNER had two important predecessors in landscape painting
in England, Gainsborough and Wilson; but neither man
created a tradition. In general, works by foreigners from
Claude to Zuccarelli were what the connoisseurs wanted;
and these, together with the products of visiting artists from
abroad, did much to set the standards and modes of appreciation. English landscapists tended to paint inferior versions
of Dutch works or scenes of a topographical kind. Philip
James de Loutherbourg, an Alsatian who became a member
of the French Academy, arrived in London in 1771 as stage-
designer for Garrick; his landscapes mostly belonged to what
we may call the cosmopolitan school and showed many signs
of scenic arrangement. But some of his work anticipated
George Morland, son of a minor portraitist and genre-painter,
who helped his father in restoring and faking Old Masters,
including Dutch landscapists; Morland applied what he had
learned from painters like Brouwer to English scenes; despite
some feeling for common life, he never got beyond the
cosmopolitan style. (In 1786 he married the sister of W. Ward,
who popularized his paintings in excellent engravings.) The
school of faking was indeed one of the gateways into the
practice of landscape. J. C. Ibbetson, who belonged to much
the same group as Morland, had also graduated out of copying
or faking Dutch paintings as well as the work of Wilson and
Gainsborough.[1]

At some points the topographical outlook merged with the

trends developed by Morland and Ibbetson. From early in
the century draughtsmen were employed by the antiquarian
rich to depict edifices or scenes. They used water-colours,
usually a greyish or brownish wash, with some odd notes of
colour; the aim was not to define effects of light and tone
as in the Picturesque, but to show the contours and lineaments
of a subject. Paul Sandby, in his long life from 1725 to 1809,
represented the development and culmination of this line.
His son stated that his aim had been "to give to his drawings
a similar appearance to that seen in a *camera obscura*",
and he "never introduced or depended at all upon violent
contrasts for effect". At times, however, he had a sense of the
particular which at some distance leads on to Constable, who
called him "the only man of genius" who painted "real views
from Nature in this country": that is, who showed no picturesque rearrangements after Gasper Poussin or Claude,
no working-up of his materials in the vein of a Canaletto.
Rowlandson, by adding a rollicking human element, may be
said to have shaken up the Sandby style.

We can, then, understand why Horace Walpole lamented
that "in a country so profusely beautiful with the amenities
of nature we have produced so few good painters of landscapes", and that the demand for Italian subjects led to
neglect of "our ever verdant lawns, rich vales, fields of hay-
cocks and hop-grounds".[2] When Catherine of Russia in 1773
ordered Wedgwood to manufacture a creamware service,
she asked for each piece to be decorated with an English view;
Wedgwood replied that there were "not enough Gothique
Buildings in Great Britain". However, the firm made inquiries
and collected 1,282 views of "the ruins, country-houses,
parks, gardens, and picturesque landscapes of Great Britain".
Gothic ruins and the mansions of topographical interest came
first, with the landscapes well to the rear.[3] However, something
was stiring; there were potentialities in the situation not to be
found on the Continent. Grosley, a Frenchman who came on
a visit in 1765, was attracted by the landscapes at Spring
Gardens, and confirmed the opinion of the previous French
traveller Rouquet that the English excelled in this branch.
"Few masters surpass the English landscape-painters; they
are at present in the highest esteem." But he names none
of them.

In 1872 the Rev. J. H. Pott was still writing:

Hitherto few attempts have been made towards forming an English school. And in this branch of the art particularly, our countrymen have contented themselves with imitating the ideas of other masters, when they should have copied nature only. In this country, the merely copying from nature, would of itself give a character to the landscape of our painters, which would be peculiar, and would sufficiently establish the taste of an English school; for England has undoubtedly many unrivalled and peculiar beauties, many characteristic charms and graces worthy of the pencil.

He cites the greenness, "the beautiful verdure that prevails here through the year". Also, "nothing is to be found in any country at all resembling an English park; nature no where appears in so luxuriant a dress, so uncontrolled in her forms and so lovely in her tints".[4]

The topographical attitudes were still strong when Turner and Girtin arrived on the scene, and for long after; but the content and method were changing. Thus, Dayes declares that the basis of style in art is to be found in the national character. The gravity of the Romans and Florentines, he says, required "that justness and truth of form which they saw in the antique statues"; the Venetians, traders with the East, delighted in magnificence. "Of the French the best masters have sought perfection by bustle and show. Of our own nation, the love of locality and portraiture may be said strongly to mark the *amor patriae*, and to exhibit our charity and love for each other."[5] Thus he posits the English values in the upper classes with their mansions and their features that they wished to perpetuate. A thinker like Blake, fiercely opposed to all values based on money and power, hated particularity of scene together with portraits as expression of the property-sense and of self-conceit. However, a shift from the upper classes with their landed interests to middle classes more professional and commercial in outlook was going on. The latter sections lacked the aristocratic pride in mansion and park; but, strongly aware of the role they played in national advancement, and largely divorced from the land, they tended to look back romantically on a lost earth. Cowper depicts the various devices of the town dweller to bring some hint of the country and its colours into his drab world:

> are they not all proofs
> That man, immur'd in cities, still retains
> His inborn inextinguishable thirst
> Of rural scenes, compensating his loss
> By supplemental shifts, the best he may ?[6]

The editor of Dayes's *Works* wrote that he hoped for the book's success "at a Period when the ARTS are held in such high repute, and when TOPOGRAPHICAL INQUIRIES so particularly accord with the prevailing taste". The growth of the wider audience had been bound up with the rise of the engraving as a cheaper form, capable of multiplication, in place of the single water-colour or oil.[7]

Water-colour had grown up as a humble exponent of topography. In 1731 *The Art of Painting and Drawing in Water-Colour*, one of the earliest treatises on the preparation and use of "transparent colours of every sort", suggests that the tinting of engravings was then considered the chief or only use of such pigments.[8] Sandby, until in his old age he was influenced by Girtin, used outlines in ink, with local colour suggested by a faint wash on a shadow tint; and water-colours were still so looked down on as a minor ancillary art that in November 1804, when the Society of Painters in Water-colours was founded at the Stratford Coffee House in Oxford Street, the promoters were concerned "whether the term *painters* in water-colours might not be considered by the world of taste to savour of presumption".

Besides the home-topographers there was what has been called the Southern School of water-colourists, who looked to Italy and Switzerland. The exponents began in much the same way as the others, as the employees of rich patrons. But in this case the patrons took the artists on tours abroad to provide memorials of the striking scenes encountered. The artists thus had to meet challenges outside the range of the topographers, and were liable to come under new influences. Their culmination came in J. R. Cozens, who seems to have travelled with Payne Knight and who was in Rome in 1778–9, where he was affected by Swiss water-colourists, especially Ducros. In 1782–3 he went south again with Beckford. He discovered the grandeur of the Swiss Alps as well as depicting the more familiar classical charms of Italy. His gentle landscapes were softly lighted and muted in colour, tending to a blue-green or blue-grey tonality of lunar pallor. His mind gave way in 1793. Turner and Girtin knew his work early through Dr. Monro; and Constable said, "Cozens is all poetry." In some instructions written down for a pupil he ended with eleven lines from W. Gilpin's *Poem on Landscape Painting*, which stressed the paramount importance of the sky in casting its colours over the whole scene.[9]

In the treatment of mansions the parkland or garden could not but play an increasing role. When Wedgwood received the Russian Empress's order his first dismayed reaction was, "Why all the gardens in England will scarcely furnish subjects sufficient for this sett, *each piece having a different subject*."[10] Landscape-gardening and the picturesque aesthetic were inextricably connected, and poetry in turn was drawn in. The poets fed Capability Brown and the other landscape-gardeners, often through the nobles who patronized poets, artists, and gardeners alike. Thus it was through the patronage of George Lyttelton of Hagley, afterwards Lord Lyttelton, himself a poet and amateur landscape-gardener, that Thomson's *Seasons* played its part in the creation of what was the finest of all the gardens, if we may credit contemporary accounts, at the Leasowes, Halesowen, the home of the poet William Shenstone.[11] Mason in his poem *The English Garden* sees the place as ideally constructed for philosopher, poet ("here shadowy glades where thro' the tremulous foliage darts the ray that gilds the poet's daydream"), scientist interested in botany or insects, and painter:

> Nor if here
> The painter comes, shall his enchanting art
> Go back without a boon; for fancy here,
> With nature's living colours, forms a scene
> Which Ruisdael best might rival.[12]

Shenstone drew on the whole poetic and landscape-gardening bag-of-tricks; and said that "Garden scenes may perhaps be divided into the sublime, the beautiful, and the melancholy or pensive".[13] Lyttelton was Thomson's patron, and gained him an official pension and the sinecure of Surveyor-General of the Leeward Islands; he was also Shenstone's neighbour – Shenstone helping to get him into Parliament in 1742. Thomson often visited Hagley and from there called on Shenstone.

Inevitably the forms of the landscaped garden affected painters. Johnson remarked, not without sarcasm, of Shenstone:

Now was excited his delight in rural pleasures, and his ambition of rural elegance; he began from this time to point his prospects, to diversify his surface, to entangle his walks, and to wind his waters; which he did with such judgment and such fancy as made his little domain the envy of the great and the admiration of the skilful; a place to be visited by travellers, and copied by designers.[14]

Nature was organized in rococo style and at the same time artificially given the touches of romanticism in its first stages. The conflict of improved and wild nature was still latent.[15]

The term *picturesque* or *pittoresco* originally meant in the eighteenth century that a landscape had been so tactfully arranged by nature as to look like something come straight out of a picture (by Gaspar Poussin or Claude). Then the meaning was inverted. The term was applied to scenes deserving a direct artistic reflection. The question of the picturesque thus could not help becoming entangled with landscape-gardening in various controversial ways, and suggested a new sort of desirable art-form – neither sublime (horrific and so on) nor beautiful (smoothed and ordered in terms of various art canons), but inviting effects of wildness, irregularity, roughness, even elements of deformity. Here was a sphere in which artistic and literary elements combined, and early exponents of the picturesque in art were often theorizing amateurs like W. Gilpin. Turner took in elements from the trend, but by 1809, as we shall see, reached a point of final rejection. Here it is sufficient to cite a passage by Fuseli, written in 1794, which attempts a reduction-to-absurdity of Uvedale Price's formulations:

If the picturesqueness of objects be increased in proportion to their roughness of surface and intricacy of motion, two spiders, such as the *avicularia*, not to descend to too diminutive a scale, caressing or attacking each other, must, in point of picturesqueness, have greatly the advantage over every athletic or amorous *symplegma* [interlocking of bodies] left by the ancients.[16]

He also argued that a landscape must be topographical, picturesque, or sublime:

Landscape is either the transcript of a spot, or a picturesque combination of homogeneous objects, or the scene of a phenomenon.

The first pleases by precision and taste; the second adds variety and grandeur; the third may be an instrument of sublimity, affect our passions or wake a sentiment.[17]

Another sphere of expression that strongly affected art from the days of Hogarth onward was that of the theatre. Many artists painted actors and scenes from plays; but even when not thus directly concerning themselves with the stage they often tended to organize their material in scenic ways. Some painters actually turned out stage-scenery, such as Michael Angelo Rooker (son of a man who acted Harlequin at Drury Lane), Francis Hayman, R. Carver, David Cox, and Louther-bourg. The last-named was by far the most important of the artists connected with the theatre; and in his work [Fig. 32] we most plainly see how the theatre affected ideas of dramatic composition in painting, merging in some respects with pic-turesque elements. Loutherbourg liked broken rocks, shaggy foliage, gipsies, bandits, scenes of human or elemental violence. In Macklin's *Bible*, where he dominated among the artists, he dealt with the Deluge (which Dayes praised as his best work), the Destruction of Pharaoh's Host (in which we see the hero-on-a-crag in a wild scene destroying the enemy below), the Chariot of Elijah, the Angel destroying the Assyrian Camp, Christ appeasing the Storm, Christ walking on the Sea, the Shipwreck of St. Paul, the Vision of the White Horse. His interest in sublime and cataclysmic themes had in it far more than mere modishness; he owned a genuine sense of doom, which on the eve of the French Revolution he expressed in his sudden belief that he had the power of faith-healing. He attempted to devise machinery for embodying his sense of natural forms in movement: his Eidophusikon with its "effects of calm and storm, sunset and moonlight, the accurate imitation of nature's sounds, the approaching thunder, the dash of waves on the pebbly beach, the distant minute gun." Dayes remarks, "In agitated water he is very successful; and this is a fine feature in his Lord Howe's Victory."[18]

The Eidophusikon led to many more experiments in dyna-mic scene effects, and links with other devices such as Gains-borough's Transparencies, the Camera Obscura (used by many painters such as Canaletto), Zograscopes, Anamorphoses or Magic Mirrors, and Panoramas. Men wanted to grasp the secret of light effects, the geometries of perspective, the movements and changes of forms in various direct ways. Many of the constructions or machines that were devised were mere toys or novelities, but in a wider view we can see how they link with a general search for deeper insight into, and greater control of, the natural phenomena that most concerned the artist. The Eidophusikon and allied inventions in particular reveal the desire to understand and express more fully the dynamic aspects of nature, the moments of large-scale change and the clash of the elements.[19]

The interest in the picturesque and in the violent helped to turn attention to sea themes, especially of storm and wreck. The eighteenth century had seen a vast expansion in Britain's commercial and naval activities, with a consequent strengthening of the power of sea themes to stir and arouse people. The seventeenth century had already seen the rise of marine painting in Holland; and the arrival of the two Willem van de Veldes in London in 1672 as official marine artists brought Dutch methods to England. These artists preferred to paint a calm or a slight swell, but the younger of them produced some gale pictures. It was a long time, however, before English painters could effectively develop the tradition thus set up. P. Monamy (of Jersey), Charles Brooking, Samuel Scott, Dominic Serres carried on with the painting of sea and ships, but made no decisive advance with the genre; and topographical artists such as Ibbetson at times followed in their marine trail. The hacks producing woodcuts or engravings for the popular markets were the main exploiters of the themes of storm and wreck. In France sea themes were treated in the general high manner. Vernet, however, specialized in wrecks, nearly all variants of the theme of ship-driven-on-rocks; at times in the spirit of Salvator Rosa, with wreckers busy on the shore. Engravings of his work, and a few of his paintings, reached England, where Loutherbourg and Morland attempted the same kind of subject – the former stressing the violence, as in *Survivors of a Shipwreck attacked by Robbers*. Occasional paintings like Robert Smirke's *Wreck of the Halsewell* 1786 had a strong effect on viewers, partly because the pathetic story was well known; the same episode was incorporated in the Eidophusikon (Northcote also painted it.) The work of John Singleton Copley, however, was making a more serious contribution towards the development of sea themes; in a work like *The Shipwreck*, painted in the 1790s, despite weaknesses of construction, he conveyed an effect of terror. Brought up in a grog-shop on Long Wharf, Boston, he had early learned both to know and to hate the sea.[20]

There, then, were the main trends confronting Turner as he grew up in the 1780s and 1790s; but to understand how he considered and absorbed them, we must take into account the two great painters who did not fit into the general schemes, and the larger system of values which they implicated.

Gainsborough, with his deep bent for landscape, in his early years drew on Dutch painters such as Ruisdael and Hobbema, but later added French influences: Watteau, *via* lesser painters like Hayman and Gravelot. He broke from his original direct contact with nature (in which, however, there is already a distinctive rhythm and touch), and devised arcadian pastorals, which at their best achieved a fine lyrical richness and unity.[21] Finally, influenced by Rubens, he sought a return to the world of fact by using bits of broken stone, dried weeds, splinters of looking-glass, which he magnified and improved into rocks, trees, water. Reynolds in his 14th Discourse, an obituary on his rival, spoke of "all those old scratches and marks which, on a close examination, are so observable", and which, "even to experienced painters appear rather the effect of accident than design; this chaos, this uncouth and shapeless appearance, by a kind of magic, at a certain distance assumes form". He seems to have used very long brushes and to have diluted his paint with turpentine to the consistency of water-colour.

Gainsborough thus gained a new lyrical spontaneity and unity of effect, in which colour and brushwork played their rich part. In some respects he appears as precursor of Turner, who in his own highly complex way made a synthesis of the Dutch, Watteau, and Rubens; who created his own pastoral world and was much concerned with finding new approaches to realism; and who shocked his contemporaries with his technical methods and experiments. Turner operated in a greatly expanded sphere, with a deepened intensity and a demonic pressure of inquiry; but Gainsborough had opened doors that made his progress easier. He himself in his Lectures

paid his tribute. He is speaking of the Dutch and the conflict
between breadth and particularity of detail:

Cuyp, Paul Potter and Adrian van der Velde sought for simplicity
below commonalty which too often regulated their choice and alas
their introductions, yet for colour and minuteness of touch of
every weed and briar long bore away the palm of labour and execution. But Cuyp to a judgment so truly qualified knew where to
blend minutiae in all the golden colour of ambient vapour.

Gainsborough, our countryman, rais'd their beauties by avoiding
their defects, the mean vulgarmiss of common life and disgusting
incidents of common nature. His first efforts were in imitation of
Hobbema, but English nature supplied him with better materials
of study. The pure and artless innocence of the Cottage Door now
in the possession of Sir John Leicester may be esteemed as possessing this class, as possessing truth of forms arising from his close
contact with nature, expression, full-toned depth of colour and a
freedom of touch characteristically varied with the peculiarities of
the vigorous foliage or of decaying nature.

To this rustic simplicity of nature unadorned contrast the meretricious Zuccarelli with all the gay materials of Watteau without a
grain of Wattaeu's taste.[22]

He carries on from there with his tribute to Wilson:

His [Zuccarelli's] figures are often beautiful, but in general poor,
plac'd always to demand attention as to colour, yet they defrauded
the immortal Wilson of his right and snatched the laurel from his
aged brow. In vain did his pictures of Niobe in the possession of
Sir George Beaumont and the Duke of Gloucester flash conviction
of his powers, as Ceyx and Alcyone and Celadon and Amelia
display contending elements or Cicero at his Villa sigh for the hope,
the pleasures of peaceful retirement, or the dignified simplicity of
thought and grandeur, the more than solemn solitude that told his
feelings. In acute anguish he retired, and as he lived he died neglected.[23]

Turner's strong feelings entangle his constructions; the Cicero
in the painting turns insecurely into the Wilson who painted
him. Describing the picture, Turner describes Wilson himself.

Wilson at Rome had been influenced by the main European
trends, both those of the contemporary world and those of the
seventeenth century which were still potently shaping tradition:
Claude and Nicholas Poussin, Mompers and Cuyp, Vernet
and the Venetians of the day. When he returned to England,
his work showed a reassertion of English and Venetian

influences, which in turn struggled with elements drawn from Claude, till in the mid-1760s a fusion came about. There emerged an elastic sense of design and increased control over light and atmosphere, plus realism of detail. Wilson's work was now too far advanced for the taste of the connoisseurs, and he suffered much hardship. But after his death, by the turn of the century, his reputation swung upwards. Artists played the key part in this change, and behind them came a new generation of collectors. The prices for his work had begun to rise by the mid-1790s.

The breadth and unity of his conceptions were realized; we have seen how these aspects of his work helped to liberate Turner from topography. In many other ways as well he fore-shadowed Turner; for instance, in his appeal to a new public (over the heads of the connoisseurs) through the engravings published by Boydell. Thomas Jones in his *Memoirs* wrote of his "dry laconic manner" and "original mode of thinking", with "a mode of expressing the idea so peculiarly his own, that he oft times provoked mirth without intending it". His withdrawn and laconic manner, as with Turner, though with less intensity, derived from his sense of isolation and originality. Farington, who had been a pupil of his, said, "He had little respect for what are called connoisseurs, and did not conciliate their regard with any flattery or attention, but sarcastically ridiculed their attachment of old pictures." Again, Jones remarks, "Wilson being an unmarried man, Kept no house." But as minutes of the Royal Academy Council of 29 December 1793 refer to a son, he seems to have had illegitimate offspring. In his *Solitude* and *Celadon and Amelia* he drew on Thomson, and he is said to have cried out at the sight of Terni waterfall, "Well done, water, by God". Many of his traits and attitudes thus suggest Turner.[24]

Above all, he was Turner's precursor in breaking through contrived systems of lighting, imposed arrangements of light and shade; he sought to bind all sections of a scene by realistic lighting with its clear source and centralization in the sky. As a step towards the union of sky and earth he massed light and shade, using cloud shadows and achieving a dramatic force. In these terms he drew to some extent on Rubens, Rembrandt, Ruisdael. Cuyp had combined at times warm and cold light, with cool grey and blue-green shadow often pitched in a high key, and produced an effect of opalescent shimmer in his light. Wilson put more green and blue-green in his shadows, in contrast with the yellows and yellow-greens of the light – and in buildings, more reflected light in the shadows. From Claude he took compositional devices such as the use of dark foreground masses of trees and edifices to frame the middle and far distances; the setting-back in space of the two flanking masses (in his Rome period); the combination of trees and architectural forms in those masses; the placing of the main tree mass towards the centre; and the introduction of a building between it and the edge of the picture. There was thus a stress on silhouette in the foreground forms and an arrangement in a receding series of planes, each parallel to the picture plane; with a treatment of forms as comparatively flat masses – the scattered lights of his earlier works being left out, and detail achieved (especially at the edge of foliage) by small strokes of the brush, almost as if with pencil or chalk. Figures were placed in ways that made them subserve the purposes of the landscape. However, he took over little of the golden light of Claude's middle period or of his later work's limpid atmosphere.[25]

Wilson thus brought about a union of Claude's general systems with the more advanced treatment of light and air by the Dutch painters. Turner had to approach this particular synthesis through Wilson, and in so doing he broke away from the parochial limitations of the topographers.

There was, however, another painter whose work still had to be absorbed if Turner were to measure up to full European standards, and who could not be adequately approached through any English master. This was Poussin, who at this period was not much regarded in England.[26] Turner had already sketched his *Exposure of Moses* and his *Landscape with Snakes* – the first when it was exhibited in London in 1798, the second in a mansion at Wynnstay, which he could have visited in 1798 or 1799. Probably both sketches, in washes of blue, grey, and brown, which come close in the same notebook, were made in 1798.[27] Turner needed to grasp Poussin's powerful and massive ordering of forms in order to consolidate his own method of history-painting, especially when dealing with great moments of shock and cataclysm. He thus broke away from the dominant Reynolds type of baroque in History, and found his own fusion of classical and realistic elements.

His account of Poussin in his Lecture shows how carefully he had analysed his work, and deserves to be cited in full:

His love for the antique prompted his exertion and that love for the antique emanates through all his works. It clothes his figures, rears his buildings, disposes of his materials, arranges the whole of his picture and landscape and gives, whether from indifference or strength of his ground, a colour that removes his works from truth. The Flight of Young Pyrrhus is a tablet of his powers in Landscape composition for grandeur and sublimity by simple forms and lines. The parallel triumphal arch in the right with the foreground trees and the classical introduction of the Ancient Hermes, interrupting the parallel lines, constitutes the leading features of the arrangement. The group of frighten'd females, the suppliant with the child, the spearman throwing the dart across the allegorical stream at once show his uncommon abilities in detailing his history and his ruling passion for the antique and allegorical allusion.

The six pictures generally called his landscapes, formerly in the Louvre, are now *dispersed*. One of them, The Roman Youth in the collection of Sir Watkin Williams-Wynn [*Landscape with Snake*] The Burial of Phocion in Mr. Hope's and in the Street Scene [*Landscape with a Road*] in the late Desenfans' collection, are with us as powerful specimens of his Historic Landscape. A slight view of them is sufficient to demand our admiration and enforce respect for their purity of conception uncharg'd with colour or of strained effects. Buildings [are] classically considered and introduc'd with the rules of parallel perspective everywhere regulating and enforcing the wholesome conviction: namely, the necessity of such rules to produce propriety even in Landscape, particularly observable in Desenfans' picture where a road terminates in the middle of the picture and every line in it tends to that centre.[28]

These passages are of interest also in showing how difficult Turner found it to express himself in conventional terms. While his thought is generally clear enough, he at times uses words in an odd way, and his constructions are liable to become confused, partly through an imperfect grasp of grammar, partly through the divigatory movement of his thought. He thinks of several things at once and is unable to separate them out in the normal logical way, as when the picture of Cicero in retirement fused with the image of Wilson in neglect. Now he goes on:

To these proofs of his abilities of Historic grandeur and pastoral
subjects we possess another truly sublime in the picture at Ashburn-
ham House of Pyramus and Thisbe whether we look upon the
dark, dark sky sparingly illumined at the right-hand corner by
lightening there rushing behind the bending trees and at last
awfully gleaming, her power reborn, its dying efforts upon some
antique buildings on the left, while all beneath amid gloom scatter'd foliage and broken ground lies the dying figure of Pyramus.
And in the depth and doubt of darkness all is lost but returning
Thisbe.

The phrase "the depth and doubt of darkness" is an example
of the way in which his untutored use of words at times has its
felicities. In the passages that follow we may note the term
"contending elements", for it meant much to him. In his
poem on Willoughby, about 1808, he made a prolonged effort
to express the idea:

> Thro the drear void contending horrors roll
> And jarring elements in uproars heap the pole . . .
> Contentious as the warring clouds
> At Winter Eve the aerial power crowds . . .
> Confused and various all contentious rush
> Reprisal seeking and the world to crush . . .[29]

Now he deals with Poussin's *Deluge*, a work that much
interested him:

From this effort of conception of contending elements let us consider
one where Nature struggles for existence and the last twisting to
the overwhelming waters of the Deluge, bearing along Earth's
perishable materials under one tone and the residue of Earthy
matter is the impression of this famous picture. Richelieu is said
to have declared that it absorbed his mind from all wordly concerns and that he could remain before it for hours as his only
pleasure. The picture is now in the Louvre and is called the Deluge.
   For colour it is admirable. It is singularly impressive, awfully
appropriate, just fitted to every imaginative conjecture of such an
event. But without which very colour Richelieu, or Poussin's
greatest admirers, could not have remained long enough before it
to have known its subject. [It is] deficient in every requisite of line,
so ably display'd in his other works, inconsistent in his introductions in the colouring of the figures, for they are positively red,
blue and yellow, while the sick and wan sun is not allow'd to shed
one ray but tears.[30]

Turner's character, his whole artistic bent, drove him to absorb all significant trends in the art of his world. All the trends or positions that we have outlined in this chapter were taken in by him and steadily transformed in terms of his own dominant purpose: all the forms and forces to be found in topography, the Southern School, the English Garden, the Picturesque, the surviving elements of rococo, the theatric influences, the art of Gainsborough, Wilson, Poussin, and Claude, and of the marine painters. Poussin and Claude – and to a lesser degree such Dutch artists as Cuyp and Ruisdael – represented important stages in the art of landscape which he felt impelled to master– not out of a mere feeling of rivalry, a need to excel, but out of his desperate impulse to take in and re-express the whole artistic sensibility of his epoch. Nothing less could satisfy him; nothing less could give him a sense of security and achievement. We have seen how on one side this driving force of his was connected with his early life of hardship and the anguish of a home which was shadowed constantly by the incalculable rages of his mother; art became a refuge in which he could feel safe only while he was working hard and extending his masteries. On the other side the driving force drew sustenance from the whole trend of the eighteenth century after Thomson, to seek out romantic excitements and intensifications of sensibility, and linked with his deep and fascinated love of all the active manifestations of nature, the forms of movement which most richly revealed their patterns in wind and water. "Contending elements" became his obsession, in which psychological, social, and aesthetic aspects were inextricably fused.

Chapter Five

The World of Poetry

TURNER'S developments might be defined solely in terms of his technical struggles and the influences such as those we have just discussed. Yet such an account would, in fact, be badly incomplete. For Turner was throughout deeply affected by poetry; his ideas and impulses in the sphere of art were inseparable from his ideas and impulses in the sphere of poetry. We do not know when he began reading poems; but it seems certain that he found out his need of them early in his career. The first scribble of verse in his hand is dated 1793 or earlier. A card has five small figure sketches in pencil, perhaps grave-diggers with a despairing woman. On the back are some partly defaced lines:

> Trusty brother strode
> Shall do for him what he has done for thousands . . .
> Prone on the grave of the dead she drops.[1]

But the first clear indications of his deep interest come in the citations to the pictures of 1798 and 1799. In 1798 five landscapes have lines: from Thomson four times, from Milton once. Next year, Thomson is once cited, Milton twice, Mallet and Langthorne once each. In 1802 come references, without words, to Ossian and to Akenside's *Hymn to the Naiads*. In 1800 we meet for the first time passages that seem to be by himself; in 1812 appeared the first quotation from what purports to be a long poem of his, *The Fallacies of Hope*. Thornbury quotes a friend as saying, "Turner's manners were odd, but not bad. He was fond of talking of poetry." Lupton, the engraver, said, "Turner among his social friends was always entertaining, quick in reply, and very animated and witty in conversation. He was well read in the poets."[2]

Trimmer, describing Turner's house, says, "I next inspected his travelling-box. Had I been asked to guess his travelling library, I should have said Young's 'Night Thoughts', and Isaac Walton; and there they were, together with some inferior translations of Horace. His library was select, but it showed the man." That he knew much verse by heart is shown by his way of citing a passage with variants introduced by himself. Thus, in his annotations to Shee's poem, he cites Mason's *Du Fresnoy*, compressing five lines into two and changing the phrases.

Why did Turner feel the need to add passages of verse? His long efforts to write poems of his own show that he was doing more than follow a fashion. He knew well enough that the picture stood or fell by its own powers of definition; yet he wanted the extra heightening of consciousness which the verses provided. He felt that they gave an insight into his creative processes; they had helped him and so should be able to help the spectator.

The central part played by Thomson in his views on poetry is amply demonstrated – by his citations, his references, and his sustained effort to pay him homage in verse: the only poem over which he continually worked. At every phase of his work he turned back to Thomson for inspiration, for verification of his impulses. It is to Thomson, then, that we must turn if we wish to grasp what poetry meant to him.

Thomson himself had had a strong response to painting. Indeed, we might say that he drew over into poetry various aspects of sensibility generated by the most significant artists of the later sixteenth and the seventeenth century: the Venetians, Claude, Poussin, Salvator Rosa. This art-response did much to help him in creating a new dynamic intensity of image in his verse, a new conception of nature which in effect created the Romantic Movement. Turner transferred this dynamic element back into art.[3] Such a formulation oversimplifies what happened, but it points to an essential aspect. Take, for instance, the lines from *Summer* that Turner put under DUNSTANBURGH CASTLE, subtitled "Sun-rise after a squally night".

> The precipice abrupt,
> Breaking horror on the blacken'd flood
> Softens at thy return. – The desert joys,
> Wildly thro' all his melancholy bounds,
> Rude ruins glitter; and the briny deep,
> Seen from some pointed promontory's top,
> Far from the blue horizon's utmost verge,
> Restless reflects a floating gleam.[4]

We see there the new Thomsonian elements, a strong sense o
the unity of a scene together with a dynamic exposition of the
interrelations. Nature ceases to be a static pattern, of which
the parts are separately described, and is realized as something
in ceaseless movement and change, with violent clashes and
overriding harmonies. This inner movement of nature involves
continual contrasts and collisions of opposites: here stark
cliff and softening light, desert and fertility, horror and joy,
nearness and distance. Light itself is not a mere incident,
one factor among many; it becomes an active principle linking
the parts, not something spread passively over the scene.
The recession of planes and colours into great distances is
centred on a point of light, which is both the stabilizing key-
stone and the heart of disquiet. Everything flows into it and
yet swings out again. The balance is caught at a sudden moment of comprehensive revelation, and thus is fixed in a stable
pattern; yet is essentially transient, making way for new
dynamic symmetries.

This is the standpoint from which Thomson seeks to catch
his landscapes, and it already represents Turner's ideal,
though he cannot yet pack all he feels of pattern and transience
into a picture. The poetry stands for his vision, the direction
he is taking and determined to keep on taking. Note that he
misquotes. He is scribbling the words down from memory – or
even if he has the book before him, he knows the passage
so well that he reads what he wants to see. For the less active
word "projecting" he substitutes "breaking", which gives an
alliterative jar to the line. Also he changes the stop after
"bounds" to a comma, making the run of the lines more fluid,
more ambiguous in construction, and sharply jostling desert
and ruins. Slight points, these, which, however, reveal the
bias of Turner's mind and the way in which he reads and uses
poetry. In 1799 he again tampered with a quotation from

Summer, attached to WARKWORTH CASTLE, NORTHUMBERLAND
– THUNDERSTORM APPROACHING AT SUNSET.

> Behold slow settling o'er the lurid grove,
> Unusual darkness broods; and growing, gains
> The full possession of the sky; and on yon baleful cloud
> A redd'ning gloom, a magazine of fire,
> Ferment.[5]

He cut out, after "the sky", some lines that extend the metaphor of artillery and chemical explosion:

> surcharged
> With wrathful vapour, from the secret beds
> Where sleep the mineral generations drawn.
> Thence nitre, sulphur, and the fiery spume
> Of fat bitumen, streaming on the day,
> With barbarous-tinctured trains of latent flame,
> Pollute the sky.

He thus confuses the grammar, making gloom and fire
ferment, instead of the combining chemicals. No doubt he
felt that the full passage distracted from his own colour
scheme of stormy sunset; but, in fact, the metaphor of
thunderstorm and artillery warfare was potently present
in his mind, and he transferred it to THE BATTLE OF THE NILE,
to which, in the same exhibition, he attached lines from the
sixth Book of *Paradise Lost*, describing the hellish invention
of artillery, "chained thunderbolts and hail of iron globes".
Thus by the collocation of the two paintings and the verses
he brings out his symbolic linkage of storm, warfare, gun-
powder, explosion, hell. This sort of metaphoric thinking
is characteristic of his mind. Doubtless it had been going
on for some time, ever since he started reading poetry and
realized the kinship of the poetic and the artistic image.
Now, as he matures, he discovers that by the use of verse
tags he can make his world-view explicit. (The way in which
analogies of war, artillery, chemical combustion, storm,
were playing in his mind can be further illustrated by looking
at Mallet, from whose *Amyntor and Theodora* he cites a
passage to illustrate CARNARVON CASTLE, also exhibited at
the same time. Though it describes an evening calm, a few
lines later we find a long account of sea storm and shipwreck.
Mallet in *The Excusion* tells of an earthquake, preceded by

"a sullen calm", using the Miltonic images of chemical combustion, sulphur, and nitre, an "enkindled mass, mine fir'd by mine in train" that "disploded bursts its central prison", releasing thunder and lightning, and begetting the cataclysm. Turner was soaked in these poems.)

In the nine lines from Langthorne's *Visions of Fancy* attached to MORNING he shows that he is already concerned with the problem of Hope, which was to become central in his thought. The lines link morning, "radiant colours", youth, joy, hope, fancy, and draw the lesson of decay, dark clouds gathering, the betrayal of hope. Here in simple moralizing form is stated a conflict which was to obsess Turner. The first two poems (1800) which seem to be his own work are not of much moment. His DOLDABERN CASTLE (with its ruined tower through which gleams an eye of light, suggestive of Wilson's towers) has five lines linking "majestic solitude" with the captive champion of liberty; as often in contemporary symbolism, the medieval tower in ruins represents the overthrow of feudal tyranny. For CARNARVON CASTLE (1800) he wrote lines imitative of Gray, in which the bard is linked with "Mona's distant hills' and again the champion of liberty is posed against the feudal tyrant.[6] In DOLDABERN CASTLE the human actors are not shown, but are expressed by the symbols of rugged mountain and threatening tower, with the thrust of light to represent the ultimate triumph of freedom. In CARNARVON CASTLE an aged harper plays to listening "swains", but the main emphasis is on nature and man's structures in their conflict and harmony.

It is from Thomson, then, that Turner drew the primary bases of his aesthetic which drove him beyond mere topography and naturalistic genre. From him he gained not only the mode of vision that looked always for movement, light change, contrasts of all kinds in landscape, but also the system of art-values that lay behind this mode. Before he directly tackled Claude, the Venetians, Rosa, Poussin, he must have had them in mind as territory that was waiting to be mastered. In the *Castle of Indolence*, Thomson succinctly set out the canon.

> Whate'er Lorrain light touched with softening hue,
> Or savage Rosa dashed, or learned Poussin drew.[7]

Liberty expanded this viewpoint. Thus, the Venetians gained from Liberty "the magic art of colours melting into colours".

> Theirs, too, it was by one embracing mass
> Of light and shade, that settles round the whole,
> Or varies tremulous from part to part,
> O'er all a binding harmony to throw.[8]

And he tells how painting came with Poussin, and

> ancient design, that lifts
> A fairer front and looks another soul;
> How the kind art, that, of unvalued price,
> The famed and only picture easy gives,
> Refined her touch, and through the shadowed piece
> All the live spirit of the painter poured.[9]

Furthermore, Turner was deeply impressed by the whole message of *Liberty*, which raises the typical eighteenth-century question: Why did the great Graeco-Roman civilization break down?

> Destructive, from the conquered east
> In the soft plunder came the worst of plagues,
> The pestilence of mind, a fevered thirst
> For the false joys which luxury prepares . . .
> Thus luxury, dissension, a mixed rage
> Of boundless pleasure and of boundless wealth,
> Want wishing change, and waste-repairing war,
> Rapine for ever lost to peaceful toil,
> Guilt unatoned, profuse of blood revenge,
> Corruption all avowed, and lawless force,
> Each heightening each, alternate shook the state.[10]

Was Britain, now spreading out in a great mercantile empire, to go the same way of disastrous greed and corruption? Thomson's answer was that Liberty had now found a secure home in Britain, since the Glorious Revolution had replaced the Stuarts with William, and there would be an endless expansion of the "Sciences, Fine Arts, and Public works".[11] His poem ended with a prospect of the great future, with Britain triumphantly repelling the baffled storm of History; but there was a deliberate ambiguity in the four lines that followed:

> As thick to view these varied wonders rose,
> Shook all my soul with transport, unassured

> But Vision broke; and on my waking eye
> Rushed the still ruins of dejected Rome.

The problem of actualizing the Vision and of escaping the fate of Rome still remains.

In his early years Turner clearly accepted the Vision as a plain prophecy which was being steadily brought true; he felt a deep patriotism as an artist playing his part in realizing the potentialities of the national character. How doubts set in, and how on his waking eyes rushed the full truth of complicated Britain, we shall see later.

Incidentally he must have been pleased with the final stanza of *The Castle of Indolence*, which would have revived memories of his childhood in the country town where his uncle was a butcher:

> Even so through Brentford town, a town of mud,
> An herd of bristly swine is pricked along;
> The filthy beasts, that never chew the cud,
> Still grunt, and squeak, and sing their troublous song . . .

Indeed, Turner must have found much in the poem to console him. He must have felt the hero close to himself: a Knight of Industry and Art born of lean Poverty, who is frugally brought up in a world of woodland nature and who is granted by Minerva and the Muses a fertile genius "in every science and in every art". He does not scorn hard work at plough or loom, but

> To solace then these rougher tools he tried
> To touch the kindling canvas into life;
> With nature his creating pencil vied –
> With nature joyous at the mimic strife . . .

The link of Thomson with landscape-painting had early been recognized. His poems were scanned for passages that could be directly transplanted on to the canvas.[12] Thomas Warton pointed out that "scenes of Thomson are frequently as wild and romantic as those of Salvator Rosa, pleasantly varied with precipices and torrents, and 'castled cliffs', and deep vallies, with piny mountains, and the gloomiest caverns. Innumerable are the little circumstances in his descriptions, totally unobserved by all his predecessors."[13] The linking of the *Seasons* with landscape-painting became a commonplace among literary critics, as in the chapter "On Thomson's

Powers of Description" in James More's *Strictures, Critical and Sentimental,* on *Thomson's Seasons,* 1777; Twining in 1789 observed that "the Greeks had no Thomsons because they had no Claudes". Percival Stockdale in 1793 saw Thomson as sage (philosopher) and poetical painter; by the end of the century, as Turner was reading his works, the *Seasons* were often compared with painting in terms of the precision, accuracy, and vividness which had become identified with imaginative power.[14]

Thomson had a predecessor in Dyer with his *Grongar Hill,* and he was expressing a tendency which would have found its expression if he had never existed – compare, for instance, the sense of colour stimulated also in Savage by Newton's work on the spectrum. Still, it was he who gave the first great utterance to the new trends, and his influence permeated the poets who followed him. To an extraordinary degree the poet looked at nature consciously as a painter. Consider how impossible in a pre-Thomsonian world would have been these lines from Mason's *English Garden:*

> Of nature's various scenes the painter culls
> That for his fav'rite theme, where the fair whole
> Is broken into ample parts, and hold;
> Where to the eye three well-marked distances
> Spread their peculiar colouring. Vivid green,
> Warm brown, and black opaque the fore-ground bears
> Conspicuous; sober olive coldly marks
> The second distance; thence the third declines
> In softer blue, or less'ning still, is lost
> In faintest purple.[15]

Hurdis, Professor of Poetry at Oxford, opened his Lectures in 1797 with a comment that the poet:

is strictly a Painter with colours and canvass before him, and the whole Creation is his subject – things animate and inanimate, intellectual and corporeal.

The first and most obvious features which he copies from *inanimate* nature, are the *changes* of the *day,* and of the *year.* Nothing therefore is more common with every Poet, than descriptions of the *morning,* the *noon,* the *evening,* the *night,* and the several *seasons,* as will readily appear from the many instances I am about to produce.[16]

Such a statement would have sounded ridiculous to any previous period; no one was likely to contest it among those whose taste had been formed by Thomson and his followers. But how close Hurdis's schematic analysis could be to the ideal structure of a poem of the period on a grand scale we can see by taking the Contents of Mallet's *Excursion*:

Invocation, addressed to Fancy. Subject proposed. A short excursive survey of the earth and heavens. The Poem opens with a description of the face of Nature in the different scenes of morning, sunrise, noon, with a thunder-storm, evening, night, and a particular nightpiece, with the character of a friend deceased. With the return of morning Fancy continues her excursion, first northward – A view of the Arctic continent and the deserts of Tartary. – From thence southward: a general prospect of the globe, followed by another of the midland part of Europe, suppose Italy. A city there upon the point of being swallowed up by an earthquake: signs that usher it in: described in its causes and effects at length – Eruption of a burning mountain, happening at the same time and from the same causes, likewise described.

What has been added to Hurdis is the large-scale use of the Prospect and the advent of Cataclysm: both elements present in Thomson and coming to a climax in Turner.

In view of the importance of Thomson in general, and in particular for the outlook of Turner, there are two points that need to be stressed. One has already been made – the dynamic quality of his vision – but we need to grasp further all that it implied; for Turner was the one disciple who absorbed all those implications, and by applying them to landscape painting introduced a new passion, a new transformative fervour. Thomson seeks to define the moment of inspiration, of extreme tension between the poet-artist and the world of nature. The viewer needs himself to catch "the landscape, gliding soft athwart imagination's vivid eye", or to lie "lost in lonely musing in a dream" of solitude, "where mix ten thousand wandering images of things". In such a moment "nothing strikes your eye but sights of bliss, all various Nature pressing on the heart" – "quick-urging through the nerves the glittering spirits in a flood of day" – "and every beauty, delicate or bold, obvious or more remote, with livelier sense, diffusive painted on the rapid mind". Again, "the swelling thought, ten thousand thousand fleet ideas . . . crowd fast into the mind's creative eye. As fast the correspondent passions rise, as varied and as high." This nervous urgency permeates all the descriptions, and is felt to make the poet-artist responsive to all the flickering and immense changes going on around him, to harmonize him with the patterns, colours, tones, and transformations of nature in the smallest and the largest aspects of universal life.[17] (Hence the importance for the Thomsonian aesthetic of participles as adjective: lengthening, softening, roughening, deepening, brightening, sharpening, darkening, quickening, whitening and so on. What for an earlier poet would be bright, for Thomson is brightening. He wants the image that impacts and expresses motion, change.)

My second point is that this world of incessant movement is in one sense outside man; it is ruled by its own laws (of which Newton is considered the prophet) – though the notions of colour and light as active principles from the first introduce a contradiction and refuse to enter a universe of mechanics in which they are meaningless. Hence a paradox. At the very moment of announcing a new active unity of man and nature, a deep division is driven between them reducing man to the role of mere observer, dreamer, muser-in-solitude. Thomson is not aware of this inner conflict in his world; he is overwhelmed by his sense of the great new potentialities revealed; but a consciousness of it slowly grows and reaches its first full expression in the great Romantics. However, from the outset it begets certain tensions and posits certain problems which underlie rococo art and come to a head with Turner. It has been observed that even in early Gainsborough we find certain rhythms which "form the core of the rococo style", some of the marks of which are: an element of detached performance, which implies a recognition that painting is only painting: a loneliness, and a certain loose-linked but firm rhythm".[18] The sense of deepened alienation from nature at the moment of increased mastery links in the social and economic spheres with the advent of the first phases of industrialism and the mechanistic science which it needs, the first phases of expropriation of the peasantry on an enlarged scale and the swelling of the cities with crowds of workless labourers and craftsmen. Hogarth expressed this historical stage; and it was no accident that his art with its restless rococo rhythms and systems begot, in his *Analysis of Beauty*, the first attempt at a formal aesthetic – one approached from the artist's viewpoint and concerned primarily with problems of form, structure, interrelations. The artist of *Gin Street* was also the producer of the first abstract designs.[19] Here we see the way in which a new consciousness of technique and of the forms of artistic expression emerge as part of the break between man and nature, man and society, which is implied on one side of the Thomsonian outlook. Thomson sees life "ever rising with the rising mind". Here nature and man are seen as united; but, applying the same sort of attitude, Hogarth defends his notions of Intricacy and of the Serpentine Line by declaring, "The active mind is ever bent to be employ'd. Pursuing is the business of our lives; and even abstracted from any other view, gives pleasure. Every rising difficulty, that for a while attends and interrupts the pursuit, gives a sort of spring to the mind, enhances the pleasure, and makes what would else be toil and labour, become sport and recreation."[20] A related tendency to abstraction of certain aesthetic elements (here light and colour) appears in Payne Knight's *Analytical Inquiry* as something independent to some extent of association and as "merely visible beauty abstracted from all mental sympathies or intellectual fitness".

Turner was not alone among artists in writing verse. Apart from Blake, whose poems he would not have known, Lawrence had composed pleasant light verses without publishing them; Shee produced two long poems on Art in 1805 and 1809; Fuseli wrote much verse in German, and though his few attempts in English were mostly unpublished, Turner may have read his specimen of Klopstock's *Messiah* (370 lines) in the *Analytical Review* of June 1791; Richard Westall in 1808 published *A Day in Spring*; Allston *The Sylphs of the Seasons* in 1813. Northcote wrote *Fables*; James Ward used verse in his description of his *Allegory of Waterloo*.[21] However, Turner was alone in seriously and consistently trying to link verse and painting, and thus deepen his consciousness of aims.

Yet the idea of this sort of alliance was deeply embedded in the contemporary outlook. We have seen how poetry kept looking to painting; in the same way painting kept looking to poetry. In 1772 Alexander Cozens, that man of incessant systems, drew up a scheme: "A Sketch of a Great Work by Alexander Cozens MORALITY, Illustrated by representations of Human Nature in Poetry and Painting, *In Two Parts*."

PART I

This part may be carried out by forming or writing a poem, upon each of the human Virtues and Vices that may be thought important enough for the purpose. Each poem to be similar to the Iliad of Homer in comprehensiveness.

Thus a system of Epic Poems would be produced. This part may be proper to be undertaken by a University.

PART II

This part may be carried out by painting a picture of each of the human Virtues or Vices that may be thought important enough for the purpose. Each picture to consist of the most extensive subject that can be procured. Thus a system of the first class painting will be produced.

This part would be proper to be undertaken by an Academy.[22]

He seems to have made no effort to implement the idea, which is none the less significant. In fact, the essence of the project was carried out by Boydell and Macklin, who built galleries, commissioned paintings that illustrated the poets, and issued engravings of them.[23] The extensive production of engravings that went on in the later eighteenth and earlier nineteenth century was initiated by Boydell's commissioning Woollett to reproduce Wilson's *Niobe* in order to counteract the influx of French works. Boydell's patronage culminated in his Shakespeare Gallery in Pall Mall (later the British Gallery), which he himself built. Before his breakdown in 1804 through the war situation, which prevented exports, he commissioned works, illustrating Shakespeare, from most of the eminent artists. In the catalogue for pictures exhibited in 1789 he stated:

In the progress of the fine arts, though foreigners have allowed our lately acquired superiority of engraving, and readily admitted the great talents of our principal painters, yet they have said with some acerbity, and, I am sorry to say, with some truth, that the abilities of those who, in less than half a century, will be lost in oblivion, while the noblest part of the art, historical painting, is much neglected.

To obviate this national reflection was the principal cause of the present undertaking.

An enterprise equally important from our point of view was Macklin's Poets' Gallery. In 1787 a prospectus of a hundred paintings was issued; in 1788 came the first catalogue. It stated:

"The object of all the arts is precisely the same; it is the awakening of the generous and social affections, the humanising of the heart, and the imparting of a general taste and relish for beauty and excellence." The common distinction between the arts was made. "The principal difference is that what the Poet or Historian achieves by long and laboured detail, the Painter accomplishes by an instantaneous effect." Reynolds had recently discussed the relation of the arts in his Eighth Discourse; but the more philosophic approach of Wincklemann, Lessing and others on the Continent was in England broken down into this simplified and direct relation of history-painting and poetry. The way was thus opened, it may be complained, to the anecdotal and sentimental genres that triumphed in the Victorian era; but a more important result was the rich fusion of poetry and painting or design that appeared in Blake and Turner.

An inquisitive character like Turner certainly would have known Boydell's and Macklin's Galleries well in his formative years. But it is of interest to note that in December 1794 the Royal Academy students subscribed "a shilling each to pay for advertisements of thanks to Messrs. Boydell and Macklin, for the privilege granted them to go into the picture Galleries without expence". Six sets (24 engravings) were published between 1788 and 1799. Meanwhile Macklin had initiated the scheme for his great Bible, which has 1791 as the date of dedication to the King and was completed in 1800, the year of Macklin's death. He had declared in the 1790 Catalogue, "The present state of the Arts in this country appeared particularly favourable to these undertakings. Genius at present wants only the stimulus of public favour to revive or eclipse all that may be boasted of the ancient schools."[24]

The poets whom Macklin's artists illustrated were Shakespeare (1), Collins (2), Gray (2), Thomson (3), Somervile (1), Spenser (2), Chaucer (3), Mrs. Barbauld (1), Gay (1), Pope (1), Shenstone (1), Jerningham (1), Mallet (1), Prior (1), Goldsmith (1), and two ballads. Among poets for whom illustrations were painted but not engraved were Milton, Young, Prior, Dryden, Jago, Parnell. The artists included Reynolds, Fuseli, Angelica Kauffmann, W. Hamilton, Macklin, Stothard, Opie, Peters, Rigaud, Ramberg, and Wheatley, who had all worked for Boydell; but Macklin got also Gainsborough,

Maria Cosway, Bunbury, and Artaud. Loutherbourg painted
the shipwreck from the *Tempest*. Of the paintings from Thomson, Reynolds did *The Gleaners* (in fact, a conversation-piece
of Mr. and Mrs. Macklin, with a girl, Miss Potts, who later
married John Landseer), and Gainsborough did *Lavinia* –
both illustrations to *Autumn* – while Opie did *Damon and
Musidora* from *Summer*. Somervile, Jago, and Shenstone were
included as lesser representatives of the Thomsonian rural
Muse.[25]

It is, then, in the works produced for Boydell and Macklin –
and also for Bowyer with his illustrated version of Hume's
History – that we must look for the specifically English flower-
ing of history-painting. Here the main basis of inspiration was
poetry, and the commissioning of pictures was made possible
because of the link with engravings, for which the public was
largely middle class. Turner and Blake, as we said, were the
great artists who germinated in this soil, though each proceeded to develop in his own highly idiosyncratic and adventurous
way. A recognition of the way in which Boydell (and therefore
also Macklin) had founded the specific English school of
history-painting, or rather made possible the expansion of
history-painting which was being baffled by a lack of patrons,
is to be found in Jerningham's poem, *The Shakespeare Gallery*
(1791):

> Too long, as with the iron power of Fate,
> Hath Custom bolted the Historic Gate;
> Enlighten'd Boydell bursts th' opposing bar,
> On their rude hinge the pond'rous portals jar;
> While the rapt Arts salute, with loud acclaim,
> This rich accession to their rising name.
>   Genius of Painting! thy bright car ascend,
> Bid glowing Energy thy steps attend,
> Triumphant ride thro' th' unrifled land,
> And seize thy plunder with victorious hand. . . .[26]

These developments securely linked poetry and history-
painting, but little was said of landscape. All the same, the
strong Thomsonian element in any contemporary notion of
poetry ensured that, in fact, landscape and history would to
some extent be connected; and the example of Wilson was
present as a proof of the possibilities in that connexion.[27]

As one more example of the closeness of contemporary

poetry and the images evoked in Turner's art, we may consider
his early drawings at Bristol, dealing with Hotwells and the
Avon Gorge, and compare them with these lines from an
anonymous *Elegy written at Hotwells* (1791):

> Now gains the struggling light upon the skies,
> And far away the glist'ning vapours sail;
> Down the rough steep the accustom'd hedger hies,
> And the stream winds in brightness through the vale.
>
> How beauteous the pale rocks along the shore
> Uplift their bleak and furrow'd aspects high;
> How proudly desolate their foreheads hoar,
> That meet the earliest sunbeam of the sky!
>
> Bound to yon dusky mart, with pennants gay
> The tall bark, on the windy water's line,
> Betwixt the riven cliffs plies her hard way,
> And peering on the sight the white sails shine . . .[28]

Finally we meet the direct linking of landscape, history, and
poetry in the club which Girtin and Louis Francia organized.
The latter, born at Calais in 1772, had come to England as a
child; he learned drawing at Barrow's school in Furnival's Inn
Court, together with John Varley; between 1795 and 1821 he
showed 85 landscapes at the Royal Academy, but failed to
gain admission; he returned to Calais in 1817 and played a
part in Bonnington's development. He was probably the moving spirit in the club, with Girtin's encouragement. On the
back of one of his drawings we find written:

This drawing was made on Monday May the 20th 1799 at the room
of Robert Ker Porter of no 16 Great Newport Street, Leicester
Square, in the very painting room that formerly was Sir Josuah
[*sic*] Reynolds', and since has been Dr Samuel Johnson's; and for
the first time on the above day convened a small and select society
of Young Painters under the title (as I give it) of the Brothers;
met for the purpose of establishing by practice a school of Historic
Landscape, the subjects being designs from poetic passages: Ls.
Francia
    The Society consists of—

	Worthington	Ts. Girtin
J. Cs. Denham—Treasr.	Ts. Underwood	
Rt. Kr. Porter	Ge. Samuel	
	& Ls. Francia, Secrty.	

Robert Ker Porter had been a fellow with Turner at the Royal Academy schools, where he and Henry Aston Barker were "great companions and confederates in boyish mischief", to the botheration of old Wilton the Keeper. Barker was the son of an Irish artist who introduced Panoramas to London. Porter himself had been admitted to the schools at the age of 13, and two years later won the silver palette of the Society of Arts for history-painting. Worthington and Denham were amateurs, the former a pupil of Girtin. Underwood was an amateur in the group working at Dr. Monro's. Samuel was a landscapist who exhibited at the Royal Academy between 1786 and 1823. Members who later joined were A. W. Callcott, pupil of Hoppner, who became a disciple of Turner, J. S. Cotman, and Paul Sandby Munn. A minute-book records its last meeting as 11 January 1800; there seem to have been further gatherings, though the organization may have been changed.

The group met every Saturday evening, at 7 p.m. (though the the first three meetings in the minute-book are on Mondays), at each other's houses. The host, called the President of the Night, selected the passage of poetry to be illustrated: one "more particularly tending to landscape". The proceedings paused at 10 p.m. for the artists to partake of "simple fare" with "Ale and Porter"; at midnight they went home. The host had to supply strained papers, colours, pencils, as well as refreshments, and in return "All the productions of the evening shall be given to the President of the Night". Thomson we may be sure was used; but the poets we hear of include Cowper (*The Task*), Ossian, and John Cunningham. Porter's sister, the handsome brunette who wrote *Thaddeus of Warsaw*, chose the passages.[29]

Why was Turner not a member? As reason for his failure to join, it has been stated that he disliked giving up a drawing. But the real reason was certainly that he blenched from asking such a group to his cramped home with his incalculable mother in its background. These were the years when she was growing so violent that she soon had to be put in an asylum. Though in 1800 he moved to Harley Street, he may have felt that he must still hold to his refusal to join; in any event he was now too taken up with other matters.

Chapter Six

Academician

THE members of Francia's club and Turner seem to have had other interests in common. The elder Barker, we noted, had introduced panoramic scenes (of Edinburgh) from Scotland about 1789. Some three years later he and his son produced a panorama of London viewed from or from near the Albion Mills on the Surrey side of Blackfriars Bridge, which Reynolds praised. In 1793 the Barkers opened a permanent building in Leicester Square, starting with a full-circle view of the Grand Fleet at Spithead. In 1799 was staged *The Battle of the Nile*. Ker Porter, too, who was doing scene-painting at the Lyceum Theatre, showed about this time a panorama of the Battle of Seringapatam, 120 feet long. Girtin was involved in work of the same sort. He painted pantomime scenes at Covent Garden; in Paris, 1801-2, he did a dropscene to be used by Tom Dibdin; on his return to London he resumed work on a huge panorama of London, the Eidometropolis, which he exhibited in 1802. In 1802 Barker produced a panorama of the Battle of Copenhagen, which drew high compliments from Nelson. (Girtin's panorama was later shown at St. Petersburg, certainly taken over by Ker Porter, who had been appointed history-painter to the Tsar.) Dayes, too, did some panoramic work; and Demaria exhibited a Paris panorama in 1802.[1]

It seems very probable then, that Turner, who liked to try his hand at all the forms of expression coming up in his milieu and who was extremely curious about all variations of landscape, all devices and effects of light and perspective, was the artist responsible for a panorama of the Battle of the Nile, which was advertised in *The True Briton* on 13 June 1799:

BLOWING UP OF L'ORIENT, with the Representation of the whole of the BATTLE OF THE NILE, aided by the united powers of Mechanics, Painting, and Optics, from its commencement on the Evening of Attack, until its glorious termination on the ensuing morning. The whole in motion, the respective Vessels taking their stations in the order in which the combat began, with the State of the Fleets on the ensuing Morning; part of the French Fleet effecting their Escape; the zealous Capt. Hood bearing down on them, and firing and receiving their Broadsides as she passes; the English boats rowing in different directions, taking possession of the vanquished ships, and saving the Frenchmen from the wrecks, is now exhibiting at the Naumachia, Silver Street, Fleet Street, every Evening.[2]

The notice stated "The whole designed and executed by, and under the direction of Mr. Turner". The only other possible Turner would have been George Turner, who in 1800 exhibited at the Royal Academy *The Blowing up of the L'Orient on August 1 1798, with the whole of the French and English Lines in their Stations*. But his other known work consisted mainly of genre-pieces; and it seems more likely that he had been stirred out of his ordinary run by painting by a visit to the panorama of another Turner than that he had conceived, designed, and organized the panorama itself. (As the advertisement shows, no one could have produced or run the thing single-handed.)[3]

Additions were made to Turner's *Battle of the Nile* from time to time. By 7 November 1799 there was included, "BUONAPARTE'S LAST AND MOST DESPERATE ASSAULT UPON ACRE" – a subject taken up by Ker Porter in a panorama at the Lyceum in the spring of 1801. On 5 December there came in "a truly grand and awful Representation of a Storm at Sea, accompanied with Thunder, Lightening, Rain, &c" (reminding us of Loutherbourg's storm in his Eidophysikon). In February 1800 we find the *Battle* followed by "ERUPTION OF MOUNT VESUVIUS VOMITING forth Torrents of Fire, environed with spiral streams of Burning Lava, and in her utmost state of Convulsion, as seen from across the Bay of Naples". And further a New System of Music was introduced before the show closed in April 1800.[4]

Transparencies were used, as *The True Briton* on 10 July

1799 stated that "The two elements are represented by Transparent Mediums, in motion, upon a scale of 30 ft by 12 in. height". Turner, as we would expect, was interested in such things. A sketchbook dated about 1796 has a transparency. The water-colour shows a cottage and peasant leaning on the wall and smoking a pipe, with a lighted lantern on the ground; on the back the scene is darkened with indigo and black, except where the light of the lantern comes, and a sunset effect is on the sky; when held up to the light the day scene is transformed into one of evening.[5]

The Vesuvian theme is again something close to Turner's heart; and though he did not paint an eruption till 1815, it had affinities with the explosion of *L'Orient*. Also, he no doubt knew what Gilpin had said about fires. "In all these operations, however grand, the fire ravages only the *works of man*. To see a conflagration in perfection, we must see the *elements engaged*. Nothing is eminently grand, but the exertion of an element."[6] Gilpin then proceeds from his account of a sea battle to one of the eruption of Vesuvius, based on Sir W. Hamilton's paper in the *Philosophical Transactions* for 1779. (Turner would have seen or known of the companion pictures of eruption and fireworks by Joseph Wright of Derby, *Vesuvius* and *Girandola*, shown in 1776. Pott wrote of Wright, "His representations of the eruption of Vesuvius, are the most sublime and celebrated of his works.")[7]

The likelihood that Turner designed the Naumachia is increased by an anecdote which Thornbury reports:

Mr. Trimmer's eldest son was very fond of drawing. One day he scrawled a man with his legs close together. Turner, being at Heston and seeing this, said, "Why do you draw the legs together?" The boy then took to battle-pieces, stimulated by the rage of the day, little queer men, all swords and plumes, men slashing and horses kicking. Turner, used to like to run over these, with a good-humoured grin, "That's better"; "Not so good"; "He'll never hit him", &c. He told me I should change my style, there being no play for talent in military costume. In fact he said, "I *commenced as a battle-painter myself*."[8]

It is hard to see how Turner could make this remark, in however joking a mood, unless it had some slight basis in fact; and from what we know, the Naumachia alone would justify it.

On the last day of March 1800 George Dance made his drawing of Turner. The features are like those of the earlier portraits, but something youthful seems already gone. He had
just finished the first large history-painting (apart from the
contemporary theme of the Battle of the Nile), THE FIFTH
PLAGUE OF EGYPT, which set him in midstream of the European
tradition and which Beckford bought for 150 guineas. Perhaps
he had been stirred by the passage in Thomson's *Summer* on
the Plague, which comes after the account of the Simoom
(later inspiring his *Slavers*) and precedes the chemically described gunpowder-sunset used in 1799 for WARKWORTH
CASTLE.[9]

In Thomson's view the Plague is the child of Nemesis; the
beasts escape it, but "intemperate man" succumbs as the "destined prey"; the cloud of death covers his "guilty domes".
Note in Turner's painting, which was generally praised, the
cloud billowing round in a great swirl. This was something he
learned from Wilson rather than Poussin, from whom, however, comes the organization along the strong horizontal
line.[10]

Turner had swung from his venture into contemporary history to the grand themes which permitted a more philosophic
statement. He seems to have been working now for some time
on AENEAS AND THE SIBYL, where Wilson's influence is paramount. Both this work and THE FIFTH PLAGUE have a clear
reference to his own state of perturbation. In the latter we see
the cataclysmic earth visited with destruction as a result of
guilt: in the former, an image of the earthly paradise, *Pius
Aeneas* (the hero devoted to his father) consults the earth
mother in her mantic chthonic form. Mrs. Turner was growing
worse in her schizophrenia; her violence must have been considerable. On 27 December, William and his son gave up the
task of looking after her at home and she was admitted to
Bethlehem Hospital. When we consider the reticent and strong
family feeling of the Turners, we can be sure that the admission
would have come about only as a last desperate resort.

Aeneas, as we shall see, was a hero of much significance for
Turner, and in many respects a self-image. He rejects and
betrays his woman at the call of a higher destiny (Rome or
Art); he is devoted to his father, not his inhuman mother; he
goes down into the earth as a prelude to his hero-work. The

Sibyl is the strange initiator into a hell-harrowing experience,
and so here seems to stand for both Mrs. Turner and Sarah
Danby. Turner was very consistent in his use of certain symbols,
and it is noteworthy that he painted the related GOLDEN BOUGH
(1834) as he was starting off with Mrs. Booth. THE BAY OF
BAIAE (1823) has again a related theme, though here the theme
of love-betrayal is uppermost, and the hero-artist, Apollo, has
turned the mantic tables on the Sibyl, who becomes manifestly
a doublet of Dido. Whether this third picture has its link with
some important love-attempt or hope we do not know; certainly Turner's women should have found in his choice of
Aeneas-Apollo as the acclaimed hero something ominous for
their relationships with him.

Farington had lost his wife in January, and his Diary loses
much of its interest in the business of this world. On 10 July
he drank tea with Turner at Harley Street and discussed what
Beckford was paying for drawings. Next day he and Turner,
in warm clear weather, went to Hoppner's at Fulham at two
o'clock and dined there. Hoppner was as well as could be expected after his accident when driving into London. The
scared horse had overturned his chaise. Turner went back
with Farington to his home.

But Farington was not the person with whom he could un-
bend. As we have seen, he often turned to the Wells family,
whom he visited both in London and at Knockholt in Kent.
He had a high respect for Mrs. Wells as well as her husband.
In 1806, after a visit to Kent, he wrote, "There is not a quality
or endowment, faculty or ability which is not in a superior
degree possest by women – Vide Mrs. Wells, Knockholt,
Oct." Wells, a teacher of drawing, had travelled widely; he
showed water-colours at the Royal Academy from 1795 to
1804, then in 1805 transferred his work to the Water-Colour
Society, of which next year he became President. He published,
with Laporte, a series of softground etchings after Gainsborough's landscape drawings, 1802–5, and he published a
Treatise on Anatomy, with plates which he himself engraved.
He had a decisive mind, and his character appears in the lines
he cited from *Measure for Measure* when urging the need of
the Water-Colour Society against the fainthearts: "Our
doubts are traitors, and make us lose the good we oft might
win by fearing the attempt."[11]

It was probably about this time that Turner wrote a poem on love in a sketchbook that has his Harley-street address:

> Love is like the raging Ocean
> Wind[s] that sway its troubled motion
> Women's temper will supply
>
> Man the easy bark which sailing
> On the unblest treachrous sea
> Where Cares like waves in fell succession
> Frown destruction oer his days
> Oerwhelming crews in traitrous way
>
> Thus thro life we circling tread
> Recr[e]ant poor or vainly wise
> Unheed[ing] grasp the bubble Pleasure
> Which bursts his grasp or flies.[12]

The New System of Music introduced into Naumachia in 1800 perhaps derived from the musical circles into which Sarah Danby had brought him. The poem, with its characteristic image of sea-storm, suggests that all was not going well in his relations with her.

So far we have noted a struggle of varying tendencies in his art: Poussin's strong design, Claude's atmospheric quality, fine water-colour effects from Cozens and Girtin freeing him from topography. Wilson's example of ways in which to use Claude and Cuyp for English subjects, Wright of Derby's contrasts of natural and artificial lighting, baroque and rococo elements of organization developing into the first stages of his own circling or elliptical rhythms in composition. Though venturesome, he had on the whole kept within the bounds of the generally acceptable canon. Now he was beginning to chafe against the bounds. At the 1801 exhibition his DUTCH BOATS IN A GALE was admired. Fuseli thought it "quite Rembrandtish"; West called it "what Rembrandt thought of but could not do". Beaumont, while conceding its merits, held the "sky too heavy and water rather inclined to brown"; Bourgeois felt "it wanted firmness"; Constable rated it high, "but says he knows the picture of W. Vandervelde on which it is formed". Still, the signs of a new technique were found worrying. *The Monthly Mirror* saw "a single and consistent image", but wanted a "greater distinction" in foreground objects. *The Porcupine* in April admitted a "comprehensive view of nature", but with "an affectation of carelessness".[13]

The disquiet came into the open with the (now lost) history-painting THE ARMY OF THE MEDES DESTROYED IN THE DESART BY A WHIRLWIND, for which Turner used a quotation from Jeremiah to universalize the disaster as a threat to all mankind.[14] *The Porcupine* called it "all flags and smoke". *The Star* on 8 May declared the army to be buried "in the sand of the desert with a single flourish of his brush". Turner's attention had probably been drawn to Jeremiah by the third stanza with its note in Thomson's *Ode to Aeolus's Harp*.[15] But there is also the contemporary reference to Napoleon's failure in the Near East as well as the general prophetic theme of doom on a warring world.

Turner was feeling the strain of his mother's final collapse, his relations with Sarah, and his ambitious hurry of work. In June he complained of "being weak and languid" to Farington.[16] On the 19th he said that he was going off next day to Scotland for three months with a Smith who lived in Gower Street; and Farington promised to send directions as to picturesque spots. But Turner arrived and "complained of imbecility – of feeling lost and worn out.[17] However, at last he got away, and, avoiding sites visited in 1797, he reached Scotland via York, Scarborough, Durham. He spent three weeks, not three months; we do not know if Smith went with him. His sketches and more careful drawings show an effort to renounce topographical detail and conventional colour, concentrating on atmospheric greys. But the results are rather vapid; perhaps he was still suffering from "imbecility".

In 1801, or perhaps even in 1800 or earlier, he had taken rooms in 75 Norton Street, Portland Road, while presumably keeping on his place in Harley Street. The address appears in the Royal Academy catalogues; but in Holden's *Directory* it is stated that he shared the house with Roch Jaubert. (The name is given as William Turner, which probably means his father. It seems then that the lease was legally in the name of Jaubert and Turner the elder.) The reason for residing in Norton Street was certainly to be near Sarah Danby at Upper John Street round the corner. The connexion is established by his co-tenancy with Jaubert, who was certainly a friend of Sarah. He had published Danby's posthumous Glees in 1798 as well as having his name down for two copies in the list of subscribers. As he was not normally a publisher or seller of music, he

must have lent Sarah his name for the occasion. What happened after 1803 at Norton Street we do not know; Turner stopped
using it as his address for the Royal Academy and it therefore did not figure in any directory of tradesmen. However, as
we shall see, there is reason for thinking that Turner and Jaubert kept the house till 1809, and that it served as the basis for
domestic arrangements with Sarah.[18] Evelina had been born
in 1799–1800; and Sarah already had four young children.
Turner must have shouldered financial responsibility for them
all to some extent. Exactly what part Jaubert played in the
system is not clear; but Turner seems to have used him as a
cover and perhaps as an agent to deal with the day-to-day
problems of the household. This rather devious and complicated arrangement was the sort of thing that gave Turner as
much sense of security as possible in a difficult situation.

When we add the fact that this year Turner's mother was
discharged, still mad, from Bethlehem Hospital, and put in a
private asylum in Islington, we can see that he had cause
enough to feel crushed into "imbecility". But he was tough,
and now as always refused to let anything get in the way of his
incessant work-drive.

Three vacancies for full membership of the Royal Academy
had come about.[19] Farington was still strong for Turner, and
drank tea with him on 6 February 1802 (presumably at Harley
Street). He admired the large drawings of Scotland. "Turner
thinks Scotland a more picturesque country to study in than
Wales. The lines of the mountains are finer, and the rocks of
larger masses." On 12 February, Turner was elected Academician, defeating the architect Bonomi. For his diploma picture he sent in DOLDABERN of 1800, then took the unprecedented step of adding another work. The Council replied that the
first work was unanimously approved. Turner attended his
first meeting on 14 April, when he was duly elected.

About this time his Devonian grandmother died at Walcot,
a village near Bath, where for some months she had been
staying with her youngest son Jonathan, a baker and biscuit-
maker – having come from a long residence with her daughter
Mary in Devon. She did not have much money, but what she
had was spread over several banks or lent out at lawful interest. On 11 March, Jonathan wrote to his brother Price,
saddler, of Exeter, complaining of her tantrums. For four weeks

she has had to be fed with a spoon; and for six weeks out of twenty she has had to have an attendant provided for her.

Now she is a cripple and carried up and down stairs like an infant In respect of her health she is as hearty as I am. I have done everything that laid in my power but no content between her and my wife, one grumbling and the other greeting [weeping]. I am almost mad, for my business is such I cannot wait on her as she expects. Now if you are a brother, think on me and come up and settle it. The best place I think [for her] is Sister Mary's, for we cannot do it any longer. Poor mother is so uneasy, for nothing will please her.[20]

No answer came. On 24 April Jonathan wrote again to inform Price that their mother was both dead and buried. After complaints, he adds, "Mother gave me all but her clothes is for sister Mary, and if there is no dispute between you four brothers, which are not in want, I will freely give up the fifty [pounds] to Mary. But if there is I can keep it all. I have not sent to London [to William] not neither shall I. It was expensive enough last summer." As postscript he states, "I am sorry you did not come up to Bath, for she desired to see none but you. I have had a sick house for a long time. My wife has been very ill with the fatuge [fatigue]." With a final detail, "Mother was so very heavy that she brought her almost to the grave with her."

But the sons, if uninterested in looking after their mother when alive, became intensely concerned when any money was at stake. Price got into touch with John, Governor of the Workhouse at Barnstaple; and John, being the best businessman of the family, gave prompt instructions.

I beg you'll go to Barings Bank and know what property she has there, and desire them not to deliver it to any person on any pretence whatsoever until they hear further of the business. And if you know of any other place that she has any property, go and stop payment . . . I will stop payment of what is in South Molton, and I think to go to Bath as soon as I can hear from you, and will see that we have justice done us.

Price found to his horror from the Exeter bank that his mother's money there had been withdrawn in January. Jonathan, asked by what authority he claims his mother's assets, passed the letter to a solicitor's clerk to answer. Sister Mary rushed in to state that her mother, when leaving her house in April 1800, had had £201 in cash and IOUs, plus a calaminco coat and gown, bed and bedding, a large silver cup and cream jug, six silver teaspoons, two large silver spoons, a pap spoon, and a parcel of books. She added that the jug had been promised to her and the pap spoon to Jonathan. Joshua, storekeeper at the Excise Office in London, suggested that the effects should be equally shared out. William, however, was more bellicose. Writing from Norton Street on 27 May he wanted strong action, especially as last summer in Bath he had heard his mother say that all should share alike; let Jonathan have his lawful expenses, no more beyond that than his proper portion; if Price won't pursue the matter, the brothers can depend on him, William, bringing Jonathan to account; he therefore means to visit the Commons to find the best way of proceeding. A fortnight later he again stresses his resolve not to let things drift.

Mr. Narraway of Bristol is now drawn in. John wrote to Price on 21 June:

I have recd. a letter from Brother William dated June 12th – saying he is willing Jonathan should be brought to heel, and is waiting an answer from me – I shall write him this day to say I am waiting an answer from Mr. Narraway he was here last week and if something extraordinary had not happened here I should have went up with him & he will assist me in the Business – I expect him here this week again concerning the Election for Cleveland – he must be here – then I mean to go with him, & he will go to Bath with me, and you may depend on hearing what the result may be. I intend writing Brother William & Jo – from Bath. & shall if the occasion require write you also – perhaps we may meet all together there to put a finish to it – for I am resolvd. to Push the Matter to the last extremety shod. he prove tardy and will not dilly dally with him.

However, Jonathan realized that the forces against him were too strong; he gave in and agreed to put the effects into a common pool from which each of the five descendants should draw their fair share. In the Letters of Administration the whole estate was sworn to be under £300 in value.

The episode has its interest in revealing the hard-headed grasping stock of the Turners (including William) and in foreshadowing the reaction of the surviving Turners when news came that William's son had died a rich man with a hare-brained scheme of helping artists and the like.

This year J. H. Serres with two colleagues founded the British School, meant to serve as a sort of auxiliary of the Royal Academy. Later one of the others told Farington that "the exhibition was broken in consequence of the pecuniary embarrassments of Serres, for whom Field and Ashford became responsible to the amount of £1,000". The venture failed by the end of 1803 – another object-lesson to Turner of how disastrous wives could be.

Besides two sea-pieces, Turner again exhibited a history-piece dealing with a cataclysm, the Smiting of the Firstborn in Egypt. Critics were again bothered at the breaking of stereotypes. Thus, the sea was not shown as transparent green where it has lashed up on chalky and sandy soil. Farington shared the reaction. Turner, he says, "strives for singularity and the sublime but has not strength to perform what he undertakes. His pictures have much merit, but want the scientific knowledge and Academick truth of Poussin, when he attempts the highest style, and in his shipping scenes he has not the taste and dexterity of pencilling which are found in such excellence in the Dutch and Flemish masters." He could not conceive that Turner had different aims from Poussin and the Dutch; for these were assumed to have set the eternal standards, so that any deviations were due to incompetence. But some younger artists and members of the public, with no vested interest in the established canon, glimpsed what Turner was after.[21] THE TENTH PLAGUE indeed had close links with Poussin in its monumental frontality, but like THE FIFTH PLAGUE it fused Wilson's *Niobe* with Poussin's structures in the rhythm of the resistances to the heavy diagonal. Both seascapes dealt with men's struggles against the sea, evoking a sense of the dark forces with which they must perpetually strive. FISHERMEN UPON A LEE-SHORE showed a mature power to express the volume and movement of the sea, and the menace of the elements combining in storm. Akenside and Ossian are referred to in the catalogue.

On 1 October 1801 the Treaty of Amiens had been signed, and France, after almost ten years' closure, was open again for visits. Girtin had got there in 1801 with the aid of a patron, Undersecretary of State; and Turner was anxious to follow. "Turner sets off for Paris tomorrow," Farington noted on 14 July, "on his way to Switzerland". The crossing was done in

boisterous weather; and at Calais the packet had to wait outside the bar till the tide rose. Turner and some others could not
bear to wait and land at the pier; they went ashore in a boat
which got into trouble at the bar and was nearly swamped.
Once ashore, Turner hurried to the pier, to watch the waves
breaking on the timbers and the fishermen putting out. Then
he hurried on to Paris with a party who clubbed together to
buy a cabriole for thirty-two guineas – to be sold at the end of
the tour. They took with them a Swiss servant at five livres a
day, who paid his own expenses. They themselves had to pay
out each about "7 shillings a day – all their expences except
travelling at half a guinea a day"; but it was necessary all the
while to bargain hard for everything everywhere "or imposition will be the consequences". They took four days to Lyons,
the country being "very bad"; then went by the malle-poste
route through Auxerre and Macon. For three days at Lyons
they enjoyed the buildings, but did little, as the town was not
settled enough". And it was dear, six livres a bed. Two days
took them to Grenoble with easier charges. Much "romantic
matter" was found in the defile of the Grand Chartreuse. Then
on they went to Geneva and Chamonix, where Turner did
some climbing and made the tour of Mont Blanc; passed over
the Val d'Aosta, crossed the Great St. Bernard to Martigny,
then moved down the Rhône valley to Vevey and went on, it
seems, to Lucerne and the St. Gothard Pass as far as the
Devil's Bridge. Retracing their steps, they visited Zürich, the
great Fall at Schaffhausen, Basle, Strasbourg, and were back in
Paris some time before 30 September, when Turner met Farington in the Louvre.

He described his journey, and said that Switzerland was in a
troubled state, but the people were well inclined to the
English. "The lines of the landscape features" he considered
"rather broken, but there are very fine parts." He noted "fragments and precipices very romantic and strikingly grand", but
disliked the houses – "bad forms, – tiles abominable red colour". However, "the Country on the whole surpasses Wales,
and Scotland too". The wines of both France and Switzerland
were "too acid for his constitution being billious. He under-
went much fatigue from walking, and often experienced bad
living and lodging. The weather was very fine. He saw very
fine Thunderstorms among the Mountains."[22]

Turner also met Abraham Raimbach, an engraver, who says that he found Paris irksome, "partly from his want of acquaintance with the language and partly from the paucity of materials offered to his peculiar studies".[23] However, he was finding enough of interest in the Louvre, studying Italian, Dutch, French, and Flemish Masters, making comments and twenty-five copies (for example three coloured drawings from Titian's) as well as analysing the Fête Champêtre, which, like others of the time, he took to be Titian's. The colour of the *Entombment* fascinated him. He made a partial copy of Poussin's *Eliezer and Rebecca*, plus detailed notes on four Poussins and colour-comments on five others, as well as mentioning four more in passing. Only Rembrandt and Titian attracted as much notice from him. He differed from other artists who found Poussin cold and austere – terms which he himself would have kept for the contemporary French neoclassic. *The Israelites gather Manna* he called "the grandest system of light and shadow in the collection"; and he found in Poussin a subtle link of colour and theme or emotion. He remarks of it:

Two figures of equal power occupy the sides and are color'd alike. They carry severally their satellites of color into the very centre of the picture, where Moses unites them by being in Blue and Red. This strikes me to be the soul of the subject, as it creates a harmonious confusion – a confusion of parts so arranged as to fall into the sides and by strong colour meeting in a background to the side figures which are in Blue and Yellow, so artfully arranged that the art of causing this confusion without distraction is completely hid. The centre has been touch'd, particularly Moses, and I think all the Red draperies in the shadows.[24]

He is working out his system of what he called Historic or Poetic Colours. In one of his lectures he later tried to state the function of colour in works that went beyond the naturalistic level. Colour

comprehends a vast portion of power in the practice of the arts. Lines and forms are defined, harmonic proportions or situations adjusted and established, subjects rendered intelligible and compatible with Nature by combinations pleasing if not fascinating. For colour often clothes the most inauspicious formalities arising from rules . . .

That is, colour does not have a mere function of decorating or emphasizing what is defined by form, but itself defines, adjusts, establishes, renders intelligible.

While light and shade can be classed without colour, producing like gradations of tone by compatible strengths of dark to light, while colour possesses the like properties as strength, [it] has others of combination, productive and destructive of light or distance, as well as appropriate tones to particular Subjects considered, or allow'd, or call'd Historic or Poetic colours.[25]

Colour does not merely produce a stronger tonal system than black-and-white with its gradations; it also has its qualities of emotional evocation, symbolism, and expression. Turner attempts further to explain Historic Colour by turning to music and to the associative theory:

Historic colour – were we to allow the musical distinctions offered to the designated styles or tone of colours of grave, soft, magnificent as has been ascribed to Poussin – with qualifications of colours innate as those of fury and anger for Pyrrhus, gracious and delicate in the picture of Rebecca, languor and misery in the Gathering, of Manna. Every tone must be Dorian, Lesbian, Lydian, Ionic, Bacchanalian. All would be historical, theoretically and practically. Confusion desiring those tones of inexplicable commixture that appall by gloom and drag the mind into contemplation of the past on his Picture of the Deluge, distracting theory by the uniformity with which he has buried the whole picture under one deep toned horrid interval of approaching horror in gloom, defying definition, yet looking alluvial, calling upon those mysterious ties which appear wholly dependent upon the associations and ideas . . .[26]

He must have "association of ideas" in mind, but by breaking the phrase up he deepens it; associations are set side by side with ideas, are merged with them, without the ideas being reducible to the associative process, as was generally done by the exponents of the theory. Colour in its full range of contrasts, harmonies and "confusions", its full tonality, ceases to be a naturalistic reflection of things and obeys other laws according to the "mysterious ties" of association and the unifying idea with its emotional modulations. The struggles over the last few years to absorb and master Wilson, Claude, Poussin, together with the revelations of the pictures in the Louvre, help to bring Turner towards a deepened comprehension of his aims and methods. At the same time, now facing the

Old Masters assembled together, he critically analyses them and realizes that he need not feel daunted.

He was still in Paris on 4 October, but back in London by the 20th. On 9 November Girtin died, and two days later Turner, with other artists, attended the funeral in the Covent Garden church where he himself had been baptized. "We were friends to the last," he later told Trimmer, "although *they* tried to separate us." *They* were the friends and hangers-on of Girtin who saw the two artists as rival tradesmen. The comment, "If Girtin had lived, I should have starved," was probably an invention, but it may have been made in a generous effort to throw back the rivalry in the face of those who had fabricated it. As late as 1840 he wrote in a notebook, by the sketch of a tower on a rock, "Tom Girtin".[27]

At the start of 1803 Turner took his place on the Royal Academy Council. A sharp struggle had been going on inside the Academy since 1799. George III in founding the Academy in 1768 had hoped to have something like the French body, with the use of history-painting to glory the Crown; but the demand for portraits and the social situation which that demand expressed prevented the Academy from ever becoming anything like its French counterpart, in which, as the Revolution loomed up, a profound conflict of political ideas went on. A theoretical homage was paid to History and periodic attempts were made by painters to show their capacity for it. The society with its forty members remained in control of its own policy and methods, and did not draw on any public money; its finances were based on the yearly exhibition. Exactly what was the relation to the Crown was never tested – until the question now came belatedly to the fore.[29] In 1799 a new member, the Irishman Tresham, was annoyed at not being promptly voted on to the Council. Using Beechey, who was in high favour at Court, he appealed to the King, who ordered that in future all Councils should be appointed by rotation. Many Academicians resented this inference. (The King's suspicions had, in fact, been earlier roused. Farington tells us that in 1794 "the academy was under the stigma of having many democrats in it", so that the King did not go to the Exhibition.)[30]

Two parties formed, one for Court, one for Academy. West, once a royal favourite but now driven into the Academical camp, was ordered to stop his history-painting at Windsor Castle and lost his pension. Having visited Paris in 1802, he was regarded by the King as "democratical" (which at this time was almost as strong a term as revolutionary). Leading royalists were the American J. S. Copley; Sir F. Bourgeois, son of a Swiss watchmaker, who boasted a Polish title and was the royal landscape-painter; Beechey, the Queen's portrait-painter, and Wyatt, Surveyor-General, who was building her a Gothic Palace at Kew; the two latter were the Court contacts. So Turner found himself on a Council with four royalists and three democrats; he espoused the cause of the three, Humphrey, Soane, and Rossi. The first clash came over the move to increase the salary of Yenn, the Treasurer, and other officials. On 4 March, Turner seconded Soane's proposal that the committee of inquiry be invited in; the Court party at once read out a protest against any delegations of authority, and walked out, so that there was no quorum. Next week a General Assembly condemned the four royalists, who then sent a threatening address to West, asking him to learn from the King if an Assembly had power to appoint committees. Resolutions of censure were carried unanimously against them.

Two incidents further increased the heat. Copley wanted extended time for sending in a large portrait group. West was absent; so the royalists voted Turner into the chair to deprive him of a vote and gained Copley his permission. Protests began; and at an Assembly on 6 April, Farington moved a vote of thanks to Turner, Soane, and Rossi for their struggle "to maintain the usages and resolutions of the Academy". Copley sent his work along in time. But he soon got his own back by pointing out that a painting by West had two dates, 1776 and 1803, while the rules forbade re-exhibition of a picture. Secretary Richards was told to write to West, but later denied receiving instructions. West first learned of the trouble through an attack on himself in *The Morning Post*. In defence he argued that he had substantially repainted the work, and as he had left both dates on he could not be accused of deception. He and others were angered at the deliberate leak of Academy matters to the Press. On 25 April an Assembly decided to apply a test to members in order to discover the guilty man, who was thought to be Copley.

On 3 May the Assembly asked Council members to sign a statement that they had had no hand in the Press leak. Copley did not attend; but Humphrey, Rossi, and Turner signed, and Smirke proposed a motion approving their conduct. Soane about this time was won over to the Court camp, and as Humphrey was often away Turner and Rossi had to lead the fight for Academy rights. At a Council meeting called for some trivial matter the royalists ignored the agenda and Copley read a resolution that the Council was not answerable to the General Assembly. West was asked to submit the resolution to the King, after a second meeting had confirmed it; he managed, however, to have this meeting held up and called an Assembly for Monday, 30 May. The Academicians voted for the suspension of the five royalists, and committees were set up to watch events. On 10 November, West told the King of the suspensions. The King replied by ordering the resolution to be expunged. The Secretary interpreted this reply as referring to all matters connected with the suspensions; but the five royalists wanted the declaration of the Council's independence from the Assembly to be left on record. West, Turner, and Rossi supported the Secretary; but the King gave his decision against them, in what West called a "tyrannical" mandate. At the Annual General Meeting the royal letter, twice read out, was heard in complete silence, and West was re-elected President. The Academicians feared that the King would refuse to accept the new Council and would be persuaded by Wyatt to insist on the previous Council continuing in office. However, perhaps he or his advisers realized that this would be pressing things dangerously far.

Turner had throughout taken an active part against the Court. He, West, and Rossi had led the Academicians; and tempers were frayed. At an Assembly on 24 December there were arguments about awards. "Daniell heard an altercation between Bourgeois and Turner", says Farington. Bourgeois said that when premiums were to be adjudged for architecture and sculpture, he voted according to the views of those "most conversant with those respective studies". Turner sarcastically suggested that he might do the same when painting or drawing of the figure was in question. Bourgeois then called "Turner *a little Reptile*, to which Turner replied by telling Bourgeois that he was *a great Reptile* – with ill manners." Bourgeois, by stressing Turner's smallness, had managed to hit him on a sore spot.

This year Turner exhibited CALAIS PIER, FESTIVAL AT MACON, and HOLY FAMILY. The considerable discussion the works caused showed how much he had been coming to the fore. The voices of disquiet grew louder. Hoppner, as one of the older artists, "reprobated the presumptive manner in which he paints, and his carelessness. He said that so much was left to be imagined that it was like looking into a coal fire, or upon an Old Wall, where from many varying and undefined forms the fancy was to be employed in conceiving things." Northcote saw only "novelty", a compound of much art in an eclectic way, with "too little of nature". Beaumont, while admitting that far and middle distances were "finished", saw the foregrounds as "comparatively *blots*, & faces of figures without a feature being expressed". The sea in CALAIS PIER was like "the veins in a marble slab". Farington thought of the works that "the *novelty of the manner* imposes beyond what their real merits would claim". However, Opie admired MACON as a work where the painter "obtained most of what he aimed at", compared with others in the room. Fuseli liked CALAIS and MACON as showing "great power of mind", though the foregrounds were "too little attended to – too undefined". Garvey remarked later to Farington that "this praise of such crudeness was extravagant and a Humbug". Constable described the whole exhibition as "in the landscape way most miserable".

The critics generally followed the line of the older artists. *The Sun* saw only genius lost in "affectation and absurdity" and complained that "under the idea of generalising his objects he often produces nothing but incongruity and confusion. The sea looks like soap and chalk." The sky "is a heap of marble mountains". The figures are flat and not "enlivened by dabs of gaudy colour. In short this picture exhibits a waste of ability." *The British Press*, while admiring much, pointed out what it considered defects, since "many young artists slavishly imitate *all* his work." *The True Briton*, on 16 May, declared that Turner had so debauched the taste of the young artists "by the empirical novelty of his style of painting that a humourous critic gave him the title of *over-Turner*". Constable, following Beaumont's lead, was surprised in talking with a group of young artists that they indeed looked on Turner's work as being "of a very superior order" and refused to agree that they were "in any extreme".[31]

All this is important in showing how quickly Turner had developed his style to the point of challenging the main accepted standards. Hoppner's comment is of interest in bringing out the relation of his "indistinctness" to romantic reveries. Blake had said, "I can look at a knot in a piece of wood till I am frightened at it." Coleridge abounds with reverie effects:

I bent down to pick something from the ground . . . as I bent there came a distant vivid spectrum upon my eyes; it was one little picture – a rock, with birches and ferns on it, a cottage backed by it, and a small stream. Were I a painter, I would give outward existence to this, but it will always live in my memory.[32]

His poem *Daydream*, dealing with images that come from the shadows dancing on the wall, is an epitome of the romantic attitude in this important matter. But for Turner there is the connexion both with this sort of poetic method and with the Blots of Alexander Cozens' system. (Note how Beaumont underlined the term *blots* in describing Turner's new mode of painting.)[33] Cozens had written:

An artificial blot is a product of chance, with a small degree of design; for in making it, the attention of the performer must be employed on the whole, or the general form of the composition, and upon this only; whilst the subordinate parts are left to the casual motion of the hand and the brush.

He adds in explanation, to make clear that he is not thinking of haphazard meanderings:

A true blot is an assemblage of dark shapes or masses made with ink upon a piece of paper, and likewise of light ones produced by the paper being left blank. All the shapes are rude and unmeaning, as they are formed but with the swiftest hand. But at the same time there appears a general disposition of these masses, producing one comprehensive form, which may be conceived and purposely intended before the blot is begun. This general form will exhibit some kind of subject, and this is all that should be done designedly.[34]

He cites with interest da Vinci's comment on the value of looking at old dirt-covered walls "or the odd appearance of some streaked stones", where you can decipher "several things like landscapes, battles, clouds, uncommon attitudes, humorous faces, draperies, &c. Out of this confused mass of objects, the mind will be furnished with abundance of designs and subjects perfectly new."[35] The aim is thus the shaking off of stereotypes and the attainment of a fresh vision. Coleridge's reveries lead to precise images; Cozens seeks to express a creative tension between accident and purpose, conscious and unconscious elements, in the process of composition. The Blot theory stresses the unity and inner consistency of structure and effect in the creative act.

But it was inevitably misunderstood. No reviews are known of *A New Method of Assisting the Invention in Drawing Original Compositions of Landscapes*, published in 1785. But the book was clearly well known in all advanced art circles. Barry mentioned it in his Lectures, and Uvedale Price in his *Essays* of 1798. Here there was no distortion, even if the full consequences of the idea were not grasped. But Henry Angelo and Pyne showed what a parodied version of the Blot was generally spread. Pyne says:

Will it be believed hereafter, that a professor of painting should undertake to splash the surface of a china plate with yellow, red, blue, and black, and taking impressions from the promiscuous mass, on prepared paper, affect to teach his disciples; and those persons of education and elegant mind to work them into landscape compositions?[36]

A game was made up on these lines. Metrical instructions in MSS. under the initials "C.D. 1816" have twice turned up.[37]

We may surmise that Dr. Monro, with his interest in the Cozenses, would have had *A new Method* in his library; and Turner, with his eager curiosity, must have read it there or elsewhere. Monro had some of Alexander Cozens's work, for he bought drawings of his at the sale of 1781; and Turner seems certainly to have owned one of the four versions known of the 13th Blot in *A New Method*.[38] In passing we may note the comment made by Samuel Palmer, "The first exhibition I saw [in 1819] is fixed in my memory by the first Turner, *The Orange Merchantman at the Bar*; and, being by nature a lover of smudginess, I have revelled in him from that day to this. May not half the Art be learned from the gradations in coffee-grounds?"[39]

The importance of these points lies in the extent to which

they help us to understand how Turner had the courage to
drive on against the whole weight of established contemporary
opinion into his great grasp of the unity of light and colour.
In the last resort there was a creative necessity which he could
not control and for which he had no words. But at the same
time he needed to draw on all aspects of theory and practice
in his world which helped to give him encouragement. Without
his love and knowledge of poetry he could never have carried
on as he did; and Alexander Cozens's *New Method* was one
of the many factors that strengthened him in his resolve to hold
fast to his conception of imaginative unity. We may recall his
own statement, "Always take advantage of an accident."[40]

Another factor that helped him towards simplifications
was the way in which he early trained himself to memorize
forms and effects of light, colour, and atmosphere. Memory
can play a creative role, selecting and reconstructing in terms
of some unifying image or concept. Akenside, the poet whose
formulations helped Turner to deepen philosophically the
ideas taken over from Thomson, states in *The Pleasures of the
Imagination:*

> But some there are
> Conscious of nature, and the rule which man
> O'er nature holds: some who, within themselves
> Retiring from the trivial scenes of chance
> And momentary passion, can at will
> Call up these fair exemplars of the mind;
> Review their features; scan the secret laws
> Which bind them to each other; and display
> By forms, or sounds, or colours, to the sense
> Of all the world their latent charms display:
> Even as in nature's frame (if such a word,
> If such a word, so bold, may from the lips
> Of man proceed) as in the outward frame
> Of things, the great artificer portrays
> His own immense idea.[41]

If for "great artificer" we read "the laws of natural process",
and for "at will" we read "in the creative act", we come close
to a statement of the way in which memory functioned for
Turner in the production of a landscape. In fact, he applied
and developed in his own way two positions: that of Cozens
which required the immediate setting-down of the main idea
or structure of a scene, with details for later elaboration (if so

wished); and that of Hogarth, which advocated a shorthand system for fixing forms and attitudes that could later be strung together in the completed paintings.[42]

If we look closely at his sketchbooks we see how experimentally free his mind already was, though he was cautious as yet in following up his momentary intuitions. He was ready to bide his time, giving the intuitions their space of play, but also determined to master the whole tradition of significant art in his world. He already has a strong sense of the unity of earth and sky, especially with water as the mediator. A sketchbook of about 1800 "has two scribbles of sunset, clouds and water, integrated as one mass; another early instance (1802) is a wonderful little drawing – the Finberg catalogue says probably of Brienz – made up of abbreviated hooked strokes. The miniscule mosaic of angularity, the richness in the poverty, suggest Klee to us. Much earlier, in 1795, when Turner was twenty, he could achieve a not dissimilar effect of the greatest delicacy, such as the twin drawings of two mounted figures descending a hillside near the sea. Other drawings conjure up Cézanne; even in many grand paintings some values of the sketch are obstinately maintained." The technique of some late oils where "calligraphy overlays an unbroken cake of paint, is foreshadowed by very delicate pencil drawings on paper prepared with wash rubbed out for the lights".[43]

Chapter Seven

Cataclysm and the Earthly Paradise
(1804-5)

In 1804 intrigues continued in the Royal Academy, beginning with the election of a new Keeper. Turner refused to say for whom he voted, but in fact supported Smirke against Rigaud of the Court party. Beechey and Wyatt at once told the King what a dangerous democrat Smirke was; he had remarked after Marie Antoinette's execution, "The Guillotine might be well employed upon some more crowned heads." But when two days later West called the King had again gone mad. There was a widespread feeling that the Royal Academy would break down, with important members seceding. In this atmosphere Turner decided to build a gallery of his own and according to James Ward, meant to charge for entry and stop exhibiting at the Royal Academy. By April his gallery (some 70 by 20 feet) in Harley Street was finished on the first floor, carried out in part on supports over the back garden. Beaumont complained to Farington at Turner showing so many pictures together and at the lack of correspondence between the strong skies and the other parts in them.[1]

However, Turner did exhibit at the Royal Academy and did not charge at Harley Street. His pictures provoked the usual insults. Northcote said he would have thought Turner had never seen the sea, and Opie said the water looked like a turnpike-road. This year a proposal of Farington's led to the institution of a varnishing day before the opening of the show. There was still tension in the Royal Academy, and on 11 May, Turner was at a Council meeting with West, Smirke, Rossi,

Bourgeois, and Farington. Bourgeois took Smirke and Farington aside into the Model Academy to discuss a scandal caused by Tresham circulating verses against the collector Hope at the Academy Dinner. "On our return to the Council we found Turner who was not there when we retired. He had taken my Chair and began instantly with a very angry countenance to call us to account for having left the Council, on which moved by his presumption I replied to him sharply and told him of the impropriety of his addressing us in such a manner, to which he answered in such a way, that I added his conduct as to behaviour had been a cause of complaint to the whole Academy."

Turner had recognized the withdrawal of the three as the sort of intrigue and faction-making of which he disapproved. But Farington's parting shot suggests that he had been throwing his weight about, perhaps on the lines of his scathing comment to Bourgeois.[2] However that may be, the episode certainly sickened Turner of the whole business of caballing in the Royal Academy, and he attended no more Council meetings that year, ignored the King's Birthday Dinner, and for some time kept away from the Academy Club and the General Assemblies.[3]

His nerves must have been upset badly by the death of his mother around 15 April at the Islington asylum. A month earlier his master Malton died – his brother James having shot himself in Marylebone Fields the year before. And, near the end of May, Dayes committed suicide.[4] Under these various pressures Turner seems to have been hardening. Tales of his appetite for money begin. However, the attempts to make him out a miserly character miss the point. On the one side there was a strong fear of insecurity, a determination to be quite independent at all costs; in this sense his care over money represents a consolation, a counter-weight for his resolute drive forward into his own style despite all the attacks and the refusal of the connoisseurs to buy his work. On the other side there was a pleasure in being able to damn the world and go his own way, without the need to defer in any way to patrons. Thus, he dunned the Marquis of Stafford for twenty guineas for a frame. He was within his rights; but Edridge, who told the tale, was amazed at his shortsightedness in annoying a wealthy client over a small sum. That, however, was precisely the reason for Turner's action; he wanted to show he was no respector of persons.[5]

This year he exhibited BOATS CARRYING OUT ANCHORS AND CABLES TO DUTCH MEN OF WAR IN 1665, showing the same energy as CALAIS PIER and FISHERMEN UPON A LEE-SHORE. *The Sun* said that it seemed to be "painted with a birch broom and whitening", and the *St. James's Chronicle* found the sailors "all bald or like Chinese".[6] In fact, his rendering of the sea was growing ever more dramatic and deeply felt. His experiences at Calais had given a new directness and a fullness of feeling for the movements of the sea and their effects on men and man-made vessels.[7]

We have seen how, after the tentative AENEAS AND THE SIBYL and the lost BATTLE OF THE NILE, he had landed squarely in the European tradition of history-painting with THE FIFTH PLAGUE, completing the trend begun by Wilson and for the first time embodying Poussin in the English line: Wilson and Poussin merge. THE TENTH PLAGUE carried this fusion further.[8] In THE DESTRUCTION OF SODOM and THE DELUGE, which followed, he continued his exploration of the Poussin world; but he did not show these at the Royal Academy. He probably put them into his own gallery in 1805, though later, in 1813, he sent THE DELUGE to the Academy. It seems, then, that for the moment he felt disinclined to display such works in the sphere of the connoisseurs and the art critics. The themes were still those of cataclysm brought on man by his corrupt backslidings. THE DELUGE he no doubt felt impelled to do in order to show how to treat the theme without the weaknesses which he felt in Poussin's work.[9]

Between 1800 and 1805 he had been driven to develop the fully fledged historical-painting; and certainly one main reason for this turn was his conviction that in such a form alone could he adequately express his deep intuition of the doom that men were bringing on themselves by corruption, greed and violence. (THE BATTLE OF THE NILE with its Miltonic tag was the prologue to the series.) But thereafter, for some five years, he dropped prophetic themes and concentrated on direct landscape.

Meanwhile, however, at the same time as he developed his Poussinesque visions, he was maturing his control of sea themes, steadily infusing them with the same emotions and symbolism as he put into the history works. He was organizing them on the same general principles, of which the gyre and vortex were the fullest expression. Take CALAIS PIER, for example. The movement-out of the pier in the right corner draws the eye round in a curve into the packet lying far off in a line parallel with the horizon and its thin stretch of seething white – into the bowsprit of the boat with brown, blown sail, outlined against the distant gloomy glow: a pattern repeated with variations in the central boat. The balance of the boats and their masts is subtly linked with the diagonal, and a host of further lines and curves plays its part in giving strength and variety, inside a complex organization of interwoven and contrasting light and dark, of shifting tensions of cloud and wind, wave and wind, boats and water. The curling wave on the left balances the pier, while carrying us into the circling turmoil which finds its point of stress and stability in both the blue oval rent of sky and the swinging sail below. The many elements drawn on, which include aspects from his own earlier work, are united in a new way, which is already pure Turner. We are hurried into the gyring scene, and yet contemplate it from a raised position, feeling both the detachment and the intense participation of the painter. (We may add that here, in his effort to pack everything in, he has forced his tone-values, wanting to make his contrasts as wide as those of nature.)[10] We may compare MACON, with its scene of harvest rejoicing drawn by the great river curve into a vast serene distance of faint glimmering tones. In CALAIS PIER and MACON, then, we can see two elements that always stayed with Turner, essential ingredients of his vision of earth: a sense of elemental violences against which men struggle either in vain or with success, and a sense of radiating harmonies of pure enjoyment and peace – the fact of deepening crisis, and the belief in ever-greater potentialities of happiness.

We can now begin to understand more fully what was meant by our earlier statement that Turner needed to match himself against all the main trends of his day, to absorb them and divert them to his own uses, not out of any simple impulse of rivalry or wish to shine, but because in no other way could he feel secure and happy. Threatening all the established art canons by his need to find and express his own standards of truth and beauty, he felt an incessant anxiety and instability, which he could only overcome by never pausing in his work, never pausing in his effort to make it both more comprehensive and more true to his deepening vision of reality. Thus, his need to absorb all that was most significant in the art trends was only another facet of his need to drive ahead on a lonely track of devotion to his personal vision. He judged art in terms of its revelation of quest. To Munro he said later, after looking at a characterless sketch of his, "What are you in *search of*?"[11]

The maturing crisis of eighteenth-century society had issued in two great revolutions, the American and the French. It was at the moment issuing in the general anti-feudal upheaval that accompanied the Napoleonic wars, and in the steady growth of the first forms of industrialism in England, with all the inevitable scientific and technological changes. The art which expressed the main political conflicts was that of history-painting as worked out in the area of most direct struggle for State power, France. David's paintings had been the plainest expression of the conflict of ideas. But the sense of continuing and confused crisis found its outlet in many forms, in pictures of storm wreck, natural disaster, battle clash, romantic horrors and wildnesses. The taste for the horrific, the desire for works of art that produced a shudder, had kept on growing, and was expressed both in pictures and in romantic verse and the Gothic novel. Turner could not but respond to such fashions, which had their roots in the real conflicts, pangs, and dilemmas of the epoch, even if they too often were vulgarized in expression, made melodramatic, morbid, overpitched or inflated. The depth and the force of his reaction to the themes of disaster rescued them from the weaker aspects of the mode. He poured his most passionate concern and anguish, his deepest insights, into them, till the storm on land and sea became for him a complex and finely articulated image of social and spiritual crisis.

At the same time his growing fascination with the face of nature in violent convulsion cannot but have links with his long-drawn-out sufferings from his mother's violent spasms. He takes the violence of mother earth into himself and masters it: just as he preluded his step into an art of mature realism and symbolism by his painting of the Father-loving Aeneas about to enter the Underworld with the aid of the mysterious sybilline Mother. He is wresting the secrets of fury and tumult, of suffering and inner discord, from the universe; and the tempestuous clouds and waters are like his own spirit, his mother, and the disturbed society that surrounds him with war, violence, division, and worsening crisis.

His inability to draw people stems from this complex of emotions. Only once he succeeded in staring someone in the face and plainly putting down what he saw.[12] The face was his own, and the result was the early self-portrait (reproduced on the dustjacket) out of which he insistently stares – a work produced in a desperate struggle to maintain self-respect through the dark yet exciting years, when his mother raved and he went on mastering his art. His weakness in depicting faces did not come from any inability to draw. When he was not thinking of figures as persons he could often draw them effectively enough; he could master ships and buildings, mountains and seas, trees and rocks and streams; he could master men at work, as long as they were part of the scene of action and did not intrude as persons. (Mayall the photographer, who knew him near the end, mentioned that in speaking Turner kept his eyes on the ground and did not look his companion in the face). The rough indications of people in his foregrounds, to which critics strongly objected, were thus a psychological necessity which could not be separated from the whole set of forces making him the artist of nature in movement and forcing him out of all accepted formulas into a sheer vision of light, colour, and form, in a new dynamic unity.

The Royal Academy was now further threatened by the formation in November 1804 of the Society of Painters in Water-Colours, in which Wells had played a leading part (water-colours were often badly hung at the Royal Academy). The new Society must have come about with Turner's blessing, though as an Academician he could not contribute. Its first show, in April 1805, was successful. And a new rival to the Royal Academy itself was coming up, the British Institution for Promoting the Fine Arts, which was founded on 4 June. Its aim was to foster British art, but the connoisseurs took it over and soon inverted its function. One of its worthy aims was to create a National Gallery.[13]

This year Turner did not contribute to the Royal Academy; he had his own gallery to think of. Apparently it opened in early May and closed on 1 July. Thriftily he sent invitations for the Academicians in bulk to the Royal Academy Secretary. Henceforth for many years his own gallery was the main place from which he sold his paintings and drawings. Now in 1805 his most important exhibit was THE SHIPWRECK (at first called *The Storm*), a work which powerfully carried on the methods evolved in CALAIS PIER. The older artists hated this painting, with its great sense of furiously moving space and maddened water. A strong diagonal, given variety and a set of inner tensions by the lines of masts, stays, spars, waves, is partly broken down and swallowed up by the central maelstrom, a sort of bursting lozenge which, with its local whirls and upheavals, creates a vortex. The covering of distance by spray and the use of a diffused light (in place of the cloud rent) provide a greater unity than in CALAIS PIER. The human figures, despite all the turmoil, are given a power and tenacity of action, which makes us feel that they may yet somehow control the situation – while Turner seeks to focus the tragic sense on a woman generalized into something of a madonna.[14]

We have seen how early Turner was haunted by elliptical forms of organization. He was certainly in part influenced by his broodings over perspective and the nature of vision. A picture's corners, if filled with distracting details or forms, spoiled the effect of unity. The compositional heart, the light centre, must also be the point at which the eye looked into the picture; and all the elements of form and colour should take this fact into consideration. Indeed, in later eighteenth-century art, in the rococo style with its restless movement, there had been a certain trend to develop a circular form of composition, sometimes moving round and spiralling into the centre. When J. Burnet in 1828 published *A Practical Treatise on Painting*, in the first part "Practical Hints on Composition in Painting", he treated of Angular (Diagonal) and then of Circular Forms. But Turner as usual gave his own dynamic to ideas that he drew in from others. For him the circular or spiral form became a tumultuous vortex; and till the end of his days this remained one of his main obsessions. Wilson's *Niobe* was an important predecessor of his method.[15] Here the diagonals are modified by the strong tower-punctuated horizon line; the drive of the wind, expressed by the cloud, Apollo, and the tree in the right top corner, and by the bushes below, comes in against the main diagonal, which is repeated in parallel form by the lower rock mass with a separating burst of fire. A set of resistances to the static diagonal is set up, showing the first stage towards the Turnerian vortex: a tension between the two light centres and the movement of cloud and wind. (Also, J. R. Cozens in the *Coast under Vietri*, painted for Beckford, fused land and storm clouds in something of a vortex.)[16]

The link of Turner's history-work with Wilson's *Niobe* was recognized. Thus, C. O. Bowles of North Aston, a collector, remarked that his pictures of 1800–1 were "the best that had been exhibited since the *Niobe*".[17] And it was probably as a response to those works that we find Loutherbourg exhibiting in 1804 *An Avalanche in the Alps, in the Valley of Lauterbrunnen.* Here a rugged rock mass on the left provides a sharp diagonal outlined against a strong splash of light and turmoiling heaps of snow, rock, fire, and swirling mist; in the lower right corner a cottage is being crushed by an avalanche. The effect is of a central explosion. Loutherbourg here exerts all his forces, no doubt stimulated by Turner's work, recalling *Niobe*, and in turn affecting Turner, who was later to repeat the demolished cottage in a yet more dramatic depiction of an avalanche with falling rocks.[18]

Hoppner remarked of Turner's gallery that it was "like a Green Stall, so rank, so crude, and disordered were his pictures".[19] West saw the water as like stone and Turner's work in general as "tending to imbecility". Wilkie, now a probationer at the Academy, wrote in a letter much praise of some of Teniers' works "which for clear touching certainly go to the hight of human perfection"; while, as for Turner, "I really do not understand his method of painting at all his designs are grand the effect and colouring natural but his workmanship is the most abominable I ever saw and some pieces of the picture you cannot make out at all and although his pictures are not large yet you must be at the other end of the room before they can satisfy the eye." However, Sir John Leicester bought THE SHIPWRECK for 300 guineas and C. Turner engraved it. When the print appeared in January 1807 it marked the start of a series of large engravings after Turner that did so much to spread his name among a new public. The list of subscribers shows only Beechey, Soane, Stothard among the R.A.'s, but at least fourteen young artists.[20]

On 21 October the battle of Trafalgar was fought. About noon, 22 December, the *Victory* entered the mouth of the Thames, bearing Nelson's body, and anchored off Sheerness. Turner sketched her as she entered the Medway. His sketchbook shows that he went aboard and drew marines and bluejackets, flags and uniforms; he also interviewed the men, noting down their characteristics. Thus, of the marines: "Undress a red jacket; sometimes a red fancy shirt." "Mr. Atkinson, square, large, light air, grey eye 5–11." "C. Hardy wore B. gaiters, 4 sailors carried some officers down about the time L.N. fell, on his left arm. Some one forwarded to help him A marine to every gun stands aft 8 others. C. Hardy looks rather tall, dreadful (?), fair, about 36 years. Marshall, young, long tail, round face, proud lips. 5.2." Next year he showed an unfinished version of THE BATTLE OF TRAFALGAR in his own gallery.[21]

At the Royal Academy, West, depressed and harassed by the royalists, wanted to resign. On 10 December Wyatt became President. Lawrence and others boycotted the meeting, but Turner voted for Wyatt. He seems to have lost all interest in Academy politics, seeing them only as a shadow fighting of no significance. Henceforth he did what he could to make the running of the Academy efficient, but that was all. Alaric Watts declared later that he used to grumble, "What has the Academy done for me? No one has knighted me, Callcott has been knighted, and Allan has been knighted, but no one has knighted me." But it is extremely unlikely that so reticent a man would have spoken like that. The words seem rather to express what everyone felt sure he must be thinking. (C. R. Leslie merely says, "I think it possible he was hurt.")[22] A more authentic ring appears in the anecdote about Haydon. Thornbury tells us:

The day poor wrong-headed Haydon ended his untoward life, Maclise called upon Turner to tell him of the horrible catastrophe. The narrator's imagination was roused to the uttermost by the suddenness and ghastliness of the event. To his astonishment Turner scarcely stopped painting, and merely growled out between his teeth.

"He stabbed his mother, he stabbed his mother."

"Good Heavens!" cried Mr. Maclise, so excited that he was prepared for any new terror. "You don't mean to say, Turner, that Haydon ever committed a crime so horrible?"

Still Turner made no other reply, but slowly chanted in a deep, slow voice, "He stabbed his mother, he stabbed his mother."[23]

Only later did Maclise realize that he had been referring to Haydon's attacks on the Academy.

This story tells us a great deal about Turner. He was a man of strong and stubborn affections, when once his fears and suspicions had been broken down. A powerful family sense had been riveted on him by his home sufferings. His deep love for his father never changed, though as time went on the relationship in a sense became inverted. In his anguish at William's death he told Trimmer that he felt the loss "like that of an only child".[24] And Trimmer adds that he "never appeared the same man after his father's death; his family was broken up". At the same time he diverted on to his art the emotions inhibited from a normal flow into a fuller family relationship; what he could not give to Sarah and her children he gave to his paintings. We have seen how Clara Wells stressed the fact that he looked on his works as his children and grieved at being parted from them. His dislike of selling them developed in time into his scheme for preventing their dispersal and for giving them a united home; he even bought his works back. In a codicil to his will he underlined the cherished aim "of *keeping my works together*". (This emotion in turn led to his feeling that any one of his works in separation had little value. He objected to people wanting to buy "scraps". Ruskin says, "When he heard of any one's trying to obtain this or the other separate subject, as more beautiful than the rest, 'What is the use of them,' he said, 'but together?' The only thing he would sometimes say was 'Keep them together'; he seemed not to care how they were injured, so that they were kept in a series which would give the key to their meaning." He disliked one being singled out for special notice or criticism; he considered the interrelations within the whole development to be alone of interest.) The Academy had become a maternal protecting figure under whose aegis, despite all the back-biting and intrigues, he had been able to consolidate his position and achieve independence. So, after the period of disillusioning struggle, he returned to an acceptance of it as a sort of necessary evil modified by many useful functions. He did not drop his independent activities, but saw them as ancillary, as an insurance against further disruptions or breakdowns of the institution.

We see here, then, at least a partial explanation of his own failure to achieve a family, despite his connexion with Sarah. He had made his art children and the maternal Academy the sole source of his satisfactions and security. To become a normally married man meant to break this set of ties or at least to force them into accommodation with another set; and this he could not bring himself to do. No doubt he visualized such a step as a loss of independence, as a surrender of his easy roving ways and his periods of total concentration n work. But the compulsion went deeper than any such rationalizations. The fractious Academy mother, with all her failings, was something which on the whole he could understand and control. A real woman, such as Sarah, held mysterious depths of resistance and betrayal against which he did not feel capable of securing himself. Security was his great aim; and yet his creative needs kept on driving him away from all the systems through which he could have built a safe reputation and income, a normal place in the society of his time. Here lay the drama of his life, and he feared to complicate it further with an emotional relationship in which he would be incalculably at the mercy of someone else, though his strong sexuality prevented him from cutting himself away from the world of women.

He had a deep need not to interfere or be interfered with. George Jones said, "My great intimacy with him arose from his confidence (that I had his confidence Turner proved by his appointing me his executor in 1831, without my knowledge) – that I had no desire to know his secrets, control his actions, or suggest changes in his course of life. He never interfered with nor condemned the habits of others; if he thought them incorrect, he was silent on the subject, and if any excuse or palliation could be made, he was always ready to accept, adopt, and promulgate the excuse. I never heard him speak ill of any one." Thornbury adds, "He never appeared morose and displeased but when people had been trying to cajole or defraud him, or when he observed in any one an unbecoming desire to pry into his private affairs. That he never forgave." In his later years the secretive element in him became obsessive. His desire to hid himself in a neutral attitude, an obscurity or anonymity, was all part of his wish to build a secure and self-sufficient sphere or family out of his art.

Much more evidence as to Turner's hiding-away of himself and his work could be adduced. Thornbury tells of Britton forcing his way into the Maiden Lane bedroom by coming up the back way; Turner covered up his drawings and sharply expelled him. He may be working up some anecdote; but the tale is true in essence. Again, he says, not long before his death Turner took refuge from a shower in a public house, where he sat in the farthest corner. An artist who knew him came in. "I didn't know you used the house; I shall often drop in now I've found out where you quarter." Turner emptied his glass and said as he went out, "Will you? I don't think you will." An acquaintance chanced to find him on the steamboat going up from Chelsea to the City. "Seeing Turner clean shaved, his shoes blacked, and looking as if he had just left home, he made some remark about his living in the neighbourhood, wondering to see him there so early, 'Is that your boy?' said Turner, pointing to the gentleman's son, and evading all questions as to his own 'whereabouts'." He even evaded friends when there was no apparent reason at all. The Rev. Mr. Judkins once came on him at Boulogne. "He did not much like the 'Why, who expected to see you here?' Mr. Judkins saw no more of him till just as he was leaving, when he caught a glimpse of him in a boat, bobbing off the shore, drawing in an anxious absorbed way, and heedless of all else. He also met him once on a Margate coach. They had, he found, been travelling together for some time. Mr. Judkins reproached him with his shyness, and Turner, said in fun, 'Why, how could I venture to speak to a great divine?'" (On this last occasion he might have been going down to stay with Mrs. Booth.)

There is a further point. The Academy mother (art on its visible and its social aspects), on which he continued passionately to beget his countless art children, was a surrogate for his actual mother; the relationship involved a sense of guilt as well as an enveloping satisfaction. (In all this we see a pattern which is to be found generally in creative activity, but which in Turner is carried to a special intensity because of his mad mother.) The repressed guilt-sense did not appear in his direct relationship to art, except as part of the dynamic forcing him into unresting activity; but it came out tangentially in his inability to build an open and stable relationship with any women. He would find satisfaction only in a socially-guilty (adulterous or promiscuous) connexion. His powerful sexuality is apparent from his art itself, with its rich sensuousness, its finely felt textures and elements of touch, its pervasive sex-symbolism in its forms and rhythms of organisation, quite apart from the drawings in which he depicted copulation. His sexuality could find a partial outlet in his unceasing art activity, but only a partial one; his sex needs drove continually out through his art and beyond it, into relationships that were momentary or remained unsatisfactory, cored and hedged round with doubts, fears, inhibitions.

Also, as I have said, there can be no doubt that as a result of all this Turner suffered a keen anxiety and that he had to keep on driving down or evading a fear of madness. Anyone who had lived through the close experience of a member of the family going violently to pieces could not but have such fears, however well they were diverted or held down. Turner's remark about Haydon expressed not only a devotion to the art mother, but also a nexus of murderous hate; he would not have visualized Haydon's actions in such terms unless they stirred something deep in himself of an allied kind. Here the link is with the actual mother, whose paroxysms, destructive of family happiness and stability, must have stirred embittered responses in the son – death wishes going back into the lost world of infancy and stirred afresh, obscurely and powerfully, at the mother's actual death in 1804.

We may add the revelation of Turner's deep and hidden emotions in his remarks about being buried in his paintings.[25] We see there much more than a passing fancy; Milman had to be assured of the absence of any such pagan cerements before he allowed Turner's burial in St. Paul's. Turner was imagining himself as the art mother finally enclosed about with the art children. The escape from a difficult and disturbing reality was achieved. Womb had become tomb, and vice versa. The desired relationship of harmony and peace had been won, but at the cost of giving up all struggle. The self-sufficient sphere was complete and finally isolated.

There is yet another point of importance to be made in this connexion. Turner became supremely the painter of natural forms in movement, in clash and convulsion. On the one hand, as we have seen, his images of natural violence can be related to the world outside, to his vision of men's heroic struggle with the elements and to his concept of the doom that they bring upon themselves by their betrayal of their own higher aims, their surrender to corruption and division. But on the other hand, those images are also born of personal anguish. Representing the face of nature in a raging fury, they also represent the demented mother in her spasms of hate and torment. (From Thomson on, the term Face of Nature, with its various changes, had become a common property of the poets.) While the former set of meanings give depth, objectivity, universality to the images, the second set provide a restless dynamic without which the aesthetic quest would never have been carried on with such force and persistence. It is of special interest, therefore, that in Mallet's *Excursion*, certainly well known to Turner, the detailed pictures of earthquake and volcanic eruption have sandwiched between them a passage which links madness with natural cataclysm:

> Sulphureous damps, of dark and deadly pow'r,
> Stream'd from th' abyss, fly secret overhead,
> Wounding the healthful air, whence foul disease,
> Murrain and rot, in tainted herds and flocks;
> In man sore sickness, and the lamp of life
> Dimm'd and diminish'd; or more fatal ill
> Of mind, unsettling reason overturn'd:
> Here into madness work'd and boiling o'er
> Outrageous fancies, like the troubled sea
> Foaming out mud and filth; here downward sunk
> To folly, and in idle musing warp'd,
> Now chasing with fond aim the flying cloud,
> Now numb'ring up the drops of falling rain.

That passage must have hit Turner hard when he read it, and sunk in deep. (He took from this poem the phrase "congregated clouds", which he repeated in his own verses.) It is important too that in another passage Mallet analogically identifies natural cataclysm with "the tyrant's law" and "the arm of Pow'r extended fatal" to crush where it should protect. Must we "homage hell", he asks, or bend the knee

> To earthquake or volcano when they rage,
> Rend earth's firm frame, and in one boundless grave
> Ingulf their thousands ?[26]

We are now beginning to grasp the complex of fears and resistances that prevented Turner from finding a happy married relationship despite his strong family feeling. He now had a second daughter Georgianna; and he must have been keeping Sarah and her four earlier children (Marcella, Caroline, Theresa, and another who died some time before 1851) as well as his own. A touch of the repugnance he felt at a furtive relationship appears in his will, where he limited the recipients of his projected charity to persons born in England and of English parentage, and of lawful issue. A minor source of discord between Sarah and Turner was no doubt also to be found in the matter of religion. Turner had no religion whatever; but John Danby had been a Roman Catholic of a seriously professing kind. Sarah must have been a Catholic by birth or conversion; and she brought up her children by John as Catholics. Her daughter Caroline Melissa married the composer H. G. Nixon (1796–1849), who was a Catholic, organist first at St. Andrew's Chapel, Glasgow, and then from 1839, at St. George's Cathedral, Southwark. He died of cholera, after his wife had borne him thirteen children, one of whom also became a Catholic composer and organist, another a violinist; she herself died in 1857. It seems, then, that Sarah kept up her musical as well as her Catholic connexions; and she cannot but have chafed religiously as well as morally against the conditions of her relationship with Turner.[27] Turner, who carried on the eighteenth-century tradition of the Catholic Church as the embodiment of feudal tryanny and bigotry, cannot have been happy in her attitudes.

As he drove ahead in his art, and broke down old stereotypes, various forms of abuse and protest were used. That which he must have found most galling and distressing was the accusation that he was mad or on the way to madness. We have seen Hoppner talking of his tendency to imbecility. At the opening of the 1806 exhibition James Boaden of the

Oracle remarked in front of *Schaffhausen*, "This is madness", and John Taylor agreed, "He is a madman." In 1814 Hazlitt saw "a waste of morbid strength", and in 1823, "visionary absurdities . . . affectation and refinement run mad". Of the BOCCACCIO of 1829, the *Atlas* said, "It would excite pity if painted by a maniac", and the *News*, "a daub of the most ridiculous kind . . . The figures are mere blotches . . . The whole group seems more like Bedlam broke loose than a family of ladies and gentlemen." In 1831 *The Times* wrote that Turner "disgraced the high powers that dwell in him by caprices more wild and ridiculous than any other man out of Bedlam would indulge in", and Richard Westmacott remarked of his exhibits, "Only one was very mad – a Medea raving in the midst of her bedevilments and incantations. You can conceive how Turner would out-Herod Herod in such matters." In 1838 the *Athenaeum* declared, "It is grievous to us to think of talent, so mighty and so poetical, running riot into such frenzies; the more grievous, as we fear, it is now past recall." In 1839 Thackeray wrote in *Fraser's* that Turner's exhibits "are not a whit more natural, or less mad". Thornbury himself continues the tradition when he says of Turner's later work, "the colour, that of fireworks, rising almost to insanity, and occasionally sinking into imbecillity".[28]

A variant was to declare that Turner was sick or diseased. An essay in the *Tatler*, probably by Leigh Hunt, in 1831, spoke of "his present disease (ophthalmic or calenture) which leads him into the most marvellous absurdities and audacities of colour that painter ever ventured on. This is very melancholy, but we feel that a timely application of blistering and phlebotomy may arrest the current of his disorder." The *Athenaeum* in 1841 described his works as "wonderful fruits of a diseased eye and a reckless hand".[29] After his death a fashionable oculist, Professor Liebreich, gave a learned lecture explaining away Turner's yellows and his opalescent colouring as due to a pathological condition of the lens.[30] Frith summed up the situation: Before *Modern Painters*, "there was not an art writer who did not vilify and ridicule the great man. In the picture by Turner of the burial of Wilkie in the sea, one of the most poetic of the painter's works, the steamer, which is, of course, dark in the moonlight, is called a black fish-kettle, and the friends of the painter are recommended to place him under such restraint as will prevent his exhibiting insults to the public!"[31] From time to time, it is true, someone spoke out with some feeling for what Turner was after; but in general what Frith said was all too true. And the insinuation that he was suffering from some mental disease must have been especially hard to take. Despite his toughness in many respects, he was very vulnerable to criticism. It could not deflect him from his purpose, but it made him suffer acutely. We hear of him with tears in his eyes as he read newspaper criticisms.[32]

Chapter Eight

Pause and Renewed Stress (1806-10)

THE wealthy committee of the British Institution had bought Boydell's Gallery in Pall Mall and fitted out three rooms to look like a sumptuous mansion. The first show opened on 17 February 1806. Many Academicians contributed. Turner sent NARCISSUS AND ECHO and THE GODDESS OF DISCORD CHOOSING THE APPLE OF CONTENTION IN THE GARDEN OF THE HESPERIDES. The latter work completed his first series of history-painting, seeking to combine the images of the earthly paradise and the threat of disaster. (He had struggled to compose verses on the theme, but they were not attached to the picture.)[1] Beaumont, expressing the doubts of the connoisseurs, told Farington that Turner's paintings "appeared to him like the works of an old man who had ideas but had lost the power of execution". He was surprised when a young artist, W. Havell, who had a picture hung near Turner's DISCORD, spoke of the latter "as being superior to Claude, Poussin, or any other". A few weeks later he summed up: Turner "is perpetually aiming to be extraordinary, but rather produces works that are capricious and singular than great".[2]

Other young artists were following Turner. An Academician uncle remarked that W. Daniell "appeared to be engrossed" by his work; he thought the Bridgewater sea-piece "a finer work of art" than Cuyp's evening scene with boats in the same collection. Augustus Callcott and S. W. Reynolds were of his school, we hear, as well of John Crome of Norwich exhibiting at the Royal Academy this year.[3] Boaden com-

mented on *A Landscape* by Crome, "There is another in the
new manner – it is the scribbling of painting – so much of the
trowel – so *mortary* – surely a little more finishing might be
borne." Such comments were now the fashion. Northcote
said of Callcott's *A Calm, with figures shrimping*, that the
artist "had founded himself on Turner's manner, which several
others had adopted, and 'had leapt out of the frying-pan
into the fire' – to avoid the appearance of oil in their pictures,
they now seemed as if executed with mortar".

Turner had opened the way in thus freeing the use of paint;
but Crome and Constable, each working along very different
lines from Turner, were the only artists who had the vision
or driving-force to make use of the new possibilities; and they
were both men who would have found their way forward in any
event, in terms of their own sensibilities. Callcott and the others
soon lost their small experimental energy, and it was left to
French artists to carry on. When a new general style did come
about in England it was pre-Raphaelitism, taking no advantage
whatever of the chances of breadth, freedom of handling,
colour range, and so on, that Turner had opened up. The
dead weight of the Victorian bourgeoisie was too great.

In the later summer Turner was at Knockholt, where Wells
suggested a project that turned into the *Liber Studiorum*.
Ever since 1793 Turner had been producing views for
publishers who wanted them engraved, but he had been
working to narrow instructions. What Wells proposed was
a series in which the various kinds of landscape composition
would be illustrated and the whole thing done under Turner's
own supervision. The aim was to reveal Turner's wide powers
of invention in a technically adequate way. Clara in 1853 stated
that her father had been "constantly urging Turner to undertake a work on the plan of [Claude's] *Liber Veritatis*".

I remember over and over again hearing him say – "For your own
credit's sake Turner you ought to give a work to the public which
will do you justice – if after your death any work injurious to your
fame should be executed, it then could be compared with the one
you yourself gave to the public." Turner placed implicit confidence
in my father's judgment, but he required much and long continued
spurring before he could be urged to undertake Liber Studiorum.
At last, after he had been well goaded, one morning, half in a pet
he said, "Zounds, Gaffer, there will be no peace with you till I

begin (he was then staying with us at Knockholt) – well, give me a sheet of paper there, rule the size for me, tell me what subject I shall take" – my father arranged the subjects, Pastoral, Architectural &c., &c., as they now stand, and before he left us the first five subjects which form the first number were completed and arranged for publication greatly to my dear Father's delight. This was in the October of 1806.[4]

Wells had in mind Claude's *Liber Veritatis*, rough pen-and-sepia records of his work which were engraved long after his death; the versions by Earlom had given them an insipid monotony, and Wells was thinking of this failure to grasp the character of the originals. The idea was not that Turner should vie with Claude; but that he should ensure against commercial vulgarization of his work. Turner was no doubt won over by a shrewd realization of the possibilities in the market for engravings. His misgivings appear in some verses which he wrote at Knockholt about a line of poplars outgrowing themselves.[5] "How near is pride to earth allied" – that is, to a fall-to-earth. But he ended by throwing himself keenly into the project and made arrangements with Charles Turner to do the engraving. In a draft title-page the categories were given as: History, Mountains, Pastoral, Marine, Architecture. But Pastoral was later subdivided into "E.P." – probably Epic (though Elegant and Elevated have also been suggested). The E. Pastorals tend to be Claudian in comparison with the more direct Pastoral proper.[6]

At the Royal Academy Wyatt had proved a feeble President, and knew it. He resigned and West was once more elected to the chair. Turner seems to have voted for him. In January 1807 he took a house outside London, 6 West End, Upper Mall, Hammersmith, which he held till 1811. It is now gone, but we are told that it was "of moderate but comfortable size, and its garden, intersected by the Church Path, extended to the water's edge. The house, a white one, with another house at its side, was on the north of the Church Path." The Path was a tree-fringed lane, probably fenced off from the house. Market gardens and meadows were all around.[7] The Loutherbourgs lived near by, in Hammersmith Terrace, but Mrs. Loutherbourg, a clever and vivacious woman, seems to have disliked and distrusted Turner. Thornbury says that Turner called, but she suspected him of stealing her husband's secrets; "on his next visit she shut the door in his face and roughly refused him admittance". This story is improbable; but some clash may have occurred.[8]

Turner was accompanied by his father. During his stay at Hammersmith he seems to have painted there, and kept Harley Street only for exhibitions. He may have left London simply because he wanted to be nearer scenes which stimulated him, or the changes may have been caused by some domestic difficulties. "Here, out in the open air, were painted some of Turner's best pictures", says Trimmer. "It was here my father, who then resided at Kew, became first acquainted with him; and expressing his surprise that Turner could paint under such circumstances, he remarked that lights and a room were absurdities, and that a picture could be painted anywhere. His eyes were remarkably strong. He would throw down his water-colour drawings on the floor of the summer-house, requesting my father not to touch them, as he could see them there, and they would be drying at the same time." Trimmer adds that he remembered as a child "walking with his father and Turner at night under the blaze of the great comet. Turner was fond of children; and children discovered it, and were fond of him."[9] (The date of the walks was autumn 1811. The comet "became visible to the naked eye in England at the beginning of this month [September], and continued to be a splendid and striking object during all the clear weather of the autumn".)[10]

From late April 1807 to 13 June the Harley Street gallery was open.[11] In May, West "was disgusted with what he found there: views on the Thames, crude blotches, nothing could be more vicious". On 11 June the first set of the *Liber Studiorum* were shown there.[12] At the Royal Academy, Turner showed works without the stress of their predecessors: A COUNTRY BLACKSMITH DISPUTING UPON THE PRICE OF IRON and SUN RISING THROUGH VAPOUR; FISHERMEN CLEANING AND SELLING FISH. He had recoiled into a calm mood, a homely poetic realism, and a serene meditation on light.[13] From Farington we learn how the artists were divided in their reactions. West said Turner had "run wild with conceit" and "greatly fallen off" in his sea-piece. Westall agreed. Mr. Phipps, following Beaumont, said of Turner "that he made nothing out; that he had no *execution*; and that *Loutherbourg* was superior to him – [Henry] Thomson said he would rather have a sketch by Turner than all Loutherbourg had ever done. Wilkie was present and concurred in giving a preference to Turner." Smirke also liked the Turners.

Turner had been making studies direct from nature. He often worked from a boat, as we find the river in the foreground. Wandering up and down the Thames, mostly between Walton and Windsor, he painted the woodland and the changing light. He had bought or hired a boat, and seems to have sailed as far as Margate and to have gone up-river as far as Abingdon, taking up his fishing-rod when he laid down brush or pencil.[14] In a list of expenses that cover Hampton, Ripley, Guildford, Godalming, we meet, "1st Catch 3 – 6." The same sketchbook shows him still brooding on history themes: "Ulysses and N[ausicaa]", "Ulysses & Polyphemus", and the first signs of sustained interest in Punic history, "Ascanius" and "Dido & Aeneas".[15]

It seems to have been his 1806 visit to Knockholt that started him off in *plein-air* experiments. He was now consolidating this field, painting landscapes with a spontaneous reaction to the view before him – though the larger examples must have been done at Hammersmith after he returned from his boating trips. At times he used his sketches for more elaborated oils. But in effect many of the works he produced were complete in themselves, whatever his motive in making them. As they were never exhibited, they had no effect on the course of painting, as did the related work of Constable with its stress on the particular scene in the fullness of its immediate aspects. Their importance lay in the gains which he proceeded to incorporate one way or another in the following phases of his art, and which had crucial links with his next experimental phase, in the 1820s. Henceforth, he held to the aim of embodying elements of direct spontaneous response in his work, whatever other elements he also incorporated.[16]

Again a naval event interested him. He went to Portsmouth to see a detachment of British and of surrendered Danish ships; but bad weather had dispersed them. On the twentieth and twenty-first of October some ships came up on the Downs, but were still held by the winds. At last however, in the afternoon of 1 November, two ex-Danish ships arrived at Spithead; a scene which Turner recorded in SPITHEAD, shown in his own gallery next April.[17] On his return journey he made notes of four subjects later engraved in the *Liber Studiorum*. The journey must have been hurried; for on the 2nd he was present at an Assembly of the Royal Academy, to vote for Daniell, who became an Associate. He himself was standing for the Professorship of Perspective; and though there were no other candidates, the matter was put to the vote, twenty-seven voting for him, one against. West was once more President. In a draft for his first lecture, Turner suggests that the situation "tempted the offer of my services altho' conditional if no other member offered to endeavour to be useful to our institution".[18] No doubt he valued the prestige of the office – for a while he signed himself P.P. as well as R.A. – but probably he also hoped to use the lectures to make an effective presentation of his ideas on the organization of a work of art.

In February 1808 he showed at the British Institution his completed BATTLE OF TRAFALGAR and JASON (at the Royal Academy in 1802). In his own gallery he had provided a key-plan of the main figures in the battle and an account of the action.[19] What he aimed at was a breakaway from the historical picture which concentrated on a few leading actors, as did West's *Death of Wolfe;* he wanted to present the action as a whole without melodrama or posturing.[20] In this aim of expressing the confusion and tumult of a naval engagement he was highly successful, and so his picture was condemned. West, echoing what Farington said in 1806, found the figures "miserably bad", and Robert Hunt in the *Examiner* remarked that all the men on the *Victory* had been "murdered". One critic, however, recognized "a new kind of Epic Picture," "the first picture of the kind" that had ever been exhibited; Turner had "suggested the whole of a great victory".[21]

John Landseer, who had started a new quarterly, was probably responsible for this insight. We can safely assume that he wrote the article in his June number, which was the most intelligent notice that Turner had so far received – indeed, that he was to receive till the advent of Ruskin. The writer insisted on the truth of Turner's vision and his grasp of all the variety of phenomena:

The brightness of his lights is less effected by the contrast of darkness than that of any other painter whatever, and even in his darkest and broadest breadths of shade, there is – either produced by some few darker touches, or by some occult magic of his peculiar art – a sufficiency of natural clearness. Like those few musicians of transcendent skill, who while they expose much less than others, the extremes of the compass of their instruments, produce superior melody.

His colouring is chaste and unobtrusive, yet always sufficiently brilliant; and in the pictures of the present season, he has been peculiarly successful in seeming to mingle light itself with his colours. Perhaps no landscape painter has ever before so successfully caught the living lustre of Nature herself, under all her varying aspects and phenomena, of seasons, storms, calms, and time of day.[22]

The writer thus came close to grasping what was to be Turner's revolutionary achievement: the realization for the first time in the history of art of the unity of light and colour. He also noted his mastery over atmosphere, "the delicate management of the air tint which intervenes between the several distances". Among other works at Turner's gallery he mentions the view of Pope's villa at Twickenham: a subject that was stirring Turner to much verse-writing as he combined it with his attempt to pay homage to Thomson. In the Royal Academy he had only THE UNPAID BILL, OR THE DENTIST REPROVING HIS SON'S PRODIGALITY, commissioned by Payne Knight to hang by Rembrandt's *Candle Piece*. The setting had been chosen so that the sunburst through a window might shine on the bottles and apparatus of the dentist. The *Beau Monde* said that an "unskilled spectator" was offended by the pervading "air of indistinctness".[23]

For part of the summer Turner visited Sir John Leicester's seat, Tabley House, in Cheshire, where another visitor, Henry Thomson, said he spent more time fishing than painting. What his thoughts were as he fished, we can gather from notes jotted down about reflections in water. He meditated on "a white body floating down a River (the Dee)". Though its whole surface was light against the water on which a dun cloud was reflected, "yet the reflection of the white body had not any light or dark reflection, but on the contrary had its reflection dark". Another note begins:

Reflections not only appear darker but longer than the object which occasions them, and if the ripple or hollow of the wave is long enough to make an angle with the eye it is on these undulating lines that the object reflects, and transmits all perpendicular objects lower than the spectator. But in receding lines, as well as objects, rules seem to lose their power, and those guides to enable us to find some cause to near objects lose their application or become enfeebled by contraction to remote ones . . .[24]

He has been watching the elongation of image or reflection on a ripple, but cannot find a formula for the reflections of receding lines as they reach the eye. If there were neither current nor motion on the surface, the water would be flat as a mirror, and the theory of mirror reflections would apply. But use that theory to deal with water reflections in motion and the result is most "fallacious to the great book of nature – when painting art toils after truth in vain". This concern with finding out where rules are useful and where they break down is characteristic of the Lectures he was now seeking to prepare. Not that he was quite ready. In December the Royal Academy Council wrote to ask when he proposed to begin; whatever he replied he did not lecture in 1809.

We can tell from his art how much he had pondered over water and its laws, its momentary effects and its fundamental patterns of movement. With a moment to spare he could not resist squatting on his haunches and staring at moving water; once he was seen near Westminster Bridge in this uncomfortable position, watching the ripples at the edge of the tide for over half an hour.[25] Hence his love of fishing, which provided just the excuse he needed for haunting waterways; it gave him something to do, something to attend to now and then, while the observation of the water was his main preoccupation. In the same sketchbook as the note on a floating white body, we read, "Fishing Rod, Great Coat, Paints Box, Canvas."[26] And in 1825, while on the Seine, he made a note about bait. "Provide yourself with plenty of gentles" in the corner of the jacket pocket; "if the aforesaid be old so much the better because they (the maggots) will work through the same cleaning themselves the while".[27] G. Jones relates, "I was often with him when fishing at Petworth, and also on the banks of the Thames, when we were making our annual visit to Sir J. Wyattville at Windsor Castle. His success as an angler was great, although with the worst tackle in the world. Every fish he caught he showed to me, and appealed to me to decide whether the size justified him to keep it for the table, or to return it to the river; his hesitation was often almost touching, and he always gave the prisoner at the bar the benefit of the doubt." Rose of Jersey adds, "I fancy I can see him trudging down the avenue something after the manner of Paul Pry, by which I mean that an umbrella invariably accompanied him; rain or sunshine, storm or calm, there was that old faded article tucked under his arm. Now, the umbrella answered a double purpose, for by some contrivance the stick could be separated from the other parts; this then formed a fishing-rod, being hollow, with several joints running one into the other. I have seen him sitting patiently for hours by the side of a piece of water belonging to the property, his piscatory propensities keeping up his excitement, though perhaps without a single nibble; yet it must not be understood that he was always unlucky, for when fortune favoured him in securing any of the finny tribe, it was not long before we were made acquainted with his success, at which he appeared as much pleased as a boy from school."[28] (As he had an umbrella with swordstick handle for protection against brigands while roaming in Switzerland or Italy, we can see how important such an article was for him.)[29]

Fishing comes into his verses. Thus, about 1809, he wrote a lamentation about the incessant rain which drives the fisherman under a tree "in doubtful shelter," while "the anxious angle trembles in his hands" as he looks out "between the falling rills", peering for a ray of sunlight. (This is the poem from which we have cited the picture of the boy launching his paper boat.)[30]

On 8 January 1809 "A Constant Reader" in the *Examiner* satirized the professors of the Royal Academy for giving no lectures, and suggested a cudgelling of "those sons of indolence" absorbed in consuming turtle soup and venison. That evening the Academicians, in fact, had a dinner with Turner as speaker. We find him drafting a reply "So we may expect a thrashing unheard next Saturday. It is hard you cannot have a few friends to-day and, if you please, give them turtle soup and venison, without giving umbrage to a constant reader . . ." (The episode has the interest of showing how closely he read the criticisms.) Soane at least was pricked into starting his architectural lectures on 27 March, Turner helping him with the illustrative drawings.

At his own gallery, among other works, he showed THOM-
SON'S AEOLIAN HARP: young people carrying out some rite
of homage to the poet, with the Thames at Putney as background. At the Royal Academy he had SPITHEAD and THE
GARRETEER'S PETITION. His Tabley pictures brought him in
more commissions, including some from Lord Egremont for
views of Petworth and Cockermouth Castle, and from Lord
Lonsdale for two views of Lowther Castle. He spent most of
the summer in collecting material for these works, gave
assurances that he would lecture in 1810, and produced a
design to improve the lighting, while Soane redesigned the
seats.

Round this time he was writing much verse. From both its
themes and the fact that we have nearly all of it in his sketchbooks, we may assume that he scribbled it down in the open
or at the end of a sketching day. He seeks above all to express
his sense of the charm and variety of nature; but his idiom,
drawn from poets like Thomson, Akenside, and Mallet, is
inadequate. If he read Coleridge, it was scrappily; Wordsworth, who followed Beaumont in disliking his work, seems
unknown to him; and he cannot have read the poems of Keats
and Shelley, who in different ways would have given him
something of an idiom nearer to his aims in art. But perhaps
that was as well. Better for him to have absorbed the
Thomsonian universe and then set himself to develop its
dynamic qualities in terms of paint; if he had found a poetic
idiom that approximated to his own rich sensuousness and
elemental vigour, he might well have been distracted between
the two arts. As things were, he could handle words well
enough to give us some insight into what he wanted to say,
but not well enough to lure him away from paint for any
length of time.[31]

His most sustained effort was *Thomson's Aeolian Harp*,
which he kept on trying to revise as well as printing it for his
gallery.

> Then kindly place amid the upland groves
> Th' Aeolian harp, attun'd to nature's strains,
> Melliferous greeting every air that roves
> From Thames' broad bosom or her verdant plains ...
>
> Bind not the poppy in the golden hair,
> Autumn! kind giver of the full-ear'd sheaf;

> Those notes have often echo'd to thy care,
> Check not their sweetness with thy falling leaf . . .

The line about armies linked the image with HANNIBAL; it also no doubt reminded Turner of the time when the Grisons were in the news, in 1798, shortly before the Battle of the Nile, and it seems fitting that Bloomfield, an eighteenth-century rural poet belated in the nineteenth century, should have gained his living by making them. For Turner it was a deeply felt symbol of the kindred forces that issued from Thomson's poetry and from nature to produce the harmonious art-image. Since music, too, was implicated, he felt here a fusion of art, music, poetry, natural process. As well as the printed verses, he wrote a poem *On Thomson's Tomb* ("the Aeolian Harp soft tuned to Natures strains") and a poem on the Harp itself, in which Thomson is described as singing his lays to its music. The tribute in these poems to Thomson was, then, the best possible expression of the stage in Turner's art where he was turning directly to nature; their keynote appeared in a line of which he wrote at least seven variants and in which the essential point was: "He looked and Nature sparkled in his eyes" – "The truth of Nature sparkled in his eyes".[32]

Turner was doing well financially. He must have made at least £2,000 in 1818; from notes of 1810 we learn that in August he held £7,216. 16s. 2d. in Funds, while a later note shows that he was also owed some £1,600. Altogether he seems to have owned about £12,000 to £13,000.[33] Yet despite this affluence and the lyrical note of enjoyment in his verse (which we may pair off with the direct paintings from nature), he was suffering from strain and an increasing sense of failure and alienation. In the Cockermouth sketchbook, with some details of itinerary on the first page, he wrote:

> Adverse frown[s] my wayward fate
> Fast telling on my poor estate
> O Heaven avert the impending care
> O make my future prospects fair.[34]

And on the next page he followed with a rambling statement about the linkage of opposites:

Speaking of the sublime Tom Paine who we may reasonably conclude to be dest[it]ute of all delicacy of refined taste, yet has conveyed a tolerable definition of the sublime, as it is probably

experienced by ordinary and uncultivated minds, and even by acute
and judicious without or are destitute of the vigour of imagination,
says that the *sublime* and the ridiculous are so often nearly related
that it is difficult to class them separately. One step above the
sublime becomes ridiculous and one step above the ridiculous
makes the sublime again.

> The beard of Hudibras and the bard of Gray
> The spinning of the earth round her soft axle
> Ample room and verge enough
> So nearly touch the bounds of all we hate.

This outburst seems to be connected with the picture he
painted for Payne Knight: a ridiculous subject to pair off with a
Rembrandt, whom Knight considered a ridiculous painter.[35]
(Knight wanted to build up a collection of paintings that
would show "the moderns can stand with" the Old Masters)[36]
Knight also stated that the ridiculous seems "always lying in
wait on the extreme verge of the sublime".[37] Turner had
probably heard him discussing some of these matters, or had
read his books; and it seems significant that about this time
he did two works (THE GARRETEER'S PETITION and THE ARTIST'S
STUDIO) in which we find something of a Rembrandtesque
treatment of related motives, one serious, one satirical. These
works depicted the pangs of artistic creation in a world of
deprivation or philistinism, with touches of irony.[38]

So Turner seems to be pulling himself up in a moment of
uncertainty, anxiously aware of the pitfalls all round him and
of the ways in which failures can be rationalized as successes
by the artist driven in on himself with no secure standards.

About this time he severed his last connexions with the
Picturesque. At this gallery in 1809 he showed SANDBANK
WITH GYPSIES, a Picturesque theme. This and SKETCH OF COWES
were the last works that he described as sketches – and
"sketches" were Picturesque.[39]

He did not lecture in 1810 after all. He went to Oxford to
draw the High Street (from a hackney, it was said) and make a
commissioned painting. Among the works in his own gallery
was COTTAGE DESTROYED BY AN AVALANCHE (later, FALL OF AN
AVALANCHE IN THE GRISONS), a return to the theme of menace,
picking up from Loutherbourg's painting of 1804, but with a
realism of disaster that left him and Wilson far behind. The

small house of domestic life is crushed by forces totally outside its control. The terrific lapse of the great crashing stone was all his own. He was still using diagonals, but in terms of violent thrust and resistance of avalanche, driving rain, earth, rolling boulders. About this time, too, he was painting THE WRECK OF THE MINOTAUR (later, OF A TRANSPORT SHIP). Here he developed the form created in the WRECK of 1805. Just as we feel the crash of the avalanche rock, here the huge overturning hulk seems about to come down on the survivors. The closer focus brings us more directly into the event. Again diagonals are used to hold together the lashing fury.[40]

In AVALANCHE, while drawing on art memories and his own experiences in Switzerland, he was at the same time, as so often, remembering Thomson, in whose *Winter* we read of hills where:

> In peaceful vales, the happy Grisons dwell,
> Oft, rushing sudden from the loaded cliffs,
> Mountains of snow their gathering terrors roll,
> From steep to steep, loud thundering, down they come,
> A wintry waste in dire commotion all;
> And herds, and flocks, and travellers, and swains,
> And sometimes whole brigades of marching troops,
> Or hamlets sleeping in the dead of night,
> Are deep beneath the smothering ruin whelmed.

The line about armies linked the image with HANNIBAL; it also no doubt reminded Turner of the time when the Grisons were in the news, in 1798, shortly before the Battle of the Nile, when their country "fortified by nature, and inhabited by a brave and hardy people, equally fond of their liberty, and able to defend it," was threatened, liable to be crushed between the French and the Austrian armies.[41]

But with his remarkable power to move between the para-disaic and the world-end image, he also exhibited at the Royal Academy two views of Lowther Castle and PETWORTH: DEWY MORNING.[42] He had been learning to unite the freshness of his open-air works with considered composition and light effects. He was oscillating between the classical order – the strong horizontals and verticals of WINDSOR CASTLE FROM THE RIVER (painted about 1805), with slight diagonal assertions through the jetty and the complex variations of shifting light and shade, but without much concern for showing the move-

ment of air – and a fresh realization of the pervasive impact
of light, on a higher level of vision. SUN RISING had provided
a temporary synthesis, but he kept moving on, even when he
still spent some time on topographical exactitude. In LONDON
FROM GREENWICH (1809) he combined the curve of river with
a suave lozenge structure, to draw the eye into the central
point, St Paul's dome against the sky: a movement subtly
punctuated by the two near towers, while the evanescent
diagonals of light are balanced by the wind-blown smoke.
Here we still meet a strong horizontal element, as in WINDSOR
(shown the same year), where the frieze of people at work in
the foreground is linked with the castle line and the rows of
trees, and with a series of delicate recessions that draw the
eye up and out into the sky, opening in gentle vanes of light
and air. In PETWORTH: DEWY MORNING and ABINGDON the
same systems are variously used, mist being employed to give
a gentle luminous unity.[43] SOMER HILL (1811) shows an extremely fine control of the recessions leading up to the house on
the hill-top, with regard to structure, placing of detail, and
rhythmic treatment of light and shadow: a masterly union of
strong recession and delaying or balancing elements. Turner
had completed his transformation of the topographical
tradition into a lyrical image; the idyll was drawn into
reality; a clear classical structure merged with movement
of light and air.[44] The fusion of casual country activities with
a finely realized atmospheric scene reached its climax in
FROSTY MORNING (1813) – via pictures like ABINGDON and
FISHING UPON THE BLYTHE-SAND, in which all adventitiously
anecdotal or trivial aspects were eliminated from the representation of men at work.

   At the same time, partly stimulated by his use of the white
paper in water-colours, he began to realize the possibilities of
a white ground for oils in his movement towards a high
tonality. "In his Thames sketches on panel he had shown his
appreciation of the colouristic possibilities of the mahogany
veneer, but this made for a low tonality; in the oils made
immediately afterwards he continued to use the relatively
subdued colouring of Wilson and Titian, though in a more
naturalistic form. For the sketches on canvas Turner had
used a white ground for water or sky, but other landscape
forms seem to have been painted over a pale brown ground, a

differentiation of function reminiscent of the traditional process followed in his first water-colours."[45] But he was steadily moving towards the idea of a canvas primed in white. Hence the way in which Beaumont and the connoisseurs savagely attacked him as the White Painter.

We must realize how completely the sensibility of the period had been fixed to the notion that a low-toned work was artistic or beautiful. In the eighteenth century gentlemen took round with them what was called a Claude Glass, which enabled them to see the landscape varnished with the golden tone of a Claude. The exponents of the Picturesque had, if anything, strengthened such attitudes; while they talked of wildness, they wanted in colour an inexpressive harmony. They disliked white. Gilpin disparaged the Isle of Wight for the chalkiness of its coast; and though he at times found a small area of white acceptable, he and Price both rated it a glaring hue that should be avoided.[46] Lock of Norbury declared the white of snow to be "so active, and refractory, as to resist the discipline of every harmonising principle." On clear days "the Glaciers are always out of tune". Gilpin said that the Picturesque eye "would range with supreme delight among the sweet vales of Switzerland; but would view only with a transient glance, the Glaciers of Savoy".[47] Joshua Kirby, whose manual on perspective was used by Turner for his lectures, noted the difficulty of getting white into an orderly place in aerial perspective.[48] Turner's interest in the white body floating down the Dee now gains more point. The question of the way in which white could be used, and the solution of the problems it raised, became central in Turner's attempts to drive his tonality up and to bring it finally to the brilliance of daylight itself. One turning-point appeared in his WATTEAU STUDY of 1831, to which he added a couplet from Mason's version of Du Fresnoy:

> White, when it shines with unstained lustre clear,
> May bear an object back or bring it near.

Interestingly, to a certain extent his aims were grasped, but were rejected as intrinsically bad. A critic of *La Belle Assemblé* in 1810 said that he would not have supposed Turner's pictures to be his but for the catalogue. "It was manifestly

Mr. Turner's design to express the peculiar hue and pellucid-
ness of objects seen through the medium of air, in other words
to express the clearness of atmosphere." But this was wrong-
headed. The correct way was "to select those dark material
objects which served as a foil to aerial lights and so to produce
atmosphere by their contrast. Mr. Turner has neglected to use
these necessary foils and has thus made a confusion between
aerial lights and the appropriate gloom of objects. Failing
in this forcible opposition, without which a painter can
never express atmosphere, the appearance of a picture is that
of a mere flimsy daubing without substance or distinction,
without either shape or colour. A man of Mr. Turner's
experience should have understood better the principles of
his art."[49]

By reversing the traditional method of working from the
darkest tones up, Turner had indeed introduced a revolutionary principle which ultimately broke up all the accepted
"principles of art", and which brought about the notion of
the unity of light and colour. One obvious logical consequence
appeared in the Impressionists, though, in fact, their method
was only an abstraction of one aspect of the Turnerian
revolution. It omitted the element of structure, which was
always as present in Turner as in Cézanne (though approached
from a different angle). And though nothing could be further
from Turner's intention than abstraction as such, by carrying
to a new intensity the self-consciousness that we noted in
rococo and the Thomsonian aesthetic, he opened up the
way to the various forms of abstraction as one aspect of the
new potentialities embodied in his art. Strangely enough,
Hazlitt in early 1816 realized all that – though the pictures
shown by Turner in the previous year (CROSSING THE BROOK
and DIDO BUILDING CARTHAGE) seem to our eyes to show
nothing of what he finds there.

... Turner, the ablest landscape-painter now living, whose pictures
are however too much abstractions of aerial perspective, and
representations not properly of the objects of nature as of the medium through which they were seen ... They are pictures of the
elements of air, earth, and water. The artist delights to go back to
the first chaos of the world, or to that state of things when the waters
were separated from the dry land, and light from darkness, but as
yet no living thing nor tree bearing fruit was seen upon the face of

the earth. All is without forms and void. Some one said of his landscapes that they were *pictures of nothing, and very like.*[50]

By his sensitiveness to the way that Turner was breaking up all the stereotypes and conventions, Hazlitt was thus able to prophesy what, in fact, did not happen till the last works of Turner – or rather what then appears as one facet of their definition.

An art form which helped to free Turner in the same sort of way as poetry, though to a lesser degree, was music. We have seen how, about 1798, he grew very interested in music, apparently as a result of his connexion with Sarah Danby. Songs are written down in his sketchbook, including one for alto, soprano, bass.[51] He himself sang no doubt in a bass key, as we know he had a deep speaking voice. Among his effects were six books of music and "sundry ditto" as well as a volume of Scots Airs.[52] The Swiss sketchbook of 1802, on the inside endcover, has a pencilled version of *I am a Friar of Orders Grey.*[53] The words "And down the valley I take my way" would have been appropriate for his tour of the moment. A little earlier, probably 1801, we find him trying to train himself in song and an elementary grasp of music; he wanted to grasp more than the mere tune; he set out the clefs for soprano, mezzo-soprano, alto, tenor, and bass parts, the names of the space-notes of the treble staff, then the sub-divisions of time as well as the ascending scale from E and the signs of sharp, flat, natural. He learned to play the flute and "Gamut for the Flute" occurs in one notebook.[54] In the interest in part-singing we can surely trace the effect of Sarah.

His Exeter nephew had some musical talent. After some attempts at painting, he became a choral singer, and in 1834 visited London to sing at a Royal Musical Festival connected with Handel. He stayed some three weeks, and called on his uncle. "I saw and had communication with him and he immediately recognised me as the son of Price Turner." Turner seems to have kept an eye on musical events; for he "told me of my engagement in London having seen my name in the printed programme and I say that he never asked me to sit down in his house or to call again or to take any refreshment and that I felt I had met with a cool reception from him but notwithstanding that I then gave him an invitation to my house at Exeter which he never accepted and that therefore I never afterwards paid him a visit or communicated with him".[55]

Turner was interested in the relation of music and art. In the same way as he saw art and poetry meeting in the laws of formative process which they shared with nature, so he saw music as part of the same system. The theory of the eighteenth century was generally in accord with such positions. Newton had noted, "May not the harmony and discord of Colours arise from the proportions of the vibrations propagated through the Fibres of the Optick Nerves into the Brain, as the harmony and discord of Sounds arise from the proportions of the Vibrations of the Air? For some Colours, if they be view'd together, are agreeable to one another, as those of Gold and Indigo, and others disagree." The common use of the term *striking* to express the impact of Thomson's imagery is linked with this notion of the analogy of sound and sight, sound and touch. L. de Pouilly tried to explain emotional responses by the theory that "there is a chain with chords in unison, which convey from one brain to the other the vibrations of the fibres of another". Murdock suggested that a reader failed to respond to a poet when his "faculties are not *tuned in a certain consonance*."[56]

Turner was aware of the analogical theories. They were set forth at great length by his acquaintance G. Field.[57] Reynolds used the analogy of *striking*. Distinct colours "strike the mind more forcibly, from there not being any great union between them; as martial music, which is intended to rouse the nobler passions, has its effect from the sudden and strongly marked transitions from one note to another which that style of music requires; whilst, in that which is intended to move the softer passions, the notes imperceptibly melt into one another."[58] And Turner himself, when in his last years he read Goethe on Genuine Tone – "If the word tone, or rather tune, is to be still borrowed in future from music, and applied to colouring, it might be used in a better sense than heretofore" – commented, "Very likely because even Music hath bounds which can only be transgressed by talent." Goethe went on, "For it would not be unreasonable to compare a painting of powerful effect with a piece of music in a flat key, while the equivalent may be found for the modification of the two leading modes." Turner remarked, "Too general to make much of."[59]

He himself used musical analogies. We have seen how in discussing historic colour with "qualifications of colour innate as those of fury and anger", he added, "Every tone must be Dorian, Lesbian, Lydian, Ionic, Bacchanalian." And his work was at times compared in its subtleties of tone and colour with music. "His paintings in their variety and effect have aptly enough been compared to Brahm's singing", said the *Monthly Messenger* in 1802.[60] In a poem *The Origin of Vermillion or the Loves of Painting and Music* (about 1808) he tried to work out an allegory of the relationship. Once, he says, Painting was a mere transcript of actuality; it aspired to take over Music's harmonizing qualities – while Music wanted Painting's direct links with life. The pair seem to embrace; Music's blush became Vermilion. "Ready Love supplied what niggard Nature here deny'd." "Nimbly the princely course of color trace As snails trail o'er the morning dew He thus the line of Beauty drew." The reference is to the Hogarthian Serpentine Line of Beauty, the snail-shell apparently suggesting a spiral or maze.[61]

Turner's work has an abundance of musical and festival moments, drawn directly from daily life or expressed in classical or romantic form. He was interested in fairs and theatres, dances and processions, as well as in musical instruments. In 1802 he made a drawing of a Swiss girl lying naked abed, with a companion at her side – her festival clothes scattered on the floor: a charming record of some inn incident. Looking at a proof of the engraving of PLYMOUTH DOCK, he asked Cooke, "Can you make the fiddle more distinct?" and drew it on the margin. Certainly his growing appreciation of music helped to strengthen him in his bold and delicate harmonies, and to give him the courage to release his full sensibility, achieving a sheer enjoyment of colour in its infinite concords and contrasts that had no parallel in previous art.[62]

Chapter Nine

Hannibal Crosses the Alps

IN the summer of 1810 he visited Sussex, but returned to
London in late July. On 17 August, Farington met him,
apparently in the street. Turner "had been in the country and
proposed going to Yorkshire" – to Walter Ramsden Fawkes
(of Farnley Hall near Otley, overlooking the River Wharfe),
who had been buying his work. Born in 1769, Fawkes had
been an active member of the Whigs, sitting as M.P. for the
county of York in 1802–7; he was interested in history and
wrote *The Chronology of the History of Modern Europe* (1810);
with two others he founded the Otley Agricultural Society,
one of the first of its kind in Europe; his park at Caley Hall
had in it red and fallow deer, zebras, wild hogs, and a species
of deer from India; he was prominent in the anti-slavery
movement and spoke strongly in the debate before the passing
of Wilberforce's measure. He had inherited relics of the Civil
War from one of the Fairfax family, and later Turner made
drawings of various items. A warm friendship grew up between
him and Turner, who liked his open-hearted directness, his
mixture of radical politics with country-rootedness.[1]

Turner was back in London by 12 December, when he
addressed a letter from Queen Anne Street, where he had
now bought a house adjoining his place in Harley Street. A
little earlier he had bought land at Richmond for £400, and
at Lee Common, Bucks, for £102, not to mention ten £5
shares in the Atlas Fire office. Normally his holdings were in
the Funds, managed by his stockbroker William Marsh of

Sweeting's Alley. He suspected banks and never used them; when he needed money, he sold stock.[2]

Some upheaval seems to have occurred in his domestic arrangements during 1809. Joseph Dupuis, who later married his daughter Evelina, wrote in a letter of 15 December 1853 that Evelina and Georgianna were well schooled and brought up "in the expectation of always enjoying a respectable position in society". When he married Evelina (in 1817) things were done with "the consent and approbation of her father." He added, perhaps with exaggeration, that his wife was for several years recognised as Turner's daughter.[3] At least till that date, then, Turner was in close contact with his daughters – and so, we presume, with Sarah Danby. The year 1809, however, provides us with the first, and indeed the only, recorded notice of the liaison. On 11 February, Callcott called on Farington and told him something of the relationship. "A Mrs. Danby, widow of a Musician, now lives with him. She has some children." Callcott, as one of Turner's devoted disciples at this phase, seems to have been in his confidence at least to the extent of being informed that Sarah had now come to stay with him, apparently at Harley Street. Whatever system had been arranged at Norton Street and Upper John Street seems to have broken down. According to the rate-books Thomas Williams, attorney, held the lease of 46 Upper John Street from 1803; as there are no earlier books, he may have been tenant for several years before. A Directory shows him there in 1802.[4] In 1809, however, he vacated the premises; the rate-books show the house as empty.[5] In 1810 Roch Jaubert appears as Cheesemonger at 7 Marybone Street; he carried on till 1813, but in 1814 fades out from the trade directories.[6] In view of the unusual name, we may assume that this cheesemonger was the friend of Sarah. Further, around this time Turner was concerned about properties in Norton Street, perhaps selling out. A notebook with material ranging from 1809 to 1811 has a draft of an advertisement for the *Herald*, which is far more plausibly interpreted as being inserted by Turner rather than as a memorandum of a property that interested him.

Herald. Thursday Aug –9. We are authorised to state that the lease and possession of the desirable premises in Norton Street, Mlbone and communicating through the garden to PR (omitted by accident in the advertisements which announced the sale of the wines, library furniture only) will be sold by auction in the second days sale of to-morrow.

Hodgetts   Sale – 90 Norton St.[7]

However this complex of facts centring on Norton Street and Upper John Street is interpreted, it suggests that some considerable change in Turner's system for Sarah and her children had been forced on him. It is safe to surmise that he would not have taken the family into his own house unless he had no choice. His retreat to Sandycombe Lodge – at first he named it Solus Lodge, a place where he could be alone – was no doubt connected with this invasion of his privacy. In passing we may note that Callcott must have known the Danbys. His brother, John Wall Callcott, ranked with John Danby as one of the most popular of glee composers; he, too, was an organist; and he subscribed to the Posthumous Glees, being there described as "Mus. Bac. and Organist of the Asylum".[8] Augustus Callcott, as a disciple of Turner and an acquaintance of the Danbys, was thus in an excellent position to know the facts about Sarah. Though he imitated Turner's work in his mediocre way and was at times praised by the critics as his superior, Turner always remained on the most cordial terms with him. "On being told that Callcott had painted one of his finest scenes on the Thames on commission for two hundred pounds, [he] observed, in the presence of several patrons of the fine arts, 'Had I been deputed to set a value upon that picture, I should have awarded a thousand guineas'."[9] It may well have been during this year that Hannah Danby, Sarah's niece, came into his household, doing some sort of house-work. By the time of his first will in 1829 she was firmly established in his confidence and was given an annuity. That means Turner must have been familiar with her a good many years. We know about her only in her later life, when she had become a repulsive hag, but she may have looked very different as a girl. In the 1841 census she described herself as a "female servant aged forty". In 1851 (when Turner himself again made no return) she gave her age as 64. We may accept that as more or less correct. In 1809 she would then have been about 22. She may have been the daughter of a brother of John Danby.

The system now set up in 1809 seems to have carried on till the break-up of his liaison with Sarah, or till the girls had been settled in their ways of life. Trimmer remarks of FROSTY MORNING, "The girl with the hare over her shoulders, I have heard my father say reminded him of a young girl whom he occasionally saw at Queen Anne-street, and whom, from her resemblance to Turner, he though a relation. The same female figure appears in his 'Crossing the Brook'."[10] In the girls in these two pictures we see the large Turnerian nose, and cannot doubt that this was the point of family resemblance which Trimmer noted. The model must have been Evelina. In view of Turner's inability to paint portraits, we may acquit him of any intention to depict Evelina, though it is possible she may have been sketched by him for the picture in question. No such studies are known; and so we may surmise that the fact of Evelina being about the place as he painted led him unconsciously to catch her features. But however that is, Trimmer's testimony proves that Evelina was to be seen at Queen Anne Street and that she looked like the girls in the two pictures.[11] Throughout his career Turner had a tendency to depict figures of a lumpy kind with Punchlike features; and this led later to various types of doll-forms. The girls in the two works in question have interest in showing this tendency to make people in his own image, which apparently for once worked out in producing a portrait of someone featured like himself.

By 1811 Turner realized that he could no longer postpone giving his Perspective Lectures. He had taken on the professorship with a conviction that he would be able to expound the ideas that seethed inside him; he had set himself industriously to collect material and make splendid diagrams or illustrations, nearly two hundred of which are extant. But as he went on he must have found that it was one thing to feel an explosive force of new ideas in one's mind, and another thing to set those ideas out in a logical system and communicate them coherently. Further, as we see from his MSS., even when he had fair copies made, he could not resist branching off into sidelines and divagations, so that he was sure to confuse himself in any public reading and make his line of thought even more difficult to follow.[12]

He gave the first lecture at 8 p.m. on 7 January. Landseer told Farington next day that, being somewhat deaf, "he could not well understand" what was said. Turner read too fast, and his plebeian pronunciations were a stumbling-block. Rossi said of the second lecture that Turner got through it "with much hesitation and difficulty". In the couplets Turner sent to John Taylor in thanks for a favourable notice in the *Sun* there is one that describes the lectures better than the romantic ballads he is parodying: "Commixt perplexing and obscure, Fitter to puzzle than allure."[13] Farington, who chaired the fourth lecture, says it lasted thirty-five minutes. The sixth dealt with the backgrounds to the theme, and consisted of a summary of Turner's views on the art-tradition.[14]

We have already drawn on this important statement. Turner also tried to define the relationship between poetry and art as he saw it, and the points at which rules broke down and the artist's intuitive comprehension of natural process took over. We catch glimpses of the way in which his views of optical process help him towards his circular or vortex forms of organization. "The eye must take in all objects upon a Parabolic curve for in looking into space the eye cannot but receive what is within the limits of extended sight, which must form a circle to the eye."[15] Further, he makes clear that he does not abstract the problems of perspective, of form, from those of light-and-shade and colour. "Lineal pictures then is the parent of Light & Shade and Light and Shade is that of Color. Each reciprocal elevating." He sees form as by its very nature begetting a complex unity of light and shade, and the resulting tonal systems by their very nature begetting colour.[16]

But his meaning comes through against a variety of obstructions, his inability to construct a logical scheme of argument, his idiosyncratic use of words, his elliptical forms of speech. When his muttered and hurried enunciation is added, we can well believe that at most a few intervals of lucidity appeared and that the audience concentrated on the fine illustrations.[17] Not that the Royal Academy had ever set a high standard of intelligibility among its lecturers. Reynolds is said to have been largely inaudible. A listener remarked of Soane in 1813 that he was "the worst reader he ever heard".

At the Royal Academy Turner had nine pictures in 1811, and a return to history-landscape showed itself in MERCURY AND HERSE, APOLLO AND PYTHON, CHRYSES, APOLLO expressed the conflict of good and evil in what we may call the *Niobe* tradition, while CHRYSES depicted the ancient priest knelt on the sea-shore as in his suffering he worships the rising sun.[18] The dislike of the connoisseurs was now coming to a head, and a campaign was launched by Beaumont. Callcott told Farington of the latter's "continual cry against Turner's pictures", but said Turner was too strong to be injured; Beaumont admitted "Turner had merit", but thought it "of a wrong sort, and therefore on account of the seducing skill he displayed should be objected to, to prevent its bad effects, in inducing others to imitate it".

There was no show in Turner's own gallery, for alterations were going on. Writing from Queen Anne Street, he declared that he was so surrounded "with rubbish and paint that I have not at present a room free". For a book of views published by Cooke he went on a summer tour of Devon, Cornwall, and Somerset for two months. He wrote a good deal of verse in an interleaved copy of *The British Itinerary*, amid pencil sketches.[19] At Barnstaple, he stayed one day at the Castle Inn and called on his Uncle John, Master of the Poorhouse, as well as John's son. Also, at his father's request he called on his Uncle Price at Exeter, and chatted with his son and daughter.[20] It is worth while to insert here, as further illustration of the characteristics of the Turner family, a letter written on 5 March this year by Jonathan to John:

I recd. your Letter and was glad to Hear From you And Happy To think that you are please to hear of My Well Doings and wish me better than all the Best Since I have Been in Business I have Done very Well so since April the 19 Next I have Been In Business Twelve years I have a House Worth £700 and Bought a Flour Loft £160 and Some Money Beside To carrey on Trade So I will Leave you to Judge Whether I have Don Well or Not and if I Live and I be in Business so Long has you and Brother Price I shall Be Cock of the Walk Brother William was at Bath three weeks since and Brother Joshua is comming soon and going to Devonshire and when he Returnes I shall be glad for you to Come With him to Bath and B Price at the same Time and I will send for B William to come to Down that we may Hall meet togeather in this World and hope We shall all meet in the Next.[21]

We see that William had visited Bath, and that despite all the petty greed and pride there was a strong family feeling.

Turner no doubt meant to work up his verses on the tour

into a polished poem, perhaps for publication with his engraved drawings, but as usual, after the first impulse, his interest failed – or he was dogged by a sense of failure, of
inability to write in a way that would command respect. In
November, Pye's engraving of his POPE'S VILLA was to be
published in *The Fine Arts of the British School*, and John
Britton sent him a copy of the comments to go with it, asking
him to make any alterations or additions. Britton had earlier
read him a part of this essay, in which he protested against
Fuseli's description of landscape-painters as "the map-mak-
ers, the topographers of art"; now Turner found that his
passage had been omitted through a friend's advice. From Farnley, where he was making a brief second visit, he protested:

I rather lament that the remark which you read to me when I called
in Tavistock Place is suppressed for it espoused the part of Elevated
Landscape against the aspersions of Map making criticism, but
no doubt you are better acquainted with the nature of publication,
and mine is a mistaken zeal. As to remarks you will find an alteration
or two in pencil. *Two* groups of sheep, *Two* fishermen, occur too
close – baskets to entrap eels is not technical – being called Eel pots –
and making the willow tree the identical Pope's willow is rather
strained – cannot you do it by illusion? And with deference:
– Mellifluous lyre seems to deny energy of thought – and let me
ask one question, Why say the Poet and Prophet are not often
united? – for if they are not they ought to be. Therefore the solitary
instance of Dodsley acts as a *censure*. The fourth and fifth line
requires perhaps a note as to the state of the grotto that grateful
posterity from age to age may repair what remains. – If I were in
town, I would ask a little more to be added, but as it is, use your
own discretion, and therefore, will conclude cavilling any further
with Dodsley's lines.[22]

The reference is to Dodsley's poem, *The Cave of Pope*, *A
Prophecy*, which declares that when kings and heroes are for-
gotten pilgrims will come to the grotto, and some good old
man will tell them that the Bard lived there; they will take to
distant shores a gem or bit of moss, "boasting a relic from the
cave of Pope". Turner's comment is of great importance.
Since he identified the ultimate functions of poetry and art in
their revelation of natural and human process, he was also
saying: If the Artist and Prophet are not always united, they
ought to be. In his history-paintings he has already tried to
bring the union about; he was now on the verge of a supreme

effort that founded his mature style and his prophetic or philosophic position.

On 4 December, back in London, he was voted into the chair at a Council meeting of the Academy, West being absent through his wife's illness. And on the 10th he was elected one of the Visitors in the Schools, with Callcott, Shee, Phillips.[23] In January and February 1812 he repeated his lectures, and in the first half of the year was busy with the management of the Schools and with Council meetings.[24] At the Royal Academy exhibition, dissatisfied with the hanging of his two Oxford pictures, and HANNIBAL CROSSING THE ALPS, he thought of withdrawing them. Large history-works by West and Fuseli seem to have caused the trouble; but finally HANNIBAL was better hung and attracted attention. Crabb Robinson considered it the most marvellous landscape he had ever seen, and Flaxman admired it. After the discussion about its hanging, Callcott dined with Smirke, Farington, Dance, and Howard; "we had conversation upon art, which became more pointed", Farington recounts, "by Callcott saying '*That Novelty is the essence of art.*' – This led to much discussion and it was the opinion of a majority that a principle which might have a good meaning yet if expressed in such words would be very dangerous in an Academy of Students."

Though the theme of HANNIBAL CROSSING THE ALPS was ancient, the image came from the Yorkshire moors. Hawkesworth Fawkes, the eldest son at Farnley, told Thornbury how Turner once called him out to admire a thunderstorm passing over the Chevin and the Wharfe valley. All the while Turner talked he made notes of its form and colour on the back of a letter. "I proposed some better drawing-block, but he said it did very well. He was absorbed – he was entranced. There was the storm rolling and sweeping and shafting out its lightning over the Yorkshire hills. Presently the storm passed, and he finished. 'There,' he said, 'Hawkey; in two years you will see this again, and call it Hannibal crossing the Alps.' "[25] The comment about two years suggests that the storm occurred in 1810, when we hear of violent storms in July and August in London, rather than in 1811, when there was bad weather in early November – though the familiar term "Hawkey", if not a Thornbury touch, would fit better the later date.[26] However, the point is trivial; for clearly Turner had long been gestating the idea in a general way, and he must have worked on the painting in the last month of 1811 and early 1812.

Now began Turner's consistent use of imagery drawn from the struggle between Rome and Carthage to express what he most deeply felt of the rivalries between the two great imperial and commercial powers, Britain and France. Even the dim-witted Thornbury comments, "In Turner's mind there seems always to have been a sense of some analogy between Carthage and England."[27] For Turner there were indeed two strands of interest in Carthage. One came from Virgil and was concerned with Pius Aeneas, the devoted father-loving hero who betrayed and left his beloved at the call of duty – as Turner told himself that he must put art before love. In this relationship Carthage appeared in a Claudean glow and merged to some extent with the earthly paradise, the city of hope, where the curse of corruption and betrayal might have been overcome.[28] The god-guided desertion of Aeneas para-doxically destroyed this possibility and ensured the hostility of the two city powers. The other strand of interest came from Roman History (probably in Goldsmith's version).[29] As usual, Turner's interpretation followed the lines set down by Thom-son. Part V of *Liberty* tells how a nation falls if it neglects "science, arts, and public works" which complete the fabric of Liberty:

> However puffed with pride and gorged with wealth
> A nation be: let trade enormous rise,
> Let East and South their mingled treasure pour
> Till, swelled impetuous, the corrupting flood
> Burst o'er the city and devour the land –
> Yet, these neglected, these recording arts,
> Wealth rots, a nuisance; and, oblivious sunk,
> That nation must another Carthage lie.[30]

The fact that both Hannibal and Napoleon crossed the Alps was a secondary matter, though it played a potent part in stimulating Turner's imagination. The great emotional signi-ficance of the painting manifest in its aesthetic power, drove him to write for it the first passage from his supposed epic *The Fallacies of Hope*. And it is noteworthy that the second use of that work came in 1815 in another mountain-landscape, this time of explicit reference to the Napoleonic Wars, THE BATTLE OF FORT ROCK, VAL D'AOUSTE, PIEDMONT, 1761.[31]

The verses are of the utmost importance for elucidating what he had in his mind. Those on Hannibal begin, "Craft, treachery, and fraud". Even in the Alpine heights the struggle for loot was going on, with ambush and continual attack. "Still the chief advanc'd, look'd on the sun with hope." Despite all his difficulties, despite the storms that blocked his way down from the mountains, desite the bloody passes, he carried on with his purpose. And yet his heroism, his undaunted resolve, was to be frustrated by the very success of his aim. "Still on Campania's fertile plains – he thought, but the loud breeze sob'd, 'Capua's joys beware!'" The escape from hardship will mean the sapping of heroic energies by corruption.[32]

Once again Thomson sets the key. Describing the downfall of Rome, he writes:

> First from your flattered Caesars this began:
> Till, doomed to tyrants an eternal prey,
> Thin peopled spreads at last the syren plain,
> That the dire soul of Hannibal disarmed.[33]

The verses on FORT ROCK put something of the same moral in a simpler way. The invading army is itself imaged as an elemental force, the wild waters of the Reuss which roll on despite all obstructions till they reach the plains and there produce devastation.[34] What was heroic in its lofty onset becomes a mere thing of rapine and destruction in its triumph below.

The image of Hannibal on an alpine height had long been in Turner's thought. C. R. Leslie tells us of J. R. Cozens, "He exhibited but once at the Academy, in 1776, 'A Landscape, with Hannibal on his March over the Alps, showing to his army the fertile plains of Italy.' This, I have heard, was an oil picture, and so fine that Turner spoke of it as a work from which he learned more than from anything he had then seen."[35] The painting is now lost, but is said to have survived in the family of Cozens's sister till it was sold in 1876. However, a roundel has come down, in which ill-drawn figures of Hannibal and his generals are set in a row half-way across the centre, oversized and flat against a rock, yet bringing out effectively from their dizzy height the plain of Italy stretched below.[36] No doubt it was this sort of contrast between the soldiers on high and the outspread lowlands, between the rocks of lonely struggle and the fertile fields of common life, that struck Turner with such force. The lines from Thomson provided the moral interpretation. Turner in 1830 returned to the image with his PALESTRINA. Here the human figures have disappeared; they exist only in Turner's mind in their sharp contrast with the loveliness, the paradisaic dream, which they destroy:

> Or from yon mural rock, high-crowned Praeneste,
> Where, misdeeming of his strength, the Carthaginian stood,
> And marked with eagle-eye, Rome as his victim.[37]

The hero in his high eyrie has become the bird-of-prey. (This picture was one for which Turner had a special affection.) Again in 1836, while wandering in the region of Mont Cenis, with mountain prospects and Roman memorials about him, he tried to recall the lines of Hannibal and jotted them down with several variations; but the chief who looks with hope through the storms, and the winds that bid him beware of Capua, are clearly there.[38]

The image of the lonely hero on a height belongs to a series of sublime conceptions which appears in both art and poetry. "High on the Alps he took his warrior stand", wrote Mason in his version of Du Fresnoy, long before Napoleon and without any thought of Hannibal, merely evoking the image of a conqueror. But the most striking example of this sort of thing was Gray's Bard hurling his prophetic defiance from a lofty rock on to the enemy below. As the epoch's sensibility grew more intense, the horrific dizziness of the height duly increased. Thus, in the 1776 edition of Gray's poems, one of the two plates shows the Bard harping on what is meant to be a rocky height with water far below, but which has no more effect of giddiness than if he stood on a flat river-bank. In the 1800 edition, Fuseli treated the same theme; but now the Bard stands on a craggy eminence in wild contortions of denunciation; there is rhythmically an effective relationship to the terrified horseman who stares up at him.[39] (Fuseli saw Gray as having been himself inspired by the figure of the Lord in Raphael's *Vision of Ezekiel* and by Parmigianino's *Moses*.)[40] When in 1817 John Martin painted *The Bard*, he took over Fuseli's idea and added a vast up-swinging mountain background.[41] A variation of the motive appeared in Loutherbourg's *Destruction of Pharo's Host* (for Macklin's *Bible*), in which the hero Moses lifts his wand of power as he stands on a rock above raging waters, with explosive skies beyond.[42]

Turner's image of Hannibal seems to have belonged originally to this series. But his deep ponderings, which issued in the statement of the verse-tag, transformed the image into something far more complex. The melodramatic gesturings of the hero were lost in the collective struggle with its tragic dilemma; the relationship of men and the elements was incalculably enriched; the diagonals of obvious oppositions faded out into the great gyres of a universe in the process of chaos and creation.

We have seen how Turner's steady rejection of the old methods of contrast – between the "appropriate gloom of objects" and the unpenetrating light of the sky – was breaking up the stereotypes of *chiaroscuro*. But that involved in turn a discarding of the various schemes by which compositions had been organized. As his lectures had shown, for him what affected form affected light-shade affected colour; the three aspects were indivisible. And so, by driving up his colour-tonality he also burst through the diagonals, pyramids, and other constructions that had so far been the basis of compositions. In their place he put a dynamic form of spiral, an explosive vortex, a field of force.

No development, however revolutionary, lacks its roots, its prefigurings. Mannerism had its serpentine recessions; and it has been remarked that after Turner's visit to Italy in 1819 "his compositions give up all pretence of classical constructions. They are based on an extension of the Mannerist scheme rather similar to that evolved by Brueghel, and often involve serpentine recession on an inner and outer circle, which, to the classically conditioned eye, gives a slight feeling of *mal de mer*."[43] But, in fact, this sort of circling vision goes right back to his first exhibited oil, FISHERMEN AT SEA, though it was only after long struggle and the full exploitation of classical forms that Turner let himself go with it. The absorption of Poussin and Claude ensured that he would make no glib use of vortex systems; at all times he based those systems on a thorough grasp of elemental movement in wind, cloud, water; of the tensions between natural forces and the more stable structures in a scene – trees, rocks, men, man-made objects.

Again, the grandiose rhythms of baroque and the lighter fussier kinetic patterns of rococo often laid stress on circling effects. In Du Fresnoy's *Art of Painting*, dealing with chiaroscuro, the Latin text says, "Let only a single globe of light and shadows be made." Mason, in his 1782 translation, adds a Thomsonian dynamism: "One globe of light and shade o'er all she flings." A few lines later he writes of rays brighter than nature, which "reflect each image in an orb of light", and then, where Du Fresnoy merely counsels rounded (*rotundas*) forms, he bids the artist throw "on all thy rounded groups the circling glow". The tunnel or cone of chiaroscuro tends to start spinning.[44]

In the Thomsonian universe we find that revolving, wheeling, circling movements are central. Various scientific concepts played their part in this development: the changes of history ("revolving ages shake the changeful earth"), the circulation of the blood and of the elements ("impelling and impelled in endless circulation"), the dance of atoms ("in elemental round") – this last phrase is Akenside's.[45] Here are some typical passages from Thomson:

A trembling variance of revolving hues. High-beat, the circling mountains eddy in. In his own loose-revolving fields the swain disastered stands. [Cattle] sip the circling surface. The circling sky, the wide enlivening air. [Evening shade] a deeper still, in circle following circle, gathers round to close the face of day. Far as the circling eye can shoot around.[46]

The last-cited line shows a Turnerian sense of the gyres of vision.

Akenside writes of the moment of inspiration, which is also the moment of a Turnerian image's advent:

> A flashing torrent of celestial day
> Burst thro' the shadowy void. With slow descent
> A purple cloud came floating through the sky,
> And pois'd at length within the circling trees,
> Hung obvious to my view, till opening wide
> Its lucid orb, a more than human face
> Emerging lean'd majestic o'er my head,
> And instant thunder shook the conscious grove.[47]

Here we have lightburst, light centralization, light opening out within the circling trees (which cannot be equated with mere surrounding trees). And finally, out of a century of poetry that throngs with such images, we may take two lines from Campbell's *Pleasures of Hope*: "I watch the wheels of nature's mazy plan . . . The mazy wheels of nature as they play." No doubt the notion of clockwork mechanisms lay behind such formulations; but there was much more than that to them. The idea of natural process as involving a spiral or labyrinthine pattern was not uncommon in the eighteenth century, whether in the views of the mathematician Bernouilli or in the principles laid down by Hogarth for his serpentine line of beauty. Akenside describes how man "exulting measures the perennial wheel of nature". He is thinking of astronomy, but with many contributory images of maze movement.[48]

In HANNIBAL the artist for the first time works out with full logic his system of internal vortex stresses, and essentially throws aside all previous systems of holding the forms of a picture together. The tendencies we have been analysing since 1797 come to a head: the complex entanglement of diagonals with resistant and billowing forces, the subtle tensions and swirls of form with form, and of form with light and shadow. At last he achieves the structures he had been seeking as most fully expressive of movement, conflict, change. The dark storm clouds are set against a summer sky of pale blue and white. In a vast cavern of churning elemental fury, foreground and distance are merged and separated by the spiralling tumult. Men emerge distinct in violence and rapine, though driven into patterns obedient to the storm, or are swallowed up in whirls of mist and light.

The surface pattern Turner used consists of a series of intersecting, irregular arcs. The principal outline of the valley and mountain forms one such arc, sweeping in from the left and curving upwards on the right-hand side. The other main arc is defined by the underside of the clouds, and curves down to meet the first, enclosing the sky in a spatula-shaped area of light. Another parabolic shape, with the sun as its focus and downward-sweeping clouds as its boundaries, overlays the first almost at right angles to it. There are further repeated arcs to the right where the snow falls, and other, smaller arcs which cut into the main ones. And so on. It shifts and reforms itself in irrational, unpredictable ways . . . In place of the controlled, static, and rational systems used by earlier artists, Turner had created an uncontrolled and dynamic one, a system that made possible a much looser and more modern type of pictorial organisation.[49]

That is well said; but the method is irrational only in terms of the stereotypes that had taken over the terms *nature* and *reason.* It has its own reason, its own controls, but they function within a new concept of nature, a concept that totally rejects the old mechanistic system of connexions and relationships, and which sees instead a highly complicated field-of-force in action.

Our analysis so far has given us some idea of the experiences and attitudes that had driven Turner to this point; but we can go much further in probing his discontents and aspirations.

Chapter Ten

Personal Crisis

THE emotional and intellectual crisis for which Turner found an artistic resolution in Hannibal had shaken all his ideas and preconceptions. Perhaps we can first begin to grasp its depth by considering several poems which he wrote in the years 1808–11. In these, often extremely difficult to decipher, he sets out the sense of despair and disillusion that threatens to drag him down. The first full expression of this mood comes in a poem jotted down while he was fishing; the sketch-book he used has many notes for his lectures.

> O Apathy untimely power
> Tho[u] foe to merits [b]rightest hour
> Sure no genial ray of morn
> Ere glimmerd when tho wert born.[1]

He paints as darkly and unpleasantly as possible the scene of Apathy's origin. "Nature's self appear[d] dismaid." But the picture of Apathy and the universal repudiation it arouses slides into one of the painter himself, with "Remorse of wild ambition born". "Indifference then lent her aid Futurity even gave her curse." Next come some passages easier to decipher:

> ... To plunder merit[s] richest soul
> And from his lips to dash the bowl
> That fame delivered to his hands
> Rich with the worth of distant lands
> Leave him to disappointments thirst
> To feel by every one accursed

> Or loaded with contempt to strive
> And dead to joy and scarce alive
> To Nature[s] bliss her cheering ray
> That led him on in youthfull play
> Which brought him on to manhood[s] hight
> With prospects gay & pleasures bright
> To leave him to thy baneful sight
> That thou has his sad disagrace
> Entaild upon his future race

However, nature is a healing presence; and by feeling afresh his place in a great chain of natural process the sufferer can be relieved.

> Thanks, dearest Vale, thou alone
> Hast broke dire Apathy[s] sad throne
> Where thought was drown'd and lost
> Like shipwrecked mariners are tost
> Lost all joy unknown their way
> But hope with thine yet holds her day
> Amid the blackness of the unknown land
> Still glimmers, still enervates the hand
> To brave the dire misfortunes sternest day
> And through contending evils work their way
> Long lost in thy entangling toils
> My mind sunk deep within the coils
> Each pleasure that my former powers
> Had given to fishing anxious hours
> Below the summer hours they pass
> Thro water gliding clear as Glass
> The finny race escapes my line
> No float or slim[m]er thread entwine
> Nor urge my hand to catch a fly
> So careless so indifferent am I
> Whatever passes pass it may
> No moment urge the rising lay
> The wind it is too high too scant
> Fro East or North, not what I want
> The sails they give me so much trouble
> And what is pleasure but a bubble
> When set I wish they were unfurled
> And fain would give evn them a world
> A world if indifference I think
> Nature denies. Nature hold[s] each link
> In the great chain that is a zone
> Where cause and its effect are one

Next in a sketchbook that contains material ranging from 1809 to 1811 (the one with the note on 90 Norton Street), we find a few strange lines:

> Where's the distance throw[s]
> Me back so far, but I may boldly speak
> In right, tho proud Oppression will not hear me.[2]

Also, some blank verse in an unusually resigned mood:

> World I have known the[e] long & now the hour
> When I must part from thee is near at hand
> I bore thee much good will & many a time
> In thy fair promises repos'd more trust
> Than wiser heads and colder hearts w'd risk
> Some tokens of a life not wholly passed
> In selfish strivings or ignoble sloth
> Haply these shall be found when I am gone
> Wh[ich] may dispose thy candour to discern
> Some merit in my zeal and let my works
> Outlive the maker who bequeathes them to thee
> For well I know where our possessions end
> Thy praise begins & few there be who weave
> Wreaths for the Poet[s] brow, till he is laid
> Low in his narrow dwelling with the worm.[3]

These lines are suspiciously smooth and tame, but even if Turner copied them from a book, he must have been much moved by their sentiment; all the other poems in this sketchbook are certainly his. Just before *World* are some lines stating that Flattery has "muddled all the fecund brains of Wilkie and of Bird". Further on comes a long and important poem, in which he compares his lot with that of Otway, Bruce, Columbus, Ralegh. He uses these men as the types of creative and adventurous discoverers whose exploits lead to disaster, ingratitude, rejection. Fancy is the decoy that draws the rash spirit on.

> Oh Fancy didst thou not lure
> The tender Otway from a parents side
> By Arun sedgy stream to feel the powrs
> Of fortune adverse tho rich in thy strength
> And full in thy realm of gay conceits
> Didst care to cast his eye that scorn[d] to shed
> The tears of weak complain[t]s . . .[4]

A particular effort is made to depict the sufferings of James

Bruce, who discovered the source of the Blue Nile and the
confluence of the Blue and the White in 1770–2, and whose
story was received with incredulity on his return to London.
Turner had probably been reading the 1805 edition of his
Travels, in which his autobiography was published.

> . . . gaze enchanted saw
> In the minds eye alone the splendid Nile
> . . . across the world[s] cold eye of sense
> And sends all headlong in the wild pursuit . . .
> Thought a madman or a fool
> Deservedly sent to perish not explore
> What could but then seem but inexplicable
> To search for what to them but fabled nonsense
> And such it proved to him What to him
> The hard hard bed and burning suns
> Pouring intense heat upon his head
> Fevering his thought to madness and despair
> And disappointment keenest made by mockery . . .
> . . . grandeur, with all the full form shown
> Of Abessinian beauties like the Hesperides of old
> Attending all to charm its labours irigating earth
> Where odoriferous sweets perfumed each gale
> Creating delight like to Mahomets heaven
> All proved but a dream . . . cleared of the mist
> That thou for many an age had hung around
> The source at length he saw and thy deceits
> Lookd down with wonder at the tepid pool
> And shed his baffled sense . . .

What he says here about Fancy is obscure. Bruce's discovery
makes clear "that Nilus and the Thames but bubble into day"
(he was uncertain whether to write Thames or Niger) – that is,
establishes the rule of general law, and we accept this fact
"without further search yet to compress by cold denying
good". The deepest and most profound of discoveries have
been caused by "various accidents"; thus, "the laws of Gravity
thou assisted to inspire" – but Fancy goes no further. "The
first great cause cannot be ascertained." And so it is only "by
analogy we judge eer of effects of causes which we know are
true". He tells Fancy: "Thou triumphs ever by investigation
which when brought to the point at issue Thou always yet
has fled the trial. Who then can hope to be successful in thy
cause ingrate [?]." He seems to be saying that thought
(fancy) quails before final issues and that this evasion is

somehow linked with the rejection or betrayal of the poet or
explorer who braves the unknown. Ralegh died in disgrace,
and the shame cannot be washed out for England "even with
Fancy's utmost tears to come." The Deceits of Fancy as in
some sort the Fallacies of Hope.

Two points are worth noting: the image of the Hesperides
brought down to earth by the Nile irrigating of its own accord
amid the Abyssinian girls. And the dislike of the World's
Cold Eye of Sense. Fancy is further bidden (after Otway's
downfall).

> Then on the World cast that reproving Eye
> That tells severely thou has done thy worst.

This fear of the Eye is related to what we have said of his
inability to draw portraits.

Next comes a poem probably written as he was leaving for
his second tour of the West Country in 1813 – though it is
barely possible Turner composed it at Farnley in 1811, as
some of the sketches in the book seem to have been made
there; and we find studies for MERCURY AND HERSE (1811).[5]
In the first line I take "discarded" to refer to "thou", not to
"London".

> Discarded London thou must now forgo
> The praises of the great the very few.
> Among the many who delight to prate
> To keep the chit chat of the tables round
> Alive, by nothingness yet talk of taste
> Must thou depart, so soon to quit
> The splendour that thou helped to give
> Displaced the[r]ough friendship, victim to desire
> And love of change that treading constant on
> The Heel of talent goods it to the fate
> Of all that toiled before, down thoughts
> That trouble. But to see the placid unheedfull
> Recreant against that wall, which echod oft
> That blushed a higher glow at such delights
> To feel the breast that fears thy hapless charge
> Like the once favourite, fallen. Meet the eye
> Of those who knew [thee] in thy lost estate
> Shut the chil eye, or bid the pliant tongue
> Tell all the misery, thou knowst thyself
> Was once beloved, respected honored
> Held high to make thy fall the greater
> Envidious exalltations woke the blast

Note the intrusion again of the feared Eye. Turner goes on to develop the image of the wintry blast that breaks down foliage, introduces the destructive avalanche, and ends with a brie glimpse of Summer.

> Or scattered as the leaves of Autumn heaped around
> Tell too loudly all impending fate
> That some day these vegetating powers
> Calld by the quick[n]ing sun to tender shoots
> Through the hard rind which brave[d] the Winter frosts
> And pendant icicles gleam[s] the first of green
> Gay livery of the groves, that curling runs
> Round vegetation in her vary[y]ing course
> From the banefull nightshade dark intwined
> In the low quicksets to the topmost bough
> That yelling in the breeze of alpine hights
> Bears the greay lichen midst the upmost storm
> Where ed[dy]ing snows and cracking glaciers fall
> Wide dealing round destruction
> To the calm sunny vale where Summer binds
> Her auburn ringlets by the yellow gourd
> That lost by brightness yields the conquest poor.

The same notebook has a series of efforts to write a lyric in a small pencilled script, beginning:

> The widowed heart
> In life[s] gay May
> A prey to grief
> Sees no relief . . .

Also several attempts to compose a punning epigram on a man named Howe, who is connected with a Phipps:

> Doth prying Phipps continue now
> To practice or lie still
> To look to lie – but he at will
> Must not since he knows Howe. . . .
> Doth Phipps eer hope to practice on [the] pair
> Credulity on British fair –

These attempts develop oddly into a joke about Pope's Grotto (rhyming with hope) seen as the mating-place of Aeneas and Dido.

> So Eneas retired
> And Dido required
> Both practice and practical care

> Lecher lie still
> To lie on and look at his ease
> Ah Dido know howe.[6]

The writing is hard to make out, but the image is certainly of lovers embraced, with someone peeping. ("Dogs neer look ere they leap" gives another pun: leap as a jump and as copulation. "In darkness got a leap") The Grotto of Pope is five times mentioned; it thus merges with the Cave in which, according to Virgil, Dido and Aeneas mated. (Turner's picture of *Pope's Villa* shows a pair of pastoral lovers.) Without knowing the point of the joke about Phipps and Howe it is impossible to decipher in full Turner's meaning; but an interesting complex of imagery appears – the lying-down of lovers is equated with the lying-in-the-grave, as the original epigram suggests an epitaph. When we add that the same notebook has three lines on the theme of the earthly paradise, we see how complicated are Turner's emotions:

> They would have thought, who heard the strain,
> They saw in Tempe's vale her native maids
> To some unwearied minstrel dancing.[7]

The date of these poems is probably between 1812 and 1813. A poem, perhaps of 1813, expresses disillusionment about Love: "Oh Love thou bane of humble joys Thou gives the es[t]asy of hope." Time past present future are linked in the struggle of Hope. The heart throughout life can "look back alas a toilsome dream Forward with pleasure hopes anew."[8] The attitude of this poem is anticipated by "Woman is Doubtfull Love", about 1809, in a notebook which also has a less sceptical love poem "Broach as a Jewel guarding a Lady(s) breast", addressed to Laura (a name which in Turner's pronunciation doubtless came close to Sarah). And in the 1811 itinerary poem there is the picture of the betrayed girl as well as lines about Love – "thoughts created by the ardent mind prove oft as changing as the changing wind" – with stress on the anguish of absence: "Absence the dreadful monster to delight Delusion like the silent midnight flight . . . the intolerable smart of Love when absent ranking at the heart."[9]

Another poem, probably written during the second tour in Devon, tries to sum up the discontents, the sense of failure and frustration, the cheat of time.

> O man, that vanity alone
> should tempt us all thro life
> To give to furnish pleasure wings
> That wafts and kills with exquisite delight
> Far from what is real joy
> We hurry onward, in madning zeal
> In wooing trifles, our Employ
> Still time, and death.
> Neglecting time, tho time we steal
>
> For as the shadow passeth on
> So man neglectful soon destroys
> Looks anxiously for....[10]

The elements of conventional diction and of incoherence must not blind us to the passionate sincerity of these poems. Turner, so reticent about his personal life, could not have made any statement about himself in prose; but in verse he felt protected by the form, as if it purged the outburst of particularizing points of reference and universalized what he had to say.

What do his verses reveal? A sense of extreme dislocation, of alienation from the whole social and artistic scene, of regret and loss. All the promise of happiness and success with which he began has been vitiated. As soon as he penetrated into "the horror of the world unknown" (as he says of Bruce), and "through enchanting prospects passing o'er", he found only the deceit of fancy, the fallacy of hope, and the total misunderstanding and ingratitude of the world.

These emotional and intellectual positions have a number of ramifications. Certainly one strong contributory factor was his inability to achieve any settled relationship in love. Sarah Danby remains a figure lost in the shadows; we cannot estimate with any clarity what part she played in Turner's life. But we are not likely to go far wrong if we consider that elements of fear, doubt and suspicion, generated in Turner by his early home life, wrecked the relationship before it began, or at least harshly limited the area of its possible development. His ingrained attitudes affected him with increased uncertainty and deepened his sense of isolation, unhappiness and frustration; only in his contemplation of nature and the pursuit of his art could he find release.

Another factor that worked along the same lines, intensifying loneliness and instability, was the mis-comprehension of his aims in art, the attacks in the Press, and the organized attempt to boycott him led by Beaumont. We have seen him hard-hit by criticisms. "No one", said Trimmer. "felt more keenly the illiberal strictures of the newspapers, and I have seen him almost in tears, and ready to hang himself, though still only rating their opinions at their worth.[11]" Again, Ruskin tells us, "To censure, Turner was acutely sensitive; owing to his own natural kindness, he felt it for himself or for others, not as criticism, but as cruelty. He knew that however little his higher power could be seen he had at least done as much as ought to have saved him from wanton insult, and the attacks upon him in his later years were to him not merely contemptible in their ignorance, but amazing in their ingratitude. 'A man may be weak in his age,' he said to me once, at the time when he felt he was dying, "but you should not tell him so.'"[12]. The verses cited above show that he felt pain, despair, and a sense of ingratitude in his early manhood as in his later years.

His ideas about critics and connoisseurs, about the artist's need to trust in his onward inner convictions, are to be read in the marginal notes he added to Shee's *Elements of Art*, 1809; we may assume that these were jotted down soon after publication.[13] (It was probably this poem by Shee which more than any other stimulated him into conceiving his own project of a poem that set out his main positions.) He declares, "It is not the love of arts that prompts a critic but vanity and never ceasing lust to be thought a man of superior taste." The critic immolates new works "under the mark of attention to the art but really only to be consider[ed] a man of taste".[14] And "how misled must they be who blindly follow the dictates of the connoisseur or the manner of the model, for imitation at best is but a secondary merit, and in Reynolds words must be content in always being behind". Rather, "the external evidence of merit" (i.e. the actual artistic definition) "should be confided in instead of sounding opinions signifying nothing."[15] In the existing situation, "it is natural that there should be more dictators than encouragers more critics than students more amateurs than artists".[16]

He therefore holds that the artist must try things out for

himself, experiment, ignore teachers, find his way by practice, and then work out the rationale of his position.

The power of thinking is not allowed, but rather check'd in the mode of tuition and overwhelmed with elementary matter and Aphorisms in art that must not be violated and each of which is sufficient for his whole life to attain even to a small degree of perfection, how can he then between contending differences dare before he can be said to see without rational analysis what he thinks he sees, while his instructors load him [with] the various beauties and defects, but which are neither one or the other to him without he proves to himself that they are so.

It is this power that may be justly call[ed] the learning of the Arts, the reflection of years increased by thought analytically considered and by a vigour[ou]s intellectual power distild from the maturity of mind, a selfformed knowledge.[17]

This distillation comes about "imperceptibly like the accumulation of drops imbibing the surround[ing] objects of Study" and "swelling to a stream that forces a channel to itself".

He is therefore against theory, against all the established canons. "The lesson is not so impressive as the illustration of the use of practical observation and reflection how far useful in preference to all the splendid Theory of Art."[18] Taste (the prevailing canon) is the result of creative effort, not the other way round. "Genius may be said to be the parent of taste, as it gives that enthusiastic warmth to admire first Nature in her common dress to consider of the causes and effects of incidents to investigate not with the eyes of erudition but to form a language of his own."[19] Genius, the inner drive, "rises with its subject its power amalgamates itself th[r]o everything and can never be said to feel more or less than its subject". That is, true art is not achieved by the imposition of the stereotypes of taste on a chosen subject, but is the expression of a vision which is one with the method used and the image resulting.[20]

As a public lecturer Reynolds was excusable in encouraging the students to individual practical study, that the Germ of their Genius would fill itself and that industry might help to ambitious views the mind of many who are less apt to catch the fleeting show of Nature, [considering] that it would be better to deny the existence of innate powers, when the principle [means] that it would be to[o] depresing upon young and feeling minds to say that all precept, industry and assiduity avail but little without Genius.[21]

Finally he states plainly his own credo.[21] He flatly disagrees with Shee about misguided youth who "midst Error's windings, miss the tracks of Truth". He asks, "Presuming true talent to exist what danger can arise from chance directing even supposing it to be erroneous." He demands the right to go wrong as the essential counterpart of the right to be creatively and adventurously right. Free choice, with its enthusiastic warmth,

is necessary to accompany him amidst errors and find the track of truth. Must he not find it himself by his own observation [and] perception by contrasting, combining and rejecting but how can he reject if insensible of error. Can precepts systematic rules explain them. No . . .

[The artist will] dare to think for himself and in that daring find a method not so afraid of choosing for himself listening to every pretender, whose utmost knowledge is a few practical terms or whose greatest pride is to point out the beauties of his own collection expecting a humble deference to his opinion, lamenting the dullness and apathy of the rising youth who are incorrigible in not following what he has condescendingly defined "the direct road to taste". These are the fatal windings the labyrinth of contrarieties and fluctuating systems – to have no choice "but that of the Patron" is the very fetter upon Genius, that every coxcomb wishes to rivet but Choice should even a beggar stand alone.

This stand is mine and shall remain my own.[22]

This is written opposite a passage about the British Institution.

We can see, then, that while the attacks upon his art caused him great anxiety and suffering, they also stiffened his resistances and drove him more strongly along his reprobated way. Still, in terms of the total situation, their effect was to make him doubt and test all his preconceptions, his social and political ideas as well as his artistic ones. They cannot be separated from the whole complex of thoughts and emotions making for the fundamental concept of the Fallacies of Hope.

That concept was linked with a long series of poems which sought to utter a considered philosophic judgement of life, often gathering what were defined as the experiences making life worthwhile under the heading of Pleasures. So we get the Pleasures of Imagination, of Hope, or Memory, and so on. Hope and Memory were generally taken as basic forms of imaginative and emotional activity. Memory looked back and sought to comprehend the past, to distinguish a coherent or significant structure in all that had gone to make the poet (who appears as the type of Man); Wordsworth's *Prelude* belongs to this tradition. Hope looked forward and sought to define a valuable goal in history and in individual experience. Out of the conflict and harmony of Hope and Memory was defined the full psychology of that experience, which in turn revealed the universal pattern of human process. In its deepest aspects the psychology of Memory and Hope went far beyond the treatment of those faculties as mere random recollection or expectation. Memory was needed to grasp both the essence and the structure of past experience, their inner meaning and nodal points of development; Hope was concerned with the next step as it emerged out of a total movement of the self (or of society) as that self was driven on by its deepmost needs, its concrete involvement in the reality of time and space. We cannot here analyse the large number of important poems which come under these headings or show in various ways the impact of the Hope-Memory complex; but it is necessary to mention Akenside's *Pleasures of Imagination* and Campbell's *Pleasures of Hope*, both of which exercised a crucial influence on Turner. Later we shall have more to say of Akenside; for the moment it is sufficient to point out that Campbell in his poem cogently set out the goals of hope, of constructive effort, which were acceptable to advanced opinion in 1799. He wanted the full development of the arts and sciences in terms of the existing perspective, the working-out of the new possibilities of Improvement (i.e. of industry, technology, and the like), the ending of the slave trade, the liberation of India and Africa.[23]

In his revulsions Turner could not simply accept this scheme. Not that he rejected the aims set out by Campbell. What he wanted to do was to add what he felt had been left out – an omission that undermined the system. He wanted to define the inner flaw, the unrealized contradiction which in the last resort prevented the working-out of history on the plain progressive lines of Campbell's picture. To the Pleasures of Hope it was necessary to add its Fallacies. In this sense his imagined poem belonged to the dissident series, of which another example was Robert Merry's *Pains of Memory*, 1796, which refused to accept Rogers's *Pleasures* as a true picture. Memory, Merry tried to say, is a painful process of realization, not a rich man's meditation in a mild evening as a large dinner is being digested. Turner similarly criticized Campbell's views by his insistence that the heroic exploits and intentions of men continually miscarry and are inverted into their opposites by uncomprehended contradictions. His sufferings and broodings, long driving him towards this conclusion, came to a head in 1811–12 in HANNIBAL CROSSING THE ALPS, its aesthetic definition and its verse-tag.

A slight event may be cited, which perhaps played its part in pushing Turner to the edge of the final decision, the total break with his world and its values which he made in HANNI-BAL. In 1811 Callcott had been picked out by Robert Hunt in the *Examiner* with praise that was meant to hurt Turner. Hunt wrote that Callcott was "beginning to share with Mr. Turner the highest honours of the Art". In fact, "he is the best painter of figures of all our eminent landscape painters. Mr. Turner always gives the suitable action and character, but Mr. Callcott superadds to this, more carefulness of delineation." In the Academy Exhibition of this year Callcott showed what was, perhaps, his most ambitious work, *Apollo slaying the Sons of Niobe at the Altar of Latona*. Hunt wrote, "The sublime demands what is here given with a just but daring hand, – the clash of elements, the opposition of colours, of line, and of angular forms. The revengeful aspect of Apollo as he launches his destructive arrows, the bluster of the wind, and the contrast of gloom with the celestial blaze, – the flight of victims, the piteous prostration of the dead, the more pathetic deprecation and fears of the living who are doomed to death, and the contrast with all this of complacency and quiet in the statue of Latona, before which the havoc and horror are displayed, exhibit a picture of the most terrific sublimity."[24]

Turner, with his need to absorb all tendencies of the period and to drive beyond them, could not but have felt a challenge at such praise of Callcott's direct attempt to outdo Wilson's *Niobe*. In HANNIBAL he brings together the whole complex of forces he has drawn from *Niobe* and from Poussin's works, and lifts them on to a new level. This is his answer, not so much to Callcott's work (which he must have estimated at its true worth), but to Hunt's overvaluation of it. Against talented imitation he sets a work of adventurous exploration, in which elements of the old are transformed inside a new aesthetic unity. Callcott's painting, and Hunt's praise of it, by themselves could not have brought about such a step; but at the point of development he had reached in 1811 they may well have played a part in touching off the new explosive image.

It is worth noting, as well, that the personal crisis of Turner which we are discussing was linked with something of a crisis in the patronage system of the arts: the breakdown of the system of eighteenth-century aristocratic patronage and the first tentative stages of the emergence of a middle-class public. We can indeed trace this crisis back to the days of Hogarth and Gainsborough; but now it showed up, in a more general and persistent way. Its growth appeared in the changes of attitude to Wilson. He had been more or less neglected by the noble patrons of art; and the rise of his reputation coincided with the rise of the new public. The swing in his favour began with the 1790s and was definite by the turn of the century. It was largely brought about by the artists, but gradually had a wider effect.[25] By the time of Turner's twenties vanguard taste had reached the point at which Wilson's poetic simplifications and his atmospheric feeling for English landscape were appreciated. A new social stratum of buyers appeared, who were keen to collect his work. The price rise began in the mid-1790s. On 15 July 1794 Vendergucht, a painter and dealer, told Farington that Wilson's pictures "are getting into greater request, at comparatively high prices". On 17 May 1806 Seguier spoke to him of a "great rise in the price of Wilson's pictures. Twenty-five or six years ago they were so far a drug that Wilson solicited Segar to purchase some of Him, which the latter answered by saying that He had some already which were not disposed of. If the result could have been forseen it wd. have been a good speculation to have bought many of them."[26] There was still, however, an opposition led by men like Payne Knight, the Marquess of Stafford, Charles Long (later Lord Farnborough), Sir A. Hume; and many leading collectors had no enthusiasm for Wilson.[27] But the movement went on, culminating in the exhibition in 1814 at the British Institution, in which Wilson (eighty-four works, with four added), was shown with Hogarth and Gainsborough.

Prominent dealers also grew interested. The professional and mercantile men had come up as buyers; they wanted pictures, but could not afford Old Masters. Many of their

names are to be found in Farington's *Diary*. They included
lawyers, bankers, linen-drapers, merchants, authors, physi-
cians, clergymen, and came from Liverpool and Manchester
as well as London. An analysis of the men who lent pictures
to the 1814 exhibition shows twenty-one early patrons, eight
new-comers from the landed gentry, fifty-nine members of the
middle class; the rest, of whom little is known, seem to include
dealers, professional men, and a few inheritors from earlier
buyers.[28]

Turner's first break-through brought him to a level generally
appreciable by this new public. His work then reposed on their
response. But he soon drove on farther ahead, and his oil-
paintings in particular often found no understanding, even
after the arrival of Ruskin. However, the middle-class public
continued to like his work when translated into engravings;
and it was mainly through the money he made out of the
drawings for this public that he was able to build up his
fortune and maintain a strong though oblique contact with
the taste of his period. With his peculiar mixture of caution
and recklessness he both completely defied all critical opinion
and kept a broad public for one section of his work. Because
of the comparative lack of connexion between the two fields –
oil-paintings and engravings – these tactics did not involve
any compromise on his part. Or perhaps it would be truer to
say that the meretriciously romanticized elements which at
times made their way into the engravings did not at all
impede his obstinate clinging to his own vision in the more
important sectors of his work.

He was thus driven more and more to feel that he painted
for himself alone – in the sense that he could find no criterion
in the general taste or in the opinions of the critics and
connoisseurs. Trimmer described an argument between him
and Henry Howard, R.A.: "Howard, though far below Turner
as an artist, was his superior in education; and although doing
ample homage to his genius, he often got into warm professional disputes with him. But Turner was mostly in the
right. They once, I remember, had a very hot dispute, and for
the time being lost temper. Howard maintained they should
paint for the public; Turner, that public opinion was not
worth a rush, and that one should paint only for judges. But
according to all artists, no one but an artist can judge of the

difficulties of painting, and consequently of the merits of a picture."[29] In fact, however, Turner painted no more for any "judges" than he did for the general public; he was probably more likely to get some appreciation from a wholly un-instructed layman than from the critics, and, as we have seen, many of the more influential artists considered that he had taken a wrong turning. In such a situation he had to rely on his own sense of what was truly the course of creative discovery; and inside, as we have seen, he was continually shaken with doubt and anguish. Yet these pangs were one aspect of the creative force that drove him restlessly on; they were the pledge of his ceaselessly renewed sensibility with its raw edges as well as its obstinate core.

This lonely and assailed position of his – though prefigured in lesser ways in the lives of Rembrandt, Hogarth, and Wilson – cannot be truly paralleled before the days of Impressionism and Cézanne, and is one of the many signs marking him out as the founder of modern art. A profound cleavage, with disastrous results, had arrived between the general public (including its critics and connoisseurs) and the creator in the sphere of art. The artist with an adventurous spirit cannot be blamed for his development; he is indeed seeking all the while for new integrations and thus for the end of the cleavage. But he is fighting against an overwhelming pressure of alienation and disintegration.

Chapter Eleven

Politics and Symbolism

THERE are yet further elements of the spiritual and aesthetic crisis in Turner to be examined. We have noted in a general way how he took over the social and political ideas expressed in *Liberty*; but we can see more precisely how those ideas worked in him to play their part in begetting HANNIBAL. The later part of 1811 had its ominous comet trailing across the sky; and someone so responsive to natural phenomena in a portentous guise as Turner was must have been emotionally stirred by its presence, recalling Thomson's comment, "The guilty nations tremble."[1] The simple patriotism with which he had begun his career had received several shocks. His love of ships and seamen had led him to commemorate naval engagements of the wars. He was fond of Charles Dibdin's nautical songs, two of which he transcribed at length about 1798.[2] What seems to be his first attempt at a sustained verse effort is the poem about Willoughby attempting the north-west passage in the sixteenth century, written about 1808. It opens, "O Gold thou parent of Ambition's ardent blush", and sees the exploit as representative of British valour and exploring energy; no conflict appears between the gold motive and the aims of exploration. Turner's main interest lies in the account of elemental fury, "contending horrors", that threaten world end – to "loose the frozen chain that binds the whole". Something of the notion of fallacious hope appears in the total disaster of the venture, though this is not brought out.[3] Lines on the Silver Thames merely admire

Commerce, as also does the poem attached to LONDON (1809). In verses on the Extended Town he sees the meeting-place of merging opposites, poor and rich, good and evil, which Hope draws together "to a concentred focus".[4]

In his notes to Opie he discusses the neglect of history-painting and the "great national point of view"; the argument is obscure, but he suggests that commerce justifies its dignity "only by diffusing its ornament to civilise men", and that it should seek "to assist and maintain art that it has been the fruit of every nation to support". However, all this leads to stereotypes, to a "rigid adherence of forms and costume". Any new adaptations are carried out in terms of the prevailing prejudices. "Hence the contraction and character of different nations have their different ideas of taste." Learning and erudition in the sphere of the arts aims at keeping "what has gone before instead of thinking what is good or bad". He then goes on to speak of the necessity of "more allurement to the higher walks of Landscape as Historical" (in place of the lower walks and the portraits which displace history-painting).[5] He is thus beginning to have doubts about commerce and national character as aids to art; but he still feels a strong patriotism when he thinks of British art. In his notes to Shee, recalling his visits to the Louvre in 1802, he remarks of the French:

they have returned with all the exquisite production[s] of ransacked countries [yet] look with cool indifference at all the matchless power of Titians glowing tones because precision of detail is their sole idol, it was no small wonder to see their choice of study. Nationality with all her bitterness came upon me but I could not refrain contrasting ourselves to them with advantage to our Endeavours generally to have been able without the aids without this power and against the ungenial influence according to Winckelmann of our Northern climate we may claim justly to be Painters [even] if we are deficient as draughtsmen.[6]

In the lectures he again refers to the theories that English climate forbade a flourishing of the arts. Here he insists that the climate is stimulating, and goes on:

the exertions of the higher departments of our art have most completely refuted the long admitted axioms of Winckelmann and Mirabeau about our Northern climate that we may not be blind to abundant advantages which nature has given us but that we may prove her superiority in a Northern line of demarkation of Genius, not in theoretical characteristics but practical exertions.[7]

And he expresses the hope that his fellow countrymen "will rise superior to the rest of the world in the polite arts as they have already in the sciences".[8] This sort of sentiment he never lost; his will shows his unfaltering sense of unity with art in general and British art in particular. Indeed, we might say that all his social and political emotions were turned in on art; but that does not mean he gave up making judgements in his own terms on the events and movements in his world. In a way the in-turning sharpened his critical sense; but what he thought and felt became solely material for his art, transformed into the symbols and images which he felt to reveal the inner significance of processes and things.

In his itinerary poem of 1811 he shows a keen interest in industrial activities, such as the rope-twisting works at Bridport. He patriotically discusses the possibilities of growing hemp in Britain in order "to meet the direfull length of continental hatred called blockade".[9] He sees a peaceful countryside, which he contrasts with medieval days; the farmer is able to gain "the recompense of labours all his own; and little troubled seems the humble cot". The barons wrung a charter from the king:

> And to maintain its freedom all have died
> The parched tracks of Memphis arid sands
> And planted laurrels wreath in hostile lands
> With native bravery, Liberty decreed
> Receive the stimulus, act from Runnymead.[10]

He wants the continual reassertion of freedom, but gives no hint of what he thinks the struggle in his own day entails. However, as we noted in dealing with the image of the boy with the little ship, a note of disillusionment creeps in. From such small beginnings come about, not the planting of laurel wreaths abroad, but forms of oppressive power, "the great Demagogues that tyrannise on earth".[11]

It may be no accident that this note of disquiet appeared in 1811 after he had met Fawkes. Luckily we know what was in Fawkes's mind in 1811 and 1812, and the sort of thing he talked vehemently about during Turner's visit on the eve of the painting of HANNIBAL. A passionate Whig of the Fox school, at this time he was uttering sentiments so radical as to approach a revolutionary despair and anger. While HANNIBAL was hanging on the walls of Somerset House he made a speech on Parliamentary Reform (23 May 1812) at that radical rendezvous, the Crown and Anchor Tavern. He called for the restoration of the Constitution, "which has been so long and loudly extolled in theory, and so strangely perverted in practice". He cited with full approval the Memorial of the Committee of Association of the County of York, which declared that "the representation of the Commons of England, is virtually annihilated; and an institution, which was intended to be the people's defence against Aristocratic domination, and Royal despotism, is now become an engine, in the hands of the Minister, to tax, oppress, insult, and enslave the People of England". (He was himself an active member of the Association.) The statement went on to say: "Now, that the national substance was wasting fast away, by the profusion of expense in this rash and unfortunate war; now, that the influence of the Crown, fed by this very prodigality, and increased in full proportion to it, is swoln to a most dangerous magnitude; now, that the system of corruption has reached its maturity, and that the crisis of our Country has arrived, the amputation of that poisonous tumour, the excrescence of our vitiated constitution, must be resolved on, or Political Dissolution must be the inevitable consequence."

The identity of interest between Government and governed, Fawkes added, "is completely lost, done away, and extinguished". The consequences of "perseverance in this corrupt and inadequate system, are now daily, I might almost say hourly, exhibiting themselves to our view. And so, we have every reason to apprehend, that the terrible crisis, if not actually arrived, is yet rapidly approaching." He saw in the French Revolution "an awful warning". Charles I and Louis XVI were "their own executioners".

He summed up, "Power I do covet – but it is only the power (would I had it), to point out distinctly to my Countrymen, the brink of the frightful precipice on which they are trembling, and the necessity of their withdrawing themselves from its hollow and crumbling edge."[12]

There we have the height image, of which HANNIBAL is one version. The whole of Fawkes's speech illuminates the social

situation and its urgencies which meet and merge with
Turner's personal and artistic pressures. At Farnley, Fawkes
must have been discussing the political and economic impasse
with the directness and frankness that were his characteristics
and which ring through his speech. Coming from such a man,
his remarks must have strongly affected Turner, linking his
inner struggle with the outer world and its problems. In
1811–12 the Luddite movement was in full swing. In early
1812, in Glasgow, delegates met to work out their campaign.[13]
The Government was driven to draft 12,000 troops into
Nottinghamshire – a larger army than Wellington took to the
Peninsula; and an act was passed that made the destruction
of machinery punishable by death. While Turner was at
Farnley in November 1811 there were bread riots and loom-
wreckings at Nottingham.[14] Such matters, closely affecting
Yorkshire, Fawkes would have analysed as proofs of the
terrible crisis he foresaw.

On his return to London, Turner must have brooded on
these matters and been deeply interested in the powerful
speech made by Byron in the House of Lords on 27 February
1812 against the law carrying the death penalty, mentioned
above. A few days later the first two cantos of *Childe Harold*
were published. They evoked the fierce struggle going on in
Spain. "They fight for freedom, who were never free", while
"fresh legions pour adown the Pyranees"; then turn to
Greece and contrast the heroic past with the apparent resignation of "hereditary bondsmen". Such a poem could not but
stir afresh all Turner's memories of Thomson's *Liberty* and
its question as to how long a mercantile empire could resist
corruption. He prided himself, Thornbury stresses, on being
well informed on all the leading issues of the day. "He was
rather desirous to obtain a repute for general knowledge,
and was a reader of all the best books and reviews of the day.
The 'Edinburgh Review' in its best days, was one of his
special favourites."[15]

Thus, there was every reason for Turner to apply to the
Britain of 1811–12 all the ideas and emotions which were for
him associated with catastrophe, storm and elemental
violence. Fawkes's eloquent radicalism must have thoroughly
shaken him up, and was an important factor contributing to
the love he felt for him. But even though he may well have

shared his attitudes at this point, that does not mean that he interpreted the situation in the same way as Fawkes; and the question of just how he did interpret it is of crucial importance for his work. Because of the inner tensions and conflicts which we have analysed, he had to transform the social, economic or political issue into an image, an aesthetic symbol, before it could penetrate his innermost self and move the depths of his being. Then what came out in Fawkes as a call to immediate action came out in him as a picture like HANNIBAL. Art was for him activity, not comtemplation, not comment linked with something outside itself; it was activity which was complete in itself, however much of its material and its stimulus might emerge out of the external world and go back into it. Art, in such a conception, is not a substitute for social action, though it does not seek to deflect men from such action in so far as it is relevant and necessary. Its own activity assumes and draws on social reality, because it assumes and draws on all aspects of reality, human and natural. It needs to be in the dead centre of the historical process as well as to achieve its aesthetic independence.

These points can be made clearer by seeing how Turner carried on his work of absorbing and transforming the material of history as well as of nature. HANNIBAL exemplified the process. Into its making went the complex of personal, aesthetic, and social forces we have discussed; yet in itself it remained something quite new. To understand it at all fully we need first to make the exploration of Turner's mind; yet after that we must stand back and look at the work for its own unity of judgement, definition, comprehension.

While these considerations may be true of all significant works of art, what we are trying to bring out here is the new consciousness of relationships, and the consequently new kind of asthetic image, that we find in Turner – an expression of all the aspirations, contradictions, and integrations of the Romantic Movement as revealed in his work. (It could be argued that only he and Beethoven show these elements in their supreme form.)

Now let us consider further the way in which Turner viewed his material, the symbolizing activity in his method which in the last resort was one with his aesthetic definition and its penetration into reality. We could paraphrase Coleridge's distinction between fancy and imagination, and say that in the more superficial levels of his mind Turner allegorized, while, when his depths were stirred, he fused symbol and reality. His allegories then reveal his imaginative energies at a level of playful fancy.

Thornbury tells us, "In the original sketch of Elgin Cathedral, made by an amateur, the windows in the nave were closed or built up; but in the revised drawing by Turner he left them open. On being spoken to about this a few years after, he said, 'They ought to have been open; how much better it is to see the light of day in God's house than darkness.'" The open windows were an allegory of anti-medievalism. He made this point clear in another work. Thornbury goes on, "Turner was always quaint in giving his reasons for what he did. When Mr. John Pye engraved the plate of Wickliffe's birth-place for Whittaker's 'Yorkshire', Turner, in touching the proof, introduced a burst of light which was not in the drawing. Mr. Pye asked him his reason for so doing. He replied, 'That is the place where Wickliffe was born, and there is the light of the glorious Reformation.' 'Well,' said Mr. Pye, satisfied, 'but what do you mean by these large fluttering geese in the foreground?' 'Oh, those – those are the old superstitions which the genius of the Reformation is driving away'."[16]

No doubt he made up that explanation of the geese on the spur of the moment; but it is clear that as he worked his mind played over everything in a picture, its texture and its smallest detail, and found this sort of fanciful meaning there. In passing we may note that once again an image of his goes back to Thomson, who wrote how

> The returning light
> That first through Wickliff streaked the priestly gloom,
> Now burst in open day. Bared to the blaze,
> Forth from the haunts of superstition crawled
> Her motley sons, fantastic figures all.[17]

And it is in the key of *Fallacies of Hope* that immediately before this passage we are told the Papacy was a power, "wild at last, to plunge into a sea of blood and horror", while immediately after it we learn that the dispersal of monastic wealth begot Trade with "guilty, glittering stores" that destroyed the Indians.

Turner felt strongly about the various liberation movements

in Europe, as befitted an admirer of *Liberty* and *Childe Harold*. His friend George Jones he used to call Georgey and Jones alternately. But "Turner, though I believe a Tory, loved liberty and those who fought for it; so when his friend's villainous namesake betrayed the Hungarians, he said to Jones, 'I shall not call you Georgey any more!' the name was henceforth hateful to him." (Thornbury's calling Turner a Tory is based on no facts; the friend of Fawkes could hardly have accepted such a description of himself. The truth is that no party label has any meaning in connexion with him.) He expressed his feeling for the cause of Greek independence by the two paintings shown in 1816, THE TEMPLE OF JUPITER PANELLENIUS RESTORED (signed and dated 1814) and VIEW OF THE TEMPLE OF JUPITER PANELLENIUS, IN THE ISLAND OF AEGINA, WITH THE GREEK NATIONAL DANCE OF THE ROMAIKA: THE ACROPOLIS OF ATHENS IN THE DISTANCE. The Restored Temple of Zeus of the United Hellenes can only be an emblem of the national restoration that the picture prophecies; and the introduction of the national dance, with the view of the Acropolis, makes the same prophecy from a different angle. The titles underline Turner's intention; and yet no one at the time, or since, has noticed the obvious fact. Turner was here a better political prophet than Byron. The latter in *Childe Harold* expressed no hope for the Greeks; and it was not till 1821 that the decisive war of independence flared up. (An earlier drawing has the alternative titles: HOMER RECITING TO THE GREEKS HIS HYMN TO APPOLLO or ATTALUS DECLARING THE GREEK STATES TO BE FREE.[18]) The verses attached to the first painting carry the image of a restored nation farther; by identifying the temple pillars with the pines throwing their shadows in the early morning, they suggest the restoration of harmony between man and nature. The light, entering the forest depth, acts as a transformative force. The direct political theme thus deepens into the theme of man's freedom altogether from alienation.

A more complicated example of political allegory appears in THE PRINCE OF ORANGE, WILLIAM III, EMBARKED FROM HOLLAND, LANDED AT TORBAY, NOVEMBER 4TH, 1688, AFTER A STORMY PASSAGE. This picture was shown in 1832, in the midst of the struggles for the Reform Bill. It obviously glances back at the Glorious Revolution and links it with the contemporary situation; Fawkes would certainly have seen the Bill as a true working-out of the principles of 1688. The *Athenaeum*, however, merely commented that Turner had squandered his powers "upon a subject which has lost somewhat of its feverish interest in the hearts of Englishmen". Turner's reference is to a vague History of England, but in fact he was thinking of Part IV of *Liberty*, which ends with a long apostrophe to William as a man who saved England from bigotry and oppression. Thomson stresses the storm as emblem of the counterrevolution. Liberty speaks:

> Immortal Nassau came. I hushed the deep
> By demons roused, and bade the listed winds,
> Still shifting as behoved, with various breath
> Waft the deliverer to the longing shore . . .[19]

In the context of 1831–2 the demonic storms refer to the desperate resistance of reaction to the Bill, with such consequences as the semi-insurrection at Bristol. But Turner with his ironies and his sense of fallacious hopes could not be expected to leave the statement at the simple identification of William's ship and the Bill. He added a note to the picture, "The yacht in which his Majesty sailed was, after many changes and services, finally wrecked on Hamburg Sands, while employed in the Hull Trade." That is, the ship-of-state has been sold to the commercial interests and thus in the end brought to shipwreck. The triumph of the revolutionary ship is shadowed by the hint of inner betrayal. A note in his last sketchbook, some eighteen years later, runs: "Geece and Goslings hissing at Pigs – The Reform Question." Here we again have allegorical geese, and we see the quizzical detachment that went with his deep feelings.[20]

In one poem, we may note, Turner set out his belief that men should unite and cease to be "niggard of their store". As with the poem on the Temple of Jupiter Panellenius, an image drawn from natural process is used; and the characteristic emblem of crisis and disaster is shipwreck.

> Hoarse on the rocky margin of the deep
> The tide swell falls in constant flow
> And the pale welkin gathering darkness creep
> While the low bark plows heavy at the prow
> Sabler at every pitch the pashing waters heavier dash
> but only to be wreck't

Insated rise to s[e]ize the fated prey
and strive to gain the deck
Oh few escape howeer the floating waste
Throw back their ineffectual splash
Shines on the bows by Cinthia[s] light bedecked
Repulsed not humbled miriadlike they join
United portions roll but onward to the shore
Giving a daily lesson to combine
To Man himself, so niggard of his store.[21]

A good example of Turner's play of fancy is his poem on the architectural orders, where Tuscan is seen as a labourer, Ionic as a courtesan, Corinthian as a full-blown matron. Ionic is further linked with the pawnshop: "The little dentals in suffite Show grinding power here complete And placed as the teeth of Shark", thus expressing the usurer who swallows up the poor. Turner was fully aware of the multiple meanings he put into a work of art; and he would dearly have liked to be understood. Hence the clues of the verse-tags. Ruskin said, "The want of appreciation touched him sorely, chiefly the not understanding his meaning. He tried hard one day, for a quarter of an hour, to make me guess what he was doing in the picture of 'Napoleon', before it had been exhibited, giving me hint after hint, in a rough way; but I could not guess, and he would not tell me." Where Ruskin so signally failed, how could he expect understanding elsewhere?

Roberts adds this comment about his pleasure in puzzling folk in general: "I was myself too much occupied to trouble myself about his private affairs, for his life partook of the character of his words; it was mysterious, and nothing seemed so much to please him as to try and puzzle you, or make you think so; for if he began to explain, or tell you anything, he was sure to break off in the middle, look very mysterious, nod, and wink his eyes, saying to himself, 'Make that out if you can'."

More examples of the allegorizing and symbolizing tendencies of Turner's mind will come up as we go on. But before we pick up again the thread of his life, I should like to analyse something of his debt to Akenside. Thomson had given him the pervasive sense of a dynamic universe; Akenside with his more ordered philosophic poem gave him a clear system and raised the main points which throughout his life obsessed him. Akenside attempted to show that the Pleasures of the Imagination arose from natural objects and from works of art; the first set begetting problems of greatness and beauty, the second begetting those of truth and morality as well as of the circumstances proper for arousing us to laughter, pity, fear, and other passions. Connected problems, Akenside said, were those of novelty, association of ideas, national habits, and so on. Finally there was the problem of genius itself, to which the Pleasures most powerfully belonged.[22]

Inevitably the problem comes up: Is Beauty (or Imagination) a lie, a pleasing delusion? That was one of the central questions of eighteenth-century thought – essentially resolved in the positions of Blake, Coleridge, Keats, Turner himself. Akenside helped Turner to formulate it and to come to grips with it. He came down strongly in his poem on the side of Imagination as a validly integrative factor, and this is what makes him in particular a precursor of Keats. Can beauty deign to dwell "where active use and health are strangers . . . the herald of a lie, to hide the shame of discord and disease?" No, he replies.

> The generous glebe
> Whose bosom smiles with verdure, the clear tract
> Of streams delicious to the thirsty soul,
> The bloom of nectar'd fruitage ripe to sense,
> And every charm of animated things,
> Are only pledges of a state sincere,
> The integrity and order of their frane,
> When all is well within, and every end
> Accomplish'd. Thus was beauty sent from heaven,
> The lovely ministress of truth and good
> In this dark world: for truth and good are one,
> And beauty dwells in them, and they in her,
> With like participation.[23]

He is thus close to Keats, and far from the moralists of the century in general. He defends passion, insists that "the gleam of youthful hope" should not be chilled or clouded, and seeks to work out a scheme of stages in the growth and liberation of the imaginative faculty.

> It now remains,
> Through various being's fair-proportioned scale,
> To trace the rising lustre of her charms,
> From their first twilight, shining forth at length
> To full meridian Splendor.

Lowest in degree is "the effusive warmth of colours mingling
with a random blaze" as beauty's dwelling. Then "higher in the
line and variation of determin'd shape, comes the level, where
truth's eternal measures mark the bound of circle, cube, or
sphere." The third ascent "unites this varied symmetry of parts
with colour's bland allurement". Loveliest of all:

> Is nature's charm, where to the full consent
> Of complicated members, to the bloom
> Of colour, and the vital change of growth,
> Life's holy flame and piercing sense are given,
> And active motion speaks the temper's soul.

These positions draw on the widespread concept of an inter-
linked chain of being, which was beginning to stir with the
first breath of evolutionary ideas. The stirring shows here in
Akenside in the dialectic of colour and structure opposed and
uniting to beget a living form in "the vital change of growth".
(Akenside, son of a butcher, was a capable doctor.) Life is
seen as at root a quest for truth, for self-fulfilment in terms
of an organic relation between man and nature. There is a pervasive sense of the "energy of life", of systems of natural
correspondences. When everything is harmoniously developed,
an idyllic relationship is born in which the earth becomes
Hesperidean, a "visionary landscape".

We have here the key to Turner's continual attempt to
depict the earthly paradise, whether by mythological evocation
or by an intensification of natural harmonies in a more or less
realistic scene. By seeing nature as restlessly moving towards
this paradise, a scale of values is established, moral and
aesthetic. Men make the universe their true home, and are
themselves transformed, "men genuine and according to
themselves".[24] Not that Akenside sets out this scheme in
uncritical optimism. He is aware that there has occurred a
dissociation of the imaginative act from the whole man, a
break between heart and mind, a "separation of the works of
imagination from philosophy". How has this come about?
he asks. The dissociation has resulted in the "abuse among
the moderns" of both imagination and philosophy; but he
sees a "prospect of their re-union under the influence of public
liberty".[25] The cause of the break has been "the rage of dire
amibition and gigantic power", which has driven the intel-

lectually inclined from the fields of public activity and "civil commerce".[26] (He adds the effects of a distortion of fancy or appetite in early years; but does not explain the connexion between this individual twist and the general dissociation.)

Just as Turner accepted the worth of Campbell's goals of Hope, but considered that there were all sorts of unrealized contradictions in his account, so he accepted the truth of Akenside's picture of man's place in the universe and his need of integration, but considered that the problem was far more complicated than had been allowed. Hence his *Fallacies of Hope*, in which he sought to express the contradictions and the complexities. But we cannot understand what he is saying unless we first grasp that he is making his judgements or criticisms inside the universe of Thomson and Akenside.

Three examples of Akenside's influence on Turner will suffice. The Argument of his *Hymn to the Naiads* runs:

The Nymphs, who preside over springs and rivulets, are addressed at day-break in honour of their several functions, and of the relations which they bear to the natural and to the moral world. Their origin is deduced from the first allegorical deities, or powers of nature; according to the doctrine of the old mythological poets, concerning the generation of the gods and the rise of things. They are then successively considered, as giving motion to the air and exciting summer breezes; as nourishing and beautifying the vegetable creation; as contributing to the fulness of navigable rivers, and consequently to the maintenance of commerce; and by that means, to the maritime part of military power. Next is represented their favorable influence upon health, when assisted by rural exercise: which introduces their connection with the art of physic, and the happy effects of mineral medicinal springs. Lastly, they are celebrated for the friendship which the true Muses bear them . . .

Turner exhibited in 1802 THE FALL OF THE CLYDE, LANARK-SHIRE: NOON. – VIDE AKENSIDE'S HYMN TO THE NAIADS. The Clyde was an industrial and mercantile river; Turner introduces the Nymphs in order to make the picture a paean to Britain's sea-power, her trade, and at the same time to pay a tribute to the cleansing and fertilizing waters. Akenside's argument brings out well his way of interconnecting things; above all, human and natural process. And this it was that impressed and influenced Turner.

Akenside's doctrine of the twofold realm of imagination,

nature and art, also helped Turner to his own position in this matter. The idea of the connexion of art and nature here has nothing of the Picturesque thesis. Nature and art come together in the dialectical unity of human and natural process. Turner thus expressed his position in his notes on Opie:

He that has that ruling enthusiasm which accompanies abilities cannot look superficially every glance is a glance for study: contemplating and defining qualities and causes: effects and incidents, and developes by practice the possibility of attaining what appears mysterious upon principle every look at nature is a refinement upon art, each tree and blade of grass or flower is not to him the individual tree grass or flower but what [it] is in relation to the whole its tone its contrast and its use and how far practicable admiring nature by the power and practicability of his art and judging of his art by the perceptions drawn from Nature.[27]

Finally there is the important use of passages in the lectures to define the power of art to reclaim the evanescent forms o life "from the waste of dark oblivion; thus collecting all the various forms of being"; its power to grasp in the changing and crumbling shapes "the pure forms of Triangle or Circle, Cube or Cone", the underlying and enduring structures.[28] The "pure forms", however, Turner saw as dialectically entangled with the "crumbling shapes", not as abstractly transcendent.

Chapter Twelve

Gathering Strength

RATE-BOOKS show that Turner's Hammersmith house was empty in 1812. By the next year he had completed Sandycombe Lodge at Twickenham, probably staying in the intervening period at Sion House Ferry, Islington.[1] He had taken much care over the new building. At first he called it Solus Lodge, then Sandycombe Lodge; the hillocks, sandy combes, and tree clumps at the back must have reminded him of Devon. One old oak tree is still called Turner's Oak.[2] With its considerable regularity of plan and outline the house suggested the country cottages favoured by the pattern-books; Gandy in 1806 described a symmetrical cottage with an Italianate touch as Picturesque; and A. Watts later spoke of the Lodge as based "on the model of some nobleman's fishing lodge".[3] However, the main idea, the small wings and the chamfered corners, suggest Dr. Monro's Fetcham cottage, which Turner had known years before.[4] The decorative motive of Doric triglyphs remind one of Turner's interest in architectural structure and ornament that had strongly increased during his preparations for the lectures. Perhaps we can see Soane's influence in the inner porch and hall, but in a lighter, brighter form.[5] And Turner did not forget Pope's villa in dealing with the outside, using the tunnel-motive of the grotto at the rear.

We have noted how his mind was playing with the idea of the Grotto as the Love Cave of Dido; and the Isleworth sketchbook has a study for the painting of the Queen and

Aeneas, which, shown in 1814, depicts the sunrise and the woodland ride that led to the Cave.[6] The composition with its central round of water belonged to the series of AENEAS AND THE SIBYL and THE BAY OF BAIAE, as well as later works like LAKE NEMI (painted about 1828). In Turner's mind the radiant sunrise of hope was contrasted with the fall or betrayal that it preluded. As we saw, Dido in the Cave was an emblem of the earth-mother; and in the series, Aeneas and Apollo, Dido and Sibyl, were interchangeable. Ruskin reminds us of the legend connected with the BAY OF BAIAE, "The Cumaean Sibyl, Deiphobe, being in her youth beloved by Apollo, and the god having promised to grant her whatever she would ask, she, taking up a handful of earth, asked that she might live for as many years as there were grains of dust in her hand. She obtained her petition, and Apollo would have given her also perpetual youth, in return for her love; but she denied him, and wasted into the long ages; known at last only by her voice. We are rightly led to think of her here, as the type of the ruined beauty of Italy."[7] No doubt, but the picture meant far more than that to Turner. The paradisiac scene, in which rabbit and snake are to be seen as well as god and Sibyl, stands for the cheat of hope, the betrayal, which ends the harmonies. Baiae then, instead of being an Eden, becomes the haunt of corrupting pleasures which bring Hannibal down.

By the end of the year 1812 Turner was again feeling near collapse. Farington, who had recently been told by Beaumont of his determination to continue the crusade against Turner, records on 4 November that the latter "complained much of a nervous disorder, with much weakness of the stomach. Everything, he said, disagreed with him – turned acid. He particularly mentioned an aching pain at the back of the neck. – He said he was going to Mr. Fawkes' in Yorkshire for a month, and I told him air, moderate exercise, and changing the situation would do most for him." By 16 December he was back in London, and on the 28th a letter of his was read at a Council meeting, in which he asked to be excused from giving his lectures till 1814 "on account of Indisposition".[8]

Trimmer records his impression of Sandycombe Lodge:

It was an unpretending little place, and the rooms were small. There were several models of ships in glass cases, to which Turner

J. M. W. Turner, after a drawing by George Dance dated
31 March 1800

Selborne: the Wakes, engraving, after W. Howell

Frosty Morning, exhibited 1813

Nude study. Watercolour, c.1811

Turner varnishing a picture at the Royal Academy, after the painting by T. Fearnley

Lovers in moonlight (East Cowes Castle), 1821. Crayon and

Old man and children. Pen and ink

Sketchbook study for *Crossing the Brook*. Ink and wash

had painted a sea and background. They much resembled the large vessels in his sea pieces. Richmond scenery, greatly influences his style. The Scotch firs (or stone-pine) around are in most of his classical subjects, and Richmond landscape is decidedly the basis of "The Rise of Carthage". Here he had a long strip of land, planted by him so thickly with willows, that his father, who delighted in the garden, complained that it was a mere osier-bed. Turner used to refresh his eye with the run of the boughs from his sitting-room window.

From the upper rooms there was a wide view of the river and of Richmond Hill. He grew water-plants to introduce in his foregrounds. At the end of the garden was a square pond, covered with water-lilies, which Trimmer thought he himself dug and into which he put the fish he caught. "I have been out fishing with him on the Old Brent, with a can to catch trout for this preserve; but the fish always disappeared; at last he discovered that a jack was in the pond; and Turner would have it that it had been put in to annoy him." He loved the blackbirds and chased away bird-nesting boys, who in retort called him Old Blackbird.[9]

I have dined with him at Sandycombe Lodge, when my father happened to drop in too, in the middle of the day. Everything was of the most modest pretentions, two-pronged forks, and knives with large round ends for taking up the food; not what I ever saw him so use them, though it is said to have been Dean Swift's mode of feeding himself. The tablecloth barely covered the table, the earthenware was in strict keeping. I remember him saying one day, "Old dad," as he called his father, "have you not any wine?" whereupon Turner, senior, produced a bottle of currant, at which Turner, smelling, said: "Why, what have you been about?" The senior, it seemed, had rather overdone it with hollands, and it was set aside. At this time Turner was a very abstemious person.[10]

William was much respected in the neighbourhood, was a regular attendant at the parish church, and worked hard in the garden. Trimmer says that Turner gave up the Lodge because of his father's continual colds through this work, though the old man wanted to stay on. He looked after the gallery in Queen Anne Street and was very upset at the expense of going up daily, until, a week later, a friend saw him "gay, happy, and jumping up on his old toes". He explained, "Why, lookee here, I have found a way at last of coming up cheap from Twickenham to open my son's gallery –

I found out the inn where the market-gardeners baited their horses, I made friends with one on 'em, and now, for a glass of gin a day, he brings me up in his cart on the top of the vegetables."[11] He also went up now and then to dress the wigs of old clients of his Maiden Lane days.

The elder Trimmer undertook to teach Turner both Latin and Greek in return for painting lessons; but found the task too difficult.[12] Once they all went, with Henry Howard, on a trip to Penn, Bucks., in a post-chaise. They halted in a copse full of wild flowers. "I can see now vividly before me my father and Howard, both standing legs a-straddle, and Turner at a little distance in a ditch", all painting hard. After a while Turner emerged with a water-colour, saying that he'd got in the ditch to avoid the sun. Howard whispered that it was to avoid having his methods overlooked.[13]

Besides his boat, Turner had a gig and an old horse, a crop-eared bay, "or rather the cross between a horse and a pony". He drove out to sketch, with his materials under the seat. Trimmer recalled an expedition to Staines and Runnymede, where he made sketches (later the basis of a painting). "We went, I remember, a very steady pace, as Turner painted much faster than he drove. He said, if when out sketching you felt at a loss, you had only to turn round or walk a few paces further, and you had what you wanted for you." His old crop-ear was used as the model for both horses in FROSTY MORNING, a picture which was one of his own favourities. "He said he was travelling in Yorkshire, and sketched it en route. There is a stage-coach in the distance that he was on at the time."[14]

In 1813 Beaumont's campaign was intensified. In March and April Farington noted down Callcott's complaints; as a disciple of Turner he, too, had suffered; for three years he had sold nothing at the Exhibition and had gained no commissions through it. "He said Turner had also suffered from the same cause, and had not sold a picture for some time past. Turner called upon Callcott at Kensington a while since and then said he did not mean to exhibit from the same cause that prevented Callcott, but he has since altered his mind and determined not to give way before Sir George's remarks."[15]

However, Turner wrote to the Hanging Committee that he

would send in only one picture and demanded the right to place it himself. Such a demand was not likely to be accepted, but it had its effect. He sent in two pictures, which seem to have been well hung.

The pictures were THE DELUGE, which had been in his mind since 1802, and FROSTY MORNING, a masterpiece of careful construction and atmosphere, with an effect of casual directness. Time and bad cleaning have eliminated the sparkle of frost, but unimpaired is the way in which the work indicates a moment of advancing time, of growing sun and lessening frost. This ability to express the movement of time is one of Turner's great qualities.[16] The girl in the picture, we noted, was recognised by Trimmer as Evelina.

At the Royal Academy Dinner, Constable sat next to Turner, opposite West and Lawrence. "I was a good deal entertained with Turner. I always expected to find him what I did. He has a wonderful range of mind."[17]

The summer Turner spent in Devon, sketching.[18] Cyrus Redding, then editing a local newspaper, has left us a detailed account of some three weeks of the tour. One of their trips was an island in Bigbury Bay, with an army officer in a new gaudy uniform and the artist Demaria. A heavy swell was running into the Sound, and the sea had a dirty look. Demaria was mutely sea-sick, and the drenched officer collapsed on to the rusty iron ballast, where he was held down with a spar. Turner, however, sat in the stern-sheets, delightedly watching the scene; as the boat rode on a wave's crest, he murmured, "That's fine! – fine!" They managed to land on the island by getting round to leeward. Turner climbed to the highest point and set to work, appearing to write rather than draw with the pencil. Later, they walked across the sands at low water to Knighsbridge and slept there. They visited the house where Dr. Wolcot (Peter Pindar) had been born, and walked most of the twenty miles home. "Turner was a good pedestrian, capable of roughing it in any mode the occasion might demand."

They also visited the mansion at Saltram. "Zuccarelli's best paintings adorn this hospitable mansion, but I could not extract from Turner any opinion regarding them." He also could not be induced to say more than "Fine" at Stubbs' *Phaeton* in the billiard-room. He seemed to pay no attention to the Old Masters, "though they might have drawn more than I imagined, for it was not easy to judge from his manner what was passing in his mind." On the way to bed Redding remarked on the works by Angelica Kauffmann on his bedroom walls; Turner merely said, "Good night in your seraglio". However, when they had to put up for the night at an inn without beds and talked till midnight, "I found the artist could, when he pleased, make sound, pithy, though sometimes caustic remarks upon men and things with a fluency rarely heard from him. We talked much of the Academy, and he admitted that it was not all it might be with regard to art". Finally, Turner leaned his elbow on the table and put his feet on a second chair, while Redding stretched out across three or four chairs; and they slept.

Once there was an argument with Demaria about painting as they looked at a seventy-four lying under Saltash. "You were right, Mr. Turner," said Demaria, "the ports cannot be seen. The ship is one dark mass." But he still demurred, "The ports are still there." Turner replied, "We can take only what we can see, no matter what is there. There are people in the ship – we don't see them through the planks."

Redding described him as at this time rather stout and bluff-looking, rough, reserved, and austere in manner – somewhat like the master of a merchantman. However, they had a picnic with some ladies on Mount Edgecumbe, where Turner supplied the food and wine, "Never was there more social pleasure partaken by any party in that English Eden. Turner was exceedingly agreeable for one whose language was more epigrammatic and terse than complimentary upon most occasions."[19]

At Plymouth he met Eastlake, who had been a student at the Royal Academy, and they stayed for a couple of days with the landscape-painter Ambrose Johns at a cottage near Calstock. Eastlake says that Turner sketched "by stealth", but could not resist using a handy painting box that Johns had fitted out, and so became used to working in Johns's presence. He was proud, says Eastlake, of the speed with which he worked.[20]

He was back in London by November, and at Farnley in mid-month. There he did two paintings, of grouse- and woodcock-shooting. Shortly before his death, in January

1851, he wrote, "A Cuckoo was my first achievement in killing on Farnley Moor in earnest request of Major Fawkes to be painted for the Book" (of Ornithology).[21] What he really felt when out shooting may be read in the poems he wrote at Farnley. In them he expresses the utmost revulsion from blood-sports, in terms that would have astonished and mortified Fawkes. "Oh, why unfortunate victim to my zeal . . ."

> Not the coarse ling or splashy spring
> Prevent. No, tis alike to him
> Wades falls or swims alike pursues
> And wet with blood his hand embrue[s]
> Again the thundrous gun then plies
> Again another helpless lies.[22]

But he had reached the stage where he did not feel capable of, or interested in, stating to others what he felt about anything – apart from his expression in art. The world would have to puzzle it all out from his pictures and his verses, or learn nothing of his thoughts and feelings. At most he was driven, under the pressure of attack or excessive stupidity, to make some caustic or aphoristic comment.

While at Farnley, he corrected the proof of an engraving for SOUTHERN COAST, which Cooke was rushing out to beat a rival publication. Turner had composed an essay to go with the engravings, but the editor, W. Combe, thought it the "most extraordinary" thing he had ever read, and told Cooke it was scarcely admissible "in its present state". Cooke seems to have told him to write his own account of the plates, using as much of Turner's essay as possible; but Turner, hurt, at once asked for his manuscript to be sent back without anything of it being used.[23]

In 1814 he failed to give his first lecture through leaving his materials in a hackney-coach. Obviously his heart was not in the matter. He advertised. The portfolio with drawings was found, and the lecture was given on 10 January.[24] The sixth or last lecture was given on 7 February. That day the ninth show of the British Institution was opened, in which was included APULLIA IN SEARCH OF APULLUS. VIDE OVID. (The names are a confusion taken over from the translator Garth, who read *Apullus pastor*, Apulian shepherd, as a proper name.) Turner, like West, had entered his work for the premium or prize, but failed. The *Examiner* mentioned both West and

Turner, but singled Turner out for attack, arguing that such competitions were not for eminent artists, that Turner was ineligible as having sent in his picture a week after everyone else, and that his work was not original, being a mere copy of the Petworth Claude.[25] Beaumont, as Turner must have known, was one of the judges; and Turner seems to have wanted to show how hopelessly prejudiced he was. For APULLIA was made as close as possible to the kind of art he admired; Hazlitt, defender of the Old Masters against innovation, thought Turner was leaving his aberrations, his "waste of morbid strength" and working correctly "in the trammels of Claude and N. Poussin". Of course, his work failed to win the premium; but it had had the effect he seems to have wanted. The competitions were stopped.[26]

In January had come out the first parts of Cooke's *Picturesque Views of the Southern Coast of England*, with four plates by Turner. An important extension of his work, involving a new and wider public, had begun. The elimination of colour, while removing much of the creative richness and originality, brought the forms and the tonal range closer to what people expected and wanted.[27]

At the Academy he showed DIDO AND AENEAS.[28] For his own gallery he does not seem to have done much, though he opened it till 20 June. Then on Thursday, three days later, he was at Portsmouth sketching the Review of the Fleet held to please the Russian Emperor and the Prussian King. At the end of the sketchbook he scribbled a few lines about floating bulwark and holy cross unfurled, something that shows the saviour of the world. "Hence gloomy evil infamy's . . ." He does not seem to have been happy at the spectacle.

Meanwhile the British Institution had been holding an exhibition of Hogarth, Wilson, Gainsborough, and Zoffany. Hazlitt attacked the purposes of the show. "Patronage and works of art deserving patronage rarely exist together, for it is only when the arts have attracted public esteem, and reflect credit on the patron, that they receive this flattering support, and then it generally proves fatal to them." For once Turner would have agreed with him. Callcott was making similar comments to Farington. "They are not patrons of Artists, but breeders of Artists" – of the kind they wanted. Some of his comments show that Turner shared this attitude.[29]

He seems to have gone to Farnley in November, spending about a month there. The war had ended with the fall of Napoleon, and London was full of foreign visitors.

In 1815 he duly lectured, and in the Royal Academy exhibition showed THE BUILDING OF CARTHAGE and CROSSING THE BROOK, THE BATTLE OF FORT ROCK and BLIGH SAND, with a water-colour of a volcanic eruption.[30] Beaumont was stirred to yet greater virulence.[31] He thought the paintings "*weak* and like the work of an Old Man, one who no longer saw or felt colour properly; it was all of *pea-green* insipidity". But retribution was coming. Roused by the British Institution's show of Flemish and Dutch Old Masters, some opponent (or a pair of them) wrote and published *A Catalogue Raisonné of the Pictures now Exhibiting at the British Institution*, a work of hard-hitting satire and serious comment, which was sent round by post. The attack on the conceit and insolence of men like Beaumont, Payne Knight (who had called the Parthenon frieze "second-rate sculpture"), and their group, was in the key of Turner's broodings against connoisseurs and critics, but expressed with a savage sarcasm that he could not command in a lengthy statement. The pamphlet was attributed to Reinagle and Smirke, to Henry Thomson and Callcott; the latter two may have had a hand in it. And Fawkes may have helped the publication.

On 29 June we find Turner putting off an invitation from the artist James Holworthy, as he had to go to Twickenham for his father's seventieth birthday. A letter to Trimmer of 1 August was twisted by Thornbury into a desperately bashful declaration of love for some lady, but, in fact, it reveals only a hope that she'll come to the point and buy the Lodge. His desire to get rid of the house on which he had lavished so much care may reflect his lessening income under Beaumont's onslaught, though he still had substantial sums in the Funds. He may have merely been feeling restless; he mentions that he had been able to stay in the Lodge little that year and hoped to be on the Continent in 1816.[32] Or he may have had some important change in his domestic system forced on him. The girls were now growing up. We may accept Trimmer's recognition of the girl in CROSSING THE BROOK as Evelina. Turner had completed his idea of that picture when he merged the delicate great vista and its Claudean flanking trees with the episode of the girl wading through the water. He probably got the idea of the girls from H. Thomson's *Crossing the Brook*, 1803, which shows a girl leading a smaller child across stepping-stones. There is no aesthetic relation between the two pictures; but possibly Turner took from Thomson the idea of girls crossing water, which he then developed in his own way. Knowing the way in which his fancy worked, we may take Evelina's brook-crossing to symbolize her arrival at womanhood. Another girl (Georgianna) remains on the bank; Evelina steps into the flowing waters and crosses into the new life of maturity. Above her, and ahead, looms the cleft which plays so crucial a part in many of Turner's pictures; here it provides the stepping-point between foreground and distance – the vaginal passage from the familiar present into the adventurous light-lost distance of the unknown. (We have seen how strong an emblem for him was the stream or river as human life in its remorseless flow and changes.)[33]

He went to Farnley in August, and meant to make a tour of the Lakes. But instead he went to York, Ripon, and other Yorkshire sites. Early in November, in London, he was arranging for BLIGH SAND and JASON ("an old favourite with some") to be exhibited at Plymouth. In December he was elected as one of the Visitors in the new School of Painting, with Callcott, Phillips, Thomson.[34]

In 1816 his two Royal Academy pictures were those depicting the Temple of Jupiter Panellenius. We cannot be sure whether he held a show in his own gallery: if he did, it was the last. Beaumont's campaign would seem to have been successful, and Turner was giving more time to work for the engravers.[35] He set off northward, calling at Farnley (early this year Fawkes had remarried.) The Fawkeses went on with him on 17 July through heavy rain, returning home on the 25th, when Turner departed alone, striking over the hills into Upper Wharfedale and on to Richmond.[36] He persisted despite the bad weather, going to Barnard Castle, then along the Tees, crossing the Fells to Appleby. From Richmond he wrote to Holworthy about an arrangement made for a meeting at Langold. "Weather miserably wet. I shall be webfooted like a Drake – excepting the curled feather – but I must proceed." The heaths and the peatbogs were soaked, and he is said to have almost lost his life. Back at Farnley, he wrote again to Holworthy: "a most confounded fagg, tho' on Horseback – still the passage out of Teesdale leaves everything far behind for difficulty – bogged most completely Horse and its Rider, and nine hours making 11 miles."[37] He had returned via Lancaster, arriving before the middle of August. On the 12th, shooting on the moors began. Next day Fawkes's youngest brother was hurt in a shooting accident, and on the 16th he died. The party broke up, only Turner and two others staying on. He was almost one of the family and he wanted to make some more sketches. Perhaps at this time he wrote in one of his attacks on blood-sports: "Away, then all sport of the fields Its pleasure and its pain I joyfull yield . . . The gun too oft its owner wound[s] No[r] brings the winged quarry to the ground."[38]

The bad weather showed in hasty sketches he made, though the water-colours made later from some of them owned a serene sunlight.[39]

While Turner was away a second *Catalogue Raisonné*, stimulated by the British Institution's show of Italian and Spanish pictures, had appeared. It mocked at the four directors appointed by the Government as a Committee of Taste in the competition for the Waterloo Monuments, and denounced West as a traitor to the Royal Academy, bought by the £3,000 for his *Christ Healing the Sick*. The Earl of Egremont was said to have financed the pamphlet. Haydon, who hoped for patronage from the Institution, drew in Hazlitt, who in three papers trounced the Academy as a "body of low traders". He called Turner's pictures daubs and said that the public saw "the quackery of painting trees blue and yellow to produce the effect of green at a distance".[40]

Turner applied in December for permission to omit his lectures in 1817. Refused, he applied again, mentioning the pressure of "present engagements", and this time had his way. Much of 1817 was, in fact, taken up with work for the engravers. To the Academy he sent only THE DECLINE OF THE CARTHAGINIAN EMPIRE. The verses spoke of Hope's delusive smile, which was linked with the portentous setting of the "ensanguined sun" in a stormy haze.[41] The various drafts of the poem suggest that he had in mind the situation after the defeat of Napoleon and the falsities of the imposed peace. Rome, taking over the treacheries of Punic faith, "Held forth

the peaceful olive but round the stem insidious twined the
asp" – "Revengeful twined the asp" – "Urged her fresh
demands to break the league to give but colour to her pur-
posed hate".

Turner did not manage to visit Italy, but used a few weeks'
leisure to see Waterloo and explore the Rhine from Cologne
to Mainz. He sailed back from Rotterdam about the middle
of September. A note in his sketchbook records a mishap:

Lost in the Walett. A Book with Leaves ditto. Cambell's Belgium
3 Shirts. 1 Night ditto. A Razor A Ferrel for Umbrella A pair of
Stockings A waiscoat ½ Doz. of Pencils 6 Cravats. 1 Large ditto
1 Box of Colors.[42]

Later he made some fifty water-colours on white paper prepared with a light grey wash, which Fawkes bought. But now
he went on commissions to Durham, From Raby he wrote to
Holworthy that Lord Strathmore called and took him away
to the north. Two sketchbooks show his itinerary.[43] In mid-
November he reached Farnley. A letter to Holworthy reveals
his mood: he had been moving rapidly – "my fugitive disposition from place to place" – and had once again found arrangements about Langold in confusion:

"No Leaves" No day No weather to enjoy see or admire. Dame
Natures lap is covered, in fact it would be forestalling Langold,
to look at the brown mantle of deep strewed paths, and roads
of mud to splash in and be splashed – as you have got me in the
mud so you I hope will help me out again and place me in as good a
position as possible.[44]

He adds as a result of his protracted wanderings, "that the
day of the Season is far spent the night of winter near at hand
and that Barry's words are always ringing in my ears – Get
home and light your lamp". Holworthy was getting married
and Turner was helping him in some building operations. He
ends, "Every one seems happy why do you delay, for the
world is said to be getting worthiless, and needs the regenera-
ting power of the Allworthy part of the community."

In 1818 he gave his lectures twice weekly so as to get them
quickly over. In the Royal Academy he had four pictures: the
rich high-pitched DORT, the graceful TIVOLI, RABY CASTLE (with
hunters and hounds), and THE FIELD OF WATERLOO. The latter
was not liked; indeed, it was a sort of parody of the Waterloo

Competition, for it deliberately omitted all aspects of grandeur and national pride, and showed only the suffering in the after-night. Here, though no doubt he did not know it, he was following a French trend, strong in Gros and Géricault.[45]

On 4 June he went to see the boat-race at Eton with the Fawkeses, who had two sons at the school. Mrs. Fawkes records, "Little Turner came with us." But generally he was hard at work for the engravers, and in late October went to Scotland to get material for a work to which Scott was to write the text.[46] He dashed through his work of sketching in and round Edinburgh. The sister of an artist with whom he breakfasted wrote: "We intended to have had a joyous evening on his arrival, but finding him such a *stick*, we did not think the pleasure of showing him to our friends would be adequate to the trouble and expense." The portraitist Nicholson complained that "after preparing a feast and having ten fine fellows to make merry with him, Turner never made an appearance". Turner was not the man to break a definite appointment; we must assume there was some confusion, and he was probably feeling very hurried and out of sorts. However, he managed to reach Farnley in November, and it was now that he painted A FIRST-RATE TAKING IN STORES (which we discussed in our first chapter). Back in London by December, he was elected once more to the Royal Academy Council, with his friend the amiable Chantrey.

This year he had bought land at Twickenham. As he later allocated it for an almshouse to shelter decayed artists, he may already have had in mind the scheme which he set out in his will. He was busy with kindred matters, acting as Chairman of the Board of Directors as well as Treasurer of the Artists' Benevolent Society, and taking an active part in the business of joining this body with a recent rival, the Artists' Annuity Fund.[47]

Late in 1817 Evelina had married Joseph Dupuis, who was employed in the consular service and who may have been related in some way to the organist T. S. Dupuis. In his letter of 15 December 1853 he remarked, "I have been married now upwards of thirty-six years."[48] As he seems to have been a precise man, his arithmetic sets his marriage in 1817, when he was on the verge of going abroad. The date is verified by his *Journal of a Residence in Ashantee* (1824), which is worth a few words since it provides us with the only glimpse we have of the life of Turner's children. Further, it helps us to understand why Turner seems to have disliked his son-in-law and to have refused to help him in any way. Dupuis outlived Turner, who, however, ignored him so thoroughly that he could not recall his name correctly, spelling it Dupree in his will.

In 1817 the Governor of Cape Coast Castle had sent an embassy to Comassy, capital of Ashantee (I use Dupuis's spellings), and a convention was concluded. Dupuis tendered his services in a memorial to the Lords Commissioners of the Treasury, and in January 1818 he was appointed Consul for Ashantee. However, he was delayed nine months in England and did not sail till November. "We left the Downs with the wind at north-east, which increasing to a gale, conveyed us to Madeira in six days. After a detention at Funchel short of a week, we finally weighed anchor for Cape Coast Castle." He landed in January 1819 and found himself in the midst of local intrigues, which he did not understand for some time. He also contracted fever and had some bad bouts. That Evelina was with him and that she had borne him a child is shown by the following passage, dealing with his return from a cruise in the open sea which he had taken to better his health:

During my absence on the cruise, a Mr. Wm. Hutton, a writer in the service of the company, landed at Cape Coast. I had once before accidentally seen him at Gravesend, when, it seems, he contemplated returning to Africa, this I knew at the time I sailed myself, and this was the limit of my knowledge of the gentleman. When I returned from the cruize, he shewed me the respect of a common place visit of congratulation or condolence, (for I had unhappily lost an infant member of my family during my absence) . . .[49]

Dupuis had thus taken good care of his own health, but had left his wife and child to suffer during the period of the rains. The slightly fussy and meticulous style of the passage cited also serves to illustrate his character. From his book he appears as a conscientious official, who took much care to keep detailed records; he shows a genuine interest in the Africans, and the illustrations, engraved after his own sketches, prove at least that he was interested in art. But his struggles in Cape Coast and Ashantee appear to have exhausted him, and he made no further mark in his career. He and Evelina arrived back in England in late August 1820; and Turner seems to have kept him henceforth at arms' length, afraid that he might press his wife's claims and become a hanger-on liable to waste his father-in-law's fortune.

He himself probably never felt secure in his position. Some verses written during these years show how he still held, as no doubt he always held, the ideal of a modest stubborn independence, in which he was able to go his own way and bow to no master.

> Sweet independence rough in this nature pure sincere
> Tho[u] gives the humble roof content devoid of fear
> Even of tomorrows fate and adds a blissful joy
> To its perhaps lone inmate ever without alloy.

"To thee the social being carrolls as he goes", secure in his family circle and in "acts which telling make the bosom glow". Such a man "scorns the power of wealth" and "owns no constraining power". He is saved by "a personal estate far beyond purchase or the grasp of state".[50]

In 1819 Turner again gave his lectures. A scheme for thirty-six drawings of the Rhine fell through, anticipated by another publication. But two London shows were held in his honour by collectors, Sir John Leicester and Fawkes, and did much to help his reputation. Lawrence was writing from Rome, urging that Turner was the one artist capable of truly rendering Italian scenery, and that he should come out. Turner was only too keen to go, and in August he set forth.[51] At the Royal Academy he had shown ENTRANCE OF THE MEUSE and RICHMOND HILL.

We can now pause and glance over his work between HANNIBAL and the departure for Rome. There is no dramatic advance, as with works like CALAIS PIER, SHIPWRECK, WRECK OF A TRANSPORT, HANNIBAL; no attempts to depict catastrophe except with the unimportant ERUPTION OF THE SOUFFRIER MOUNTAINS and THE DELUGE. THE BATTLE OF FORT ROCK was a comparatively prosaic appendage to HANNIBAL, and THE FIELD OF WATERLOO a night-piece aimed against heroics. The period saw, however, a considerable consolidation of his forces. He made his last direct reaffirmation of the Claudean landscape. APULLIA was overtly based on *Jacob with Laban and his daughters* at Petworth; the connected works, DIDO BUILDING CARTHAGE; OR THE RISE OF THE CARTHAGINIAN EMPIRE and

THE DECLINE OF THE CATHAGINIAN EMPIRE, again looked to
Claude, though with more Turnerian transformations – as
also the two pictures of the Temple of Jupiter Panellenius
(mixed somewhat here with elements from Poussin).[52] In
these works we can detect a pattern on which he variously
drew for a series of landscapes that reach well into the 1830s.
At the same time he extended the Claudean system to English
landscape, most successfully with CROSSING THE BROOK, where
browns are kept for the foreground and the rest is a delicate
gradation of blues and greens. RICHMOND HILL, the largest
canvas he ever painted, might be called a Wilsonian subject
on a grand scale – or a more naturalistic version of the Claudean paradise such as we see in MACON. Incidentally, he is here
finding a way of dealing with figures without distracting detail.
which leads on to the Petworth water-colours of about 1830.
In FROSTY MORNING he finally achieved a casual effect of directness on the basis of carefully organized form and atmospheric
definition; in DORT he used the stimulations of his visit to the
Netherlands and his revived memories of Cuyp to achieve
another kind of direct vision, without any Claudean distil-
lations, but with stress on light diffusion.[53]

With CROSSING THE BROOK, FROSTY MORNING, and DORT
we can say that Turner reaches the climax of the first half of
his career. They represent a lyrical realism which is all his
own. The vortex is absent in them, but in due time it will
reassert itself, as his lyricism grows stronger and more confi-
dent, and the drama of "contending elements" returns.

A desire to break through into greater freedom and fluidity
can, however, be read in the seventy-nine cloud studies made
in a single sketchbook, which can probably be dated around
1818. Here he does not have to concern himself with detailed
forms, and is able to concentrate on an endless variety of
moving shapes and their tonal modulations. He uses a simple
range of colours and gains textural contrasts by setting against
the blue sky-washes the wetly mixed grey-blues and pinks of
the clouds. At most he enriches the scheme with oranges, to
bring out such forms as the moon. His interest in the structure
of movement, of complex but unified light sweep, distinguishes
his work here from Constable's studies with their concentration on weather.[54]

Chapter Thirteen

Italian Light

HE took the usual *malle-poste* road, which he had taken in 1802, to Switzerland. Then he went on from Chambéry, over Mont Cenis, to Turin and Como, and on to Venice, where he stayed about a fortnight. Then he went down to Rome, possibly arriving before Chantrey, who was there on 13 October.[1] Tom Moore gives us a glimpse of Turner on the Capitol in a strong wind: a gallant captain snatched his umbrella to shelter the Princess of Denmark, and it was blown inside out, with some ribs snapping. Hearing that Vesuvius was active, he hastened to Naples by way of the Pontine Marshes, and visited Pompeii, Herculaneum, Paestum. Soane's son wrote:

Turner is in the neighbourhood of Naples making rough pencil sketches to the astonishment of the Fashionables, who wonder what use these rough draughts can be – simple souls! At Rome a sucking blade of the brush made the request of going out with pig Turner to colour – he grunted for answer that it would take too much time to colour in the open air – he could make 15 or 16 pencil sketches to one coloured, and then grunted his way home.

Between his arrival at Rome and his departure he made some 1,500 pencil sketches, many of them works of art. Christmas he seems to have spent in Florence. At Turin he found the snows had held up coach services to Switzerland. Despite grave warnings, he and some other urgent travellers secured a coach and set out. On 15 January 1820, at the top of the Cenis pass, the coach turned over and the passengers had to climb out of the window. In 1826 Turner wrote about the episode to Holworthy. "Mount Cenis has been closed up some time tho the papers say some hot headed Englishman did

venture to cross a pied a month ago, and, which they considered *there* next to madeness to attempt which honor was conferred once on me and my companions de voiture, we were
capsized on the top." He adds, "The Guide and Cantonier
began to fight & the Driver was by a process verbal put into
prison [tear] so doing while we had to march or rather flounder
up to our knees nothing less in Snow all the way down to
Lancesleyburgh [Lanslebourg] by the King of Roadmakers
Road not the Colossus of Roads, Mr Mac Adam but Bona-
parte fill'd up by Snow and only known by the precipitous
zig zag."[2]

In 1820 at the Academy he showed a large-scale and over-
ambitious attempt to express what Italy had meant to him,
ROME FROM THE VATICAN. He here combined the Roman
and the Renaissance scene, with a view of the distant hills
thrown in: Antiquity, Raphael, and Claude.[3] Fawkes again
opened his house in Grosvenor Square as an exhibition.
Turner often dined there, as well as accompanying the
Fawkeses to Eton and Greenwich. He attended Council
meetings, but made no tour, occupied with enlargements of
his Queen Anne Street house. On Monday, 13 November, he
wrote to Wells:

Many thanks to you for your kind offer of refuge to the Houseless
which in the present instance is humane as to cutting you are the
cutter. Alladins palace soon fell to pieces, and a lad like me cant get
in unsheltered, and like a lamb. I am turning up my Eye to the Sky
through the chinks of the Old Room and think shall I keep you a
bit of the old wood for your rem[em]brance of the young twigs
which in such twinging strains taught you the art of wiping your
Eye of a tear purer far than the one which in revenge has just
dropt into mine for it rains and the Roof is not finish'd. Day after
day have I threatened you not with a letter but your Mutton but
some demon eclypt Mason Bricklayer Carpenter &&& . . . has kept
me in constant oscillation from Twickenham to London from
London to Twik that I have found the art of going about doing
nothing "so out of nothing, nothing can come – however joking
apart, if I can find a day or two I'll have a peep at the North Side
of Mitcham Common, but when it is impossible to say, whenever
I have been absent either something has been done wrong or my
wayward feelings have made me think so or that had I present it
would not have occurred that I am fidgetty whener away, when this
feeling has worn *itself* away at least I shall become a better guest.[4]

A letter to Cooke mentions that he had had an accident, and
on account of it and the rebuilding he was coming up to
London only once a week. This year he inherited his share
of the small Marshall property, four freehold cottages in
New Gravel Lane, Wapping, in a section then called the New
Crane. He converted the cottages into a tavern, *The Ship and
Bladebone*.[5]

In 1821 he gave his lectures, but was still much taken up
with building operations.[6] This year he had no commissions
and did not exhibit at the Academy. Fawkes was in London on
22 March, but did not show his pictures. Turner spent Christmas at Farnley.[7]

In 1822 he omitted his lectures. In February, Cooke held
a show in Soho Square of his drawings. He included works
by the Old Masters, Reynolds, Gainsborough, Girtin,
Cozens, but these were mainly used as a setting for Turner's
water-colours.[8] The Fawkeses again came to London. Turner
was a guest at the marriage of the youngest daughter. "A very
long day," wrote Mrs Fawkes. "Had a large party to dinner.
All tipsey". Turner was now at last able to open his new
gallery; but the critics were more interested in John Martin
showing at Egyptian Hall, or J. Glover, called the English
Claude, at 16 Old Bond Street – while West had a large display
in Newman Street. Turner stood unsuccessfully for the office
of Royal Academy auditor; he had a project of big engravings
on the scale and standard of those made after Wilson by
Woollett;[9] but meanwhile he went to Scotland by sea. George
IV was on the way there; and Wilkie, who had decided to
paint some of the events, was surprised to find Turner on
the quay at Leith for the King's landing. Turner's main aim
was to draw scenes for Cooke, but he made two unfinished
paintings of the royal ceremonies. Returning by sea, he was
sketching on the Medway in September or October.

In 1823 he gave no lectures. On 1 January, Cooke opened
a second exhibition. R. Hunt said that Turner was using
"very little besides yellow, grey and blue", but agreed that
principle and practice both "feed and satisfy" the imagination,
The Literary Gazette, on 18 January, however, took up the
line that henceforth Turner's adversaries stressed: his works
were "the vagaries of a powerful genius showing little or no
connection with nature". The idea itself was not new. *The*

True Briton (3 May 1802) had said, rather in praise, of FISHER-
MEN UPON A LEE-SHORE: "always attempting something extre-
mely bold & sublime, & therefore generally leaves poor Nature
behind him." Hazlitt in 1814 had said of DIDO AND AENEAS,
"It is not natural nor classical".[10] But now the accusation of
brilliance with no basis in nature became the usual thing.
At the Royal Academy this year Turner showed the BAY OF
BAIAE, carrying on the use of a light key and rich colour.[11]
(The idea that Turner's later work was somehow false
persisted right into our own day. Finberg in 1910 wrote,
"The *Frosty Morning* of 1813 is really the last work in which
the inspiration rings true throughout, in which form and
content are absolutely indissoluble.")

At the start of May came the dinner of the Artists' General
Benevolent Institution. Lord Liverpool was in the chair;
but when he vacated it, "Mr Turner, R.A., was unanimously
called upon to fill it. He obeyed the universal desire, and kept
up the good humour and conviviality of the meeting."[12]
This month he added two works to Cooke's show: of stormy
shipwreck and of sunrise (Margate) – his typical contrasts,
between elemental violence and an idyllic rendering of men
at work (here whiting-fishing). On the first day of August,
Cooke published the first part of *The Rivers of England*; a
publication mainly to be made up of Turner's work, with a
few illustrations after W. Collins and Girtin. Turner seems
to have spent a part of the summer at Folkestone, Hythe,
and near by, and to have sallied into the Channel as far as the
French coast.[13] The latter part of the year was taken up with
work on TRAFALGAR, the one piece of his commissioned by
the Crown, which was to serve as a companion for Louther-
bough's *First of June* – as part of a scheme to fill three big
galleries in St. James's Palace. In October, however, Hobhouse mentions him at Farnley, "making designs for a museum
intended to contain relics of our Civil Wars, and to be called
Fairfaxiana". In December he succeeded in becoming an
Auditor, with Chantrey and Soane. Two of his sketchbooks
show how seriously he took his duties.[14]

In 1824 he again lectured. By May his TRAFALGAR was hanging in the Palace. G. Jones had made Wellington conspicuous
in his paintings of Vittoria and Waterloo, but Turner disliked
spotlighted melodrama. So he displeased the Government,

the courtiers, the ambassadors, and the sailors. Jones tells us that he was "criticised and instructed daily by the naval men about the Court, and during eleven days he altered the rigging to suit the fancy of each seaman, and did it all with the greatest good-humour".[15]

On 30 April he wrote to Holworthy, who had retired to Derbyshire, about some drawings that he had meant as a sort of wedding gift. The letter shows the somewhat disturbed state of thought and emotion provoked in him by his friend's marriage – rather than his inability to come to the point about a gift, as it has been interpreted:

Dear Holworthy I shall feel uncomfortable if anything should in this note give you any pain but when I look back upon the length of time you took to acknowledge the recipt of the Drawings and withheld the pleasure I expected of at least hearing if Mrs. Holworthy (to whom in your mutual happiness I certainly presented one) approved; and your letter treats them both so like a commission that I feel my pride wounded and my Independence roused – I should be happy to receive any presents of recollection you may with Mrs. H. think of to send me and will keep alive my high considera-tion but money is out of the question in the present case. It gives me great pleasure to hear from Mr. Phillips of your comforts at Green-hill and I may perhaps, if you have as great a regard as Auld Lang sine as myself witness *all* and tho I may not ever be blest with [a] Half yet you may believe me that it gave me the greatest pleasure to hear and will continue to give to the end of this sublunary turmoil for I do not mean my comfort or miseries to be my pleasure of the like in others. When you come to town I have a great many interrogations to make, not in doubts but for want of Experience in these matters and I do not hesitate to acknowledge it in offering my respects to Mrs. Holworthy. Believe me to be dear Holworthy Yours most truly JMWTurner.[16]

Holworthy seems to have been a likeable fellow, to judge from the tone of Turner's letters to him; to nobody else did he write so unbosomingly. In the earlier letter about the marriage we found him punning on Holworthy-Allworthy. There as here the thought of Holworthy begetting children excited him; and the gift of two works of his to the bridal pair (recall the identification of his works with his children) had disturbed and led him to write, it seems, with extra obscurity, so that he now found himself hard put to explain his meaning. Later in April 1827 he wrote again to Holworthy: "What may become of me I know not, particularly if a lady keep my bed warm, and last winter was quite enough to make singles think of doubles. Poor Daddy never felt so cold."[17]

We do not know when his connexion with Sarah Danby ended; but from these letters to Holworthy we get the feeling that he was now on his own, troubled by the need of someone in Sarah's place. This feeling is reinforced by a couple of sketchbooks, which show him in the grip of a strong sexual emotion or which record actual experiences. William Michael Rossetti tells of Ruskin finding several indecent drawings, "which from the nature of their subjects it seemed undesirable to preserve"; they were "burned by him on the authority of the Trustees" of the National Gallery. Rossetti had been helping Ruskin to sift the Turner material; and neither he, Ruskin, nor the Trustees were swayed by the fact that Turner had evidently considered the sketches desirable to preserve. However, either their standards were not excessively severe or their sifting not very thorough. In a sketchbook probably dated 1824 (it has notes on Academy finance dated 1821 to Ladyday 1823) we find many rapid pencil drawings of copulation by naked lovers, in some of which the genitals are plainly shown, even enlarged. Later, in 1834, we have what seems the record of an episode in an inn (on the Rhine perhaps). A set of delightful little paintings show a serving-girl undressing, a couple tumbling in the large bed, compositions derived from their embraces, and what are almost pure effects of colour and light derived from the experience. Indeed, Turner had a fondness for painting bedrooms.

Not that he seems to have been averse at any time from imaginings or experiences such as those the sketches reveal. The most successful of his lyrics is that beginning "Be still my dear Molly" about (1809–10) with stanzas like these:

> By thy lips quivering motion I ween
> To the centre where love lies between
> A passport to bliss is thy will
> Yet I prithee dear Molly be still
>
> By thy Eyes which half closed in delight
> That so languishly turn from the light
> With kisses I'll hide then I will
> So I prithee dear Molly be still . . .
>
> By the touch of thy lips and the rove of my hand

> By the critical moment no maid can withstand
> Then a bird in the bush is worth two in the hand
> O Molly dear Molly I will.[18]

The pencil sketches show a liking for the upturned Omega of a girl's buttocks as she lies on her side. As an example of the sort of thing that was said about Turner – though we cannot take it as proving anything further – we may note that Thornbury says he left four illegitimate children, and cites an unnamed friend:

I once heard Mr. Crabb Robinson (the friend of Wordsworth) casually mention a remark dropped by the late Miss Maria Denman, when the two of them were out for an excursion with Rogers (I think), and had put up at inn in a village near London. "That," said the lady, pointing to a youth who happened to pass, "is Turner's natural son."

I have referred to the strong sexual symbolism in Turner's scenes. The V of light with its effect of turning vanes, noted in KILGARRAN CASTLE and CROSSING THE BROOK, has its meaning as a birth-tunnel, a vaginal passage of rhythmic convulsion. Kindred forms play a very large part in Turner's composition and finally appear in the pure gyratory whirls of the vortex. The sense of descent between two rising masses goes deep in his dynamic constructions; the movement into gushing light through clefts or flanking hillsides, the upswing of vast palpitating masses as in the "two ridges of enormous swell" which Ruskin noted as divided the sea of SLAVERS. The great spout of waters dashed on the mounded clouds of FIRE AT SEA is in turn linked with the rich curves of a retreating tunnel or whirlpool of sunset-light, against which is thrust a powerful length of unfolding cloud-dark. What we see here in its most violent and tumultuous form can be traced in countless variations that include ahe most delicate lyrical expressions, with an irridescent hole of light as the point to which all forms are related. Without this fascination with the movements in-and-through a scene we cannot conceive Turner's achievement at all. More, it is not a simple passage in-and-through; it continually involves a tension of contrary pulls or motions, of which the head-on collision of wind and tide is the plainest example, but which is to be found in all sorts of meetings, mergings, thwartings, involvements, resistances clashes between two forces or movements In speaking of sexual symbolism here, I am not trying to reduce all these patterns and images to a simple basis in sex. They have their deep truth in nature, outside the artist; but the intensity, the consistent drive, of his realization of these vortices and copulations owns its sexual as well as its intellectual side. Otherwise the powerful union of his own organic being with the vital processes of nature would not thus appear in his art.

A passage in the Fifth Lecture shows how well he was aware of the powerful effects to be gained by contrasts of simultaneous ascent and descent. He is discussing Titian's *St Peter Martyr* and refers to the sublimity of the "arrangement of lines which by its unshackled obliquity and waved lines obtains the associated feelings of force." Additions in pencil and ink describe this effect as "eruptive expanding," a "continuity, that rushes with the ignited spark" or flame, "struggling in the ascent from Earth towards Heaven." He then introduces the image of a Rocket: "and when no more propelled by the force, it scatters around its falling glories" (or "ignited embers") "seeking again its parents" (or "Earthly Corner") and "while diffusing around its living radiance in the descending cherub with the palm of Beatitude to the dying Martyr, sheds the mellow glow of gold th[r]o the dark embrownd foliage."

This year he had nothing in the Academy. *The British Press* says that he "returned thanks in a neat speech" at the Benevolent Institution's dinner on 25 May. Cooke again held an exhibition – in April, a little before the Academy opened – with fifteen water-colours by Turner and Gainsborough's landscapes on glass for his Show Box. Sketchbooks of summer and autumn show him at work along the coast from Colchester to Yarmouth, also at Brighton and Portsmouth.[19] On 19 November he was at Farnley, where he stayed till 14 December. This was to be his last visit; for Fawkes died in London in October 1825, and Turner could never bear to visit Farnley again.[20] (Later, in 1836, the last sketchbook he had used there he gave to Munro while drawing in the Val d'Aosta. It contains a sketch of a coach stopping outside Wakefield on a stormy evening, and various Farnley drawings and cloud studies. As Turner turned the pages over, he must have felt oppressed; he took the unprecedented step of giving a sketchbook away.)

The following year (1825) he sent in an oil, HARBOUR OF DIEPPE, and a water-colour. Critics found DIEPPE not at all like nature; *The New Monthly Magazine* called it "perhaps the most splendid piece of falsehood" by Turner or one of his followers; *The Literary Gazette*, "a brilliant experiment upon colours, which displays all the magic of skill at the expense of all the magic of nature". The terms had been found for evading and misrepresenting Turner's bold and powerful quest for new truths. The *Gazette* a month later warned artists still using Turner's early manner not to be tempted by the light of his sunshine to desert their correct and unaffected style "in order to catch the eye or serve as an exhibition-trap".[21] Artists like Etty and Collins were following the line in calling Turner's work unnatural. Etty spoke of "fiery abominations", and said, "When he abandons nature, I must abandon him."

In Turner's view colour, form, and depth (light-shade) were all indivisible. But when his work was reproduced in engravings the colour was left out and the tonal system hardened: hence the engravings remained popular. A critic praised the mezzotints as divested of the meretricious display of colour". In 1841 *The Art Union* wrote, "In the engraving [of MERCURY AND ARGUS] we cannot perceive the defects so generally attributed to the picture", and argued that "the good qualities of the work have been preserved, while the wilful follies of the great painter have been entirely abrogated". When Dr. G. F. Waagen, director of the National Gallery at Berlin, visited England in 1835, he was eager to see the originals of Turner, whose work was known throughout Europe "in beautiful steel engravings". He was very disappointed when he saw the paintings.[22]

Turner's reaction to this sort of thing was to stiffen his prices.[23] On 27 August he dined with the Fawkeses, though his old friend was in a bad way, and next morning he left for the Hague. He travelled across Holland to Cologne, then went to Antwerp, Ghent, Bruges, Ostend – returning via Dover and Deal. He found a financial crisis in full swing. The value of British and foreign securities was deteriorating; near the end of the year many banks failed, all over the country.

A failure at Wakefield caused heavy losses to the Fawkeses, and Scott was ruined by his publisher's collapse. Turner must have congratulated himself on avoiding banks; but he was indirectly hit in various ways – for instance, the print-dealers Hurst and Robinson could not meet their bills. Turner certainly helped the Fawkeses now with money, though we need not accept Thornbury's tale of sending £80,000 to an early patron in trouble.[24]

A letter to Holworthy in January 1826 showed that he had left Sandycombe Lodge (though the address appeared in the Royal Academy Catalogue in May). He gave thanks for a turkey. "Daddy being now released from farming thinks of feeding, and said its richness proved good land and good attention to domestic economy." A severe frost was reigning. "The Thames is impeded below bridge St. James's and Serpentine both frozen in spight of every attempt to keep them open by follow and rashness so the advantage is by the side of the trout stream in more ways than one look at the crash in the commercial world of mercantile speculation and the check which must follow but the trout will be found in the pool and the gudgeon on the shallow but everyone seems to have had a nibble and experience so bought will last longer than a day or its day." He feels that a decisive change has occurred in his world. "Who to use Allason's phrase ever contemplated what has already taken place." (Thomas Allason had published *Antiquities of Pola* in 1819). "By the bye he is getting a fortune rapidly so I am told his connection with the great men in the East [the City] prevents his looking westward now while everything jogs on as usual every one for himself but at more rapid trot notwithstanding Steam Boats liability Banks and Stoppages. Alas my good Auld Lang sine is gone ... and I must follow indeed I feel as you say nearer a million times the brink of eternity with me Daddy only steps in between as it were while you have yet *more* and long be it so say I whether I ever see her or not in London don't think that that promise of bringing [her] on your tremendous mountains will prevent my trudging up some summers-day."[25]

His personal sense of desolation and loss (accentuated by his thought of the "more" which Holworthy has) merges with his conviction of a changed world, where every man is still all out for his own benefit alone, but where the struggle of competition is vastly intensified – "at a more rapid trot". The death of Fawkes had played a considerable part in thus forcing him to face his inner sense of desolation; the financial crisis had made him look more sharply at the world where the Allasons are prospering.

This year there came up the project for *Picturesque Views of England and Wales*, to be published by C. Heath in parts of four engravings each. On 10 August, Turner left for the Meuse and Moselle via Calais.[26] He was back in London by 6 November. A letter to Holworthy states that William, hearing of a powder-magazine blowing up near Ostend, was afraid his son was in the neighbourhood, and "contriv'd to stir up others in the alarm". As a result the *Hull Advertiser* came out that great fears were entertained of Turner's safety. "However it does not appear by your letter that the report reached your quiet valley." He says that "in the Spring when the trout begin to move I am fixed by Exhibition's log; in the Summer I have to oil my wings for a flight; but I generally fly too late for the trout – and so my round of time. I am a kind of slave who puts on his own fetters from habit or more like what my Derbyshire friends would say an Old Batchelor who puts his coat on always one way. The Knot of celibacy (alias maguilpe) grows beautifully less. Callcott is to be married to an acquaintance of mine when in Italy, a very agreeable Blue Stocking, so I must wear the yellow stockings." Callcott's bride was Maria, widow of Captain Graham, who wrote *Little Arthur's History of England* and who once remarked, "I would rather be called a bitch than a prude." Callcott was only three years younger than Turner; and the latter keeps brooding on the question of marriage. He insists that "I am as thin as a hurdle or the direction post (tho not so tall) that will show me the way to Hathersage".[27]

During the year he broke off his relations with Cooke, all of whose ventures had failed.[28]

In 1827 the lectures were delayed by the death of the Duke of York; then the fifth was countermanded by advertisements mentioning a domestic affliction. *The Times* on 13 February spoke of "the death of a near relation", but this seems mere guesswork. Apparently old William was ill.[29] *Views* began appearing in March, but a publication *The English Channel* was still-born. At the Royal Academy Turner had two sea-pieces, one an act of homage to Ruisdael, MORTLAKE TERRACE, attacked as too yellow; and REMBRANDT'S DAUGHTER (in homage to Rembrandt), which attracted some ridicule.[30] In late July he again visited the Isle of Wight, as guest of the architect John Nash, and did two paintings of the Cowes Regatta. In the midst of drawings mainly connected with East Cowes Castle we meet a study for DIDO DIRECTING THE EQUIPMENT OF THE FLEET (shown in 1828).[31] Three letters to William from his son, written at Cowes, have a curt business-like tone and deal wholly with jobs to be carried out – disposal and treatment of pictures, sending of paints, canvases, and clothes ("more light Trouzers" and "White Waistcoats"), and the ejection of a tenant:

Daddy. It is of no use to talk of Smith. I have long ago desired you and Marsh to get him out, but that seems to me of no use or to give him any more time or jobs so again I say get him out at any rate . . . tell him therefore, if he does not get out of the House by next Saturday week, that is tomorrow week that Mr. Marsh will seize and will not take away the man, but sell the things – at once.

You have not said one word about whether Mr. Marsh has sent or not, or Mr. Quilly for the Picture or Mr. Broadhurst or any things which I care about. Why tease me about Smiths affair!! take the Paper about *Wapping* and get it stampt at the office Somerset House JMWT[32]

On the way home from Cowes Turner probably went to Petworth. In December he was again elected Auditor and Council member of the Royal Academy.

In 1828 he lectured and attended Council meetings till the end of July, when he went to Italy. In the Exhibition he showed the picture of Dido he had begun at Cowes, with its subtitle, *The morning of the Carthaginian Empire*. Somehow the Regatta had stirred him with this image. *The Literary Gazette* advised viewers to veil their eyes or be "overpowered by the glare of the violent colours". *The Times* said the work was "extremely beautiful and powerful; in short it has but one fault, it is like nothing in nature".[33]

Before leaving for Italy, Turner completed the water-colours for the England and Wales series and for various Annuals, as well as most of the vignettes for Rogers' *Italy*. He was in Paris by 11 August, when he wrote to Eastlake in Rome, asking him to get a whole-length canvas – two if possible – prepared and grounded, as his first work was to be a companion for the Petworth Claude. "Order me whatever may be necessary to have got ready, that you think right and plenty of the useful – but nothing of the ornamental – never mind Gim cracks of any kind even for the very Easel." His sketchbooks show that he went to Orleans, Lyons, Avignon, Marseilles, then on to Nice, Genoa, Florence, Siena, Rome.[34] Eastlake recounts that Turner stayed in the same house as he, and there painted ORVIETO, REGULUS, and MEDEA. These pictures were exhibited in some rooms that Turner later took at the Quartro Fontane, and he framed them by nailing a rope round the edges and painting it with yellow ochre in tempera.[35] In a letter written in February 1829 Eastlake says that he had worked "literally night & day here began eight or ten pictures & finished and exhibited three – all in about 2 months or little more – more than a thousand persons went to see his works when exhibited & you may imagine how astonished, enraged or delighted the different schools of artists were at seeing things with methods so new, inventions so daring, & excellences so unequivocal."[36]

Turner left Rome early in 1829. He scribbled some lines of benediction, "Farewell a second time the Land of all bliss that cradled liberty could wish and hope . . ."[37] A young Englishman travelling on business happened to be with him between Rome and Bologna and wrote to his artist friend Uwins at Naples to ask about "a good-tempered, funny, little elderly gentleman", who keeps "popping his head out of the window to sketch whatever strikes his fancy", and who was angry when the conductor wouldn't wait while he took a sunrise view of Macerata. "Damn the fellow!" says he. "He has no feeling." He adds that "he speaks but a few words of Italian, about as much of French, which two languages he jumbles together most amusingly . . . Probably you may know something of him."[38] Turner again crossed Mont Cenis. On 22 January 1829 his diligence came to grief in a snowdrift; but he reached London in time to attend a General Meeting on 10 February, when Constable was elected Academician. Afterwards Turner and Jones went to the latter's house in Charlotte Street with the news and stayed talking till 1 a.m.[38]

Turner's Rome paintings did not arrive till July. He thus sent into the Academy as oils ULYSSES DERIDING POLYPHEMUS,

THE LORETTO NECKLACE, and THE BANKS OF THE LOIRE. The first picture went back in conception to 1807–8, but seems to have been painted after the return to London. The rich colour shocked people, especially as the centre of attraction was Wilkie's paintings in a strong black manner, adopted after travels in Italy and Spain.[40] Early in June, Heath and his publisher followed the example of Cooke, holding a show of Turner's drawings in the Egyptian Hall. The feeling of urgency that had gripped Turner is brought out by a letter to Clara Wells, now Mrs. Wheeler, on 19 March:

Dear Clara, I must not allow myself the pleasure of being with you on Saturday to dinner.! Time Time Time So more haste the less Speed.

He then sketched an overturned varnish-jar spilling on to the floor, with palette and brushes turned into a human head staring with a look of indignant horror.[41]

He had meant to return to Rome and had kept his rooms there, but the delays over the transmission of his works and the thought of the July heat depressed him; he wrote on 11 August to Eastlake saying that he would not come. No doubt he was also worrying about his father's health.[42] He merely went for a short tour in France: Paris, Normandy, Guernsey, and was back early in September. His father died on the 21st and was buried in St. Paul's Church, where he had been married. Turner went broken-hearted to Trimmer, the vicar of Heston, saying he felt as if he had lost an only child. Trimmer's son said, "Turner never appeared the same man after his father's death; his family was broken up." The day after the funeral he signed and sealed his first will. This document survives only in an imperfect draft in his own hand. The main points were the bequests of £50 each to his two paternal uncles and £25 each to the eldest son of each man; £50 a year for life to Hannah Danby, niece of John Danby; the same sums to Evelina and Georgianna (described as daughters of Sarah Danby widow of John); and £10 a year for life to Sarah herself; £500 to the Artists' General Benevolent Institution (revoked 7 June 1830); funds to the Royal Academy for a Turner Gold Medal and a Professorship of Landscape Painting. The rest of his property be devoted to a College or Charity for the benefit of "decayed English artists (Landscape Painters only) and single men", to be built on his

Twickenham land and to contain a picture gallery with small houses on each side for the Keeper and the artists.[43]

We can now turn back and consider more fully what had been happening to Turner's art in the 1820s. Before he went to Italy he had been brightening his colour and driving up his tonality, but he was still far from the decisive step of unifying light and colour. What affected him in Italy was only in a secondary way the ruins of antiquity and the Claudean or Virgilian effects; primarily it was the flooding and omnipresent light of the Mediterranean world. The impact showed itself first in his water-colours, for instance in those made at Lake Como and in Venice on his way to Rome. At last he saw how fully to take advantage of the white of paper, which had long been influencing him, together with fine washes of pure colour and general economy of method. He is able to transfer to water-colour the shimmer he had obtained in oils, plus a greater intensity. And then in turn the development affects his oils.[44]

In a work like THE BAY OF BAIAE, 1823, the tones are lightened and the distances are defined by translucent blue glazes. The foreground, however, is still stubborn; it maintains much of its traditional pattern in opposition to the distances; chiaorscuro has not given way to a pure opposition of colours. The vortex is absent in its dynamic form, as indeed it is in all the pictures of the 1820s; instead we get what we may call Turner's maze system, which we have already noted in his use of spiralling recessions. The symmetries and the planes parallel to the picture surface are displaced by a complex of curves and winding lines that lead into the depth without destroying the pattern's coherence. Such a system is related to the vortex, but expresses serenity and balance – whereas the vortex expresses violent conflict. In its richness, its diversity and unity, it goes far beyond any rococo system of serpentine lines. Turner was to use this method in various forms up to the end of the 1830s: in PALESTRINA, CHILDE HAROLD, MERCURY AND ARGUS, CICERO.[45]

The main effect of the two Italian visits, then, appeared in the water-colours, which reacted on the oils, but did not yet wholly transform them. Turner began to make experimental sketches in which he tried to work out the new possibilities he felt of conceiving a landscape purely as a colour structure.

Some 390 items are gathered in one set of the Bequest [46] The works are mostly hard to date with any precision; but we may assume that they extend through the 'twenties and well into the 'thirties – indeed some seem certainly to belong to the 'forties. A few can be related to finished works or to definite scenes,[47] and identifiable sites range from England and Wales to France (Grenoble), the Rhine and Italy. No doubt Turner was often concerned to make notes or sketches that would be of use later in more elaborated works. But clearly in a great number of cases he felt delight in trying out various colour combinations and effects, drawing on his indefatigable memory for certain momentary harmonies or contrasts, and constructing a single complete colour image on the paper.

Such works become pure colour experiments of a kind unparalleled in art; and the best term we can find for them is not that used by Finberg, "Colour Beginnings", but that which he adds, "studies of the fundamental colour structures of designs". In the last resort they are not studies, sketches, or beginnings; they are entire in themselves, works of art, not to be compared with the true sketches, which, however effective or pleasant, have not the same radiant self-sufficiency.

One rough way of dating them is by assessing the amount of directly realistic elements in the colours; those with the most such elements we may take to be earlier. As Turner goes on, we find especially a use of reds and of bold primary colours.[48] Colours are used to create recession without the least element of chiaroscuro or local effects; broad bands and opposed colour masses; all sorts of technical devices, delicate and broad, to define some momentary impression – thus, he uses the texture of paper to break up a thin wash and suggest cloud or mist, or keeps a blank area of white as a high point such as the sun. At moments forms emerge with a faint persistent clarity, set securely in space, yet floating on a mist of transience. Again and again we wonder at the grip on tone and structure which makes of the least colour-wash or indication of form something that is firmly rooted in space and time, and suggests the fullness of the scene by a sort of slow breathing, a palpitation of obstinate life, like the universe on the edge of bursting out of chaos. No artist has ever been able to express so much with such slight means as Turner.

Often the structure seems to exist only in his mind, not on the paper; and yet we feel it dynamically present, glowing, steadily asserting itself yet vanishing at an effort to locate it too definitely – like a music of silence.

In these colour structures we excitingly watch him in the demiurgic act of creating a new cosmos of unified light-colour-form out of the most simple possible materials, in a revolutionary leap of sensibility. Herein lies their importance: the way in which they break through all prevailing concepts and limitations of method, and lay the basis on which Turner was to build his more fully worked-out paintings in the next two decades. Without an understanding of their experimental achievement it is impossible to understand how he arrived at his great break-through into pictures like SLAVERS, SNOW STORM, PEACE, the Venetian visions, and so on.

The visit to the Isle of Wight in 1827 helped him to apply something of his new outlook to sea scenes of calm or crowded regatta movement, and led on to his work in Italy during the second tour of 1828, when he made several oil-sketches on millboard. At times he used a tree pattern framing the depth of light and air, but he also made a direct approach.[49] The paintings with their limited tonal range, their concentration on gradations, may have been made on the spot. A group of larger canvas sketches, too, may have been painted in Italy; they show a broad and bold handling, with contrasts of blues and reddish-browns. One of them is a study for ULYSSES, the work in which his colour interests of the 1820s culminate. However, rich and daring as ULYSSES is, it still does not attempt the organization of structure in terms of colour. Colour appears in a powerful contrast of blues with reds and oranges to build a tremendous sunset of violence and pain (the giant) and of joy and relief (the escaping Greeks). There is a sort of underlying chiaroscuro ghost, though it is interpreted in terms of explosive colour elements.

We see Turner approaching this position in various oils of the late 'twenties. He tried to deal with figure subjects in BOCCACCIO and other works; he turned to Rembrandt and struggled to redefine that artist's chiaroscuro in his own glowing terms, especially in PILATE (1830), with REMBRANDT'S DAUGHTER as the prelude. But as this development carries on into the 'thirties, we may leave it for the moment.

Chapter Fourteen

The Fires of Colour

THE year 1830 opened with news of death. One of Clara Wheeler's sisters died. On Sunday evening, 3 January, Turner did his best to write a note in pious terms that would please Clara: "Your foreboding letter has been too soon realized poor Harriet dear Harriet gentle patient amiability, earthly assurances of heavens bliss possesst, must pour their comforts and mingle in your distress a balm peculiarly its own – not known, not felt, not merited by all. I should like to hear how they all are at Mitcham, if it is not putting you to a painful task too much for your own miseries, to think of before I go on Friday-Morning. Alas I have some woes of my own, which this sad occasion will not improve but believe me most anxious in wishing you may be all more successful in the severe struggle than I have been with mine."[1] But before Friday Lawrence had suddenly died – a likeable character who genuinely admired Turner and who was six years his senior. Turner wrote to Jones wintering in Rome: "Alas, only two short months Sir Thomas followed the coffin of Dawe to the same place. We then were his pall-bearers. Who will do the like for me, or when, God only knows how soon; my poor father's death proved a heavy blow to me, and has been followed by others of the same dark kind. However, it was something to feel that gifted talent can be acknowledged by the many who yesterday waded up to their knees in snow and muck tó see the funeral pomp swelled up by carriages of the great, without the persons themselves."[2]

Lawrence's death meant that the presidency of the Royal Academy was vacant. If the most illustrious artist were to be chosen, Turner was obviously the man. But "combinations and concatenations", as he calls them to Jones, were going on. Wilkie had many partisans, but they spoiled his chances by overplaying their hand and getting him promptly appointed as Principal Painter in Ordinary to the King, in Lawrence's place. The academicians in general saw this as an effort to browbeat them; and anyhow Wilkie was awkward and bashful. On 25 January Shee was chosen, against Wilkie, Phillips and Callcott. Turner was nowhere in the running. His plebian bearing and way of speech, and even more his heretical developments in art, made him a hopeless candidate. No doubt he recognised this fact, but that would not make it all any the less bitter.[3]

He sent seven pictures to the Academy. Perhaps to show that he could still paint without strong colour he showed two seascapes, FISHMARKET ON THE SANDS and CALAIS SANDS, which were generally approved. But he added ORVIETO and PALESTRINA, which were relegated to "the realm of fancy" as mere dreams, and JESSICA and PILATE, which *The Times* condemned as "trumpery", incredible products for the artist of the seascapes. The desolation of CALAIS SANDS, LOW WATER, which expressed Turner's sense of the void after his father's death, was not noticed.

George IV died on 26 June. On 7 July and during the following fortnight Cooke's stock of engravings and plates were sold by auction in Fleet Street. As reports of the Revolution in France arrived the new edition of Rogers' *Italy* with vignettes by Turner and Stothard was announced. Turner decided not to go abroad. He needed further English material and went on a tour of the Midlands, probably late in August. (In a sketchbook is a draft of a poem: "The first pale Star of Eve ere Twylight comes Struggles with . . .", which seems connected with THE EVENING STAR, a painting in which again, with its restrained blue-greys and dim pinks, we find an elegiac sense of death, an immense pathos of darkening distance. "Where is the star which shone . . ." the verses ask.)[4] He was back in London by November, writing to Holworthy in apology for not having reached his place, "I am and have been a sad truant and delinquent with your invitation, I admit and therefore to save myself from a charge of vagrancy beg leave to say I am at home again."[5] He had come near, at Castleton, but apparently did not feel up to any heartiness.

This year "A Lady", writing in the *Dublin Literary Gazette* (15 May), described Turner. "What an odd little mortal he is, wizened, and not even so good looking as Etty, who would be the ugliest man in London but for one simple cause – his pure unaffected good-nature that renders him the darling of all the students of the Royal Academy, and irradiates his countenance until you wonder you ever thought him less than beautiful." The Lady might have added that Turner as well as Etty, was very popular with the students. Edwin Landseer said of him, "Without exception the best teacher I ever met." Frith, mentioning his compliment over *Old English Merry-making*, flatly contradicts the statement that Turner did not encourage the young, "I do not know that Turner's treatment of young men, and his kindness in expressing his opinion of all contemporary work, were in exact opposition to the general notion of his disposition"[6]

About this time Turner started going to Petworth to work. He may have been there late in 1830 and early 1831 painting the four landscapes for panels in the Carved Chamber.[7] Lord Egremont carried on the tradition of the easygoing highly-cultivated eighteenth-century nobleman, who took his pleasures in an airy grand manner without any sense of shame. "Nothing will persuade Lady Spencer," wrote Lady Blessington in 1813, "that Lord Egremont has not forty-three Children, who all live in the House with him and their respective Mothers; that the latter are usually kept in the background, but when any quarrels arise, which few days pass without, each mother takes part with her Progeny, bursts into the drawing room, fights with each other, Lord E., his Children, and, I believe, the Company, and makes scenes worthy of Billingsgate or a Madhouse." Creevey said, "He has a fortune, I believe, of £100,000 a year, and never man could have used it with such liberality and profusion as he has done." His characteristics were "simplicity and sarcasm". The servants were "very numerous, tho' most of them very advanced in years and tottered, and comical in their looks." Haydon said, "The very animals at Petworth seemed happier than in any other spot on earth." There could be no question of any intimacy between Turner and such a man (now aged 79); but they seem to have understood and respected something in each other, for which no words were needed.

Egremont had at first bought works of art by old and modern masters; but several years before his death he told Phillips the portrait-painter, that he had resolved thenceforth to buy only contemporary works, since thus he could most effectively patronize the arts. He built a large gallery at Petworth for this purpose; and at his death it held 170 pictures and twenty-one pieces of scuplture, nearly all commissions or works bought direct from artists. His open forthright character can be read in a letter to Arnald about this time (19 July 1831): "Sir, the Picture, is returned, but I have been very ill, and I do not recollect whether you have been paid or not. I shall be obliged to you if you will let me know. Your humble Servant Egremont."[8]

In February, Turner was back in London.[9] He had seven works in the Royal Academy; the fine LIFE-BOAT AND MANBY APPARATUS; a painting of a naval episode of 1805; Admiral Van Tromp's barge; VISION OF MEDEA (done in Rome, 1828); CALIGULA'S PALACE AND BRIDGE (perhaps begun in 1828); the Watteau study, and an historical painting of Lord Percy's two daughters visiting him when under attainder – these last two suggested by Petworth. The success of Roger's *Italy* drew Scott's new publisher, Cadell, into suggesting an illustrated edition of Scott's poems; but Turner was loth to visit Scotland this year, especially to face the harsh weather of the western coast. But Cadell pressed and Turner at last agreed – though, unknown to him, Scott had had his paralytic attack.[10]

On 10 June he made his second will. Its terms were generally like those of the first, though more carefully set out, for he had now grasped some of the problems attached to the willing of property for charitable purposes. The beneficiaries of his bequest were named as Poor and Decayed Male Artists born in England and of English Parents only and lawful issue; the institution was to be called Turner's Gift.[11]

The artist finally set off to Scotland in later July. Scott, though still suffering from the effects of his seizure, did his best to receive him with the full honours of his hospitality, and went with him to Smailholm Crags. Turner must have been feeling irritable; for Cadell wrote to Scott, "I am sorry Mr. Turner should have annoyed you all so much – it was most absurd to be in such a pother." Leaving Abbotsford, Turner went to Glasgow, the Falls of the Clyde, and on to Oban and Skye.[12] Then he sailed by steamer for Staffa and Iona. A strong wind and headsea made it hard to reach Iona; the captain put the matter to the vote and a majority of the passengers decided not to land. The captain then promised to steam thrice round the island. "The sun getting towards the horizon, burst through the rain-cloud, angry, and for wind; and so it proved, for we were driven for shelter into Loch Ulver, and did not get back to Tobermoray before midnight." From this experience came STAFFA.[13]

He was back in London by September.[14]

In the atmosphere of militant Reform of 1832 attacks increased on the Royal Society as a body of antiquated privilege.[15] The first twelve Scott drawings were exhibited in Pall Mall before going to the engravers. Turner's six pictures in the Royal Academy consisted of CHILDE HAROLD'S PIL-GRIMAGE, an effort to sum up his feelings about Italy, THE PRINCE OF ORANGE LANDING; two more-sea pieces (with titles indicating his debt to Holland); STAFFA; and NEBU-CHADNESSAR AT THE MOUTH OF THE BURNING FIERY FURNACE. The last-named work, expressing the devotion of the righteous in the face of oppression, had its link with THE PRINCE OF ORANGE. It was furiously abused, though the *Morning Herald* observed, "Turner is not so funny this year as usual."[16] Before the exhibition closed the Government's plans to build a National Gallery became known.[17]

In August, Turner made a further effort to cover up the loopholes in his will, laying down that if for legal reasons his charitable purposes could not be carried out, his house in Queen Anne Street should be used as a gallery for keeping his works together. He clearly had in mind the way in which Soane was arranging to have his house turned into a Museum in order to foil a spendthrift son.[18] He does not seem to have gone abroad, but sketched at the mouth of the Thames and along the coast to Ramsgate. After being re-elected as Auditor, he went to spend Christmas at Petworth, whence he wrote asking to be excused from his lectures in 1833.[19]

In 1833 he had six smaller pictures in the Academy Show, including two of Venice, fairly easy to accept. About this time he began to demand big prices. Jones quotes him as saying, in connexion with THE BRIDGE OF SIGHS, "Well, if they will have such scraps instead of important pictures they must pay for them."[20] The first of *Turner's Annual Tours* (Loire and Seine) appeared in June, as well as Part XVI of *England and Wales*, with an exhibition of drawings at 6 Pall Mall. One drawing showed Nottingham in agitation during the recent elections. Perhaps in August he went to Paris. During these years he once called at the studio of Delacroix, who records in his *Journal* on 24, March 1855, after talking with a young English painter, Thomas Armstrong, who had come to Paris in 1853: Turner "lived in a miserly way with an old servantwoman. I recall having had him at my place once when I used to live on the quai Voltaire. [Between January 1829 and October 1835.] He produced a mediocre impression on me: he had the look of an English farmer, black clothes, gross enough, big shoes and hard cold demeanour."

Arnald's *Magazine of the Fine Arts* had some good comments on his work, showing that there were some at least who were able to see something of its general direction. "While other men were content to pursue their art with an apathy to all the deep and intricate beauties of nature", great painters were always the greatest experimentalists. Turner, "after having first well grounded his talent, emerged as a meteor in colouring. We are well aware that on this point he is unceasingly assailed, as sacrificing both nature and art to a *false* taste." But those who took this position, "looked to nothing but the main body of colour; they have no perception of the combination of the whole."

Instead of censuring, they ought to rejoice in having the opportunity for observing, in his various experiments, the progress and process by which he attempts to embody the most beautiful and difficult effects of nature.[21]

In December came the second issue of *Tours* (Seine) and the illustrated *Poems* of Rogers. Turner was re-elected Auditor and elected Visitor of the Life Academy.

Some time before this he had made the acquaintance of a Margate landlady, Sophia Caroline Booth. *The Athenaeum*,

immediately after his death, told how he had taken lodgings
with her. When asked for references, he replied, "But, my
good woman, I will buy your house outright." As for signing
an agreement, he was ready to pay in advance, and pulled
out a handful of bank-notes and sovereigns. She asked his
name, and he answered that if she were Mrs. Booth, then he
might as well be Mr. Booth.

The apocryphal nature of this tale is shown by the fact
that there was an actual Mr. John Booth, who did not die
till 1834, though Turner seems to have stayed with the Booths
for some six years previously. Mrs. Booth had had an earlier
husband, Henry Pound, to whom she bore a son, Daniel
John, and who died soon after, leaving her as a widow of 26
without any means. Not long after, she married Booth, a
retired gentleman with a small income. This part of her life
took place at Deal. But in 1827 the Booths moved to Cold
Harbour, Margate, where they had a cottage overlooking
the sea and took in boarders. She bore Booth a son, and
called him, in pious memory of her first husband, John Pound.
Their cottage seems to have been next to the Custom House
and alongside the Foy Boat Inn. Turner clearly found the
company of the Booths congenial.

When Booth died in 1833 he left his wife the household
effects, £1,200 in cash, and the income from the rest of his
fortune, subject to the payment of £200 to the stepson on
attaining the age of 25 and £400 on Mrs. Booth's death.
Booth's own son had died before him; otherwise Mrs. Booth
would have got only £300 in cash, though with the income
from a correspondingly larger sum.[22]

Turner, if we may judge from Sarah and Sophia, had a
predilection for widows. No doubt he felt safer with a woman
who had already been married and who would not have the
same sort of claim on him that an unmarried mistress would
have had. The executor of Booth's will was the local physician,
Dr. David Price, of whom Turner painted a miniature as a
gift for Mrs. Booth, and who in time became his own doctor.
At what time Mrs. Booth became Turner's mistress, we do
not know; but we may surmise that they came to some arrangement while he was consoling and helping her soon after
Booth's death, on the same lines as had happened with Sarah.
The relationship has not the same interest as that with Sarah,

for it does not seem to have been charged with any strong emotion. Mrs. Booth appears as a comfortable not-very-well educated body, a good thrifty housekeeper; and it is pleasant to know that for his last seventeen years Turner was able to find a certain repose in her warm companionship. He seems to have found in her someone as far removed as possible from his mother; between them there was nothing of the tension that accompanied his relations with the incomparably more cultivated Sarah.[23] Charles Turner in 1852, on 23 March, went to Turner's house in Chelsea, "where he went by the name of Admiral Booth"; on 6 September, "went to see Mrs. Booth the female Mr. Turner resided with. Exactly like a fat cook and not a well educated woman. *Muster* Turner instead of Mr. Turner when speaking to me. Everyone to his taste!!! What a pity so great a man in talent should not have a more ladylike choice. He could not have introduced her to *his friends*."[24] No doubt she was not like a fat cook when Turner met her some twenty years before, and her broad accent would not have bothered him; nor had he any wish for a woman he could introduce to his friends. There had always been a deep gap between Turner's personal life and his public career as an artist. Now that gap became final: whatever ideas he may ever have had of bridging it were given up.

In 1834 Turner was busy supplying the engravers. His five Royal Academy paintings included a Venetian view, THE GOLDEN BOUGH, FOUNTAIN OF INDOLENCE, and WRECKERS. He was in Oxford in early July, then went to Brussels for river sketches of the Meuse, Moselle, and Rhine, which were never engraved. Back in England, he visited Petworth (where the fishing episode mentioned in our first chapter occurred), then returned to London in time to witness the burning of the Houses of Parliament on 16 October. As usual, he hurried to the scene of a near disaster and made sketches from both sides of the Thames. In December the third volume of *Tours* was published, and again he became an Auditor.[25]

There had been complaints about the lack of Perspective Lectures, but once more, in 1835, he asked to be excused. At the British Institute he showed his first picture of the burning Parliament. The critics objected to the method of painting, but had to admit the work's great power. "The burst of light in the body of the flame, and the flood of fiery radiance that forms a luminous atmosphere round all the objects near, cannot be surpassed for truth," said the *Spectator*, yet "Turner seems to paint slovenlily – daubing."[26] In the summer he went to Venice via the Baltic, Berlin, Dresden, Prague, and Vienna. He had in hand the job of illustrating Campbell's *Poems*.

We can now pause to look back at the works of the previous five or six years, and sum up what he had been doing. As usual he pursued a zigzag course, taking in new influences, darting forwards, retracing his steps and resuming a previous manner, then pulling everything together in a decisive advance. The effect of Van Dyck appeared in the Petworth-influenced paintings of 1831, while Giorgione and Titian merged with Hoppner (*Sleeping Venus and Cupid*) to beget the unfinished WOMAN RECLINING ON COUCH with its remarkable luminosity of flesh, which shows how far Turner could have gone if he had concentrated on the nude. He carried on his simplifications of structure in form and colour in the melancholia, the acceptance of death, of CALAIS SANDS and EVENING STAR, and in the serene joy of PETWORTH PARK, with its marvellously balanced oval composition which returns in on itself in the tunnelling recession of the almost-vanished sun.

In STAFFA he developed further the colour effect of EVENING STAR, but in a richer, more ominous way, stressed by the orange-over-pink of the setting sun. Diagonals join with vertical-horizontals to control the tensions brought about by the movement of colour, the recessions linked with the swell of water, the sun sinking menacingly into the water on the right-hand, the looming cloud that mingles with the misty headland. There is a pulsating effect of in-and-out motion, highly complex in its tensions. The trail of smoke links the human and elemental aspects, and completes the effect of the ship struggling into the heavily circling structure of space. Colour and form merge, as spray, mist, cloud, rock-forms with their fractures also merge, distinct and indistinct at the same moment. As with CALAIS PIER, the new unity is closely linked with a personal experience of danger and stormy violence.[27]

THE MOUTH OF THE SEINE, 1833, carries on this new quality.

The dissolution of outline increases. The composition is controlled by the dialogue of towering cloud and the spray of topping wave curves, the swing of bird flight; the buildings are reduced to a lesser place as if barely able to inhabit truly the momentary and eternal sphere of the elements, where they exist in alienated opposition. The note in the catalogue about the dangerous quicksands only underlines the aesthetic effect. Turner is beginning to be interested in the pure elemental forms of violence and tension for themselves, as holding the clue to the structure, the formative essence, of natural process which men seek to obstruct. What he is saying is something far more complicated than a banal comment on man's impotence before nature. With this keen interest in the various aspects of science that impinged on art, in all aspects of technology, he knew that men were far from impotent. What he was defining was the inner flaw, the fallacy of hope, that broke men down. In these terms the elemental violence expressed the unexpected and uncontrollable forces coming destructively out of the inner flaw. In so far as man was whole, he was one with the momentary eternity of the natural pattern of movement, however tumultuous. So the artist himself, who expressed the scene of destruction but also felt one with the pattern, stood for that in humanity which survives the disaster and continues to seek wholeness. Turner is expressing both a judgement on alienated man and a resolving unity with process, which overcomes alienation from nature (and so in turn from society and from self). He is finding safety in the heart of danger instead of denying the danger by falsified notions of triumphant mastery over nature.[28]

At the same time, as we have seen, he had been trying to work on figure-subjects, drawing on Stothard, Watteau, Van Dyck, and especially Rembrandt.[29] For some while he had been seeking a way of generalizing form, while preserving the essential aspects of character and action. He succeeded at times when he was dealing with small figures engaged in some kind of activity, above all that of work; but he could not succeed in looking people in the face. That this weakness was psychological and not a failure in draughtsmanship is shown by his many life studies. Indeed, he seems to have suffered from an inability to look even his pictures in the face – that is, self-consciously, when not working on them. This is how Rippingille describes Turner finishing his work on the BURNING OF THE HOUSES OF LORDS AND COMMONS:

Turner gathered his tools together, put them into and shut up the box, and then, with his face still turned to the wall, and at some distance from it, went sidling off, without speaking a word to anybody, and when he came to the staircase, in the centre of the room, hurried down as fast as he could. All looked with a half-wondering smile, and Maclise, who stood near, remarked, "There, that's masterly, he does not stop to look at his work; he *knows* it is done, and he is off."[30]

But there was more to it than that – a strange sort of shame or fear. "A well-known collector with whom the artist had long been intimate", says Thornbury, "once invited him to be present at the opening of a new gallery which was hung round with his most beautiful drawings. To the disappointment of the connoisseur, Turner scarcely noticed them, but kept his eyes fixed upon the ceiling. It was pannelled, and neatly grained in oak. 'What are you looking at so intently?' said the host. 'At those boards,' was the reply, 'the fellow that did that must have known how to paint.' And nothing would induce him to turn to the magnificent pictures that sparkled on the walls. He never talked about his own pictures." He adds, "It was not easy to draw his attention to the admiration of his own pictures." Ruskin tells us, "I never saw him at my father's house look for an instant at any of his own drawings. I have watched him sitting at dinner nearly opposite one of his chief pictures (presumably SLAVERS); his eyes never turned to it."[31] The same complex of emotions made Turner hoard his pictures and buy them back, only to let them moulder and rot, rolled up against walls or used to keep the draughts out of windows. DIDO BUILDING CARTHAGE, which he thought so highly of that he wanted it hung with Claudes, was found after his death so neglected that the paint was flaking off in large pieces, and when it was dusted outside before being put in a van, the pavement looked, said Uwins, "almost as if a chimney had been swept upon it".

PILATE reveals Turner's characteristic failure with faces, especially of women: for example the Virgin Mary, flanked by two back-turned women. (Turner was rather fascinated by the female back, particularly in the mode of the day,

with hair parted in the middle and flowing down to the
shoulders, and with a low-cut back to the dress. He gets
something of the sexual suggestiveness out of this viewpoint
that Fuseli does).[32] But despite the incidental weaknesses
of PILATE, the total effect, the movement of light and colour
over the surface, gives an extraordinary effect of rich tumult.

Then, about the mid-'thirties, he achieved much of what
he was seeking in the sketches he made at Petworth, where,
since his father's death, he had become a regular visitor, with
his own studio. These works, mainly of the interior of the
building, though at times of the parkland, were made in
body colour on blue paper [Figs. 22–25]. They were lyrical,
simple in their breadth, highly expressive in the way they
catch a number of people in a momentary light effect, a
momentary group relationship. The climax came with MUSIC
AT PETWORTH and THE LETTER. In the latter he has absorbed
the influence of Rembrandt, does not seek to subdue his
colours to an explosive golden glow, but finds his own key.
In MUSIC AT PETWORTH he carries this development further,
dissolving contours in the light burst without losing structure.
Here, as in others of the Petworth series, the explicit theme
is music, and the aesthetic definition seems to have been
affected both by the actual mood of music and by the feeling
for a flow of rich semitones, the fine modulations of liberated
colour.[33]

In 1833 he exhibited his first Venetian oils. The only
Venetian subjects shown previously had been the water-
colours of 1820–1. And now (save in 1838–9) he kept on
showing more views of Venice till 1846. Yet before 1835 he
had visited the place briefly in 1819; in all he spent about six
weeks there. Perhaps the rereading of Byron had turned his
thoughts to the city; in 1832 he exhibited CHILDE HAROLD'S
PILGRIMAGE. One of his 1833 Venetian works was a tribute
to Canaletto (he paid a tribute also to van Goyen this year);
yet he saw Venice with very different eyes than did the painter
he complimented. In 1834 he began his series, light in tone
and glowing in colour, with THE DOGANA – at last realizing
in oils the vision of light which Italy had woken in 1819. It
was characteristic of him that he should turn first to Canaletto
and produce a work of comparatively firm and definitely
organized forms before letting himself go.[34]

The Parliament paintings started him off on a new series
of disasters: night scenes in which fire appeared destructively
or ominously. Some had Venetian settings, but there were
also FIRE AT SEA and the water-colours, FIRE AT FENNING'S
WHARF and A CONFLAGRATION, LAUSANNE. The Parliament
works allowed him to express to the full his liking for dramatic
contrasts of warm and cold colours, the reds and oranges of
the flapping flags of flame and the quiet blues of the sky;
contrasts of the violent flame and the quietly flowing river –
with the flame reflections, lurid or soft, as a connexion.[35]
Rippingille describes him at work on the British Institution
picture on varnishing day:

The picture when sent in was a mere dab of several colours, and
"without form and void", like chaos before the creation . . . Such
a magician, performing his incantations in public, was an object of
interest and attraction. Etty was working at his side [on *The Lute
Player*] and every now and then a word and a quiet laugh emanated
and passed between the two great painters. Little Etty stepped
back every now and then to look at the effect of his picture, lolling
his head on one side and half closing his eyes, and sometimes
speaking to some one near him, after the approved manner of
painters: but not so Turner; for the three hours I was there – and I
understood it to have been the same since he began in the morning –
he never ceased to work, or even once looked or turned from the
wall on which his picture hung. All lookers-on were amused by the
figure Turner exhibited in himself, and the process he was pursuing
with his picture. A small box of colours, a few very small brushes,
and a vial or two, were at his feet, very inconveniently placed;
but his short figure, stooping, enabled him to reach what he wanted
very readily. Leaning forward and sideways over to the right, the
left hand metal button of his blue coat rose inches higher than the
right, and his head buried in his shoulders and held down, presented
an aspect curious to all beholders, who whispered their remarks to
each other, and quietly laughed to themselves. In one part of the
mysterious proceedings Turner, who worked almost entirely with
his palette knife, was observed to be rolling and spreading a lump
of half-transparent stuff over his picture, the size of a finger in length
and thickness. As Callcott was looking on I ventured to say to him,
"What is he plastering his picture with?" to which inquiry it was
replied, "I should be sorry to be the man to ask him."

This account – as also that of the way he painted the water-
colour for young Fawkes – reminds us of a factor which has
so far been little stressed, but which played an important part

in freeing Turner. This was the actual process of handling paint with brush, finger, knife. Turner, with his strong concept of the unity of all the elements and methods employed in making a picture, could not but feel a close link between the rhythms of composition, the conflicts and harmonies of colour, and the method used in creating them. The colour tensions were reflected in the actual sweep, twists, turns, and pressures of the hand and its instrument. The co-ordination thus built up between hand and mind, hand and materials, gradually became more assured, more spontaneous; in Turner's mature work the free, almost self-guiding movement of the hand was a powerful factor in producing the aesthetic effect. The rococo satisfaction in the handling of paint as such, which we noted in Gainsborough, was thus carried to a new level, more comprehensive, dynamic, and liberating.

The theme of DIDO AND AENEAS had hardly appeared since 1823; but in 1834 it reasserted itself in THE FATES AND THE GOLDEN BOUGH. (The Catalogue refers to *The Fallacies of Hope*, but the editor seems to have cut out the verses.) Here the theme of the mysterious Sibyl, the Mother as the guide in hell-harrowing, the bearer of the saving bough, is found again, looking back to AENEAS AND SIBYL and BAY OF BAIAE. As in BAIAE, a snake lurks in the foreground, reminding us of the Fall. In CHILDE HAROLD Turner returns to the Claudean earthly paradise: the right-hand side, says Ruskin, "founded on faithful reminiscences of the defiles of Narni, and the roots of the Apennines, seen under purple evening light. The tenderness of the mere painting, by which the light is expressed, is not only far beyond his former work, but is so great that the eye can hardly follow the gradations of hue; it can feel but cannot trace them."[36]

There is yet one further point. Turner had been stirred by the agitation during the struggle for the Reform Bill, when Bristol was in flames and there was a threat of widespread violence. Now in the 'thirties a renewed tide of political struggle was setting in, the continuous assertion of radical and chartist demands that reached its climax in 1848. To Turner, with his way of seeing events which stirred him in terms of his poetic and artistic symbolism, the burning of the centre of government could hardly be other than an emblem

of the conflict and malaise consuming the country. As he
wrote no verses for his pictures of this event, I cannot prove
my point, but in view of the consistent evidence we have as
to the way his mind worked, I feel sure that he seized on the
event as symbolically expressive of the fires of decay and
violence at work in English society and liable to burst out
in a general conflagration. The Parliament fire of October
1834 had followed on other fires of the sort that would attract
his notice: a steamer was burned at Dublin on 6 April; sixty
to seventy houses were burned down at N. Tawton on 14–15
July; a large fire raged in the Liverpool docks on 16 August;
and on 17 August a Government steam packet at the same
place caught fire and exploded.[37] The spectacle of the burning
Houses of Parliament was highly dramatic, indeed apocalyptic. As it broke out early in the evening, vast crowds gathered,
and the army had to be called out to support the police.
A witness tells of the ceaseless tolling of the bell in St. Mar-
garet's Church, Westminster, the shouting of the firemen,
the crash of falling timbers, and the clarions of the Horse
Guards wailing through the air. At half past nine, when the
roof of the House of Lords fell in, "bright coruscations, as of
electric fire, played in the great volume of flames, and so
struck were the bystanders with the grandeur of the sight at
this moment that they involuntarily (and from no bad feeling)
clapped their hands as though they had been present at the
closing scene of some dramatic spectacle". To someone like
Turner, not concerned to make the tumult of applause appear
respectable, the clapping may well have seemed to betoken
the collapse of a political system. The *Annual Register* says
that the roof crash was "accompanied with an immense
volume of flame and smoke, and emitting in every direction
millions of sparks and flakes of fire. This appearance, combined with the sound, resembling the report of a piece of
heavy ordinance, induced the assembled multitude to believe
that an explosion had taken place."[38] It was this moment,
when the wind had veered to the west, which I believe Turner
to have set out to record in the painting.

Chapter Fifteen

The Sea of Blood

TURNER showed in 1836 at the Royal Academy three works: ROME FROM MOUNT AVENTINE, MERCURY AND ARGUS, and JULIET AND HER NURSE. In the British Institution he had FIRE OF THE HOUSE OF LORDS and WRECKERS ON THE NORTH SHORE. When the Academy exhibition closed he went with the rich amateur H. A. J. Munro of Novar on a tour of France and the Val d'Aosta. Munro told Ruskin in 1857 that Turner had dissuaded him from politics, as he saw that "I was getting on the wrong tack and that it was the part of a friend to secure me in those pursuits I have ever loved". Munro seems to have been a retiring fellow – in a letter to Holworthy, Turner mentions that he has been blushing less than usual – and Turner may well have felt him unsuited for public life. Ruskin cites an episode of the tour to show Turner's dislike "*to appear* kind". Munro had got into difficulties over a coloured sketch. "Turner looked over him a little while, then said, in a grumbling way – 'I haven't got any paper I like; let me try yours.' Receiving a block book he disappeared for an hour and a half. Returning, he threw the book down, with a growl saying – 'I can't make anything of your paper.' There were three sketches on it, in three distinct states of progress, showing the process of colouring from beginning to end, and clearing up every difficulty which his friend had got into."[1]

During Turner's absence a Select Committee on Arts and Manufactures appointed by the Commons, had been hearing evidence about the corruption and incompetence of the

Academy. Questions were asked about Turner's failure to
give his lectures. Shee stated that the Academy had not pressed
him, partly because the members thought lectures a bad way
to explain perspective and partly "from a delicacy which
cannot perhaps be perfectly justified, but which arises from
the respect they feel for one of the greatest artists of the age
in which we live. He of course receives no emoluments during
the cessation of his lectures."[2] A different sort of attack was
being launched on him by the Rev. J. Eagles of Wadham
College, Oxford, in *Blackwood's Magazine*. This essay
repeated crudely all the worst sort of insults that had been
thrown at his work; its importance lay merely in the fact
that it stimulated Ruskin, then a youth of seventeen, into
writing a reply. His father persuaded him to send it, not to
Blackwood's editor, but to Turner. Turner replied:

I beg to thank you for your zeal, kindness, and the trouble you have
taken in my behalf, in regard to the criticism of Blackwoods Mag
for Oct respecting my works; but I never move in these matters –
they are of no import save mischief and the meal tub, which Maga
fears for by my having invaded the flour tub.

He was referring to Eagles's description of his *Juliet* as
"a composition as from models of different parts of Venice,
thrown higgledy-piggledy together, streaked blue and pink,
and thrown into a flour tub".[3]

On 10 November his old friend Wells died at Mitcham.
Clara tells of his "agony of grief". "Sobbing like a child,
he said, 'Oh, Clara, Clara! these are iron tears. I have lost
the best friend I ever had in my life.' "

In 1837 Turner showed REGULUS at the British Institution,
with something of a Claudean basis, but also with his own
flood of light and restless movement.[4] He was attending most
Council meetings, but his health was bad.[5] On Sunday
evening, 12 March, he wrote to Clara about her husband's
illness. "I know your fears (I hope so) are magnified if I
were to judge by [my] own feelings having yet the baneful
effects of the Influenza hanging upon me yet daily (for it
alternates) and hourly – that the lassitude the sinking down
and yet compelled to work the same is not to be expressed
but must be borne by me if possible 3 weeks longer without
any help." Early in April, when he was working on the Hang-

ing Committee, he wrote to Emma Wells about the reply to
an invitation, which he had neglected to post: "the fact is I
thought I had put it into the Box on my way home, and only
found it to day in my Holiday-coat for any thing will do to
hang Pictures. Thank God (pardon) we have it nearly done."[6]

However, he had not been too ill to write to R. Holland,
M.P. for Hastings, about the balloon trip which he had made
in 1836 to Germany. "Your excursion so occupied my mind
that I dreamt of it, and I do hope you will hold to your
intention of making the drawing, with all the forms and
colours of your recollection." Any suggestion of a new angle,
a new approach, to the questions of perspective, colour, and
the like, deeply stirred his imagination.[7]

This year the Academy exhibited in the eastern half of the
front part of what is now the National Gallery, which had
been allotted as its premises. William IV opened the show on
28 April. Turner had sent in APOLLO AND DAPHNE and HERO
AND LEANDER, both dealing with themes of baffled love. The
first, however, was a serene landscape where the god of poetry
and art chats with the girl; the pursuit is merely forecast in
the secondary motive of greyhound coursing hare. (We may
compare the rabbit and snake in BAIAE.) On the other hand,
the second work was a great symphonic poem of frustrated
love.[8]

In June, Victoria came to the throne. Various artists were
knighted: Callcott, Westmacott (sculptor), Newton (minia-
turist), while Landseer refused the title. The choice of a minor
follower of Turner like Callcott underlined the ignoring of the
great artists. From 27 July to 2 November, Turner was away
from Council meetings, no doubt travelling; he was at Petworth in October. On 11 November, Egremont died in his
eighty-sixth year. Turner went to the funeral at Petworth and
headed the group of artists. Next day he was back at his
Academic duties, but by early December he had to give them
up. On the seventh he wrote to Maw, an amateur artist and
collector, "I am now more than an invalid and sufferer either
from having taken cold at the Funeral of Lord Egremont or
at the Life Academy, but I hope the *worst is now past*, but Sir
Anthony Carlisle who I consult in misfortune says I must not
stir out of door until it is dry weather (frost) I hope he in-
cludes, or I may become a prisoner all the Winter." However,

on the 28th he attended the Council meeting and announced his resignation as Professor of Perspective. No new professor was elected; after some delays a teacher was appointed.[9]

In the Royal Academy of 1838 he showed PHRYNE and two contrasted pictures of Modern and Ancient Italy (the latter linked with Ovid's exile). The full title of the first picture was PHRYNE GOING TO THE PUBLIC BATH AS VENUS – DEMOSTHENES TAUNTED BY AESCHINES. The processional part may well have been suggested by H. Tresham's *Phryne at the Possidonian Feasts*, which he had seen as a young man; but the combination with the orators is his own touch. We may interpret the overt theme of the work, then, as the opposition of the enjoyment of life to the political problems which intrude on that enjoyment. Demosthenes, the exponent of Greek city-democracy, is assailed by Aeschines, the advocate of Macedonian kingly power. The two aspects of the situation, the immediate release of delight and the threatening political conflict, are fused in the movement of light and colour, but are otherwise quite unaware of one another.

Turner was absent from the Council from 6 August to 20 October; he seems to have spent at least some of the time at Margate with Mrs. Booth. It has been suggested that it was while returning from one of his journeys that he saw the *Téméraire* being towed from Sheerness, where she had been guardship, to Deptford to be broken up by a shipbroker of Rotherhithe – her rusty hull covered with its last coat of dockyard-drab. Thornbury says, however, that he had been picnicking with other Academicians off Greenwich marshes in Blackwall Reaches when the old ninety-eight gunner came up. Woolner's account supports the first supposition.

One day in 1838, W. F. Woodington, the sculptor of one of the reliefs on the base of the Nelson Column, was on a steamboat returning from a trip to Margate when in the midst of a great blazing sunset he saw the old Temeraire drawn by a steam tug [actually there were two]. The sight was so magnificent that it struck him as being an unusually fine subject for a picture, and he noted all the points which he thought would constitute its glory if presented on canvas.

But he was not the only person on board who took professional notice of the splendid sight, for he saw Turner himself there, also noticing and busy making little sketches on cards.[10]

Turner's painting, THE FIGHTING TÉMÉRAIRE, TUGGED TO HER

LAST BERTH TO BE BROKEN UP, was shown in the Royal Academy of 1839. In a December letter he described himself as unable to accept a Christmas invitation to Hastings, as "I have been so idle all the summer". We may assume that he was spending much time with Mrs. Booth at Margate.[11] In a codicil he revoked legacies to his uncles and their sons as well as the yearly sums for Sarah Danby, Evelina and Georgianna; and he made Hannah the sole custodian of his pictures.

In 1840 Leslie's son gives us a glimpse of Turner's personal fantasy. He "came up to our house one evening by special appointment to sup upon Welsh rabbit". Leslie was at Henley and had been painting the Lord Chancellor. "Turner went into the painting-room, where the robes, wig, etc., of the Chancellor were arranged upon a lay-figure; and after a little joking, he was persuaded to put on the Lord Chancellor's wig, in which my mother says, Turner looked splendid, so joyous and happy, too, in the idea that the Lord Chancellor's wig became him better than any one else of the party."[12]

This year he showed SLAVERS, BACCHUS AND ARIADNE (again the deserted girl), NEAPOLITAN FISHER – GIRLS SURPRISED BATHING BY MOONLIGHT and ROCKETS AND BLUE LIGHTS. During a visit to his agent T. Griffith at Norwood, on 22 June, he met Ruskin, though unaware he had been the writer of the reply to Eagles. Another visitor noted, "Though Turner spoke kindly to Ruskin, he took no particular notice of him." Ruskin, tall and slight, with frank blue eyes, fair rough hair, protruding lower lip scarred by a dog-bite, whiskered cheeks and elegant attire, did not interest him. In his own diary Ruskin noted down that evening:

Introduced to-day to the man who beyond all doubt is the greatest of the age; greatest in every faculty of the imagination, in every branch of scenic knowledge; at once *the* painter and poet of the day, J. M. W. Turner. Everybody had described him to me as coarse, boorish, unintellectual, vulgar. This I knew to be impossible. I found in him a somewhat eccentric, keen-mannered, matter-of-fact, English-minded gentleman: good-humoured evidently, bad-tempered evidently, hating humbug of all sorts, shrewd, perhaps a little selfish, highly intellectual, the powers of his mind not brought out with any delight in their manifestation, or intention of display, but flashing out occasionally in a word or a look.

Well might he comment, half a century later in *Praeterita*,

"Pretty close, that, and full, to be seen at a first glance, and set down the same evening."[13]

Early in August, Turner went to Rotterdam, then up the Rhine and on to Venice. He returned via Munich and Nuremberg, arriving home in early October. A letter to Cobb, his solicitor, shows high spirits and a keen interest in railways:

Why! you are like a Jack of Trumps, turning up at cribbage: so two thanks for your letter from Brighton or anywhere – tho I am sorry to hear you complaining yet of illness.

Wally Strong shall be paid but confound him he will not move about the piece of Ground, so things remain (as they were). What Young has bought and paid his rent for *Heaven only knows* for I do not.

Having left the great Gates and no garden, and having locomotive Engines in progress towards you, we may meet again ere long, by rail-road either at Brighton or London: but I suppose you also are not so located by the heels, Mr. Jack of Trumps, but do come to town occasionally by the Rapid, Dart or Quicksilver: that I do hope to see you before the Chemin de Fer is completed – I should have answered your letter sooner, but have only arrived from Venice a few hours.[14]

He had six pictures at the Royal Academy. Of ROSENAU, *The Times* said that it represented "nothing in nature beyond eggs and spinach".[15] Ruskin, back from Switzerland, met Turner again at Griffith's. "Turner there is no mistaking for a moment – his keen eye and dry sentences can be the sign only of high intellect. Jones a fine, grey, quiet, Spectator-like 'gentleman'."[16] Late in July, Turner himself set out for Switzerland, where he spent much of the summer. On 1 June, Wilkie died on board ship as he sailed back from Egypt; and on 25 November, Chantrey suddenly died. Jones says that Turner "wrung my hand, tears streaming from his eyes", and "rushed from the house without uttering a word". In a letter of 9 December, declining an invitation, he describes himself as "very low, indeed, for our loss in *dear* Chantrey".

Illness or death stirred his deep fears and also released his equally deep stores of buried tenderness: "In illness," says Thornbury, "Turner was all consideration. He was as anxious as a mother or a wife, and as careful as a nurse. His friends used in this to compare him to his patron, Lord Egremont; to be ill was to secure a visit from the owner of Petworth. In some cases, when a friend had died, Turner never could be prevailed to enter the house again." When the son of the engraver Charles Turner was dying Turner called constantly to inquire about him. The parents learned of this only after the boy's death, when the servant reported that "a little, short gentle-man, of odd manners, had called every evening". At the funeral of Lawrence, on a day of snowfall, Wilkie whispered into Turner's ear, "That's a fine effect." Turner turned away in disgust. ("This", says Trimmer, "I had from Constable, who was on the other side of him, and who, when telling me the anecdote, remarked that Turner had a great deal of good feeling about him.")[17]

In these years Turner was consolidating the gains he had made in the world of colour, and finding new liberations. The years 1836–7 saw a decisive turn. On the one hand he returned to the theme of disaster. Into SNOW-STORM, AVALANCHE AND INUNDATION he packed about as much catastrophe as a single canvas could hold. Here is the climax of a series begun with his early sea-storms: with all forms recognizable and playing their parts in what we may call a coherent system of New-tonian mechanics and dynamics, though the vortex threatens to overturn all landmarks in its great swirl. So the work in turn preludes the leap into a new space, one of immeasurable clashes and indefinable transitions, in the 'forties. From now on the sea-and-fire theme grows stronger. Storm has invaded the Venetian idyll.[18] Venice indeed has become so much a place of drama for him that he transfers Juliet and her Nurse thither without explanation.

At the same time, with Egremont's death, the gracious world of elegant Petworth impressions exploded. In INTERIOR AT PETWORTH light-explosion is everything, dissolving and controlling forms. Light and colour have at last become dynamically one without any qualifications. The hall depicted, in fact, did not exist at Petworth; and the incident seems a scampering confusion of dogs that rush into the domestic privacy. We could argue that the theme is the breakdown of the old happy relationships at Petworth; the dogs that once streamed across the parkland to their master are now questing for him in vain; the Petworth way-of-life falls into chaos. True, the elemental forces have here burst in on the human space of security and withdrawal, and there is no escape. And yet the ultimate effect is one of joy. However, it may be a joy born out of bitterness and surmounting it only by a tremendous effort to regain harmony. The classicisms linked with Claude and Poussin are at last rejected – or rather, since Turner, however he dissolves forms, never dissolves structure, they are now at last fully incorporated in the vision of the gyring storms and serene pools of light.

Claudean elements continued, however, to persist when Turner turned to mythological subjects or wanted to use the Campagna for works that looked nostalgically back to ancient Rome. And similar elements with variations showed up in the works which from 1835 (following his tour of the Rhine, Meuse and Moselle) depicted German scenes. Byron provided a connecting link, for instance in CHILDE HAROLD'S PILGRIMAGE and THE BRIGHT STONE OF HONOUR (EHREN-BREISTEIN). A new method of treating the crowds of people that often appear in such works is now found. The simplified realistic figures give way to more schematic forms, who tend to lack weight and to have heads that can only be described as bubbles. This tendency is to be seen already in PILATE; it is strengthened in the BURNING OF THE HOUSES (the crowd on the left) and in PHRYNE with its clustering heads. Here Turner seems to be reducing men to ciphers; but he is also defining them as a part of nature, momently hard to distinguish as they concentrate on some great point of attention or festivity. As these bubble-heads grow steadily more dominant through the 'forties, we can leave further discussion of them till we come to the later canvases.

As the explosive sunset of ULYSSES had opened the way for the work of the 'thirties, so now the great elegiac sky of the TÉMÉRAIRE drew together the achievements of the last decade and led into the full liberations of the 'forties. Here we find all the contrasts that Turner loved: contrast of warm and cold colours, which had a deep emotional significance for him – here the left side is cool, the right hand richly warm, with the pallor of moon and pearly-white of ship against the orange-reds of the sinking sun; contrast of tall whitely glowing ship and squat brown-black businesslike tug; contrast of old and new, of life and death, of death and rebirth. The ships with their forward-thrown reflections and the sunray over the

waters converge on the artist, the spectator. Then there are the
contrasts of the smoke-line from the tug and the ray bursting
out in the same sweep – while other rays are wheeling inside
the tunnel of recession centred on the sun, which is sinking
between the closing lines of the two shores. The verticals are
subtly held on the left by the moon and its reflection in the
water. Chiaroscuro is gone, even in the form in which it
existed in ULYSSES; depth, structure, all relationships are
expressed through colour.

The work is not simply an elegy over the days of sail. In
fact, from one angle Turner exalts the triumph of the industrial
world of steam-power over the handicraft world of the old
ships. The work is permeated with a sense of historical change,
of remorseless destruction and renewal. (The fact that the
heroic ship is being sold to private enterprise for profit links it
with William of Orange's ship.) But this representation of an
epoch is also an expression of Turner's own life, which began
when London was only an overgrown country town and ended
with the Crystal Palace Exhibition announcing the full advent
of industrialism. His own sense of mortality is merged with
the definition of history. We have seen how he had been
overwhelmed by a series of deaths – his father, Wells, Egremont, Chantrey. He hated to be reminded of his age. "He
would never tell his birthday. One who was a fellow-student
with him at the Academy, and his companion from boyhood,
once said to him, 'William, your birthday can't be far off:
when is it? I want to drink a glass of wine to my old friend.'
'Ah!' growled Turner, 'never mind that; leave your old friend
alone.'"

Turner and Carew were once fishing in the pond at Lord Egremont's
at Petworth, when Carew, in his blunt, honest, Irish way, broke
silence, and said: "Turner, they tell me you're very rich." Turner
chuckled and said, "Am I?" "Yes; everybody says so." "Ah!"
Turner replied, "I would give it all up to be twenty years of age
again." "What!" says the other, "do you like it so well as all that?"
"Yes, I do," was the reply.[19]

He was so attached to TÉMÉRAIRE that he refused to sell it or
put any price upon it. In a late notebook (?1848) a draft letter
to a publisher or engraver stated, "No considerations of
money or favour can induce me to lend my Darling again".

He was almost certainly referring to the TÉMÉRAIRE, of which the engraving by Willmore had been issued that year.[20]

He was now completely out of fashion. His increasing breadth of style with its use of colour as a constructive element was totally in opposition to the prevailing trend towards meticulous naturalism and smooth finish of surface, which was soon to issue in Pre-Raphealitism. The few artists who had tried to follow in his wake had long ago fallen far astern. More than ever he stood alone. More than ever he grew uncompromising. In SLAVERS at last the division between his private and his public work, his sketches or colour structures and his finished work, was ended. We shall see later how this step worked out. But we must note how already in PHRYNE he has discarded the dark foreground. Light and colour permeate all planes, and he uses what seem at a glance to be arbitrary zones or patterns. And we must glance at the complex of ideas behind SLAVERS.

In earlier pictures such as *Wreckers – coast of Northumberland*, exhibited in 1834, Turner had been content to treat rather similar subjects with a measure of detachment but here the bloodshot sea and the dark menacing sky (the force of which enables one to accept the almost comic ravenous sea creatures which so disturbed the young Thackeray) suggest that Turner was in this case deeply moved by the terrible nature of the event. The technique of this remarkable picture is very different from that of the paintings of the early 1830s with their relatively limited range of colour and tone. Here, over the usual white ground delicately glazed in blues and pinks, a far wider range of colours is applied in a much greater variety of handling, from glazes to thick impasto, producing the most various effects. The dark areas of sea, for instance, are achieved not only by the deep browns and blacks of *Staffa, Fingal's Cave* but by a multifarious and complex harmony of pure colours, built up in places to a considerable thickness.[21]

Eastlake, who must have known Turner's painting methods well, tells us, "He depended quite as much for his scumblings with white as on his glazings, but the softness induced by both was counteracted by a substructure of the most abrupt and rugged kind. The subsequent scrumbling, toned again in its turn, was the source of one of the many fascinations of this extraordinary painter, who gives us solid and crisp lights surrounded and beautifully contrasting with etherial nothingness, or with the semitransparent depth of alabaster." Here, in SLAVERS, though the composition is held together by the skyline and the sunflare up and down from it, this criss-cross structure appears only as a momentary stabilization of the turning vortex into which space and time have been violently transformed.

In 1840–1 slavery was at its last gasp in the British dominions. The Reformed Parliament of 1833 had abolished it, with a seven-year period of transition. However, the Commons, despite the Government's objections, voted to shorten the period, and in effect slavery in the West Indies ended in 1838. We have noted how important was the theme of anti-slavery in the poetic tradition which Turner cherished, from Thomson to Campbell – as well it might be. By the Treaty of Utrecht, Britain had forced France and Spain to allow her a virtual monopoly of the slave trade. On the many millions of negroes torn from Africa and carried inhumanly to America was mainly based Britain's commercial prosperity of the eighteenth century. Turner's theme was, then, not so anachronistic as might appear. (Slave systems still ruled in many parts of the U.S.A.) The full title of the picture was SLAVERS THROWING OVERBOARD THE DEAD AND DYING – TYPHON COMING ON; and the verses from the *Fallacies of Hope* ran:

> Aloft all hands, strike the top-masts and belay;
> Yon angry setting sun and fierce-edged clouds
>   Declare the Typhon's coming.
>   Before it strikes your decks, throw overboard
>   The dead and dying – ne'er heed their chains.
>   Hope, Hope, fallacious Hope!
>   Where is thy market now?

He was probably referring to the slave ship *Zong* of 1783; the negroes aboard were afflicted by an epidemic and Captain Collingwood threw the sick into the sea. The reason was that he could claim insurance for negroes lost at sea, not for those dying of disease. At his trial a shortage of water was pleaded; but the fact was that a storm, which would have replenished supplies, was coming up. The story, which Turner may have heard in his youth, was told in T. Clarkson's *History of the Abolition of the Slave Trade*, which, published in 1808, was reprinted in 1839. But, mixed with Turner's indignation at this story, is his memory of lines from Thomson's *Summer*:

> . . . In the dread ocean, undulating wide,
> Beneath the radiant line that girts the globe,
> The circling typhon, whirled from point to point,
> Exhausting all the rage of all the sky,
> And dire ecnephia reign . . .
>   A faint deceitful calm,
> A fluttering gale, the demon sends before
> To tempt the spreading sail. Then down at once
> Precipitant descends a mingled mass
> Of roaring winds and flame and rushing floods . . .

Thomson moves on to an account of how "the terrors of these storms" are increased by "the direful shark", and he depicts the wreck of a slave ship in which "one death involves tyrants and slaves" and the shark "dyes the purple seas with gore, and riots in the vengeful meal".[22]

Turner is recognizing that the guilt of the slave trade was something too vast to be wiped out by any belated act of Parliament. What he is expressing is the crisis of his society in 1840–1, which Carlyle had tried to sum up in *Chartism* (1839), with its realization that human relationships were being supplanted by the cash nexus. The slave trader and the shark are one; the "angry setting sun and fierce-edged clouds" are one with the whole threatening situation of discord. "Where is thy market now?" is the question aimed at the society of the cash nexus, which in its blindness cannot see the disaster it is bringing on itself.

Turner's slave ship thus belongs to the series of sunset ships which occur in eighteenth-century poetry and which find their culmination in Coleridge's *Ancient Mariner* (where the guilt-complex also has its roots in the slave trade via Newton's *Narrative*). Its sea is "the sea of blood" which also keeps appearing in that tradition and which is exemplified in these lines from Coleridge's *Religious Musings*:

> Haply from this some younger Angel now
> Looks down on Human Nature; and, behold!
> A sea of blood bestrewed with wrecks, where mad
> Embattling interests on each other rush.[23]

It was characteristic of Turner that he should find a great aesthetic release through an image which concentrated his social thinking and at the same time was deeply embedded in the poetic tradition he so loved.

The Angel looking down into the sea of blood suggests the later ANGEL IN THE SUN. Turner saw in the ominous red of sunset a tinge of blood. The "sea of blood" appeared directly in his verses for WAR; and in a fairly early drawing of water (barges), church tower, amid distant foliage, and sunset, he wrote above the sun, "Fire and Blood". On another sunset sketch he wrote on the clouds below the sun, "Orpiment and blood". Ruskin, who noted the sympathetic relation between the dying rays of the sun and the ebbing life of the wounded Procris in the *Liber*, said also of a late sketch in which a dog from a wrecked ship struggles on to the shore: "The dawn-clouds have the first scarlet upon them, a feeble tinge only, reflected with the same feeble blood-stain on the sand."

Chapter Sixteen

The 'Forties

IN 1842 an old scheme for issuing large engravings for Turner's works was revived. In April a Jersey lady reported that he had been "very ill; he is now better, but it has shook him a great deal. He is living by rule." Wanting some cash in hand, he chose some fifteen sketches of Switzerland and the Rhine, and asked Griffith to get him commissions for the finished drawings, Griffith did his best, but only managed to sell nine.[1] At the Royal Academy Turner showed SNOW STORM, PEACE, and WAR. The full title of the first was SNOW STORM – STEAMBOAT OFF A HARBOUR'S MOUTH MAKING SIGNALS IN SHALLOW WATER AND GOING BY THE LEAD. THE AUTHOR WAS IN THIS STORM ON THE NIGHT THE ARIEL LEFT HARWICH. Ruskin had the following story from the Rev. Mr. Kingsley:

I had taken my mother and a cousin to see Turner's pictures, and as my mother knows nothing about art, I was taking her down the gallery to look at the large 'Richmond Park'; but as we were passing the "Snow storm", she stopped before it, and I could hardly get her to look at any other picture; and she told me a good deal more about it than I had any notion of, though I have seen many snow-storms. She had been in such a scene on the coast of Holland during the war. When, some time afterwards, I thanked Turner for his permission for her to see the pictures, I told him that he would not guess what had caught my mother's fancy, and then named the picture;

"I did not paint it to be understood, but I wished to show what such a scene was like. I got the sailors to lash me to the mast to observe it. I was lashed for four hours, and I did not expect to escape; but I felt bound to record it if I did. But no one had any business to like the picture."

"But", said I, "my mother once went through just such a scene, and it brought it all back to her."

"Is your mother a painter?"

"No."

"Then she ought to have been thinking of something else."

These were nearly his words. I observed at the time he used "record" and "painter", as the title "author" had struck me before.

Ruskin also mentions that Turner spent the evening at his father's house after critics had called the picture a mass of "soapsuds and whitewash". After dinner, sitting in his armchair by the fire, Ruskin heard him mutter again and again, "Soapsuds and whitewash." At last he went to him, and asked why he minded what they said. Turner burst out, "Soapsuds and whitewash! What would they have? I wonder what they think the sea's like? I wish they'd been in it."[2]

This abusive description at which Turner so suffered became characteristic of the way his great works of the 'forties were treated for many long years. Hammerton in 1895 summed up the verdict that after 1838 Turner's work went to pieces. The paintings thereafter

belong not merely to a period of decline, but to a state of senile decrepitude. It is therefore both a waste of time and an offence against decency to criticise them with the frankness which we rightly use in speaking of work done in the maturity of the human faculties; and as criticism which is not frank can serve no useful purpose, it is better to pass these 'dregs of life and lees of man' in melancholy and respectful silence.

And Finberg in 1910 wrote: "In the whole history of pictorial art we have never had quite the same display of senile apathy gilded and transformed by the dying shafts of an incommensurable natural capacity."

The jokes about his work even reached the pantomime stage. Wyke Bayliss tells us that when first he became a student, about 1841, he saw a pantomime scene with the setting of a Strand art shop. A crowd gather to look at the Turner in the window, all crimson, gold and white. A baker's boy enters with a tray of confectionery, trips, and falls into the window, going headfirst through the Turner. Out rushes the dealer in dismay, but he sees the tray, which, about the same size as the ruined canvas, is a mess of red and yellow

jam tarts. He sprinkles some flour over it, puts it in the frame
and produces a Turnerian harmony. A connoisseur enters and
buys it for £1,000.

About this time Turner bought back from Campbell the
twenty drawings he had made for his *Poems*. Campbell, hard
up and unable to get a good price for them, met Turner and
told him that he was going to auction them; so Turner bought
them. Redding, who heard the story from the poet, assumed
at first that Turner didn't want the drawings to come on to the
market, then felt that he had quite possibly acted out of a
"desire to befriend Campbell. He was just the character to do
such an act silently, and bluntly."[3] Near the end of May,
Turner wrote to Clara, "I expected to have intercepted you
at the Ex[hibition] but another mishap occurred in the morning to see in the Gazette Messrs. Finden's Bankruptcy – Woe
is me – one failure after another, is quite enough to make one
sick of the whole concern."[4] Two of his large water-colours
had been engraved for Finden's *Royal Gallery*, but not yet
published.

On 1 August he was at Liége on his way to Lucerne with
"friends wishing to get onward to the Rhine with all possible
speed". He crossed the St. Gothard; and was probably back
in October.[5]

That month a whale of $14\frac{1}{2}$ feet appeared off Deptford and
was dispatched by four watermen, who displayed it to the
public. Turner, with his keen interest in all marine matters,
probably went to see the whale, or heard about it, and may
have gained the first stimulations for his whaling pictures of
1845–6. His memory of the Deptford whale was given a new
life by reading accounts of whaling in the northern seas.

Ruskin had taken his degree in 1842. His mother wanted
him to be a clergyman; his father thought he would win fame
as poet or artist. In 1843 he was at work on the first volume of
Modern Painters, which had grown out of a fresh desire to
defend Turner, this time against an attack he read on his way
to study geology at Chamonix. The book was rejected by
Murray on the ground that the public "cared little about
Turner", but was published in May by Smith, Elder and Co,
as by "A Graduate of Oxford". At first it attracted little
attention, but by the autumn it had begun to have some effect.
Ruskin had felt much trepidation as to Turner's reactions.

When on 24 February he called on him, he records, Turner "insisted on my taking a glass of wine, but I wouldn't; excessively good-natured today. Heaven grant he may not be mortally offended with the work!"[6] And indeed there was much in it that Turner did not like: for instance, the neglect and rather low opinion of his earlier works, the polemical tone in general. He did not want an exaltation of his own art to depend on depreciation of other artists. Ruskin had felt it necessary to treat Claude in a cavalier way. Further, Turner knew that Ruskin had not penetrated into the deeper meanings of his imagery and that he was often confused as to the relations of art and nature. Still, the work had its nobility (especially in the later volumes, published after Turner's death); and it was fitting that what might be called one of the two or three foundation-stones of modern art criticism came about as a tribute to Turner.[7]

The new group of buyers who came up after Ruskin's work were members of the post-Reform middle class, exemplified by Gillott, the manufacturer of steel pens who turned into an art dealer with large sums of money at his disposal. Thackeray in 1845 contrasted the liberality of the new patrons with the niggardliness of the illustrious, who at the moment were making poor payments to artists for decorating the summerhouses in Buckingham Palace – while, at Prince Albert's blushing instigation, Etty's fresco was being hacked out of the palace wall.

But the new dealers and buyers belonged to a middle class that was very different from that which over the generations had supported the advanced realist and romantic positions from Thomson and Hogarth onwards. A vital element had been lost with political success. The winning of Reform had brought about a split in the radical movement, with the active sections passing over to the new threatening working class and its Chartist demands. Turner was a survivor from a dead world. The death of the deep element of dissidence and revolt which had underlain the Romantic Movement meant a surrender to philistine sentimentality, naturalistic triviality, and the rest of Victorian falsifications of art and life – with the Aesthetic Movement coming up as a weak and one-sided attempt at resistance. Ruskin and William Morris carried on as prophets of doom, but could not affect the alienating trends. Turner could not be understood in such a world; he could have no progeny.

In the Royal Academy, Turner had WALHALLA, SUN OF VENICE, and the two Deluge pictures dedicated to Goethe. The verses for the SUN OF VENICE directly attached the picture to the tradition of the sunset ship of doom. Returning from Switzerland, he found that Ruskin's book had had a certain effect on buyers, who were inquiring about his unsold pictures.[8]

The winter again made him suffer. A letter written at the Athenaeum Club and posted late at night on Monday, 12 February 1844, to Clara, said that he had meant to call and see her on Sunday, "but the Evening beat me. Time always hangs hard upon me, but his auxiliary Dark weather has put me quite into the background altho before Xmas I conceived myself in advance of Mr. Time." He apologized for "my engagements with the RA, which I really do dread. However I have got a Macintosh and with some fur round the shoulders I hope to fare better betwixt the heat and the cold. If not I will give in for every one feels the varieties of temperature in the Life Academy to be very bad."[9]

On 4 March he dined with John Murray in Albemarle Street. Lockhard and his daughter, vainly worshipped by Ruskin, were there, and Elizabeth Rigby, later Lady Eastlake. The latter wrote in her diary that Turner was "a queer little being, very knowing about the castles he had drawn – a cynical kind of body, who seems to love his art for no other reason than because it is his own. Lockhard grew black as thunder when Turner was pertinacious and stupid, and looked as if he could have willingly said, 'You blockhead.'" Two days later she saw some of his drawings of the Seine, and commented: "He does much as he likes with the brush, and if his likíngs are sometimes beyond our comprehension, this is perhaps our fault. He can never be vulgar, if vulgar means common, for his faults are as rare as his beauties." Some sort of intuitive contact seems to have been established between her and Turner. It was for her he called in his last words.[10]

An interesting example of the way that Turner turned compliments wittily aside appears in Ruskin's record of a call on 13 April. "I said the worst of his pictures was one could never see enough of them. 'That's part of their quality,' said Turner." He pretended that Ruskin was referring to their indistinctness.[11]

He had seven pictures at the Academy show, one of which was RAIN, STEAM AND SPEED, and by chance we know of its genesis. Lady Simon, an old friend of Ruskin, was travelling in the same compartment of the Exeter–London train as an old gentleman. He asked permission to lower the window as the train was passing through Maidenhead. Rain was falling in torrents, but for fully nine minutes he exposed his head and shoulders to its full violence, then leaned back with closed eyes to memorize. Lady Simon thought him a paternal old fellow with the most wonderful eyes she had ever seen, eyes that luminously, kindly, and inoffensively perused her face. Next year she saw the painting at the Royal Academy and knew that the old man was Turner.

At the end of July Stanfield took Turner to the dinner given to Dickens before he left for Italy. The day was sultry, but Turner sat, says Forster, "in a huge red belcher-handkerchief which nothing would induce him to remove. He was not otherwise demonstrative, but enjoyed himself in a quiet silent way, less perhaps at the speeches than at the changing lights on the river."[12] Thornbury remarks that about 1843, when Ruskin had been "heralding Turner as the apostle of nature", he was noticed on a Margate steamer, eating shrimps out of an immense red silk handkerchief laid across his knees. "An apostle, surely," said a bystander, "in the strangest guise."

One of the friends he was now visiting was Mrs. Moore, a surgeon's widow, who gave him the name of Mr. Avalanche Jenkinson.[13] We find him excusing himself from staying at what seems a summer-house she had taken, as he was going to Switzerland. But he found that country in a disturbed state: "a cauldron of squabbling, political or religious," he told Hawksworth Fawkes. "The Rains came on early and I could not cross the Alps – twice I tried was sent back, with a wet jacket and worn out boots." He got his boots "heel-tapped" and "march'd up some of the small valleys of the Rhine and found them more interesting than I expected".[14] He was back by October; for on the 8th he saw Louis Philippe land at Portsmouth on a visit to Victoria. On the 17th he and Ruskin were at Griffith's, and he brought himself for the first time to thank Ruskin for his book. "Boy-like", says Ruskin, "he said he would give sixpence to find the Harley Street gates shut; but on our reaching the door, vow'd he'd be damned if we shouldn't come in and have some sherry. We were compelled to obey, and so drank healths again, exactly as the clock struck one, by the light of a single tallow candle in the under room – the wine, by-the-bye, first-rate." It was probably at this time he told Ruskin that he had been too hard on his brother artists because he didn't know how difficult art was.[15]

About this time J. A. Hammersley, an assistant teacher at the Government School of Design, called on him. He waited in a "cold and cheerless" dining-room. Then he heard "a shambling, slippered footstep down a flight of stairs – slow, measured". The door opened. "I, nobody, stood face to face with, to my thinking, the greatest man living. I shall attempt no description; you know how he looked. I saw at once his height, his breadth, his loose dress, his ragged hair, his indifferent quiet – all, indeed, that went to make his physique and some of his mind; but, above all, I saw, felt (and still feel) his penetrating grey eye!" They went and looked at the pictures, which were mostly "covered with uncleanly sheets or cloths". Turner was taciturn, but chatty enough not to seem inattentive or discourteous. Hammersley came again on 26 November, only for ten minutes. Turner was extremely taciturn and restless, "and occasionally clutched a letter which he held in his hand. I feared to break the dead silence, varied only by the slippered scrape of Turner's feet as he paced from end to end the dim and dusty apartment. At last he stood abruptly, and turning to me, said, 'Mr. Hammersley, you *must* excuse me; I cannot stay another moment; the letter I hold in my hand has just been given to me, and it announces the death of my friend Callcott.' He said no more; I saw his fine grey eyes fill as he vanished. I left at once."[16]

On 28 December, writing to H. Fawkes to thank him for the Yorkshire Pie that came as a customary Christmas gift, he said that the pie was "equal good to the Olden-time" of Hannah's culinary exploits. "The rigours of winter begin to tell upon me, cough colds and more acted upon by the change of weather than when we used to trot about at Farnley – but it must be borne – with all the thanks DUE – for such a lengthened period."[17]

In 1845 he was on the Royal Academy Council.[18] When

Shee's health failed he was voted into the Chair; he was also on the Hanging Committee. He showed six works: two Whalers and four of Venice, including contrasted pairs, indeed a fourfold sequence, Evening, Morning, Noon, and Sunset. Unfortunately only the title *Fallacies of Hope* was given in the catalogue. After the Academy Dinner he seems to have been out of sorts; he apologized for not going to a dinner. "I feel the sad necessity of leaving Town tomorrow." He probably went to Margate, then across the Channel to Boulogne. By mid-May he was back.[19]

The Royal Academy was having trouble in finding a suitable President. The younger section wanted Eastlake, whom many Academicians disliked. Shee was persuaded to withdraw his resignation, and Turner, in fact, did the work. His position as Deputy-President worried Hall, a strong Eastlake supporter. He admitted Turner's genius; but there "the merit of Mr. Turner begins and ends". Shee had had all that Turner lacked, "learning, courtesy, polished manners, liberality of mind and feeling, powers of eloquence, and a most bland and persuasive address"; he was "a gentleman in the best sense of the term". But "we shall be agreeably disappointed if we find there is even one of the presidential duties to which Mr. Turner is as adequate. He has, indeed, one qualification which, in England, outbids the best: Mammon is ever lord of the ascendant in this country – and Mr. Turner is prodigiously rich."[20]

As a result, Turner could not go touring till September. Then he crossed to Dieppe and roamed along the shores of Picardy on the trail of "storms and shipwrecks". He was back in October, once more presiding over Council meetings.[21]

He was at the Ruskins' New Year party in 1846 and must have discussed his will with the elder Ruskin, a capable wine-merchant. In a note thanking him for a fishing card and "for sending us all home", he added, "I haven't yet been able to see Mr. Harpur but trust to do so soon." Harpur, his solicitor, had drawn up some of the codicils.[22] Still Deputy-President, he showed six pictures at the Royal Academy, including ANGEL IN THE SUN. Miss Rigby went to the Exhibition on 5 May: "A mighty world: Turner living by the grace of Art. Turner proves how vulgar we are." On the 20th she went to Queen Anne Street. "The door was opened by a hag of a woman, for whom one hardly knew what to feel most, terror or pity – a hideous woman is such a mistake. She showed us into a dining-room, which had penury and meanness written on every wall and article of furniture. Then into the gallery; a fine room – indeed, one of the best in London, but in a dilapidated state; his pictures the same. The great RISE OF CARTHAGE all mildewed and flaking off; another with all the elements in an uproar, of which I incautiously said: 'The End of the World, Mr. Turner?' 'Nó, ma'am; Hannibal crossing the alps.' "[23]

On 29 August he signed a codicil appointing Hannah and Mrs. Booth joint Custodians and Keepers of the Gallery of Foundation described in his will, giving each of them a yearly sum of £150, and making them Residuary Legatees. The worsening health that had prompted him to the codicil made him wish to have Mrs. Booth closer at hand than Margate. Despite his dislike of any step that might bring the curious eyes of the world peering in at his windows, he decided to bring her to London. Hearing that Etty was going to vacate his top-floor apartment in Buckingham Street, Strand, and retire to York, he went along to see him. Etty records for 3 September that as he was going out he met Turner coming down the street. "I made him turn back; as he was coming to see me. He had heard that I was going to establish a School in York! and wanted to know what apartments I had. I thought he meant in York. Not! not so! *here*. He liked my view; and seemed a little disappointed I was not going sooner. However, he was very good, drank a glass of wine; and, I believe *sincerely* wished me well, wherever I went; said he should be sorry." The view reached from Lambeth to Westminster and must have also thought that such an address would put him at the mercy of callers. So he arranged instead to take 6 Davis Place, Cremorne New Road, now incorporated in 118–19 Cheyne Walk, Chelsea, in Mrs. Booth's name. The house faced south, on a bend of the river. He built a sort of gallery on the roof; and from that and his bedroom window he could look on the flowing waters. It was also useful for observing the Vauxhall fireworks.[24] In a note to Ruskin on 3 December he stated, "I think I am better and looking forward towards the end of this month to be relieved from the unpleasant duty of acting (Pro Pre) at the Royal Academy." He refused re-election

as Auditor: a post he had held since 1824. Much of his physical
trouble around this period seems to have come from the loss
of his teeth. The Rev. W. Kingsley, in his notes on Ruskin's
collection of drawings, speaks of his weakening powers. "The
cause was the loss of his teeth: Cartwright did his best to
make him a set of false ones, but the tenderness of the gums
did not allow him to make use of them; so his digestion gave
way and he suffered much from this to the end of his life." A
surgeon dentist and cupper, W. Bartlett, of 15 Park Place
South, Park Walk, Chelsea, was called in to supply him with a
set of teeth. "But he never told me his real name; he went by
the name of 'Booth'. There was nothing about the House at all
to indicate the abode of an artist. The Art Journal and Illustrated London News were always on the Table. He was
very fond of smoking and yet had a great objection to any
one knowing of it. His diet was principally at that time rum
and milk. He would take some times two quarts of milk per
day and rum in proportion, very frequently to excess." He
adds, "During his illness I saw him 3 or 4 times a day and he
offered should he recover to take me on the continent and
shew me all the places he had visited."[25]

In 1847 he seems to have spent much time, perhaps from
July to October, at Margate and Ramsgate. In his last sketchbook he struggled to work out a poem on Hero and Leander.
"There on the lonely shore the bold brave Lover stands." We
can make out references to the pale strand, the lamp, the
distant shore, death, the lover's toil. "The refluent wave fell
sluggish on the beach." "On the lone beach beyond the hour
Stand, and on the Horizons rim" the waves, it seems, rise and
fall, replacing one another. About the same time a drawing
shows a man on a jetty looking sadly across at the sunset.[26]
A drafted letter mentions: "am so ill that [I am not] disposed
to write". However, he attended general meetings at the
Royal Academy in November and December, and wrote to
thank H. Fawkes for "the three PPP viz. Pie Phea and Pud."
(He ironically refers to Ruskin as the Under Graduate of
Oxford.)[27]

In 1848 he added two more codicils to the will, dealing
mainly with his finished pictures, which were to go to the
National Gallery if a special Gallery were built for them
within five years of his Queen Anne Street lease expiring. If

the Gallery were not built, the gift lapsed. Griffith and Ruskin were added to the trustees.[28] In the autumn he got £550 for half an acre of Twickenham land from the South-Western Railway Company. The Company had wanted only a few square yards; but Thomas Williams, steward of the Duke of Northumberland, acted so capably for him that they had to buy the whole piece. (One wonders if this Williams was the Thomas Williams, attorney, who had rented 46 Upper John Street.)[29]

Ruskin had married his cousin in April, and in October he settled into his own house. He probably saw a fair amount of Turner till he went abroad next April. Turner seems to have had an intuition of the marriage's unhappy future; and, probably in a moment of sherry-warmed musing, he wrote in November from the Athenaeum a brief note, which may be either sardonic or genuinely pleading: "My dear Ruskin!!! Do let us be happy Yours most truly and sincerely JMW Turner." (He had a trick of putting exclamations before instead of after a passage.) Thornbury remarks, "Latterly, Turner was always to be seen between ten and eleven at the Athenaeum, discussing his half-pint of sherry. As his health failed, he became very talkative after his wine and rather dogmatic."[30]

He seems indeed in these last years to have been drinking too much. W. Kingsley says that as his digestion failed, "he had to have recourse to stimulants, and finally took too much. I wanted him to come and stay with me in Cambridge and he told me he could not, because he 'was so nasty in his eating, the only way he could live being by sucking meat'." Thornbury further tells us, "At one time Turner frequented at night the Yorkshire Stingo; but he abandoned it on being recognized by a friend. No one before that had observed the little man in the corner." One wonders, then, how it was known he had frequented the place. "A friend of mine remembers seeing him often rather the worse for grog at Offley's, in Henrietta-street, at the time Macready was bringing out the "Tempest". Turner was a great theatre-goer at the time, and was very indistinctly voluble on the subject of Shakespeare, and Macready's scenic effects." It would be pleasant if we could trust this statement and imagine Turner enjoying Macready as Prospero (one of his major roles); he may well have felt in the *Tempest* his own mood of a magician renouncing his magics.[31]

The Chelsea house lay between a boat-builder, Alexander, and two beer-retailers, to whom in an expansive moment Mrs. Booth confessed that her husband was, in fact, a notability.[32] We catch a glimpse of the Booths from the account taken by the Pennells from the artist Greaves, whose father had been a waterman:

Greaves' father knew Turner and used to row him about just as the son rowed Whistler. Turner used to walk about Chelsea with Mrs. Booth who was a big loud coarse Scotchwoman, and he would ask Greaves what kind of a day it would be. If he thought it would be fine they would go off, often being rowed over to Battersea church or the fields which are now Battersea Park. If it was not fine, he would say, "Well, Mrs. Booth, we won't go far." Turner wanted to buy the house from Mrs. Booth which Greaves says he had papered with drawings but apparently there were what he calls "private affairs" between her, Turner, and the other old woman from Queen Square and it never came off. Greaves does not remember Turner but he does remember Mrs. Booth of whom when a boy, he was much afraid. Whistler, always reviled Turner.[33]

Thornbury tells us that Turner was here known to the street boys as Puggy Booth, and to the tradesmen as Admiral Booth. The tale went round that he was an admiral in reduced circumstances.[34]

Another glimpse is given us by Francis Sherrell (who did not die till 1916, at Thanet). He got to know Turner through his brother at Chelsea, who acted as the artist's barber. The brother chose a suitable moment to ask Turner to have a look at Francis's drawings. Turner decided that the lad had talent and agreed to give him lessons in return for various services. Sherrell describes him mixing his chromes in a bucket with his own hands, and daubing it on the canvas with his hands when laying the foundations of trees. A caller once claimed to be an artist. "Show me your hands," said Turner gruffly. They were spotlessly clean. "Turn the fellow out," Turner whispered; "he's no artist."[35] Mrs. Booth's son he helped to be trained as an engraver.

In February 1849, in another codicil, he limited the time in which the National Gallery could get his works to ten years after his death. In all these later codicils there was no mention of Evelina and Georgianna. The latter was dead before the

Chancery suit concerning his will came on. She was probably
dead now; but Evelina was still alive, no doubt abroad with
her husband at Tripoli (1825–34) and Sfax (1836–42). Turner
could not have seen much of her; he seems to have closed her
and Dupuis out of his mind. As we know nothing of the
details of his break with Sarah Danby, we cannot say whether
he treated her badly or not. On the face of the evidence – the
small annuity and its cancellation – he seems to have behaved
coldly and callously. But it is possible that he settled money
on her before or after the break. With his dislike of publicity,
such a step was more likely than the bequest of a large sum
in a will. However, it seems clear that after Evelina was
married he considered himself free of responsibility for her.
Perhaps he felt towards her and Georgianna some of the
bitterness that doubtless accumulated during the failure of
his relations with their mother.[36]

In December, writing to thank Farnley for Christmas fare,
he said that his health was on the wane. "I cannot bear the
same fatigue, or have the same bearing against it, I formerly
had – but time and tide stop not – but I must stop writing
for to-day." The same letter shows him interested in the
revolutionary situation in Rome and the French assault,
having heard an eyewitness account. He was mainly worried
about any damage to works of art. "Had the 'Transfiguration'
occupied its old situation, the St. Pietro Montoreo, it most
possibly must have suffered, for the church is completely
riddled with shot and balls. The convent on Mount Aventine
much battered with cannon balls, and Casino Magdalene,
near the Porto Angelino, nearly destroyed, occurred by taking
and storming the Bastion No. 8."[37] If the events of 1848-9
had occurred during his more active years, we can be sure he
would have been stirred into the creation of symbolic images
expressive of vast upheavals.

In his Chelsea cottage he painted his last four works for the
Royal Academy, which were shown in 1850. Here he returned
to the tale of Dido and Aeneas. The theme was the betrayal of
love by Aeneas at the bidding of the gods, so that he might
continue with a greater purpose: the sacrifice of love for what a
man considers his duty in life, because love is felt to be divert-
ing him from his all-consuming goal. He thus ends his art in
meditations on the Cave-Grotto of poetry and of treacherous

mating; and the constancy of his mind in such matters is underlined by his having shown in 1846 at the British Institute QUEEN MAB'S CAVE, with two citations: "Frisk it, frisk it, by the Moonlight beam", *Midsummer Night's Dream* (though no such line occurs in the play), "Thy Orgies, Mab, are manifold", *MSS Fallacies of Hope*. He is thus conceiving the Cave as the place of transformation through the embrace of love, where man is revealed in his animal nature and yet where the ass-headed boor can masquerade as a comely fascinating person.[38]

Turner's work was now finished, and we must return and consider what he had achieved during the 'forties. This decade was one of ceaseless and desperate social struggle, with a threat of large-scale violence every now and then rising up. In *Past and Present*, 1843, Carlyle saw it as a time "when a world, not yet doomed for death, is rushing down to ever-deeper Baseness and Confusion", and cried out, "Oh, if the accursed invisible Nightmare, that is crushing out the life of us and ours, would take a shape; approach us like the Hyrcanian tiger, the Behemoth of Chaos, the Archfiend himself; in any shape that we could see, and fasten on." He himself saw this pervasive intangible evil as the impersonal cash nexus replacing humanly responsible relationships; Turner, with his acute sense of crisis pressures, was seeking for cataclysmic imagery to express the "invisible Nightmare", perhaps in the Whale seeing a Behemoth of Chaos, certainly in sea-storm, in mingling fire and water, in deluge, in apocalyptic angel, and in sunset demon focusing his emotions of disquiet and doom, both general and personal. The vortex-freedom established in SLAVERS is carried on in ROCKETS AND BLUE LIGHT, SNOW STORM, YACHT APPROACHING COAST. The vortex now rules, and controls all forms and colours. There is a rich and yet simple aesthetic unity of a kind never dreamed of before in paint, and which derives in the last resort from two factors: his elimination of all intellectualized attitudes from the treatment of colour, and a realization of the pure identity of colour and light; his concentration on essential structures of movement, which are to be seen most powerfully in wind and water, but which dominate and control all forms. Even man-made forms are fused with the dynamic world in which they live and with which they struggle.

The use of zones of light and shade, warm and cool colour, often without any obvious naturalistic explanation, plays a key-part in this definition, and has certain affinities with the use of planes by Cézanne and later the Cubists. But the arrangement is not arbitrary or merely formal, nor is it primarily concerned with an analysis of the structuration of space. It is above all dynamic, linked with a profound grasp of the nature of process, movement in its fullness, violent and elemental tension. Naturalism is dispensed with in terms of a deep vision of reality, of the dynamic and fluid nature of matter and all its forms, and of the dialectical relation of the components form-colour and colour-form. Drawing in the old sense is equally thrown over; for structure is realized, not in abstraction, but as an aspect of a world of ceaseless change. The promise of a new vortex-vision, given its first full expression by HANNIBAL, is brought to its logical conclusions.

The human aspect may, however, seem to have been discarded. This is so, in a sense. But from a deeper viewpoint we may claim that the form of vision itself represents a higher level of humanity, something which transcends the levels at which the fallacies of hope operate. Man can now be present only as a pure potentiality: the artist who is able to penetrate into quite new secrets of movement and transformation. We may then correctly say there is a symbolist element. Only the artist with his control over the image of change survives as the magician of mysterious power. But at the same time, to the extent that reality is truly pierced and concretely apprehended in a new unified grasp of process, all men are implicated in the potentialities opened up.

The division between water-colours and oils now closes, too. The technique of some of the late oils is practically identical with that of the water-colours of the same period, both in the way that fine washes are used and that detail is suggested.

In the watercolours resulting from his third visit to Venice of 1840 and those of Swiss and German subjects made during the early 1840s the pigment is floated over the surface of the paper to give a transparent pearly effect, and over this is often superimposed a multitude of rapid pen-strokes in undiluted reds or greens to give an impression of detailed form . . . In a number of the Swiss and

German scenes, such as *Rheinfelden*, this method gives a gothic fairy-tale effect appropriate to the subject, but in others it is nervous and distracting. Turner's use of a similar technique in many of his late oils, involving red or blue calligraphy over thin, light glazes, likewise met with varying success.[39]

In his Venetian works he went on driving up the tonality into yet greater lightness, with whites, light blues and pinks setting the key. Signs of his weakening appear in the way that yellow tends to get out of control in his latest works, and distracting aspects such as those mentioned above are to be found. Among the English scenes, RAIN, STEAM AND SPEED is outstanding. It has been contrasted with both the detailed naturalism of Frith's *Railway Station* of 1862, and Monet's *Saint-Lazare* of 1877 with its scientifically precise vision of how things seem.[40] Turner is concerned with grasping the essentials, not only of appearances, but of movement and dynamic structure. RAIN, STEAM AND SPEED brings out clearly the way in which he expressed Time as a necessary aspect of his grasp of a changing universe. The forward rush of the engine is expressed by making the engine darker in tone and sharper in edge than any other object, so that it shoots out in aerial perspective ahead of its place in linear perspective.[41] Thus oppositions in tone and line are used to express succession in time. A careful examination would show that he uses the mingling or superimposition of different moments in order to give his significant works a direction in time as well as a pattern of tensional movements in space. The sunset darkens as we look at it; the dawnlight whitens and deepens. Ruskin says well of the TÉMÉRAIRE:

That picture will not, at the first glance deceive as a piece of actual sunlight; but this is because there is in it more than the sunlight, because under the glazing veil of vaulted fire which lights the vessel on her last path, there is a blue, deep, desolate hollow of darkness, out of which you can hear the voice of the night wind, and the dull boom of the disturbed sea; because the cold deadly shadows of twilight are gathering through every sunbeam, and moment by moment as you look, you will fancy some new film and faintness of the night has risen over the vastness of the departing form.[42]

Ruskin's poetic rhetoric is simply true. But the effects are gained, as they only can be in a painting, by methods of paint – by the particular forms of gradation and of broken, merged,

or contrasted colours. Ruskin himself, discussing the problems
of painting a mountain against light, remarks:

Turner only would give the uncertainty; the palpitating, perpetual
change: the subjection of all to a great influence, without one part
or portion being lost or merged in it; the unity of action with
infinity of agent. And I wish to insist on this the more particularly,
because it is one of the eternal principles of nature, that she will
not have one line or colour, nor one portion or atom of space,
without a change in it. There is not one of her shadows, tints, or
lines that is not in a state of perpetual variation: I do not mean in
time, but in space.[43]

He is wrong, however, in the last words. The variation is also
in time, and that is precisely what Turner understood and
defined. He knew how to merge the successive effects of a
scene before him so that the changes were not observed and
transferred in abstraction, but as aspects of an irreversible
universe.

The sea-pieces of the same year as RAIN, STEAM AND SPEED
resumed the picking-up of the Dutch tradition of the early
1830s, but in terms of the new vision and its methods of
painting. PEACE has a great glow at the centre, contrasted with
the ringing whites and blue-greys, and with the stark black
sails – their angular patterns repeated in felucca and low-
flying bird. Across the clear pattern trails the diagonal of
smoke, of human transience.[44] The Artist returns to Nature;
this funeral moment of secure balances and contrasts is also
the expression of a Peace beyond Understanding. WAR with
its figure of Napoleon and its bloody sunset was ridiculed, but
it aptly supplements PEACE. Its verses were the best that
Turner ever wrote:

> Ah! thy tent-formed shell is like
> A soldier's nightly bivouac, alone
> Amidst a sea of blood –
> – but you can join your comrades.

He compactly defines his symbolism. The soldier sees in the
sunset his field of battle; the rock limpet is a tent, but by his
actions he has cut himself off from humanity. He is alienated,
"alone, amidst a sea of blood". The limpet, however, in its
innocence is still an integrated part of nature. Wilkie as the
artist who has fulfilled himself becomes a living part of that

nature in the consecrated moment of death; Napoleon is condemned to be alone and for ever alienated.

We can perhaps link with the vortex-impulsion the tendency to a certain kind of impressionism. "Indistinctness is my forte," he is said to have remarked. His contemporaries saw all this as a mere loss of form, a kind of blurred chaos; but, in fact, the forms were merged in a new conception of air, light, and process. They were not lost; they were realized in new ways. Forms in movement, in change, cannot have the same sort of coherence as forms in static positions. Turner's concept of dynamic unity, of the relation of the pictorial image to actual optic processes, and his concept of form as something in ceaseless elemental change, came together to produce his "indistinctness", his refusal to accept the old lines of demarcation.

Certainly in many late canvases the storm of light penetrates all objects, all masses, and determines their volumes, their places in space, their planes; water, land, and sky in one sense become only variants of the enveloping light-energy. But I do not think we can describe this as a retreat to nothingness (as Hazlitt prophetically understood it). "Isn't it possible that he [Turner] saw the wraiths of landscape features" in a work like the late NORHAM CASTLE, it has been asked, "as objects that were disappearing rather than emerging? They look like the victims of an inundation of light as inexorable as a deluge. There is at least the possibility that they are the records of an exultant brush with nothingness."[45] The Castle is certainly coming up out of the deluge, reborn or purified as the earthly paradise. Turner had a special love of this scene, of which he made variants at different stages of his development. Once, passing by with Caddell, he took off his hat to the view. "Oh! I made a drawing of Norham several years ago; it took, and from that day to this, I have had as much to do as my hands could execute." He was referring to the water-colour of 1798, showing the Castle in "Summer's morn". In his final return to the scene Turner sought to give it an accolade of sheer transformation; he compressed the features, raising up the hills – partly, perhaps, for increased dignity, but also to enable the spectator to feel more the dive down and up into light which was so characteristic of him. In his later work, if he is not directly depicting the forms and tensions of elemental violence, he is driven to depict a paradisaic earth in which the tensions of light-energy compose the forms. What we see is a field of force, but one which is assembling and constructing life out of its minute gradations, its overall movement from complex asymmetries into a new controlling symmetry. Or, rather, the forms tremble on the edge of this new system; and this is what gives the definite but indefinable effect of irreversible time – something which so far Turner alone of artists has been able to master.

One effect of the concentration on vortical or circling compositions was a tendency towards the use of square canvases instead of oblong or upright.[46] No doubt Turner had been helped in this by his work at vignettes for illustrating poems – though there the designs were relatively static and aimed at charm. The first related oils were rather similar in character: BACCHUS AND ARIADNE, DAWN OF CHRISTIANITY, GLAUVUS AND SCYLLA. He here began to feel that the octagon would better suit his purposes; thus, DAWN and BACCHUS show pencil lines marking out an octagonal space, and DAWN was completed as a circle. PEACE was again an irregular octagon, though the composition was not vortical. WAR resumed the vortex, as did the two Deluge pictures. Last in the series were THE ANGEL and UNDINE, which pair together with much the same colour contrasts as the Deluge couple.[47]

THE ANGEL and HURRAH of 1846 were his last fully realized paintings – though some slight weakenings can be noted. THE HERO OF A HUNDRED FIGHTS (ostensibly a representation of the casting of the Wellington statue) and WRECK BUOY were repaintings of earlier works, while the four Carthaginian works of 1850 were roughly painted in hot colours, all variations of a single composition. Now the vortex is in confusion, and the bubble-heads float about in a lost way. Even in HURRAH the heads of the rowers are bubble-egglomerations. This massing of bubble-heads, we noted, had already arrived in the 'thirties; but in the last decade we see its presence growing more general. It seems especially used to express a group united in a festival – as in HEIDELBERG, PHRYNE, VISIT TO THE TOMB – or in some common activity – HOUSES OF PARLIAMENT, HURRAH. And its culmination appears in THE MORNING of the Deluge pair. But to grasp all it means there we must consider Turner's relation to Goethe's Theory of Colours.[48]

Chapter Seventeen

The Theory of Colour

FROM Turner's own writings and from the evidence of his work it is clear that he gave an endless amount of thought to questions of colour: its general function, its poetic and emotional values, its harmonies and discords, and their relation to the phenomena he observed. He had carefully studied the laws of both perspective and the prismatic analysis; but in the last resort his use of colour was intuitive and he had no comprehensive theory. He had been brought up against the possibilities of such a theory by the works of George Field, especially his *Chromatics or, An Essay on the Analogy and Harmony of Colours*, 1817. Field was a colour-maker, and his broodings on harmony led him to develop a fully extended philosophy of analogical relations covering the whole universe. Despite his voluminous disquisitions he never makes his system quite clear; but it assumes a unitary process at work, inside which all things are connected by analogies or correspondences, and development occurs by some sort of triadic formation. The system is thus a sort of naïve and embryonic dialectics, but without any notion of growth through the fusion of opposites. As one would expect, Field sees rather a series of reconciliations between opposites: subjective and objective, external and internal worlds, idealism and materialism. In his later writings he mentions Kant, but he does not seem to have known anything of Hegel.[1] Mind he sees as having three concurrent powers, consciousness, will, and understanding (agent, patient, and efficient), and three reciprocal faculties, reason, imagination, and memory. Memory is the passive receptacle, imagination generalizes or comprehends ("by the concurrence of the logical subject with medial or sensible objects"), and finally reason universalizes. Interestingly, he illustrates this system by citing Akenside:

> Her secret stores let Mem'ry tell;
> Bid fancy quit her fairy cell
> In all her colours drest;
> While, prompt her sallies to control,
> Reason, the judge, recalls the soul
> To Truth's severest test.

Turner was one of the subscribers to his *Outlines of Analogical Philosophy* in two volumes, 1839 – as well as Callcott, Edwin Landseer, Wilkie, Eastlake, Clarkson Stanfield, Etty, Beechey, Pyne, Reinagle, Cornelius Varley, Mulready. Field was certainly well known among artists, and the general influence of his thought must not be underestimated. His practical treatises, variously edited, continued to be published for many years after his death.

In *Chromatics* he claims "that colours have a science as distinct from any association with figures or forms, as that of musical sounds is from figurative language or poetry". And he states in italics, "the Chromatic system, like the universe is an absolute unity comprehending a relative infinity". But apart from his general analogical reasoning and his attempt to work out some colour triads or triangles, he has little to say that would be of practical use to an artist. He sent a copy of the book to Turner; and when they next met, says Trimmer, he asked his opinion. "You have not told us much," said Turner dryly.[2] The concision of the comment is ambiguous. Turner might mean that the book has nothing of interest to say, or that it is on the right lines as far as it goes, but fails to develop its concepts. What he was opposed to altogether was the notion of an abstract science of colour. Thornbury goes on:

Almost the last conversation Mr. Trimmer had with Turner was respecting colours, which were not considered by him to be reducible to scientific rules. He then called Field's book a fallacy. I told him [said Trimmer] that genius was acting by rules unconsciously, and that as canons of oratory had been deduced from Cicero's orations, of which he was not aware, his own pictures might form the basis of a scientific system of colouring. I have heard my friend Field say that Turner's most extravagant conceptions were in perfect harmony, but Nature in a very high key, as seen through a prism. He painted offhand, without the slightest effort, and produced the most inimitable effects. Constable used to say that an oil painter should never paint but in oils, and that Turner's pictures were only large water-colours. He tested this with a diminishing glass.

But Turner, though intensely opposed to any schematic analysis posing as a complete theory, was, in fact, always seeking to unite his practice with theoretical understandings. Thornbury, basing himself on remarks by Birch, stated that Thomson of Duddingston, with whom Turner went sketching, introduced him to a group at whose meetings "Turner would constantly battle with them upon the subject of light, trying to gain from Brewster and other *savans* something upon that subject. It is supposed that in this discussion upon these matters, he formed a theory which enabled him to create the varied effects that he has displayed in his works. It is said he carried the discussion to such a height with Brewster and Thomson that the subject was at length prohibited – and he then became more earnest to discover what combination of colour would produce light." Brewster, however, declared that he only met Turner once at an Edinburgh dinner, in 1834. "On that occasion he exhibited none of his pecularities." But Thornbury maintained that, even if Brewster was not one of the group among whom Turner discussed optics, the story in general was correct.[3]

Turner's interest in optics is proved by the lectures; a notebook gives his definition of colour: "Colour is a matterial [*sic*] substance indued with a quality of diversely affecting the Eye according to the matter wherein it is found."[4] This idea of colour as a *substance* is opposed to the ideas of Newton and Locke which dominated the eighteenth century, and according to which colour is a purely subjective impression. In the lines from *Fallacies of Hope* which he attached to THE FOUNTAIN OF FALLACY, 1839, he announced:

> Its rainbow-dew diffused fell in each anxious lip
> Working wild fantasy, imagining;
> First, Science in the immeasurable abyss of thought
> Measured her orbits slumbering.[5]

The (lost) painting appears to have been the same as THE FOUNTAIN OF INDOLENCE shown in 1834; perhaps he had worked over the canvas. Critics spoke of it as delightful, showing a warm and mellow happiness. There is, perhaps, a close link with the Fountain in Thomson's poem, which sends out a "drizzly dew" of Nepenthe, "sweet oblivion of vile earthly care, Fair gladsome waking thoughts and joyous dreams more fair". Turner's title shows it as the spring of fallacious hopes, and his verses link its scattering irridescent dew with the prismatic analysis of light. The next two lines, which might have come direct from one of Blake's accounts of Urizen, leap straight to a picture of the Newtonian demiurge engaged in measuring what cannot be measured, applying rules of quantity to a world of quality. It is hard to be quite sure in such a compressed verse-statement, but Turner seems to be pairing off "wild fantasy" (art as the mere embodiment of the pleasure-principle, divorced from the struggle to grasp reality in its fullness) with quantitative science, which reduces the concrete world of experience to a mere wraith. Wild fantasy and slumbering Science are then seen as the divided halves of alienated man.

In his Fifth Lecture he makes some attempt to deal with the various uses of Colour. He says that form has mostly constituted the character of the Masters, "and colouring that of the different schools of each master" as well as being used to express particular emotions or "sentiments." For instance, Yellow has been taken to Express Glory; Blue, Duty; Red, Power; "Author[it]ative Purple, Green Servitude; as compounds, they must be left with those who framed them." (I take this to mean: Let the propounders of such theories explain all the complicated meanings of graduated colour-effects.) He writes at the side, in pencil and ink: "Emblematical and Typical Illusions" and "Emblematical Conceats and Typical Allusions" – an example of the puzzles produced by his way of spelling. He probably intends "illusions" as he sometimes spells that word with an *a*.

He then goes on to discuss "tone or straight" of colour. "Comparatively, Red possesses the utmost power of attracting vision: it being the first ray of Light, received and the first which acknowledges the dimension of light, tho it is a shade to Yellow as Blue is to Red; thus far as [to] primitive strength."

In aerial perspective "yellow would be medium; Red material; Blue, distance: White in prismatic order is the union." He seems to say that the mixture of the broken-up aspects of light provides "our material colors," and in the end "becomes the opposite Darkness. Light is therefore Color, and Shadow the Privation of it by the removal of these rays of Color." The rays "are to be found throughout Nature in the ruling principle of diurnal variations: the grey Dawn, yellow morning, the golden Sun rise and red departing ray, in our changing combinations." Thus is born "an immense field of combinations." White as "the substitute of Light" is the "very inverse of colorable materials," and "mixed, produces strength or weakness." It can give lightness and what he calls "the tone of colour", or it can destroy colour and corrupt it. Colour is thus seen as a dynamic force, integrating or disintegrating in terms of light; it is seen as the materialization of light, densest in red (which in both emotional symbolism and plain fact appears as the expression of power). Turner expressly distinguishes colour from chiaroscuro or mere ornamental colouring. "Coloring not color."

In his Lectures he also showed that he had studied the Natural System of Colours of Moses Harris, entomologist and painter, which had been reprinted in 1811. (Reynolds had approved of it.) Turner adapted its colour-circle for his own purposes, making two diagrams (sometime after 1824), giving yellow pride of place instead of Harris's red; he also changed the ring of primitive (primary) and secondary colours round the circumference (with harmonizing complementaries opposed) by throwing out purple, symbol of authoritative rule, which he disliked as the foe of his beloved yellow. Harris had put three triangles inside his circle, partly superimposed, to show the three primaries begetting black. Turner, with his deep sense of dialectical opposites, added a second circle labelled in his notes Mixtures of Light. Here the triangles, made larger, show yellow, red and blue superimposed without increase in darkness. These were the "pure combinations" he had spoken of. (By devising a principle of additive and subtractive colour-mixtures he anticipated Helmholtz.)

An important glimpse of Turner and his fascination with problems of light is given us by the daguerrotypist Mayall, who came to know Turner well in 1847–9. Mayall was then struggling to make his way. Outside his shop in Regent Street he hung photographs satirizing the Railway Mania of the day. "On one side there was a Stock Exchange man radiant, shares being at a premium; on the other, the same man is maniacal despair at the Great Bubbleton railway shares falling down to tell a story. These pictures (almost the earliest attempts to make photography tell a story) attracted crowds, and among them Turner. So interested was he, that he came into the shop, and asked to see the gentleman who designed them. After this, he came so often, that an Abernethy chair was habitually placed for him, so that he might watch Mr. Mayall, without interrupting him at work. He took great interest in all effects of light, and repeatedly sat for his portrait in all sorts of Rembrandtic positions."[6]

Mayall tells us, "I took several admirable daguerrotype portraits of him, one of which was reading, a position rather favourable to him on account of his weak eyes and their being rather bloodshot. I recollect one of these portraits was presented to a lady who accompanied him. My first interviews with him were rather mysterious; he either did state, or at least led me to believe, that he was a Master in Chancery, and his subsequent visits and conversation rather confirmed this idea." (We may recall how delighted he was at being at home in the Lord Chancellor's wig; perhaps that experience encouraged the fantasy of himself as a legal bigwig.) "At first he was very desirious of trying curious effects of light let in on the figure from a high position, and he himself sat for the studies. He was very much pleased with a figure-study I had just completed of 'This Mortal must put on Immortality'; he wished to bring a lady to try something of the kind himself. This was in 1847; and I believe he did fix a day for that purpose. However, it happened to be a November fog, and I could not work. He stayed with me some three hours, talking about light and its curious effects on films of prepared silver. He expressed a wish to see the spectral image copied, and asked me if I had ever repeated Mrs. Somerville's experiment of magnetising a needle in the rays of the spectrum. I told him I had."

All this time Mayall had no idea that the visitor was a painter. But "I was much impressed with his inquisitive disposition, and I carefully explained to him all I then knew of the operation of light on iodized silver plates. He came again and again, always with some new notion about light. He wished me to copy my views of Niagara – then a novelty in London – and inquired of me about the effect of the rainbow spanning the great falls. I was fortunate in having seized one of these fleeting shadows when I was there, and I showed it to him. He wished to buy the plate. At that time I was not anxious to sell them. I told him I had made a copy for Sir John Herschel, and with that exception did not intend to part with a copy. He told me that he should like to see Niagara, as it was the greatest wonder in nature; he was never tired of my descriptions of it. In short, he had come so often, and in such an unobtrusive manner, that he had come to be regarded by all my people as 'our Mr. Turner'."

So things went on till one evening they met at the *soirée* of the Royal Society. "I think it was early in May 1849. He shook me by the hand very cordially, and fell into the old topic of the spectrum. Some one came up to me and asked if I knew Mr. Turner; I answered that I had had that pleasure some time. 'Yes,' said my informant, rather significantly, 'but do you know that he is *the* Turner!' I was rather surprised, I must confess; and later in the evening I encountered him again, and fell into conversation on our old topic. I ventured to suggest to him the value of such studies for his own pursuits, and at once offered to conduct any experiments for him that he might require, and, in fact, to give up some time to work out his ideas about the treatment of light and shade. I parted with him on the understanding that he would call on me; however, he never did call again, nor did I ever see him again."

He adds that he had just bought a large lens in Paris, six inches in diameter. "I let Turner look through it, and the expression of surprise and admiration were such that I ought at once, to have known him in his true character; however, he was very kind to me, and by some sort of innuendo he kept up his Mastership in Chancery so well, that I did not. He sent me many patrons. I used to hear about him almost daily. When somewhat desponding on my success one day, I told him London was too large for a man with slender means to get along. He sharply turned round and said, 'No, no; you are sure to succeed; only wait. You are a young man yet. I began life with little, and you see I am now very comfortable.' 'Yes,' I replied; 'and if I were on the same side of Chancery as you are, perhaps I might be comfortable also.' I was at that time fighting the battle of the patent rights of the daguerrotype. He smiled and said, 'You'll come out all right, never fear.' My recollection now is, that he was very kind and affable to me, rather taciturn, but very observant and curious; he would never allow me to stop working when he came, but would loiter and watch me polish plates and prepare them, and take much interest in the result of my labours."[7]

It is a pity that Mayall did not particularize what were Turner's "ideas about the treatment of light and shadow", but his account is valuable in showing how pertinaceous was Turner's interest in every aspect of light and colour, practical, scientific, theoretical. In 1840 Eastlake had published his translation of Goethe's *Theory of Colours*; and we may surmise that he had talked with Turner about the book before that date. We have Turner's annotated copy; and we turn to his notes and comments with the hope of here finding a full statement of his position. However, despite the copiousness of his remarks, we are still left with a large number of unanswered questions. Goethe takes an anti-Newtonian position, basing his analysis not on the spectrum but on a chromatic circle divided into plus and minus colours – the reds, yellows, and greens, associated with happiness, gaiety, warmth; and the blues, blue-greens and purples, which produce "restless, suspicious, and anxious impressions". The theory was thus concrete, relating colour to the life-process, whereas Newton's analyses were abstract, concerned primarily with mechanistic quantities.

One would think that here was a viewpoint that Turner would welcome, since it seems intimately related to a great deal of his practice. He had himself developed his art out of the notion of light and colour as vital aspects of a scene, not merely a mode whereby form became visible; on the realization of a dialectical interplay between dark and light, warm and cold masses; on a sense of the universe as composed of vortices, fields of force. And he could have found a great deal in Goethe's positions to justify his life's work and its opposition to established canons.

But, in the first place, he was extremely suspicious, as we saw with regard to Field, of any schematic analysis, any theory which claimed to cover all the facts and phenomena. Even if he had many elements (largely unconscious) of an anti-Newtonian position in his own views and practices, he was not going to surrender any of the Newtonian analyses which he felt that his own exerience had vindicated. Goethe's scientific positions he attacked at some length, at times drawing optical diagrams. He often was driven to contradictions or taunts. "Prove it – and the Newtonian principle comes in." "Oh! Oh no." "This denys gradation". "This doubtful." When he felt that the argument against abstraction had itself become abstract, he jotted down "Poor Dame Nature", "poor painting". Many of Goethe's points about colours aroused his repudiation. Worse, he either did not understand or did not accept Goethe's concept of polarity. When Goethe says, "Colour is determined towards one of two sides. It thus expresses a contrast which we call a polarity, and which we may fitly designate by the extreme plus and minus", Turner adds, "Light in shade." When Goethe says, "Every single opposition in order to be harmonious must comprehend the whole," Turner adds, "or ought to be a part".[8]

When Goethe writes of "the real red" – which was for him a symbol of Divine Majesty – that it "should not incline too much to yellow", Turner's remark is "Oh"; and later, without any obvious reference to the text itself, he writes "poor red stands for darkness". Turner also disagrees with Goethe's proposition that the combination of two colours diametrically opposed in the colour-cycle produces a harmonious effect. In a paragraph on this synthesis of opposites, Goethe writes: "If these specific, contrasted principles are combined, the respective qualities do not therefore destroy each other . . ." At this point Turner breaks in with "yet they do. The violet the green and the purple are negatives to Yellow Red and Blue." Similarly, when Goethe writes of the difference between "augmenting" the contrasted opposites Yellow and Blue (*Steigerung*), and merely mixing them to produce Green (*Vermischung*), Turner adds "this pictorially will no do [sic] . . ." Turner thus appears to reject not only the concept of *Polarität* but also that of *Steigerung*.[9]

On the other hand, when Turner feels that Goethe is not being too rigid in his rules, he relaxes in his criticism. "Goethe leaves Genius almost to herself here." "Goethe allows an ample room for practice even with all his Theory." When Goethe says, "The principles in question have been derived from the constitution of our nature and the constant relations which are found to obtain in chromatic phenomena. In experience we find much that is in conformity with these principles, and much that is opposed to them," Turner is appeased and adds, "Thus all that has been defined come back to this." And at times he seems to agree with Goethe's positions, as, for example, "opposite colours tend towards each other and become united in a third; then, certainly, an especially mysterious interpretation will suggest itself, since a spiritual meaning may be connected with these facts," where Turner comments on "simbolising power of color to designate Qualities of things". He seems to accept Goethe's comparison of the six colours of the colour-cycle with the Mystic Hexagon, though he differs about details, e.g. contentment and earthly satisfaction as embodied in Green; and when Goethe speaks of Green as "appropriated to hope", he comments that he thought the colour "stood for servitude". When Goethe wants "harmonious relations in light and shade, in keeping, in true and characteristic colouring," he replies, "Yes, this the tru[th]. Shot – but not winged the Bird." What Goethe has said is true, he thinks, but not the whole truth. Again, when Goethe writes, "a distinct style of colour may be adopted on safe grounds for every subject. The application requires, it is true, infinite modifications, which can only succeed in the hands of genius", Turner assents, "Goethe will not say how, but it may be."[10]

Apart from a general suspicion about all-too-precise theorizings, Turner's objections centre on Goethe's proposition that colours arise from the coming-together of light and darkness. Turner holds that they come wholly out of light; and he feels therefore in Goethe's proposition an unresolved duality which he cannot accept. This leads him to much of his critical attitudes in scrutinizing Goethe's Theory and its working-out. Yet it seems that after the heat of the argument, conducted on the margins of the book, he began to feel that his own ideas had more kinship with Goethe's than had appeared from his comments on particular aspects. If Goethe had presented colour in all its manifestations, light and dark, as arising from the conflict and fusion of opposites within a unitary stream of light, Turner might well have felt a complete accord. I believe that something of this realization, phrased in his own terms, came to him as he pondered on the Theory. He then painted his two pictures LIGHT' AND COLOUR (GOETHE'S

THEORY) – THE MORNING AFTER THE DELUGE – MOSES WRITING
THE BOOK OF GENESIS and SHADE AND DARKNESS – THE EVENING
OF THE DELUGE. The words seem to suggest both an agreement
and a disagreement with Goethe. If he were simply underwrit-
ing the Theory, he would have used some such title as LIGHT,
DARKNESS AND COLOUR.[11]

What he did, in fact, was to paint the Morning in terms of
Goethe's plus colours, the Evening in terms of his minus
ones. The two works together then added up to the totality
of Goethe's Mystic Hexagon. In Morning we find dominant
reds, yellows, greens; orange-red, says Goethe, expresses
"warmth and gladness", yellow and green juxtaposed are
"cheerful", and yellow has a "gay, softly exciting character".
In EVENING we have the colours that "produce a restless,
susceptible, anxious impression". Blue suggests "cold, and
hence reminds us of shade", as well as owning "an affinity
with black". The world of light, Turner might have been
saying, is indeed made up of such dynamic colour-elements,
with which we see the "simbolising power of color to designate
Qualities of things", and which therefore merge man and
nature in the concrete sphere of immediate experience. But so
far from colour being composed of a dialectic of light and
darkness, Morning and Evening show how it arises from an
inner dialectic of light itself. Turner pays his homage to
Goethe, but maintains his own position.

The lines attached to LIGHT AND COLOUR state his concept
of light as a unitary process, which is one with life itself.

> The ark stood firm on Ararat; th' returning Sun
> Exhaled earth's humid bubbles, and emulous of light,
> Reflected her lost forms, each in prismatic guise
> Hope's harbinger, ephemeral as the summer fly
> Which rises, flits, expands, and dies.

He stresses both the fragility and the ceaseless return of life.
Instead of bubble-heads we find heads encased in transparent
rainbow-bubbles; and the whole picture is enclosed in one
great bubble with iris-edges running all along the lower part.
Each bubble, each individual life, by enclosing the prism of
colour, encloses the sun, encloses the whole of light, and is a
microcosm. The vortex has become the seething womb of
light.[12] In the centre rises a green mass, with an uplifted

serpent – a symbol of the crucifixion or of life reborn out of "servitude", obstinately ignoring the brief duration of the bubble? Aloft sits Moses, recording the scene, with pen in hand amid the misty white. The artist is at the heart of the light-bubble, the life-circle, realizing its nature and setting down its laws. (Note that Moses is here made the author of *Genesis*.)

In SHADE AND DARKNESS the vortex appears in the down-sweeping sky that curves heavily over the earth, and in the involving line of dark birds that wheel above. In THE ANGEL STANDING IN THE SUN, in the apocalyptic light-storm the Angel plays the part of recording Moses in LIGHT AND COLOUR and at the same time, expels the defaulters from the paradisaic sphere or bubble of light. The summoned carrion-birds flitter in out of the upper whirl; and we feel at once the blessing of the sun that shines on good and evil alike, and the curse of light upon man who has alienated himself from nature by his violence and his corruption. The sun is both creator and destroyer. The painting is Turner's final judge-ment on life and on death. As we look at it, we feel that his death-bed utterance, "The Sun is God", is something that could not have been invented. It rings infinitely true of the man.

The Angel then is Light, is both Life and Death. But he is also Turner himself. In the first volume of *Modern Painters* Ruskin compared Turner with the Angel of the Sun in the Apocalypse; and the passage so scandalized the religious that it was omitted from all later editions.[13] Turner could not but have been struck both by the passage and by the way in which it horrified so many people. In thus picking up the image of the Angel a few years later he was supporting Ruskin's original point. But not in any narrowly personal way. Rather, he was saying that every true artist is this sort of Angel, recording, accepting life in its wholeness, loving and relentless. And, while justifying thus his life, he is accepting his death.

Chapter Eighteen

Last Days

SHEE died on 19 August 1850; and the question of the Presidency had to be settled. Eastlake let it be known he would not accept the position unless he could keep his salaried job as Secretary of the Fine Arts Commission, together with other posts. One of his partisans, C. R. Leslie, invited a group to discuss things. Turner was there.[1] He "was full of spirits on the evening, and apparently in his usual good health. He quite won the heart of my two sisters", Leslie's son recalled, "pretty girls of twenty-two and twenty at the time, flirting with them in his queer way, and drinking with great enjoyment the glass of hot grog which one of them mixed for him. He had always the indescribable charm of the sailor both in appearance and manners; his large grey eyes were those of a man long accustomed to looking straight at the face of nature through fair and foul weather alike." Eastlake was finally elected and knighted. Turner was then too ill to attend the meeting of election or the two dinners given by the Eastlakes in the New Year. In his Christmas letter of thanks to Farnley he remarks on "Farnley like former times. Old Time has made sad work with me since I saw you in Town. I always dreaded it with horror now I feel it acutely now whatever – Gout or nervousness – it having fallen into my Pedestals – and bid adieu to the Marrow bone stage." He shows a keen interest in the Crystal Palace, which "is proceeding slowly I think considering the time, but suppose the Glass work is partially in store, for the vast Conservatory all looks confusion worse confounded The Commissioners are now busy in minor details of stowage and hutting, all sent before the Glass Conservatory is ready – to be in bond under the duty to be lay'd on if sold."[2] In another letter written at the end of January 1851, with thanks for two braces of longtails and hares, he again comments on the Crystal Palace. "It looks well in front because the transept takes a centre like a dome, but sideways ribs of Glass frame work only Towering over the Galleries like a Giant."[3]

On 13 March he called on Charles Turner, who noted that he was "looking better tho' not well". He turned up on varnishing days; but at the private view P. Cunningham thought he "was breaking up fast".[4] At the Dinner, near the end, he pressed Sidney Cooper to stay and have a glass of wine with him. Cooper then gave him his arm down the stairs. Sir Edwin Landseer and the Prime Minister were by the entrance, and Landseer observed, "There is Cooper, leading out the Nestor of the Royal Academy." Turner said, "Never mind them. Never mind them. *They* shan't lead me out." He was very feeble and Cooper put him in a fly, but excused himself from seeing him home on the grounds of going to a *soirée* at Lord Rosse's house. The fly went off; and then later Cooper found Turner, too, at the *soirée*.[5]

This spring F. T. Palgrave met him, probably at Munro's house. The conversation turned on politics, and Turner talked with "eminent sense and shrewdness"; he had a "clear practical view of the subject in hand; an evidence of general mental lucidity". He spoke of "the mysteries of bibliography and the tangle of politics neither wittily, nor picturesquely; but as man of sense before all things". He seemed "as secure in health, as firm in tone of mind, as keen in interest, as when I had seen him years before; as ready in his dry short laugh, as shrewd in retort, as unsoftened in that straightforward bearing which seems to make drawing-room walls start and frightens diners-out from their propriety". Palgrave asked Turner why a large white star had been blotted out from later states of the *Fairy Queen* plate in the *Liber Studiorum*. Turner "laughed ironically, to the terror of the enquirer, and said the stars and their ways were beyond his control and responsibility". Several guests followed him down to the front door. Palgrave helped him on with his rough and old-fashioned greatcoat, when, as if to efface any effect of abruptness in his remark about the star, he pointed to Jupiter and gaily said, "I might ask that star why it pleased to shine." He then disengaged himself, laughing and talking freely, stepped sturdily through the door, "and turned down the few steps into Piccadily from our sight".[6]

However, when he was too ill to attend the Royal Academy *soirée* at the close of the Exhibition his friends grew worried. David Roberts wrote to Queen Anne Street, begging him to let him come and see him if he were ill, and assuring him that his place of residence would remain undisclosed if he so wished it. Turner did not reply, but turned up at Roberts's studio in Fitzroy Square, sadly broken up. Moved by the letter, he said, "You must not ask me; but whenever I come to town I will always come to see you." He refused to be cheered up. He laid his hand on his heart and said, "No, no; there is something here which is all wrong." Roberts could not help peering in his face. He noted "the small eye was as brilliant as that of a child, and unlike the glazed and 'lack-lustre eye' of age." Roberts was painting a large picture of the Battle of Hyderabad in an upper room. "Turner was too infirm to get up the stairs to see it, and he never before appeared vexed with me, yet on this occasion he did so."[7]

In August 1815 appeared Ruskin's *Pre-Raphaelitism*, dedicated to Hawkesworth Fawkes and written in defence of the young painters of the school. Ruskin tried to refute the charge of inconsistency in praising their meticulously detailed work as well as Turner's broad and subtle style. He sought refuge in a vague doctrine of the artist's need to "go to nature". This sort of confusion helps to explain why Turner responded so little to Ruskin, whose admiration, Ruskin himself said, gave him "no ray of pleasure". He always discouraged him "scornfully" and "died before even the superficial effect of my work was visible". (We must remember that the later volumes of *Modern Painters* had not yet been written, with their far better understanding of Turner's art.)

In October Mrs. Booth paid into his hands £59 19s. 9d. to be invested on her behalf in the Public Funds. He put the money in his pocket and forgot all about it. When she reminded him how much he owed her – the cost of five years' board and lodging, washing, clothing and nursing – he weakly murmured that he was unable to go into the accounts with her, but she might make a claim against his estate. He added that she'd be dealing with gentlemen who would do her justice. One night (she told John Pye) he called out excitedly; and so, to quiet him, she saw that he had drawing materials at hand for making notes for future pictures. Once he happened to be peering into the river just as the police dragged up a girl who had drowned herself; and he had no rest till he had sketched her face. Mrs. Booth encouraged him to keep on painting, and even when he was too ill to sit up in bed for more than an hour or so she saw that his brushes were clean, a canvas ready, and his palette set as he had taught her.

She tried the effect of a change of air, with the attendance of Dr. Price. They went to Margate. He said he felt better, but insisted on going back to Chelsea, where he soon had a bad relapse. Bartlett was treating him, but Price was now called to London. He told Turner that death was near. "Go downstairs," said Turner, "take a glass of sherry and then look at me again." Price did as he was told, but did not change his mind. "Then," remarked Turner, "I am soon to be a nonentity."

Two days before the end, looking very steadily, he repeated Lady Eastlake's name. He died at ten in the morning on 19 December in the presence of Bartlett and Mrs. Booth. "It was very dull and gloomy, but just before 9 a.m. the sun burst forth and shone directly on him with that brilliancy which he loved to gaze on and transfer the likeness to his paintings. He died without a groan."

Hannah Danby seems not to have known of the Chelsea house or Mrs. Booth. We are told that she had been anxious at hearing nothing for weeks from Turner. By accident, looking through some old clothes, she came on a letter that gave her a clue. With an old crony, Mrs. Tanner, who had helped at times at Queen Anne Street, she made her way to Cremorne and found the cottage, a short while before Turner's death.[8]

The funeral took place on Tuesday, 30 December 1851. The guests gathered in the picture gallery between nine and ten o'clock in the morning. Everything but the pictures on the wall had been removed. The coffin was in the small ground-floor parlour. As the guests waited, they gazed at the dingy gallery, "dirty in the extreme", said one of them,

R. Redgrave. "The hangings, which had once been a gay amber moreen showed a dirty yellow here and there, where the stains from the drippings of the cracked skylight had not washed out all the colour." The pictures were dropping from their canvases. A breakfast was expected, but not provided. The procession went through Regent Street and Trafalgar Square, on to St. Paul's. It took three hours. Griffith says that as the sound of the organ and the boys' choir burst out, with the coffin moving towards the choir, "there was not a dry eye" among the long line of spectators crowding the chapel. The ceremony was concluded in the crypt, where the body was placed near those of Reynolds, Lawrence and other artists.[9]

The mourners returned to Queen Anne Street and the will was read in the presence of the Executors alone. There is no need here to examine the sorry story of the attempts to upset it. The relatives on the Turner side, as next-of-kin, in whom Turner had shown no interest whatever, promptly tried to prove him of unsound mind and incapable of making a legal will. When this failed, they turned to Chancery, pinning their hopes on Mortmain. When at last it seemed likely that Turner's fortune of some £140,000 or more would be frittered away in legal costs, they came to an arrangement with the Executors. Satisfied with the money they got, they made no claim to the paintings, drawings, and sketchbooks. The nation neglected to carry out the provision of the will about building a gallery; but as the art-works were left unmolested in the hands of the National Gallery, they ended by becoming, in fact, the property of the nation, which for long treated a large part of them no better than Turner himself had done in his gallery. The Chancery settlement had frustrated all his charitable intentions. Evelina, however, had her £100 annuity vindicated, and an Account was set up in her name into which £3,333 6s. 8d. was transferred. She was the first person dealt with by the Court after settling the general issues. As Hannah had died on 11 December 1853, her heirs, the three daughters of Sarah and John Danby, had become defendants in the suit and were duly awarded their cousin's share: what was due to her as custodian of the Gallery from the date of Turner's death to that of her own, plus five Austria Metallic Bonds (each of 1,000 florins denomination) which were found in a box to which she held the key, and which she had insisted were a gift to her from Turner. In her will she had left £50 to Evelina, directing that the money be handed over to her in person and not used to pay her husband's debts. In the Chancery decision Evelina's annuity was stated to be payable to her "for her separate use".

Turner went through far too complicated a maze of development for any brief summary to do him justice. There are, however, a few key-points. He was the artist of a paradisiac earth and also of tragic catastrophe. It has been well said that in his later phases, "Natural forces, both those that he had inherited from the Sublime as images of horror, such as fire and storm, and those of light and colour, that he had discovered for himself, became the very essence of his art, embodying in their forms alone the emotions he wished to communicate. The former, fire and storm, conveyed his sense of the insignificance in the face of the immensity and destructiveness of nature; the latter, light and colour, were hymns of praise to the life-giving essences of the physical world."[10] The two aspects were not cut apart; they merged in a single vision, which is at once tragic and lyrical, expressing in one breath the fallacies of hope and man's unconquerable spirit.

He was the first artist to grasp thoroughly the unity of light and colour, and all that that implied. But he was able to take this step because he was also the first artist to be obsessed by the sense of nature as something in perpetual flux and change. He came to realize that the *forms of movement* were what he wanted to define, and that nature consisted, not of separate objects in mechanical relations to one another, but of fields of force. Hence the deep tensions that entered into his forms and his colours. (There was a subterranean link here with the scientific quest of men like Hamilton and Faraday.) As part of his capacity to define movement and change, he expressed the direction and convergence of time-factors by means of rhythms and colour-tensions. Here, as in so many other ways, he anticipated modern developments of art; but what such post-Cézanne artists as the Cubists, for example, attempted by an intellectualized analysis of spatial structures and interrelations, he defined intuitively and sensuously. (It would need a whole new book to continue this point; but I should like to say that while I consider Cubism an essential new starting-point for art, I see it as reducing all life and process, including men, to things. Therefore it hands on the problem of re-achieving sensuousness without loss of its great new analytical viewpoints. These questions are latent in Turner; but it needed the whole development leading on into Cézanne, Picasso, and Braque before they could be formulated as general issues.)

A large number of factors, which we have to some extent explored, gave him the first slight stepping-stones in this adventurous journey of his into untrodden spaces. But we cannot overemphasize the part played by poetry in giving him courage and direction, despite his world's inability to understand what he was seeking to do. From the poets he gained various dynamic conceptions, which he felt driven at all costs to re-express in the specific terms of pictorial art. His lack of education in the sense in which his world understood that term, plus his magnificent equipment along the lines most useful for his purposes, played an important role in releasing him from the established canons. The anguished experience of his schizophrenic mother also had a deep and permanent effect, driving him in on himself and compelling him to seek for an understanding, an effective definition, of the violences of nature. This does not mean that in any way his quest can be reduced to a psychological compulsion born narrowly out of his home life; but the compulsion was there, precipitating certain personal problems which he had to resolve and universalize in his art, merging them with the problems shared by all the men of his epoch and with the particular forms of that epoch's sensibility.

In his work modern art was fully and definitely born, with all the possibilities of good and evil, of violent disintegrations and of great new integrations, which we see being worked out in the century following his death.

Notes

Abbreviations: F. = Finberg's *Life*; F.Coll. = the nine volumes of his material in the Print Dept. B.M. Th = Thornbury's *Life* (with i or ii to represent the first edition; with page-number alone for the second). PTh. = Platt's 13 vol. interleaved edition of Th. in the B:M. Roman numerals in capitals refer to the sketchbooks or collections in the Turner Bequest as catalogued by Finberg; TB means the Bequest. Turner Dossier (TD) refers to the collection of papers in the hands of C. W. M. Turner of Hampstead. RB = Rothenstein and Butlin, 1964. LS = *Liber Studiorum*. BML = Letters in B.M. Add. MS. 50118–9. W. = Whitley; WP = Whitley Papers, ed. xii (Print Dept., B.M.); RD = Ruskin, *Dilecta*; RP = Ruskin, *Praeterita*. Dates attached without comment to a title indicate the year of exhibition. For the Lectures, B.M. Add. MS. 46151 A–Q; and TD.

1. *Childhood and Early Youth*

Here and throughout I do not give references for the accepted and uncontroversial aspects of Turner's life which are gathered effectively in Finberg's *Life*. Often in dealing with matters that I do not have space here to follow up, I merely refer to the discussion in Finberg – or to Whitley.

Much information about the Turner family is to be found in the Turner Dossier. The earliest known member of Mary Turner's family is Joseph Mallord, will proved 10 April 1688, Citizen and Butcher of St. Leonard's, Eastcheap. We can discount the tale (Th. i, 10) that T. in youth visited Shelford Manor House, near Nottingham, "where his mother's family lived, and I presume suffered some indignities there". Cf. the tale about his uncle John at Barnstaple.

Thornbury adds, "Dr. Shand, author of 'Gallops in the Antipodes', writes to inform me that 'Miss Marshall was first cousin to his grandmother'." He also asserts that T. used to talk of being born in the same year as Napoleon or the Duke of Wellington, though, in fact, the date was six years later.

1. Timbs (1), 155. "The Cider-cellar is now, altogether, a more extensive concern than it was in Porson's time. . . . In the first floor of the adjoining house was located, not many years since, the *Fielding Club*, a society of authors and artists, mostly; prominent among whom was Albert Smith."
2. Fred Turner, 126.
3. Th. i, 7, and ii, 39.
4. John Lees; book now in Brentford Public Library. For early work

done by stealth: Th. i, 22 (citing Bell). Dr. Monro is said to have bought early drawings at Maiden Lane.

5. Ruskin: 5th and last vol. of *Modern Painters*. Stokes adds, "bodies and jetsam in seas, or on an earth so flattened in some late canvasses as to suggest a pavement of rippled water", 74; cf. Clark (1), 116 f.

6. Th. i, 18.

7. Letter to Mrs. Moore, late July 1844: F., 402; Th. ii, 231 f.

8. The widowed Mrs. Girtin married a pattern-draughtsman of St. Martins-le-Grand, Vaughan, to whom Robert Seymour, Dicken's illustrator, was apprenticed. Turner made an earlier drawing of Lambeth Palace for Hardwick (prob. early 1789), much tamer than the exhibited work, which seems to show Malton's influence: F., 18. Tale in Th., i, 55, of T. recalling the parish stocks and the Lambeth public house with a board: Be sober, be vigilant. G. sketched from barge floating up and down Thames: Roget i, 95; G. and L., 21.

9. Livermore (3), to which I owe several points here. Domenichino, Poussin: LXXII, 36 and 41a.

10. Cf. CII, 23a, "Beside the masters desk he trembling stands, But not with fear of smarting broken brands;" rather he is "fearful he may lose the weekly prize whence all his joy accrues." The writing is difficult, but the tone seems sarcastic, referring to Mammon (cf. 12a, "Children of Mammon"), and apparently suggesting that out of such ingrained "hope and fear" British trade and prosperity has been built. The river-image is used, the stream that "pours hea(l)th and commercial vigour on their shores", with the moral that in such small beginnings is "the germ of wealth."

11. CXIX, x.

12. Cottage: XVII; L. Sketches: CVI, 15a, and CXCII, 2a. More exs.: "Woman frying. Boy looking . . . Children at tub, a girl beating the barrell" (C, 54a), "Girl breaking off sticks and putting them on the grate" and "girl filling the kettle out of a large brown jug" (XCVI, 13, 13a). More exs.: XXIX, O; XXX, 89 and 96a; LIX, 9 and 16.

13. CXLV, 107a; Ruskin cited Th. ii, 218.

14. Naples: CLXXXVI, 81a; 64 has Bay of Gaeta with Vesuvius in distance: "Boy with Ball and Ring. Men smoking . . . men wading and fishing." Cf. CLIX, 92a. Hellebore: CXLIV, 99 (also "Brooms"). Child running: CXIX, M. Also CLX, 93; CCX, 50.

15. XCVI, 25; CXCVIII, 67; CXI, 71a. Young Anglers, CXVII, i (R 32).

16. Weir: CCLXXXI, 23. Then CCV, 41a (also "Artillery Yeoman"?); 42 has woman bathing, "Wood Nymphs"; 4 and 1 (1a and 2 have studies of wildflowers; 2, "Curious effect of Sunset at Twickenham").

17. CL, 23; CCCLXIII, 2. "May 30 – Margate. A small opening along the horizon marked the approach of the sun by its getting yellow", 6.

18. Dish: CCLXXXVI, 55a–56 (?1834). Poem: CXII, 88 and 87a.

19. CXXIII, 166a; note ref. to "triumphant Argo" and "a little navy rears".

20. CVIII, 26.

21. R. Leslie (1) and (2) 57; RD 1, 3, 5. *The lost vessel*: CCLXIII, 2.

22. Th. ii, 56. For runner, see note 14 above.

23. Th. ii, 38–39, and i, 169.

24. Th. ii, 52, and Butlin (1), no. 8; Th. ii, 88, 393 (T. "tore up the sea with his eagle-claw of a thumb-nail"); Ruskin *Pre-Raph.* 1851 (1904, xii, 386).

25. Th. i, 6–7, and i, 164; for portrait by C. Turner of William and T.'s objections: Th. i, 5–6. (Th. i, 164, adds, William was "very like his son in face, particularly in his nose. He was a little, thin, common looking man, very short, and with all the barber's loquacity about him.")

26. Th. i, 74; A. Watts, 8; Th., 43. F., 26, raises the sum to a shilling.

27. TD. First letter has "Queen Ann street" at top, "Solus Lodge Twickenham" below; second, "Sandy Combe Lodge".

28. Th. i, 5–6, 10. In second edition he cuts the remark about Turner resenting references. Thornbury writes so badly that it is hard to make out whether Hannah, he, or Trimmer is speaking.

Falk, 23, speaks of a stillborn child exacerbating the condition of Mary Turner, but gives no authority.

2. *Apprentice Years*

1. Dayes, 352.

2. Ink-outline and rough wash of colour. Another wash-drawing has the same date: Clifton, Nuneham Harcourt – also no doubt a copy, as are two views from Gilpin's *Observations*, though with added details: perhaps a little later, as also a w.c. copy of a Sandby (ruined tower in Bay of Naples): see sketchbook I. Thornbury speaks of a Margate sketch made at age of 9 (i, 18).

3. Sunnywell church: II, 12 and 13.

4. F., 16–17. Thornbury says his genius was revealed at age of 5.

5. Watts, p. ix; Lovell Rees.

6. 1790–1 R.A. Catalogue; description, Th., 1–2.

7. F., 18–19, and CXCV, 113 ("worked by Malton's method"); Th. i, 49, 53, 67 (Malton), i, 54–57 (Hardwick). "All this time T. is colouring prints and washing in skies for architects. When artist friends in after life used to express their wonder at his having worked, as a boy, at half a crown a night putting Indian-ink skies to amateurs' sketches, he used to say defensively, 'Well, and what could be better practice?' He adds that an old architect, still living, told him, 'I knew him when a boy, and have often paid him a guinea for putting in backgrounds to my architectural drawings, calling upon him for this purpose at his father's shop in Maiden-lane, Covent-garden; he would never suffer me to see him draw, but concealed, as I understood, all that he did in his bedroom' " (Th., 38; cf. i, 66–67).

Wanstead: Lysons, *Environs of London* ii, 237.

Th. i, 53: Trimmer says that a Mrs. Malton and her daughter "resided at Heston in my childhood; it was with her husband that Turner was placed as an architect." Trimmer also says, "I have been told that old T. was left by a relation 200 l., with which sum he placed out T. to a landscape-painter, who, seeing some of his products subsequently, said, 'He is not indebted to me for this'." Trimmer seems to confuse things here.

8. Lowe: Falk, 25–26; W. (i) ii, 334 (Ruskin). Porden (architect who did part of Brighton Pavilion) offered to take him on for seven years, no premium: Th. i, 47; Timbs (2), 310. Protests against Th.'s picture of Porden, WP, 1547, 1579. For Tomkinson, WP, 1549; Th. i, 15–17. *Sun*, 21 September 1822, in obituary calls his Eaton Hall near Chester, "one of the finest examples of the Florid Gothic that the Art has pruduced".

Girtin: Thornbury and Roget tell the story, which H. Stokes gave verisimilitude by making the Bridewell the prison and introducing Monro (the latter's father was physician in charge here as at Bethlehem; he died 1791, but his son was probably doing most of the work for some time before that). See Mayne, 17–20, for discussion; also C. F. Bell, R. Davies (who consulted Bridewell records up to 1795), W (2), 44–46; Mayne, 26–42; Guillemard, for rels, with Monro. Also Girtin and Loshak, 21–23. If G. went to jail, it would in fact have been at Tothill Fields.

Th. i, 97, says T. and Girtin met at Henderson's house, copying the Canaletti, Piranesi, Malton. For Smith: Timbs (2), 310, citing Bryan; W (2), 196 f.; G. and L., 24 f. Crop: G. and L., 112 (Abbé Ange Denis Macquin, in Moore papers, Ashmolean.)

9. F., 20: Th. i, 66; Th., 23; see latter as to Narraways.

10. Pantheon: F., 20–21; IX, A–C.

11. *Conn.*, February 1923.

12. R. Russell, cf. VI, 3, and XXIII, O. Note XVI, G (Storm off Dover), ? 1793, with other sea-subjects; XXIII, O–Z (Storms and rocky coast, etc.), ? 1794.

13. See appendix on engravings.

14. Influences: Malton, Sandby, Hearne, Dayes (F., 21 f.), Morland, Rowlandson, Loutherbourg. Dr. Monro bought his *Anselm's Chapel*: F. (2), 19. His first review in *St. James' Chronicle*, 13 May 1794; *Morning Post* a few days later.

15. Tours: Th., 39, 45; F., 25; Oxford (for Henderson) Th. i, 67. Boxing Harry: Watts, p. xxxix.

Lists: XIII, H (rev.); XIX, XXVI; XLVI, 119a–120a; CLXXI; CLXIII, etc.

16. Industry: the author of his itinerary notes "The Iron Works" on his S. Wales tour, 1795, XXVI (TB i, 49). See XXXIII, B (foundry), E (gravel pit); XXXVIII (inside cover), "4 Drawings of the Iron Works of Richd. Crawshay Esqre at Cyfaithfa, near Merthyr Tidril – 18 miles from Cardiff – 16 from Brecon". T.'s collection of Welsh and Shropshire cards by Loutherbourg (CCCLXXII), mostly industrial, bought at Dr. Monro's sale, 1833. See further Gage (1), 22a, who points to a similar itinerary in H. P. Wyndham's anon. *Tour through Monmouthshire and Wales* (1794); T's own pencilled notes were probably made for Farington in 1799: F., 61. Note the close link of the Picturesque with Tours and their literature.

17. R.A. 1796 Register lacks till December; T. was often there, December, January, February. For R.A. Life-class: Zoffany's painting, 1771 (at Windsor Castle); engraving after Rowlandson and Pugin (PTh. ii, opp. 8).

18. Bell: F., 44; Th. i, 75–77. For relation to a LS plate: F., 34, n. 2.

Th. i, 53: T told Mr. Trimmer that his first instructions in paint were from a person who taught him to place a small piece of carmine in the centre of the cheek, and to lose it by degrees. This might have been the itinerant painter who painted his father's blocks, and who is said to have instructed him."

19. Pasquin: *Critical Guide:* RB, 8; F., 33; Peter Cunningham, 21.

20. Th. i, ch. 4; Leslie (2), 225, and RD 7; WP, 1568.

21. Th. i, 24–25; Th., 14.

22. F., 27. Trimmer, says Thornbury, took it for T. at 16. "The profusion of dark tresses which it faithfully represents recalls the enthusiasm with which the old man used to speak of his son's 'fine head of hair', a point whereon his judgment may not be questioned; and the fracture visible on the left side of the picture commemorates T.'s dissatisfaction with the work, which he expressed by knocking his fist through it." William T. gave it to Hannah Danby, who gave it to Ruskin.

23. F., 27 f., 50 f., 234. He would not have been mollified, though perhaps pleased, to read Verity (1733): "I observe that the most elevated men in art are the least in stature, particularly Mr. Zincke, enameller; Mr. Hogarth, painter; Mr. Philips Junior, painter; Mr. Scott, seapainter; Mr. P. Scheemaker, sculptor (and his brother less); Mr. Isler (?) modeller in Wax; Mr. Worsdale, painter. These gents are five feet men or less." If we may trust Th. ii, 321. T. repeated through life the statement that no one who saw his portrait would believe he had painted his works. Cf. *Morning Chronicle*, 1830 (W (3), 190): "That he should be such a poetical being would, we think, never have been presumed by Lavater or Spurzheim. Mr. Turner is a tubby little man and has every mark of feeding well, and 'sleeps o' nights'."

24. Th. ii, 55, 53. Frith i, 127, writing of T.'s generosity, says that once he joined a group discussing a picture's shortcomings, "and after hearing much unpleasant remark from which he dissented, he was forced to confess that a very bad passage in the picture, to which the malcontents drew his attention, '*was a poor bit*'." Cf. the story of his rebuking Ruskin for not appreciating the hard work that went to even a mediocre picture.

3. *Associate of the Academy*

1. In March 1794 Monro moved from Bedford Square to Adelphi Terrace (built by brothers Adam), facing the Thames, next door to Mrs. Garrick and John Henderson, rich art-patron: C. F. Bell (2), 21 n.

2. Ruskin, *Works* xiii, 405.

3. Cozens died December 1797 at Northampton House, John (or St. John) Street, Smithfield, an establishment of Dr. Monro, and was buried in St. James Church, Clerkenwell: Oppé, 119. The elder Monro was one of the doctors attending George III; the Monro connexion with madness was pronounced.

4. To Dr. Burney, Turner deprecated the drawings in 1833: "Well, perhaps they are not so bad, for half-a-crown – and one's Oysters." Pye says that the first mention of T. in Monro's journal was in 1793 and that Girtin did not work so long for M. as T. did. He adds they were paid 2s. or 3s. plus supper "to put in effects of black and white and

of colour into black lead outlines"; Stokes, 23–24. Cornelius Varley said that G. made outlines, some of which T. tinted; G. complained that this did not give him the same chance of learning to paint. Cf. Roget i, 82. See also Girtin and Loshak, 30–32.

T. told David Roberts that he and G. often walked to Bushey and back to make drawings for a few shillings. See F., 35–40, 55; Timbs (2), 312; Farington, 11 November 1798. For the "club": Roget i, 79.

5. F. Norris.

6. Hoppner, though generally disparaging, thought T.'s *Evening Sea View* "good". Pasquin in *Critical Guide* after writing in *Morning Post*, 5 May: F., 41. *Times*, 3 May: F., 41–42.

7. Green 35. Green, 1769–1815, was six years older than T. for Ewenny: XLII. Note Girtin's stormy *Dunstanborough*: Mayne, pl. 15.

8. Girtin admired Wilson and Rubens. Pyne in *Somerset House Gazette* said G. chose cartridge paper "as his aim was to procure a bold and striking chiaroscuro, with splendour of colour, and without attention to detail". See H. Stokes, 69 f.; Girtin and L., ch. 3, etc. Colourmen got up Girtin's Stopping-out Mixture; but some time before, lights were rubbed out or wiped: Cozens in 1777 (Binyon); F. Nicholson, 87 f.; Hughes, 43 f. G. probably made a tour with James Moore and others in Scotland, 1792; 1794 he and Moore visited Lincoln, Peterborough, Lichfield, Warwick; 1795 they seem in the Cinque Ports. James Moore was a rich young linen-draper, Fellow of R. Soc. of Antiquaries; already in 1786, when 24, he published *A List of the Abbies, Priories, and other Religious Houses, Castles, etc. in England and Wales*; and had drawings engraved in Grose's Antiquities, 1787. At times he got other artists like G. and T. to complete his work. An MS. note of J. J. Jenkins says that T. travelled with him (as well as G. and Dayes): C. F. Bell (5). See also G. and L., 23 f., 26–28, 51–57. Another merchant connoisseur was C. Lambert, *ib.* 27, n. 3.

9. S. Rigaud; Cust. Date: ? Saturday, 14th, to Wednesday, 18th T. had perhaps already called in at Canterbury: F., 47.

10. Whitley (1) ii, 219. At an appeal from West, Farington, and Hoppner, Pitt had "houses kept by Royal Academicians and Associates" put on the same footing as houses licensed for the reception of lunatics and places of public entertainment. Loan to Nixon: XXV.

11. Opie: F., 54; *Dunstanburgh*, F., 48–50; Wilson, F., 52; Woodall, 39, Beckett. XXXIII, I and A; XXXVII. For two paintings (at Harewood House) at Plumpton Rocks near Harrogate, showing influence of Wilson: Borenius (1), pl. lxviii–lxix; Beckett, 15.

12. RB, 10. *Norham Castle* was much praised: W. (1) ii, 223 f.

13. XLII. Letter of 1841, to H. Fawkes: F., 419.

14. Probably XXXVIII and XXXV. Hoppner's comment may refer to certain darkenings through Wilson's influence.

Farington: in *Examiner* 1808, "Connoisseur" asks if Bell, the surgeon, was aware that everything in the R.A. was done by favour and that "the Academy is ruled by a party, at the head of which is said to stand a very mediocre landscape painter, one Farington by name": W. (2), in general (3), 19–21.

In the *Examiner*, 1814, 632–3, a letter treats of the hopeless inadequacy of the R.A. Library, and after sarcastic remarks of the way the Academicians "take such especial care" of themselves, it suggests a good library be set up, open to the students, with an Academician as librarian – Farington is suggested as one "whom it would infinitely benefit to quit the brush".

For Snowdon, cf. Burke, pt. ii, sect. 16; Gage (1), 18. And XXAVIII, 76; LXX, Y.

15. Devis, a candidate, gave a dinner to several Academicians and sent his carriage to fetch them.

By 1797 Turner was well known enough to be named on Gillray's print *Titianus Redivivus*, satirizing the "Venetian secret" of Mary Anne Provis (which she claimed to reveal the system used by the great Venetians and which she sold at ten guineas a time). T.'s name comes at the end of the list of sceptics (Fuseli, Beechey, Loutherbourg, Cosway, Sandby, Bartolozzi, Rooker) on a canvas on which a monkey urinates. Next year a critic (*Monthly Mirror*, WP, 1513) praised him for keeping aloof from "these ridiculous superficial expedients". Miss Provis was under the professional care of Dr. T. Monro. See Gage (3), and n. 38, ch. 8, here.

16. Danby, 1757–98, was elected member of R. Soc. of Musicians on 6 March 1795; in 1781–94 he gained ten prizes from the Catch Club (for eight glees and two canons); *Awake* got prize medal of 1783. His masses, etc., written mostly for two to three parts, are inferior to his glees. At the benefit concert, pianist J. B. Cramer was in charge of the band.

Danby was buried near south wall of west part of Old St. Pancras churchyard, with altar-tombstone (now nearly illegible); see Roffe, *Brit, Monumental Inscriptions* i, no. 44 (sketch in appendix). He published four books of glees (including that of 1798), *La Guida alla Musica Vocale*, 1787 (elementary), *La Guida della Musica Instrumentale*. The full title of the final collection is: "Under the Patronage of their Royal Highnesses The Duke and Duchess of York; Danby's Posthumous Glees, Being a Fourth Set for 3, 4 and 5 Voices. Also the Ode to Hope. Presented to him by the Glee Club & (by their permission) included in this Work. Dedicated to the Noblemen and Gentlemen of the Catch Club, and the President and Members of the Glee Club in London. Published for the Benefit of His Widow and four Infant Children. Price 12 shil. Op. 6."

For Danby: Groves, *Dict. of Music* i, 429a (incorrectly says he died "during the performance of a concert"); DNB; Scholes, *Oxford Comp. to Music* 1956. Also *Europ. Mag.* xxxiii, 359; *Gent. Mag.* lxxiii, 1, 48; *Georgian Era* iv, 521; *Morning Herald* 18 May 1798.

Upper John Street was that part of Whitfield Street between London Street (Maple Street) and Howland Street. The continuation to the south, as far as Tottenham Street, was known as John Street, and north to the junction with Warren Street was Hertford Street. In 1867 all three parts were incorporated into Whitfield Street; no changes have gone on since then, in name or numbering. But Upper John Street is not listed as a separate name in the Tottenham Court Road (west side) rate-books, though John Street does appear, and Tompson's 1803–4 Map clearly shows the area as fully developed. It does, however, appear in the run of rate-books for the borough as a whole.

Thomas Williams is entered against no. 46 from 1803 to 1809. The book for the year 1803 is the earliest extant; in 1809 the house is shown as empty. Williams may well then have been the holder in 1798.

J. W. Callcott, son of bricklayer and builder, was a prolific composer; in 1807 his brain gave way and for five years he was in an asylum. In the 1798 Danby Glees in the list of subscribers he is described as "Organist to the Asylum". A. W. Callcott, 1779–1844, began as portraitist under Hoppner, but turned to landscape. His son was a musician; his grandson, dying young, showed musical promise.

Glee clubs grew up from the 1760s, though glees were still mixed with catches, e.g. Gentlemen's Catch Club, founded 1761. Hamerton, 368.

17. Falk, 42.

18. XLII, inside cover, flyleaf at end, 139, 130, 129, 128. The love-song, in the line that F. failed to make out runs: "But shield my Swain with all his charms". The other glee seems to start "Faint and"; 1.6 ends "night to drop"; 1.7 has "how briskly" – in the parts F. could not read. The smoothness of the first song and the complicated rhymes of the second militate against T.'s authorship. For the traveller, cf. XXVIII, F (Top of Hill).

19. CXI, inside cover; but there is also a payment to "Mrs W" of 6 gns.

20. 29 April 1799.

21. Green, 137–8. This year T.'s name was linked with G.'s: Whitley (1) ii, 235; WP, 1512, 1514; *St James's Chron.* 20–23 May 1797; J. Robert, 9; and *A Treatise on Akermann's Superfine Water Colours*, 1801; Ackermann ix, 92 f.

22. See Beckett for the variations, including one without the V. Wilson's painting seems the basis of an engraving by Elliott, published 1775 by Boydell in a series of Views of Wales all painted by Wilson. For relation to Wilson, cf. Armstrong, 47–48, "Colour, texture and even handling all betray an eye fed on Wilson" (adding "while the vigour of the chiaroscuro . . . rests lightly on Girtin"). Cf. C. F. Bell (1).

23. Gage (1), 23; *Naval C.* i, 208.

24. *N.C.*, 477. Gage cites Mitford, "Backhuysen, Vandervelde, Loutherbourgh, write their names on a piece of Board; Turner writes his in the trough of the sea, with every letter flowing into motion." However *The Dort* is signed and inscribed on a piece of board – because of its closeness to the Dutch sea-painters? Gage notes the likeness of the N.C.'s account of Moonlight at Sea to Vernet effects, also that of Turner's 1796 *Fisherman at sea*. Note Vernet in TGRM, pl. 4.

25. Gage, *l.c.*; N.C. ,517.

26. Gage, *l.c.*; Gilpin (2), 205–14. Gage cites the *Morning Post*, 3 April 1799, which while admitting the moment of explosion was well chosen "to impress the mind with an idea of the terrible and sublime", disliked the way in which "the vivid flame illuminates the surrounding objects" – this minuteness detracting from the grandeur. Not a defect of the artist, but "of the subject, in relation to the sublime".

For naval themes: note LXIX, 116, 32a–58; XLI, 25–28; XLII, 24; XLVI, 118a.

27. XL, 8a, 67, 13; cf. XLVI, 4, 79, 83.

28. French: XLVI.

29. Girtin was offered £30 a year; Elgin later got Lusieri at Naples

and other draughtsmen and modellers: LFA iv, 27 f.; *Gent. Mag.*, 1802, 1163.

30. Bought, with four smaller Old Masters, for 7,000 gns.

31. W. (1) ii, 179–81, 224–7. James Irvine was another artist-dealer at Rome. Further sales were facilitated by the counter-revolution at Rome abrogating the laws that had made family pictures heirlooms and thus inalienable. At first prices were low, but the crowds of English buyers drove them up. More activities of Fagan, W (2) ,11–12. The Orleans picture: Dayes, 333; F., 69 f. Spain: W (2), 124, 233.

32. W. (2), 4. J. Galt says of West's early days, "A fine old picture was then rarely seen except at a sale, and many of our most promising students never saw a Rubens or a Vandyke except at auction." The auctions were the great occasions. Northcote wrote home to Devon soon after becoming Reynolds's apprentice, "When I was at Plymouth I was glad to walk ever so far to see a picture by Sir Peter Lely or Vandervelde, but now I can see new ones almost as often as I choose, for there are picture sales very frequent where there are paintings of all the greatest masters." Still things were much the same by 1800. Reynolds's collection was sold in 1791. T's. commissions gave him a chance of entry into great mansions, e.g. Fonthill, where he would see a fine series of J. R. Cozens's water-colours, etc. *Examiner* (1811) 802 for B.I. scheme old masters (incl. a Veronese) to be copied by students.

33. Farington adds he had been paid 40 gns. (more than he asked) by Angerstein for a drawing: *Carnarvon Castle*.

34. W. (1) i, 41; Ridler and Savage, 197 (1776). Dayes, 262. Dayes adds, 208, "When we have made ourselves acquainted with the beauties of art, we may consider ourselves at liberty to act on our own foundation, but we are bound to show in our works, that we act from an impression made in our minds by nature, or we shall never excite similar sensations in the spectator, but ultimately sink into mere mannerists; we mean not, however, such similitude as may happen by chance."

Fuseli was much concerned with mannerism, attacking under this term all contemporary attempts at originality other than his own (Mason, 294–5, 307). "A mannerist is the paltry epitomist of Nature's immense volume; a juggler, who pretends to mimic the infinite variety of her materials by the vain display of a few fragments of crockery" (Lecture vii, 322–3, 1807); he deals with three classes of mannerists. "There are two ways of composing in poetry and painting: the one finds materials for a subject, the other a subject for materials; the one is the method of him who is said to write or work with *style;* the second is that of those who indulge in what is called *manner*" (*Analytical Rev.*, July 1789, iv. 370, in unsigned account of Macklin's gallery, attacking Stothard). Cf. "In the following too closely a model, there is danger in mistaking the individual for Nature herself; in relying only on the schools, the deviation into manner seems inevitable: what then remains, but to transpose yourself into your subject?" (Aphorism 144). Goethe called Fuseli a "mannerist of genius" (Mason, 364).

35. See Reynolds *Works* ii, 135; but cf. ii, 92 (on Gainsborough).

36. Gage (2), 75: Gilpin (3), 43–47; Price i, 59, 233–4. But J. H. Pott, W. Mason, and Payne Knight praised the beech, e.g. Knight wrote that those who judged the tree by Gilpin's drawings "will probably agree

with him; but if they view it in the drawings of Claude (with whom it was a favourite tree), and then impartially examine it in nature, they will be apt to agree with me" (2) iii, 81–89, 74; Pott, 86; Mason (2) iii, 215–18. Both Cozenses, Sandby and W. Day painted it. For Sandy: Rothenstein (3), pl. 30, Note CCX, 13(c): "Beech trees in light". And poem, J. L. (2), no. 36.

37. Serres published *The Little Sea-Torch* (trans.), a guide for coasting ship, 1801; *Liber Nauticus*, instruction in the art of marine drawing, 1805.

In 1806 his wife was landscape-painter to the Prince of Wales; in 1813 tried to prove her uncle the author of the Junius Letters; in 1817 claimed to be Princess. Though she and Serres had separated in 1804, they both died within the rules of the King's Bench, she in 1834, he in 1825.

Falk states, 27, with no authority, the Blake was T.'s pupil in 1798, found him neglectful, and in revenge withheld notification of a lucrative commission. A more unlikely story it would be hard to find (? misunderstanding of XXXIV, 67, and XXXVIII, 50a; see XXI, 4).

For drawing of event in St. Paul's: see XLIV, V.; TB i, 108–9. For Oxford Almanack: F., 61.

4. *The World of Art*

1. Faking as a school of art: Ibbetson wrote *Incidence or Gamut of Painting in Oil and Water Colours*, in which he says he has collected a prodigious amount of material for a work to be called *Humbuggologia*, anecdotes of picture-dealers, picture-fakers, and pictures. He also bids artists avoid dealers like serpents; they are to live painters as hawks to singing birds: Redgrave (3). When Morland broke from his father, he was exploited mercilessly by a dealer, Desenfans (1), 26–27, tells of the term Winchester Oven for "a manufactory where several persons were employed making copies, which, after being soiled with dirt and varnish, were thrown into an oven built on purpose, where, in the course of an hour or two, they became cracked, and acquired the appearance of age and a certain stoicity . . ."

For the role of foreigners: D. Cook; Rothenstein (3), 84. Note Canaletto's visit; S. Scott had something of his precision.

2. Clare, 114.

3. E. Stokes, 19; Finer and Savage, 144–6; Longton as to the numbers. For Sandby: Waterhouse (1), 235.

4. W. (1), 209–10. And Pott, 53–55. Cf. Mason (2) on English Garston, "Be various, wild, and free as nature's self" (ii, 92).

5. Dayes, 268.

6. Hurdis opens his ninth lecture with this passage.

7. In 1789 began *The Topographer* "containing a variety of Original Articles, Illustrations of the Local History and Antiquities of England". Topography and middle class: Girtin and Loshak, 12.

8. H. Stokes, 17; Roget. Thomas brother of P. Sandby lived 1721–98. Others were F. Towne, 1740–1816; W. Pars, 1742–82; T. Hearne, 1744–1817; T. Malton younger, 1748–1804; E. Dayes, 1763–1804. Similar work in Holland by men like P. van Liender 1731–97, W.

Hendricks 1744–1831: Rothenstein (3), 98. For early use of body-colours and direct colours: Girtin and Loshak, 5 f.

Another line contributing to landscape was the sporting or animal picture. Thus, John Wooton painted landscapes in the manner of G. Poussin; Constable, criticizing, perhaps did not know he did them in later years with failing sight: W. (1) i, 77. For the relation to Dutch animal painters: B. Taylor, 14–15; mixture of local elements and conventions of Italian and Flemish hunting-pieces, *ib.*, 21. The climax was in Stubbs and J. Ward, and to a lesser extent in Sawrey Gilpin, pupil of marine artist S. Scott. Pott. 76 f., praises Cozens's water-colours in that "they resemble painting, for the effect is not, as is usually the case, produced from outlines filled up; but is worked into light, shade, and keeping by a more artful process, the masses being determined in the first making out or designation of the parts, and afford an harmonious effect unlike the ordinary compositions of scratches and lines, which are just connected and embodied by a flimsy washing." See also W. (1) ii, 323.

9. Oppe, 116–17; Girtin and Loshak, 8.

10. See n. 3 above.

11. J. Street. Note the link of picturesque and improvement in Burgh's claim that vistas were permissible only "when they form an approach to some superb mansion so situated that the principal prospect and ground allotted to picturesque improvement be entirely on the other side."

12. Cited Hurdis, 68, Mason (2) ii, 165 ff. For the new interest in microscopic life: Thomson, *Summer*, 287 ff.

13. Shenstone's essay *Unconnected Thoughts on Gardening*. He produced false perspectives by making avenues wider at the start. "An avenue that is widened in front and planted there with yew trees, then firs, then with trees more and more fady, till they end in the Almond Willow or Silver Osier will produce a very remarkable deception." Hagley had a seat dedicated to Thomson; cf. *Castle of Indolence* I, lxvi. For Thomson and Hagley; H. Miller, 135 f.; H. E. Hamilton; R. Cohen, 217 ff.

14. *Lives of the Poets*, Shenstone. He continues, "Whether to plant a walk in undulating curves, and to place a bench at every turn where there is an object to catch the view; to make water run where it will be heard, and to stagnate where it will be seen; to leave intervals where the eye will be pleased, and to thicken the planatation where there is something to be hidden, demands any great powers of mind, I will not inquire . . ."

15. Thus, where Thomson has "To glimmering shades and sympathetic glooms where the dim umbrage o'er the falling stream Romantic hangs . . ." the Leasowes had (according to a contemporary account): "At the bottom of a valley, a beautiful place of water, shaded by hanging woods", and so on: Street. W. Mason (2) ii, 81, ". . . duly mixt, with those opposing curves that give the charm of contrast".

Gage (1), 17a: "If the later eighteenth-century landscape painter did not work exclusively for antiquarians, his patrons were mostly those landed proprietors whose parks and gardens had been clipped to the prevailing Picturesque fashion, and whose daughters had toured Picturesquely **and** taken lessons in sketching what they had seen – or ought to have seen." See further his discussion.

16. *Analytical Rev.* xx, 265, November 1794, signed R.R.; E. Mason, 335, 174–5; in the same review Fuseli argues that though the P. "be founded on ideas of age and decay", in fact children are more P. than adults, just as a sketch is more P. than a finished work, for "the elements of motion, form and growth exist, but the transitions from part to part are either not delineated, or abruptly marked". He also describes intricacy and roughness as ingredients of the P. (See further Gage (2), 79).

17. Aphorism 236.

18. Boase (2), pl. 23e (Destruction of Host); Dayes, 337. In general, Boase (2). Bonnington and J. Varley were in youth connected with the theatre at Nottingham. Sandby painted scenes at least for the private theatre at Wynnstay, for Sir W. W. Wynn. Wilkie represented on the stage: W. (3), 230.

19. Zagrascope, popular 18–19 cs: magnifying engravings with perspective views, etc. Anamorphoses, giving distorted reflections from a polished surface (generally cylindrical or conical). Dioptrical Paradox, giving a different view of a coloured picture than that got by direct vision. Later, various panoramic and peepshow effects. For anamorphoses: note Thomson, *Summer*, 1687–9. T. Malton, elder, constructed a Perspective Machine (1722). Optical Illusions were popular, e.g. the Aggrescopius of J. Belzoni (in the show of 26 February 1813 were also Musical Glasses and "the Delineations of le Brun's Passions of the Soul") C. Clair J. Belzoni, 15 f.

20. See Boase (1) for further details. Eidophusikon: D. Cook, 201. Copley: B. Nicholson, 243, and Eitner, 280. Halsewell, 336, with d. L. (2), 112.

For Boydell, F. Wheatley did wreck scene (*Comedy of Errors*), Romney also (*Tempest*). Northcote's *Captain Inglefield*, etc., 1784, had the huge bulk of H.M.S. *Centaur* ready to fall on a crowded pinnace.

Morland on the I.O.W. did smugglers, sea scenes; Ibbetson did smugglers on Irish coast, shore scenes – his *Jack in his Glory* has Morland elements with a boisterousness all its own. For I.O.W., including Turner's relations: Gage (1), 22–23. Vernet (or Loutherbourg): copy in XXXVII, 104–5.

21. Hoyland. He says of *Cornard Wood*, its rhythms are not unique to G., "they **form the** core of the rococo style". The drawing "defines every spatial position and every plane". See later, n. 18 to ch. 5. For T. and Gainsborough: **Th. i**, 179 – "praise of G.'s execution and Wilson's tone", 176. Hayes (3), **24** as fig. 3, for G.'s *Coast Scene* (1781 R.A.) with effect of outswelling incoming wind and cloud.

22. Ziff (1), 146.

23. *ib.*, 146–7.

24. In general, Constable, e.g. 26, 125 ff. (Thomson) 90–91; Ziff (1), 321, note 40. T. in his lecture recalls *Celadon*. For Wilson and Girtin: W. (2), 44; Pope, G. and Loshak, 69, 119.

St *James Chron.* in 1761 satirizes the cognoscenti who say of the *Niobe*, "None of the colouring of Claude's glowing backgrounds", etc.: W. (1) i, **174**. The son: W. (1) i, 386, and Constable, 61. For Turner's

Terni: Th. ii, 44; CLXIII, 1; CLXXI, 1, 13, 28; CLXXII, 18; CLXXVII, 55a; CXCI, 24a.

25. Constable, esp. 92–93 and 80–81. For a tale of T.'s admiration for Cuyp; Th. ii, 185. See W. (2), 144, 146. Also CCXIV, 131 (132, Hobbema), CCXXVII, 11 ("all one tone"); CCXL, 70a; CCXLIX, 39a; CCLVIII, 15; CCLXX, 52a; CCCLXIII, 27.

26. F. Cummings, 149.

27. Ziff (1), figs. 41 and 43, p. 316; sketches XLVI, 114a and 118.

28. Ziff (2), 143–4, with figs. 19 b, c, d, 315–16; B.M. Add. MS. 46151 (9 and 16), with MS. in TD. The lecture was first given 12 February 1811, "Backgrounds, Introduction of Architecture and Landscape".

29. CII, 1a, onwards; cf. CXXIII, 130a.

30. See also TB i, 188–9 (1802). T. seems to be reviving his memories through engravings; he gets right and left hand confused in his account of *Pyramus and Thisbe*. See his letter to Soane (F., 113), 4 July 1804, which seems to show borrowings to authenticate historical details in his Poussin-type paintings.

5. *The World of Poetry*

1. XVII.S. As the B.M. Print Dept. could not locate this drawing, I have had reluctantly to follow Finberg.

2. Th. ii, 152 and 37; Th. ii, 282; Shee, 14.

3. See J. L. (1) and (2), and Ann Livermore (1): Lectures, see CX, 45a–43a, and CVIII, 48a, 49.

4. *Summer*, 163 ff.

5. *ib.*, 1113 ff. *Amyntor* i, 169 ff.; he misquotes "evening's solemn hour" and "cerulean". *Excursion* i, 401 ff. In Bell's Poets, *Mallet* (1800), has the wrecked Amyntor illustrated by an engraving after Ang. Kauffmann.

6. Accepting LXX, H, as this picture. For Cozens's influence: Oppe, 160 n.

7. *C. of I*, I, xxxviii.

8. *Liberty* iv, 237.

9. *ib.* v., 561.

10. *ib.* iii, 372, 405.

11. Contents of Part V.

12. *Letters of the Critical Club*, Edinburgh, 1738: Letter xii (27 February 1738), 32–85.

13. *History of English Poetry*, 1774, i. 46: he compares a *Summer* passage with G. da Bassano.

14. See in general, R. Cohen, 198, 216 f., 251 ff., etc. See J. L. (2) for comparisons of Ann Radcliffe with Claude or Rosa, etc. The fact that there was Scottish poetry description of nature before Thomson does not touch in the least the specific element he gains from Claude, Rosa, etc.

15. Cited Hurdis, 103 f.

16. Hurdis II. On 111 he says, "From Landscape at large, let us descend to the *minutiae of nature*", but not till 195 (in a book of 330 pages) does he reach Man. Mallet's Contents for Cento II: "Contains,

on the same plan, a survey of the solar system, and of the fixed stars."

17. *Spring,* 459–63; *ib.,* 1159 f.; original *Spring* (Robertson, p. 51); *Summer,* 1750–2; *Autumn,* 1004 ff.; *Summer,* 1687–9.

Note how air becomes active, "The surging air receives . . ." (*Spring,* 746); forms also, "The valley to a shining mountain swells, tipt with a wreath high-curling to the sky" (*Winter,* 274 f.), the verb swells gets its full force through the added image of the curling mist – a Turnerian effect; movement of light and colour used to centralize, e.g. original *Summer* (Robertston, p. 76).

18. Hoyland, see n. 21 to ch. 4.

19. In the figures of the *Analysis,* 89 and 31.

20. Thomson, end of *Summer; Analysis,* ch. v (Of Intricacy).

21. Fuseli's blank verse is as clumsy in its Miltonic way as T.'s Thomsonian. "Eccentric up and down the turbid space Hell rolls, all anarchy; of swift or slow Regardless, huge." Mason, 28 f., see also 15, 17, 26 f., 78, 103, 149 f., 153 f.

Westall's weak verse, illustrated by his own designs, has *A Shipwreck* (attempting a high prospect) and an *Ode on the First of June.* One poem tells how Ignorance alone was harmless; but wedded Pride; the pair, envious, "blast the rising name".

22. W. (1) ii, 320.

23. Farington (Grieg) i, 80.

24. See Boase; W. (1) ii,; Pye; W. (2), 9–11, etc. Note also Fuseli's Milton Gallery.

25. The episodes that appealed to artists were that of Lavinia, lightning-struck Celadon, Damon spying on Musidora as she strips to bathe. Thomson was early drawn into the pictorial tradition; the 1730 edition had illustrations by W. Kent. The mannered pastoral tradition of Hayman was easy to adapt to the *Seasons,* culminating in W. Hamilton's designs of 1797, with elegant artificiality, which, however, had its charm and its moments of Fuselian intensity. (Earlier in 1777 Hamilton had been drawn into illustrations, in a weak Hayman style, with Allan doing allegorical figures of each season. Then 1784 he made four paintings for Boydell of *The Seasons;* and 1790–3 Macklin engraved his twelve months, with Wheatley as the main influence. Later he collaborated with Fuseli for du Roveray's edition of 1802. Thus he covered the whole range of reactions from Hayman to Fuseli). *Gleaners:* W (2), 10 f. In general, Cohen, ch. V.

Smirke exhibited a *Musidora* at R.A., 1800; W. William painted *Thunderstorm with death of Amelia,* 1784; one of the last commissions to Raeburn was for a *Musidora.* (The story that Emma Hart sat to Gainsborough for *Musidora Bathing her Feet* is incorrect; the work seems only *A Nymph at the Bath,* a large oval sold by his wife nine years after his death. Whitley thinks it perhaps Mrs. Hartley, (i) ii, 149; not Perdita Robinson. See TGRM, 139).

The edition of 1794 has illustrations by Conrad Metz, a German residing in England, who tried to mix Fuselian style and pastoral themes. For Constable citing the *Seasons:* W. (3), 101 f.

26. Note link of Poetry and Energy, a point hardly possible before these years. The connexion brings out what I have said of the Thom-

sonian dynamic, now expanding in all sorts of ways, e.g. in the Gothic Novel with its notion of Fettered Energies.

27. Lessing treats Landscape in *Laocoon* with contempt as incapable of the Ideal.

28. "Addressed to the Revd. William Howley" (later Archbishop of Canterbury), who had been ill; the poet also links the scene with Rev. T. Russell who died there at 26 years, a poet, and who was at Winchester College with him. (H. was Fellow there in 1794. The poem describes "gray rocks and mazy springs". Tenth stanza has "To part from every hope that brought delight" (contrast with Memory).)

29. In general H. Stokes, 46–50; Mayne, 51–53. Guillemand; Girtin and Loshak, 37 f. First meeting, 20 May 1799. In Francia's *Transport returning from Spain* (1809) we see Girtin's influence: Binyon. His *Shore Scene* (Calais) is more like a Turner. Thus elements of both T. and G. were handed on to Bonnington. (For Francia: W, (2), 219 f.)

6. *Academician*

1. Girtin's panorama is lost, but half a dozen sketches for it are in the B.M. Dates of his show: Girtin and Loshak, 45 n. (1797), but see Oppe (3), 393; Whitley (6), 13, *Morning Herald*, 1 September and 6 December 1802 (started 1800). See G. and L. further, 33–36, 105 f., 116–18; W. (6); Roget i, 103–6. Dayes worked for Barker: Dayes (2), 27 February – 2 July 1798. Turner may have known the scenic and panoramic painter James Demaria before he left for Birmingham in 1800: Solly, 7, W. (2), 38–39. J. S. Hayward and panoramas: Roget i, 189 f.; S. Kitson, 20; G. and L., 44.

For Barker: W. (1) ii, 107 f.; Roget i, 104 f. A panoramic relief, *The First of July*, 1794, was shown July-August 1795, no artist given in *True Briton* adverts. Burnet said of T., "He influenced the style of theoretical scenery and of panoramic exhibitions" (Th. ii, 199).

2. WP, 1514; Gage (1), 24 f., with full discussion on which I draw. Fawkes was somehow connected with a sketchbook that has drawings and plans of the battle showing same scheme as the Naumachia: Gage, 24, B.M. Add. MS. 41644, L. Paul – for rel. to W. Anderson. No sure evidence of link of T. and Fawkes in 1799–1800, but T. Edwards of Halifax may have introduced them: Wroot, 233; F., 61; Gage, 24, n. 63. Many stage effects of disaster could be adduced, e.g. Reynolds, *Life and Times*, 1826, ii. 350, 391: two musical dramas which succeeded "through the destruction of the Temple of the Sun by an earthquake, and of a large Moorish vessel by a waterspout".

3. Other Turners (1) Daniel, who did town-pictures, F.62; (2) William of Walthamstow, coachpainter and landscapist; (3) J., Painter and Gilder of Lincoln's Inn Fields; (4) George, genre-painter – with (5) John, navy agent, &c., of Change Alley: Gage, 25a. I have searched through post-office directories, etc., and can add to this list only; (6) Henry Turner, painter, 59 Great Wild Street, Lincoln's Inn Fields (Holden, 1805–7).

4. Vesuvius: *True Briton* 6 February 1800; end: *Monthly Mirror*, April 1800, 240. Latter magazine, December 1799, 373, mentions a new scene, "a public building, lately erected in the city".

For related T. material: XXXVII, 94–95, 88–89, 128a, 104–5 (? Vernet). For Bay of Naples, etc.: CCCLXXV, 21; CXCVI, S (in style of L, G, and LXX, K – ? 1800). Eruptions: *Souffrier Mtns*, 1815; *Vesuvius*, 1822, f. CXLI, 35a. *Annual Register*, 1799, 377–8 has "Comparison between Mounts Vesuvius and Etna; from Spallazani's Travels in the two Sicilies". Eruption: Akenside, *P. of I.* (1st) ii, 163 ff.

Fireworks and various kinds of water displays utilizing light effects contributed to the new aesthetic. (Water effects were much used on the stage near the end of the eighteenth century).

5. XXVIII, H. His *Fountain Abbey*, 1798, was perhaps varnished for the purpose; Gage, n. 69.

T. used ship models like Loutherbourg: Gage, 24, App., and n. 65–66. L.'s plan for *Admiral Howe's Victory* is B.M., 201, C5, 51.

6. Gage, 23 f.

7. *ib*., n. 56; Pott, 74 f. In general, influence of Wright: RB, 8, 10. Note also Pether as a painter of fire and moonlight: two works at Macklin's Gallery (*Examiner* 1811, 487), one a blacksmith's shop: the other, Lukin's Iron Foundry, with glare of molten iron, lamplight, moonlight.

8. Th. ii, 42. The omission of R.A. after T.'s name for Naumachia proves nothing; L. in his Eidophusikon does not appear as R.A.

9. Summer, 1052 ff.; Livermore (1), 81. Note 2 studies for *Fall of the Walls of Jericho*: CXX, A.

10. Praise: W. (2), 7. He cites *Exodus* ix, 23.

11. F. 126; F. (2), 75 f.; CVI, 67a; Knockholt in general, XCVa.

12. XLIX, cover: misread by Finberg. For T. at Fonthill: F. 68. In winter months T. was busy among other things with picture for Duke of Bridgewater, a large sea picture to companion one by W. Vandervelde the Younger. The Duke was owner of coalmines and builder of canals, and had recently done well out of the syndicate for buying ten pictures belonging to the Duke of Orléans; he found his health benefited from having galleries to walk about in: F., 69 f. Prices: F., 71.

13. F., 71; W. (2), 19 f. Study of Whirlwind: LXXXI, 165. Other studies in this notebook, besides the sea studies (e.g. Shipwreck, 6, 80–83, 132–3), include: Hannibal, 38–39; W. Tell, 36–37; Jason, 7; Parting of Venus and Adonis, 50; Death of Adonis, 52; Macon, 54, 116–17; Hero and Leander, 57; Holy Family, 60, 63; Death of Python, 68; Deluge, 120–1, 163. See also LXIX; LXX. N, Q, S, h.

14. He cites *Jeremiah* xv, 32–33; it should be xxv. (The Fifth Plague should be called correctly the Seventh.) For himself as Jeremiah: see ch. 16, n. 13. Callcott, *View near Oxford*, was also criticized as obscure by the *Star*. *Sun* compared T. and Girtin, to G.'s credit: W. (2), 21.

15. Livermore (1), 84. The sense of doom and threat is also in the water-colour of Pembroke Castle with approaching storm.

16. *Diary*, 10 June 1801. T. now had a small collection of his own: a Cozens, and in this May a dozen sketches by Rooker and outlines, and eight drawings of West Country barges by S. Scott: CCCLXIX.

17. Finberg, 73 takes imbecility to mean "some form of temporary indisposition" – typical of his fear of any entry into T.'s conflicts.

18. William T. wrote, 27 May 1802, from 75 Norton Street.

19. Deaths of F. Wheatley, W. Tyler (architect), W. Hamilton. (Romney died later in the year, 15 November.) Soane and Rossi filled the other two seats.

Farington gives some accounts of T.'s methods: 13 February "Turner called. He paints on an absorbing ground prepared by Grandi and afterwards pumissed by himself. It absorbs the oil even at the fourth time of painting over. When finished it requires three or four times going over with mastic varnish to make the colour bear out. He uses no oil but Linseed oil. By this process he thinks he gets air and avoids any *horny* appearance."

27 February "Turner I called upon. Grandi being there laying me some absorbing grounds. He uses White, Yellow Oker, Raw and Burnt Terra di Sienna, Venetian red, Vermilion, Umber, prussian blue, blue Black, Ultramarine."

At Desenfans's sales in March 1802 were sold a Vernet, Hobbema, Titian (*Departure of Adonis*), 3 Claude, 2 Poussin, 2 Rubens, 3 Cuyp, and Watteau's *Bal Champêtre:* W. (2), 32–34.

20. TD, as also the rest of the material about this episode.

21. Caldwell of Dublin wrote in a letter: "A new artist has started up, one Turner; he beats Loutherbourg and every other artist all to nothing. A painter of my acquaintance, and a good judge, declares his pencil is magic; that it is worth every landscape-painter's while to make pilgrimage to see and study his works. Loutherbourg, that we used to think of so highly, now appears mediocre." J. B. Nichols viii, 43; W. (2), 37; F., 78 f.

R. Smirke admired the *Tenth Plague* (Farington, 15 June). Opie had his *Rizpah* this year.

22. F., 82–84; LXXI and LXXXI; LXXIII–LXXX. For Girtin: Roget i, 110, but see Farington (Grieg iv, 103).

23. Falk, 47.

24. Ziff (1), 318–19; Cummings, 150; LXXII, 26a. For Poussin touched-up Ziff, 319. T. studied Raphael, Correggio, Domenichino, Ruisdael, Barbieri, Rubens, da Mola.

25. Lectures MS. 14, box 1 (marked lecture 4 of the series of 6), with note p. 24, "Finish'd Feb 16th, 1810 Copied by W. Rolls"; but the cited passages were added later by T. himself: Ziff, 319. T. said of objections to F. Danby's colour: "Sir, Danby is a poetical painter", F., 290 n.

26. *ib.* 22. Note how the term "confusions" links the lecture with the Louvre notes.

27. CCCX, 68; F., 92; W. (2), 42; Th. i, 117 (remark that he'd have starved if G. lived). G. was attended by Dr. Monro. *Athenaeum*, 27 December 1851: "The artists of his admiration – the only ones he cared to talk about – were Reynolds and Girtin."

28. J. L. (3). The phrase about the *Deluge* "distracting theory" probably means that it runs counter to Reynolds's dictum that "absolute unity, that is, a large work, consisting of one group or mass of light only, would be as defective as an heroic poem without episode . . ." R. contrasts Rembrandt and Poussin, saying that while P. is distinguished by simplicity (as Rembrandt by combination, i.e. Complexity), his works yet have "scarce any principal light at all, and his figures are often too much dispersed, without sufficient attention to place them in groups"

(8th Discourse: i, 441). T. had perhaps been drawn to note this point by Opie, 120 f.

29. F., ch. ix; W. (2), 50–55, 78–80, etc. W. takes it as a mark of respect that T. was put in the chair, but it seems pressure of politics. Royalty did not attend the Dinner this year; for the odd mixture of airs and glees: W. (2), 56 f.

30. Later, Banks's model of Oliver Cromwell was objected to as an improper object that should be removed. Hoppner's wife as an American Republican: W. (1) 11, 42, 56.

31. F., 97–101; W. (2), 58 f. *The Holy Family* was much ridiculed. The nickname Overturner was later used at Farnley when he overturned a carriage: Th. ii, 85, cf. Mrs. Millais. Constable in May letter to Dunthorne.

More pictures coming in from Italy: W. (2), 60–63. Turner on the Hanging Committee with Bourgeois: *ib.*, 56.

32. J.L. (4), 38 f.; see the whole of the essay for the fuller relations. Also Beckford's *Reverie* written December 1778; and for contemporary interest in the phenomena: J. Grant.

33. Oppe (1), 41, n. 3 notes this point.

34. See Oppe's reprint in (1) 6 f., 5 f.; also his comments 169, 168.

35. For a discussion of da Vinci: R. Clark (1) 59 f., (2); MacCurdy, *Notebooks*, ii, 231.

36. Barry i, 482; Price (2) ii, 169. Edwards gave a short note on it. Pyne i, 1823, 16.

37. Oppe (1), 41. (Fuseli on Titian's *Holy Family:* "like the embryo or blot of a great master of colouring.")

38. *ib.*, 83 and pl. 13: in coll. C. M. Turner.

39. Palmer, 343; Grigson, 7. For "smudginess", Palmer, 336. Compare Palmer's Shoreham Monochromes and Cozens's Blots for imaginative unity and stress on structure.

40. Th. ii, 343.

41. IV, 70 ff. Ruskin on T.'s work: "perhaps universally an arrangement of remembrance".

42. *Analysis*, ch. xvi. Picturesque and abstract beauty: Hussey, 70.

43. A. Stokes, 59; XLIX, 68a, 69a; LXXVII, 41; XXV, 82a. Delicate pencil drawings: LIV, LXXIX, CLXXXIII. T. "was a phenomenal draughtsman in several genres, but particularly for choice and disposition of accent and bare space in a finely controlled sea of detail; for a pointilliste employment as a youth, in company with Girtin, of pencil's point within a pattern of short strokes", *ib.*, 60.

7. *Cataclysm and the Earthly Paradise*

1. Gallery: F., 101 f. Beaumont:.F., 107. Troubles at R.A.: F. 109 f. West on his troubles: W. (2), 78. Perhaps what T. had heard in France about the methods of artists led to the idea of his gallery.

1804: more pictures from abroad, W. (2), 68. There was an eclipse of the sun (three-quarters of diameter in London), 11 February: LXXXV.

2. Farington, 4 April. T. remarked that Morland's paintings showed "the effects of living within the rules of the Kings'-bench".

3. In November the King was well enough to reject Smirke; his

partisans tried to oust West; but Wyatt was beaten, twenty to seven. Farington thought T. among the three abstainers.

4. W. (2), 73–75. T. Malton elder died 1801. Both Dayes and T. Malton younger had tried in vain to become Associates. Morland died 27 October 1804.

5. F., 113. Frames at "cost price" (1841): F., 383. Note the letter of Wright of Derby, 1774, to Secretary of Incorporated Society of Artists: asking for his *The Earth Stopper* to be delivered to Lord Hardwicke without frame. "The shabby price his Lordship is to pay for it will leave no room for his Lordship to expect the frame with it; but if he should say anything about it pray inform his Lordship that the Earth Stopper was exhibited in an old Italian moulding frame which I have had by me for many years and keep for the use of the exhibition, and on no account let him have it." For another Edridge tale that must be distorted: F., 113.

6. Joseph in *Holy Family* also called Chinese by *Monthly Mag.*: W. (2), 59.

7. See LXXXI.

8. K. Clark (1), 2, puts well the role of Poussin (but fails to note the important link with Turner): "Even the romantic side of P. was perpetuated in the work of Francisque Millet, whose *Destruction of Sodom* contains the sort of alpine panorama which Ruskin believed to have been the discovery of Turner. That P.'s influence should have declined in the Rococo period was inevitable, but in the more heroic age of classicism it was revived. Through Pierre Henri Valenciennes it dominated the early work of Corot, and although Corot himself was to discover that his true affinities were with Claude, the shadow of P. still falls across the landscapes of Millet and Pissarro, long before Cézanne made a more spectacular return to his principles."

Various later works of T. show a clear P. influence, e.g. *Narcissus and Echo*, *Hesperides*, *Temple of Jup*, *Panhell.*, etc.: Ziff (1), 321, n. 37; but, more deeply, what T. had learned had sunk permanently into his system, ensuring a sense of structure in the wildest of his colour experiments.

9. *British Press*, 8 May 1804, says he was at work on a *Deluge*; F., 113, 118. West had a *Deluge* in R.A., 1805.

10. He draws widely, from Titian to Teniers (in the figures).

11. Th. ii, 153.

12. RB, 76.

13. F., 119 f.; W. (2), 106–12.

14. RB., 19.

15. T. was familiar with the engraving: F., 161. Note also the lecture reference. A drawing in Sandby's possession was described: "the effect of a storm. It was from this sketch Mr. Wilson took the idea of painting his celebrated picture the Niobe", W. (2), 152.

16. RB, 6. Note the rotating movement in Girtin's *Village of Jedburgh*, 1800: Loshak and Girtin, 75 and fig. 58.

17. Farington, 10 June 1801. For Bowles: Britton (1), 65n.

18. Christie's, 25 June 1965, Northwick Park Coll., no. 88; engraved by J. Young. For T.'s work: H. Finberg (2); Ruskin, *Works* xiii, 122 f.; Armstrong, 109.

19. Hoppner contrasts T.'s crude work with the fine delicacy and

naturalness of Glover's drawings. Callcott at R.A.: W. (2), 88. Ker Porter had his huge *Agincourt* (2,800 feet of canvas) at Lyceum, *ib.*, 93 f.

20. F. 116–19; Leicester's house, W. (2), 106. For Shipwreck: LXXXVII–LXXXVIII.

21. LXXIX, incl. diagrams of Victory deck and position of the ships, study for Death of Nelson, etc.

22. Watts, p. xl; C. R. Leslie (3), i, 199.

23. Th. ii, 98 f.

24. Th. i, 164. G. Jones: Th. ii, 159. Note T.'s refusal to verify a picture for fear of being involved in a law court; and leaving letters unopened: Th. ii, 152. Britton, Judkins, etc.: Th. i, 389; ii, 278; i, 223. Tour with N. Lowson on condition of not sketching same views; did not show L. any of his sketches, i, 223. Keep together: i, 242, ii, 154. Note his inability to sell even to an admirer like Munro: Th. i, 351. Also his wish for Ruskin to obey his mother: F. 116; Ruskin *Works* XXXV 342; RP iii 65.

25. Th. ii, 244; i, 180 and 299 f.; Frith i, 136. *Dido building Carthage* and *Sun rising through Mist*. For the special significance of Dido to him, see later. Note both pictures are of Sunrise (Resurrection).

Chantrey's comment was: "Indeed. Well, if that bright idea is carried out we will dig you up again, and will unroll you as they do the mummies", C. R. Leslie (3), 207 f. (also for Milman).

26. *Excursion* i, 484 ff., and ii, 67; Turner, the Arctic poem in CII beginning on 1a; *Amyntor* ii, 244 ff.

27. Grove, *Dict. Music*, s.v. Henry George Nixon, organist at St. George's Chapel, London Road, 1817–20 (where he married Caroline in 1818); Warwick Street Chapel, 1820–36; St. Andrew's R.C. Chapel, Glasgow, 1836–9; in London Road, St. George's R.C. Chapel (Cathedral, 1851), Southwark, 1839, till death. His works included five masses, cantata, vespers for every festival of the year, songs, pianoforte solos. His son, H. C. Nixon, born 1842, died 25 December 1908, organist at churches of various denominations at Hull, London, Woolwich, Blackheath, Spanish Place, St. Leonards on Sea. His many compositions included overture *Titania* (18 December 1880, Cowen's Concerts), symphonic poem *Palamon and Arcite*. A brother of his, James Cassane N., was born 1823, died 1842; a violinist.

28. Boaden: Farington, F., 126; Hazlitt, F., 208, and W. (3), 43; *ib.*, 146–7. *The Times*, 6 May 1831, and W. (3), 212; PTh. vii, 319 (original); 1838, F., 370; 1839, F., 373. Th. ii, 347. Falk, 170, cites with no references "charlatanerie and the vagaries of Bedlam" in 1840s.

Cf. Herbert Spencer, *Autobiography*, 1904, 233–5, accepting the tale that T. "ridiculed the public, saying laughingly – 'They buy my freaks!'." He thought Pyne better than T., and Orchardson superior in not overloading detail; he echoes the old criticism that T.'s pictures were false by lacking contrast of dark earth and brighter sky.

29. W. (3), 213; F., 383.

30. Liebreich, esp. 5–6. "The fault is a vertical streakiness, which is caused by every illuminated point having been changed into a vertical line. The elongation is, generally speaking, in exact proportion to the brightness of the light." Thus any shapes or outlines in the way of the

streak are blurred out. T. was normal till 1830; then began the distortion, a change in colour "caused by the increased intensity of the diffused light proceeding from the illuminated parts of the landscape." By 1833 the diffusion shows verticality; by 1839 regular vertical streaks appear. So the later works are the result of a deranged eye, not, as is usually supposed, the "result of a deranged intellect".

31. Falk, 165.

32. Th. i, 173 (Trimmer).

8. *Pause and Renewed Crisis*

1. See J. L. (2), no. 45. *The Fall of the Rhine at Schauffhausen* (R.A., 1806) can be compared with *Hesperides:* contrast of diagonal crag in centre and vertical bluff on right; water rushes between, but here its diagonal thrust is met by enlarging the bluff and using the foreground figures to strengthen the horizontal structure.

2. Farington, 5 April. For 1806: trouble about hangings at R.A.: F., 124. *Windsor Castle* is signed "J. M. W. Turner, R.A. Iselworth", where he seems to have had a house 1811–13, but this must have been done at time of its sale to Egremont: RB, 19. Verses to Soane show that lectures were on his mind: J.L. (2), nos. 58–59; F. 123. Pictures from abroad: W. (2), 124 f.

3. F., 122, 125 f., 124. Farington, 28 March 1804: Daniell painting in T.'s manner. "The lights are made out by drawing a pencil [brush] with water in it over the parts intended to be light (a general ground of dark colour having been laid where required) and raising the colour so damped by the pencil by means of *blotting paper;* after which with crumbs of bread the parts are cleared. Such colour as may afterwards be necessary may be passed over the different parts. A white chalk pencil (Gibraltar rock pencil) to sketch the forms that are to be light. A rich draggy appearance may be obtained by passing a camel Hair pencil *nearly dry* over them, which only *flirts* the damp on the part so touched and by blotting paper the lights are drawn partially." If D. had learned these methods directly from T., as seems the case, he was not at all secretive with young artists trying to follow his lead. For Crome and T.; W. (3), 4; F., 126. Later, S. Palmer reacted to his work, but made no major use of it.

4. Rawlinson (2), 2nd ed.; F., 128; Th. ii, 55, same story with slight variations.

5. CXVI, C; J. L. (2), no. 34.

6. RB, 20; Clare, 85 f.; Rawlinson, etc. On back of LXXXVII, 10, not noted by F., is written: "No. 1 of Liber Studiorum being Studies for Pictures in History Mountains Pastoral Marine and Architectural Landscape. Price 15."

7. F. G. Stephens; W. (2) 195 f. Rate-books show it assessed at slightly higher rate than some houses around: F., 133. Th. i, 162, calls it Kensington Mall, corrects in 2nd ed., 116.

8. Th. i, 162; the tale that he went to be near L. is obviously incorrect. Mrs. L. was then about 59 years. L. painted her as Zara and she appears in his *Winter* (with him and Picot, who engraved the work). For the L. house: W. (2), 195 – and its view.

9. Th. i, 162 f.

10. *A.R.*, 1811, 95, *Chronicle*. Account of volcanic eruption at sea, *ib*. 32–34.

11. 20 April was day of Opie's funeral, which T. attended.

12. F., 134, for list, etc.

13. Hamerton, 160; F., 134 f. *Sun rising* has dignity and peace; verticals and horizontals used, with gentle transitions of diffused light. One of the two paintings he chose to go with the two Claudes, but no obvious link with Claude or the Dutch sea-painters. See Gage (1), 23, n. 54, for Vernet's sunrises. Dawn had little to offer, in the Picturesque view: "The thick atmosphere prevents the appearance of a colour, save the monotonous cold, grey tone", J. H. Clark, no. 9.

14. Boat: Th. i, 343, "a good deal of his knowledge of seamanship was picked up during his trips to the North, to which he always went by a collier. Once he spent a whole summer in drifting about the Thames, for he was fond of water; and at the time of his death, 'Mr. Booth's' boat was moored off Battersea Bridge. Lord Egremont used to assert that Turner had a yacht."

XCIX, 86: design and measurements, list of costs amounting to £23 (the sails cost £10).

15. XCVIII.

16. RB, 23–26. "As with Constable, light is still rendered by contrast sparkling meadows set off by dark green bushes, trees silhouetted against the sky. But they have an elegance and artifice which C. lacked, and we recognize that they are the work of a painter who is used to relying on his memory and to finding graphic equivalents for every phenomenon", K. Clark (1), 109 f. C.'s horizons usually closed; T.'s open, indicating that "the scene represented, however intimately, is only a part of a limitless whole", RB, 23 f.

17. *Spithead*, R.A., 1809, shown at his own gallery 1808 as *Two of the Danish Ships which were seized at Copenhagen entering Portsmouth Harbour*. But by 1809 the topicality gone. His most dignified restatement of the van der Velde tradition.

18. Box 1, MS. 3.

19. F., 141–2. Water-colour. Soc., 1808: W. (2), 141.

20. Clare, 79; F., 142. Only precedent for close-up view of sea-battle seems Copley's *Siege of Gibraltar:* W.(1) ii, 100, 137–9, for all the trouble taken.

21. F., 135; hanging stories, 135; Wey sketchbook, 137.

22. *Review of Publications of Art*, June; see F., 142–9, *Hesperides*, etc. Also for a work of "Runic superstitions". Troubles about advertising, F., 150.

23. See XCIX, 74a, 77a.

24. F., 151–2; CIV and CV; Romans in Britain, CV, 81a.

25. Falk, 183.

26. CIV, 4a.

27. CCXI, 42; careful details of fishing boats at Dieppe, 31a, 39a; fish, 31.

28. Th. ii, 123 and 92; cf. 42; 133, seldom went on country visit without a rod.

29. Ruskin, WP, 1567.

30. J.L. (2), no. 32; CXI, 86–87a. The image of cattle is from Thomson *Summer*, 1123–5. For sketch as Picturesque: see ch. 4, n. 16. For sketches of cattle by Gilpin: CXXIX, 8.

31. See J.L. (2), nos. 32–33, 35–40. Ziff (3), 193 f., for link of verse activity and the thinking that went into the lectures.

32. J.L. (2), intro.; Livermore (1); J.L. (2), nos. 4, 53–54; Pope, no. 5. Note John Danby's most famous glee, "Awake, Aeolian Lyre", with image of music as river, which must have impressed T.; cf. J.L. (2), 70. In Thomson's *Ode*, the Harp's sounds are described as made by the spirit of a love-lorn maid, a hermit, a sacred bard (Jeremiah) weeping his people's woes, the celestial choir, and "the wandering spirits of the wind". In the *Castle*, it represents "wild warbling Nature all, above the reach of Art".

For a mingling of musical chimes and light effect: "Merlin's exhibition in the morning and Dillon's exhibition of philosophical fireworks in the evening. During the intervals Mr. Cartwright performs on the musical glasses, the sounds of which are most harmonious, while Mr. Dillon lights up an aerostatic branch suspended from the cupola of the saloon, in which light is produced in an instant of time, which Mr. Dillon carries at will, and extinguishes in an instant", Sophia von la Roche, 26 May 1786: *Sophia in London*, 1933, 238. (For the Glasses, see ch. 4, n. 19.)

Note Danby's glee: "Let gaiety sparkle in our eyes."

33. F., 152, 170–2. Callcott fails as Academician, F., 155; letter of Lawrence praising T., 156; criticisms of Spithead, 159; summer 1809, 159 f.; Oxford commission, 160 f., 164–6. In December, 1808 A. Carlisle was elected Professor of Anatomy at R.A. and held post for sixteen years; at some time was T.'s physician. *Hastings Beach* was described, 1875, as given to him by T. "for medical attendance": W. (2), 137 f. In 1809 varnishing days were instituted. T. and Soane improved the lecture room: W. (2), 149.

34. Paine, *Age of Reason* II, 1795; cf. T. in lecture L. 8, fo. 52v; Shee (2), 75, 194.

35. Knight (1), pt. III, ch. ii, 4.

36. Farington, 11 February 1808.

37. Knight, *ib.*, 9; cf. Reynolds on M. Angelo, ii, 129, "in the highest degree sublime or extremely ridiculous".

38. In general, Gage, 79, with figs. 30, 29; J.L. (2), no. 61; Ziff (3), 207 f. Cf. Thackeray in *Fraser's*, 1845, on *Whalers*, "the unrevealed bard of the 'Fallacies of Hope', is as great as usual, vibrating between the absurd and the sublime", F., 408. (Note link of the pictures with Hogarth's *Distressed Poet*.)

The Garret drawing has notes: "Translations etc. Vida art of Poetry. Hints for an Epic Poem. Reviews Torn upon Floor and Paraphrase of Job" (that by Blackmore?). "Coll. of Odds and Ends." The torn-up reviews are shown in the painting, expressive of Turner's dislike of critics. On the door is posted a table or "Almanak of Fasts and Feasts" (in both drawing and painting); above, in the painting, is a plan of Parnassus.

The drawing for the Artist's studio shows a work "Forbidden Fruit" on the easel; at the bottom is scribbled, "Picture either Judgment of Paris (or) Forbidden Fruit", and "Old Masters scattered on floor". There is added "stolen hints from celebrated Pictures Pallets Crucibles retorts labelled bottles Mystery Varnish quiz". The painting of the dentist's room with its bottles may have helped to revive his memories of the arguments about chemical short cuts to fine painting – also Shee's lines (Elements, 288 f.): "in gums engross'd, macgilpts and oils. The painter sinks amid the chemist's toils." For the Venetian Secret: Gage (3).

39. Gage (2), 99. An important note occurs in the Shee annotations, 7. "True Genius rises with its subject its power amalgamates itself th[r]o everything and can never be said to feel more or less than its subject." He goes on: "Simplicity [of] the impression upon the mind and simplicity of subject are to me widely asunder hence the difficulty of defining the picturesque. Uvedale Price upon the Picturesque infers roughness broken and undulating lines but all these may be found in common pastoral the broken bank and crook[ed] and uneven road may be often picture-*like* but requires size to render it wild while the appearance of a practicable road reduces its character. Mr. Knight maintains that seeking for distinctness in external objects is an error and all such distinctions only exist in a well-organized mind but surely they exist in both, in Nature or the Painter could not draw his conceptions of her incidents by description however florid if they were not in Nature originate by assistance in the Poets mind or [if] such distinctions did not exist in his transcript of Nature, how could they challenge the recognition of a well organized mind." See also Gage, 76. T. thus could not accept the narrow Picturesque notion of the right to rearrange Nature to make her conform to art. Gilpin told Mason, "I am so attached to my picturesque rules, that if nature gets wrong, I cannot help putting her right." See Barbier (1).

40. *Transport Ship*, almost certainly completed 1810 for C. Pelham, later first Earl of Yarborough; T. develops the vortex type of composition of *Shipwreck* of 1805, so takes a step towards *Hannibal*. Shipwreck and avalance this year intrude on pastoral and quiet sea-pieces. For *Transport*, F. 167–8; Burnet (4), 78; RB, 30.

41. *Winter*, 413–22; *A.R.*, 1798, 106, also stressing the coveted mineral wealth of the region.

42. RB, 26 f.

43. *Windsor* also called *Ploughing up Turnips near Slough*. RB, 26–28; Clare, 80. For jetty of *Windsor Castle*, cf. *Calais Pier*. His sketches XCIII (*c.* 1806) are still Wilsonian: Butlin (1), pl. 3. For Thames sketches in general, dates, etc., Gage (2), 75, n. 2.

44. He carried on the genre, e.g. *Raby Castle*, 1818.
Note Beckford's complaint that T.'s drawings for him "were too poetical, too ideal, even for Fonthill". Yet, Gage points out, 21, T.'s vision corresponds to B.'s own notion of the spirit of the place, which "looks heavenly through the showers..."

45. RB, 28. Note effect of Cézanne's water-colours on his oils.

46. Gage (2), 75b. Gilpin (4), 94–98, and Price (3), 215, (1) i, 160–3, 174–5n.; J. T. Smith (3), 18.

47. Lock, cited Gilpin. T. early tried his hand at snow: XXXVII,

64–65, snow scene at Lewisham; LXXV, 22–23, Mer de Glace; CI
(Boats and Ice), 12, "Greenish black in shadow" (written over water),
"Ice white and grey"; CII, 31a. For the dislike of whitewashed cottages:
Gage, 75. Girtin's *White House* was thus in its way a precursor of T.'s
interest in white; for it, see Girtin and Loshak, 70 f., 29 (T.'s liking for
it); R. Davies, 19, 22; Wedmore (2), 112.

48. Kirby, 104. Note the relation to optical illusion; the fallacies of
perspective that interested the epoch and that T. often deals with in his
lectures; cf. n. 19, ch. 4.

49. *La B.A.* i, 250, 1810.

50. One of his Round Table essays in the *Examiner*. Forecasting
Cubism in which the artistic process becomes explicitly the subject or
expression.

51. See ch. 3, n. 18. Story in Th. i, 316 f., of T. telling Rev. Judkins
that his *Ulysses* was inspired, not by Homer, but by Tom Dibden's
song: "He ate his mutton, drank his wine, And then he poked his eyes
out." A joke, but showing a bias of his mind.

52. TD.

53. LXXVIII; Livermore (2).

54. LXIII, inside front cover; CV, 24 (*c.* 1808). For other expressions
of his self-education: grammar (CVI, 67); style (*ib.*, 67a–68), cf. CXX,
V (adverbs of place in six languages).

55. TD.

56. Newton, *Opticks* (4th ed., 1730), 346; cf. M. H. Nicolson. L. de
Pouilly, 104 f.; cf. Avison 20–28. Criticisms by Aikin and G. Dyer.
See Cohen 202–6 for all this.

57. Field (3), sections 26–28: "*gradations of hues and shades . . . they
may therefore be termed the melodies of colour*". Goes on to identify
analogically "accordance of two colours" and the musical term "Concord". Field in all his thinking has a vague sort of dialectical triad in
mind. He ends here: "As the relation of harmony in colours is con-
sonant, or co-expansive, and an evident triunity governing the Chromatic system, the most proper figure in which to illustrate the correlation
of colours is the equilateral triangle." He has many such diagrams.

58. *Works* i, 350 (4th Discourse).

59. Goethe (Eastlake), sects 889–90.

60. W. (2), 37. Thackeray: J.L. (2), 75; F., 373.

61. J.L. (2), 71–75, and no 56.

62. Note Baudelaire in Delacroix essay: "The art of the colourist is
evidently in some respects related to mathematics and music." Cf.
theoretical application in Chevreul, 1838: K. Clark (1), 115.

Fairground: XX. Swiss girl: LXXVIII, 1. Harpers: LXIX, 18, 86a, 87;
XLVI, 1, cf. *Carnarvon Castle*. XLIV, W. (interior Covent Garden
Theatre, from the Gallery). LXXVIII (Swiss), 5–8, procession, "Men
follow'd the Priests, Women the Men." Man with flute in *View of
Fonthill* (1799). engraved, to give the character to Beckford's mansion;
flute-player in LS, n. 8. Pipers in contemporary scenes with or without
drums; drummers in martial settings such as Looe or Portsmouth.
"Mountebank selling Eau de Cologne", CCXV, 13; "Red Cart with a
Barrow and Man singing", Gosport, "Cold Claude-like effect", CCVII,
10a; procession for rain, Martigny, LXXIV, 87; on coast near Naples,

CLXXXIV, 1, "Girl dancing with Cansoneta"; LS, no. 3, woman with tambourine (cf. Romaika in *Temple of Jup. Panellenius*, 2nd version); CLXXXVI, 69a–70, "Girl dancing to the Tabor or Tambourine. One plays, two dance face to face. If two women – a lewd dance and great gesticulation; when the men dance with the women a great coyness on his part till she can catch him idle and toss him up or out of time by her hip: Then the laugh is against him by the crowd. Boy with Ring and Ball holds out cards . . ." *French Dancer in Sabots*, with two musicians. *Virginia Water:* early study has no band or barge, they appear in 1830 engraving: see Livermore (2).

Dancers in historical works: LXX, N.

9. *Hannibal Crosses the Alps*

1. In 1823 Fawkes was High Sheriff of Yorkshire; died 24 October 1825: see *Leeds Mercury* obituary, and *Gent. Mag.*, 1825: Foster, *Pedigree of W. Riding Families*.

2. F., 170 f. Complaint to C. Turner, 169 f; WP, 1520.

3. Falk, 43, who cites TD; but C. Mallord Turner has not been able to find the letter for me. It must, however, have existed.

4. *Holden's Triennial Directories*.

5. Information from W. M. Maidment of Highgate Library, who consulted the rate-books for me.

6. *Post Office Directories*.

7. CXI, 62a–63. But there was no newspaper named the *Herald* at the time; I cannot ascertain what periodical he means.

8. Son of a bricklayer and builder; very prolific with glees, submitting a hundred in 1787 for a competition; in 1807 his brain gave way and he was in an asylum for five years.

9. Th. i, 114: despite the giving of a knighthood to C., which almost amounted to an insult to him. News of his death: Th. i, 121 – T. much moved.

10. Th. i, 171.

11. Evelina is normally mentioned first in the testimentary statements (Th. ii, 410, 415). Once when Georgianna is named first (414), we may assume that the position comes from Turner's thinking first of her, then of married Evelina. Her name he gives as Georgianna, Georgiana, and Georgia.

12. CXCV; F., 176. They include designs of the construction of shadows, architectural drawings, coloured studies of reflection and refraction (as shown in glass balls empty or half filled with water), pyramidal composition of Raphael's *Transfiguration*, prison interiors (with shadows cast by jailer's lantern), domes, steeples, pinnacles, classical facades, Trajan's Column, vaulted arch, etc.

He cites Moxon, Hamilton, Malton, Kirby, Brook Taylor, Andrea Pozzo, Peter James, Highmore, Androuet, etc. See Th. ii, 108, on Hamilton's Perspective in a problem of domes; T. keeps on saying, "I think somehow I could do that yet." In his classical swing, he turns to Dryden, Richardson, Lairesse (one of the earliest opponents of Picturesque: J. Landseer (2), 170), away from Gothic ruins, topography, humble scenes: Gage 79b. We have already noted his turn from Picturesque (absorbed partly through Hearne in water-colours, Wilson in oils) of broken brushwork and sparkling light. For Dryden, cf. 18 FFS (Lecture 4): "Dryden says that art reflecting upon nature endeavours to represent it without faults. This idea becomes the original of Art and being measured by the compass of interlect is itself the measure of the performing hand and by imitation of which imagined form all things are represented which fall under human sight." He also read Shee, Roger de Piles, Opie, Dufresnoy, etc., and re-read Reynolds: Ziff (3), 195.

For accounts, etc., of the lectures: WP, 1541a, 1557–66; F., 174–7; MacColl (3); W. (2), 178–84, etc.

13. BML, 28, 16 January 1811. He takes up Taylor's feeble poem, *The Caledonian Comet* (for comet, n. 10, ch. 8, here) meant to satirize vogue for Border Minstrelsy. T.'s poem for all its incoherence keeps more to the parody point. (For a rebuttal, that works out the comet-image: M. A. Sellon, *The Caledonian Comet Elucidated*, 1811.) The references in the last three lines (F., 175) are to the Shakespearian quotation on Taylor's title-page.

Taylor praises Shee, Westall, and Tresham as poet-painters; this may have stirred T., whose scorn here expressed for romantic medieval trappings accords with his lecture attitudes, see n. 12 above. (Taylor may have given Gainsborough his idea of a "show-box" or transparencies; for about 1766 he showed T. Sandby an invention of this kind as something new for England: W. (2), 113).

14. Ziff (2) for reprint and comments.

15. 22 FFS. He says: "This is the case in Nature of panoramic views, and they are produced by such means and the retina of the Eye being according to Mr. Hamilton a parabola or in his words nearly a plane in the centre of the eye receiving in a circle all produced produce [*sic*] at the point of intersection the parabolic curve . . .": the sentence goes on confusedly, but what he is trying to say seems to accord with the point made in our text.

Goes on to say that what "is fallacious perspective not a fallacy of vision", "such should be the course of rules and the joint coincidence of vision . . ." Cf. 26 FFS on Conic Sections.

16. 21 FFS, 35. Cf. his attack on drawing taken in abstraction from light shade and colour; notes in Opie's *Lectures*, 1809 (TD), 23; poem J.L. (2), no. 60; F., 230 Draft of 4th Lecture (Box i, 14, pp. 21, 23): cited in ch. 6 here, after "arising from rules", goes on, "lines or localities of nature by a diffused glow or gathering gloom, which destructs abstract definition as to tone, and prevents even contemplation of any formality therein existing". Also he says Perspective can determine only gradation of line, of tone, of colour; intellectual or emotional aspects ("higher qualities") "are beyond dictation". See Gage, 18; Ziff (1), 319.

17. *Annals of Fine Arts* iv, 1820, 98, says the course was "distinguished for its usual inanity, want of connection, bad delivery and beautiful drawings". The *Annals* was hostile to R.A., but no doubt its comment would have been accepted by most listeners: WP, 1557; W. (5), 256. The 1818 syllabus did not include Backgrounds; T. may have succumbed to criticisms of its lack of relevance to Perspective: W. (2), 184. For appreciations: Redgrave (1) ii, 95; Stothard, nearly deaf, was a constant attender.

18.Python: Thomson, *Liberty* iv, 163ff., Apollo expressing the triumph of Graeco-Roman civilization; cf. Akenside, *P. of I.* (later) i, 322 (Tempe Golden age).

R.A. matters: F., 177 f. and W. (2), 185; Soane, F., 178; Hoppner, 178; hangings, 178 and W. (2), 187); Prince of Wales, F., 180 f.: prices, 181; LS delays, 181 f.

19. List of places visited: F., 182; CXXIII–CXXVI. Bank-notes: F., 182. Verse: CXXIII and J.L. (2), no. 50.

20. TD; Mary Matthews, Price's daughter, recalled her uncle William "was twice on a visit to my said father" at Exeter (about his mother's effects). The son recalled T. calling at Exeter "about forty years ago", at the time of the Chancery suit.

21. *ib.* Various jottings on the sheet about corn, wheat, flour. "Price of flour 18s per Sack."

22. T. Miller; F., 184; Th. i, 235 (distorted). Britton accepted T.'s suggestions. Britton: "I have often referred to this letter with gratification, not unmixed with surprise, as its critical remarks are at once frank and nicely discriminating; though his usual tone and language in conversation was blunt, abrupt, unaccommodating, and uncourteous."

A Coll. of Poems in Six Volumes by Several Hands, R. and J. Dodsley, 1758, iii, 346, at end of volume that opens with Pope's own poem on the grotto "composed of marbles, spars, and minerals"; note 142 for poem on a similar grotto. Note the old man on left in the engraving of *Pope's Villa;* he probably comes from Dodsley's account.

23. Earlier in year, Landseer told Farington that T. wanted repeal of rule forbidding landscape-painter to be Visitor, and was told there was no such rule. Note T.'s touchiness on status of landscape. Constable not elected: F., 184.

24. He moved there should be no agent to promote sales at the Exhibition as was done 1811, see W. (2), 187; Smirke seconded; passed. Marquess of Hereford, F., 186; Oxford pictures, 186–9; T.'s gallery, 190 f. Loutherbourg died, 11 March. Reception of *Hannibal:* W. (2), 199 f.; Crabb Robinson, *Diary* v, 15 May 1812. See also Farington 10–15 April; Burnet (1), 29, 37, 44; Th. i, 211, 294; ii, 88; Hamerton, 138; Monkhouse, 66 f., 76; Armstrong, 59, 85, 88, 104, 109–11; Chignell, 55, 68; Swinburne, 156; Brion, 31; Ruskin, *Works* iii, 239; Wyllie, 50, 55; Mauclair, 19 f.; Boase (5), 286–8.

25. Th. ii, 87. Lavery thinks the setting to be the Valley of Chamonix seen from Mount Prarion, cf. LXXIII, 1 and 63, 71a, 72a; LXXV, 1(?) and 15, 17, 22, 23, 54; also water-colour *Valley of Chamounix* at Farnley. Note stress on sublime in T.'s comments to H.F. For adaptation of a scene, cf. use of Cromarty in *Mercury and Argus*, 1836 (Ross-shire seen 1831): F., 359.

26. For Weather see *A.R.*, 1810, 269, 272 f.; November 10 at Boston, 285; *Bell's Weekly Messenger*, 1810, says October was very mild, 334; and also most November, 384; July–August saw some bad weather, 248, 280, 1811, *A.R.*, 124, also 89, violent storm July–August. *Examiner*, 1811, 769, speaks of heavy rains in early November.

27. Th. i, 294.

28. Claudean: Claude's "seaports, painted in the 40s, may remind

us of that moment when Aeneas leaves the grandeur and certainty of Carthage for a shining unknown distance. But the Virgilian element in Claude is, above all, his sense of a Golden Age, of grazing flocks, un-ruffled waters, and a calm, luminous sky, images of perfect harmony between man and nature, but touched, as he combines them, with a Mozartian wistfulness, as if he knew that this perfection could last no longer than the moment in which it takes possession of our minds." K. Clark (1), 77.

29. One volume of his 1786 Roman History is in TD.; the slight drawings deal with Caesar, Pompey, Cleopatra. But on the inside covers are five suggested pictures of Regulus returning, Pompey in defeat, Cleopatra on the Cydnus, and "Hannibal crossing the Alps", "His departure from Carthage the Decline of that Empire". Note LXXXI, 38–39.

30. *Liberty* V, 381–8.

31. F., 218 f. T. passed along the road and out of Fort Roc in 1802 (F., 83); the painting has a huge overhanging rock on the left.

32. J.L. (2), 47–49; no. 8. T. may have noticed that Sir W. Drummond had claimed to have found Hannibal's burial-place in Malta, *Examiner*, 1811, 739. The use of "downward" in the verses comes from Thomson: used of sun, cave, orb, age (*Summer*, 189, 1227, 1371, 1516). The distance in the painting is concentrated in the skyline-breaking elephant with waving trunk.

33. *Liberty* i, 286–9.

34. J.L. (2), no. 9. Note the relation of *Army of Medes* (1801) to Napoleon in East. T.'s picture of Hannibal amid ice and snow just antedates Napoleon this year in Russia.

35. C. R. Leslie (3), 263; see ch. 6, no. 12, here.

36. Sotheby, 17 May 1933, lot 11; Walker Galleries, 1934, no. 22; Oppé, 125 f.

37. J.L. (2), 49, no. 14. *Liberty* i, 64, "To whom Praeneste lifts her airy brow", where the link with the lowlands is harmonious, expressing the positive aspects of Roman rule.

38. CCXCIV, 60a; Romans, 68.

39. Boase (2), pl. 21 d and e. Mason, line 779; the Latin is less romantic: *ad alpes Dun super insanas moles . . . fulminat*. Note T.'s later drawing of Hannibal crossing the Alps in Roger's *Italy*.

40. Fuseli, 11th Lecture; Antal (2), 27, pl. 64b.

41. Antal (2), 148, pl. 64a.

42. Boase (2), 167, pl. 23e.

43. K. Clark (1), 111.

44. Mason, lines 384, 396; Latin, 278 f., 290.

45. *Summer*, 724; *Spring* (original, Robertson, p. 51); Akenside, *P. of I.*, i, 517.

46. *Summer*, 158; *Autumn*, 322; *Winter*, 2781; *Summer*, 488, 1083, 1683; *Autumn*, 41.

47. *P. of I.* ii (first version), 221–30. See also, 558.

48. In one case Campbell is thinking of improvement and so of industrial machinery; in the other, of the pure patterns of nature. Akenside, *P. of I.* i, 198; cf. "to scan the maze of nature", iii, 274; "the lamp of science through the jealous maze of nature guides", ii, 127;

"mazed folly", iii, 236; "he asks a clue, for nature's ways; but evil
haunts him through this maze", *Ode*, I, vi.

49. Kitson; cf. Turner's own incoherent statement of vision, "it
always must view only a part of the circle at which [at] a time the object
must be thrown on a part of circle instead of a square and as every line is
more or less elevated to it [must] it participates of a parabolic curve
because the eye is within the area of its circle", Lectures, 22. I have put
the "must" in brackets as it seems intrusive.

Kitson writes well also of the storm action creating the unity of the
work. "Everywhere the different parts fade into each other, forming a
complex, shifting pattern of ovals and parabolas, suggestive of flux."
Of the painting, within the limited colour range, the sky-greys are
skilfully modulated; he probably began with dark underpainting
(though he had begun to prime in white), then laid on succession of
lighter greys and whites; dragged on final touches of snow, right, with
almost dry brush; probably used palette-knife for yellowish-white in
distance, left, then flattened the paint. The picture has lasted well.
the weather effect is correct enough for a mountain storm.

10. *Personal Crisis*

1. CVIII (watermark 1808). "Ennervate" is a favourite word of his,
but he seems unclear about its meaning; here it seems to mean "in-
nervate", give nervous energy. "Slimmer" is unsure.

2. CXI, 54; J.L. (2), no. 62. Note in this book the favourable notice
of *Mercury and Herse* from *Sun* written out (31 April 1811), 68a; also
Python, 17, 70a, 78, notes on LS and finance; smoking the herb Stra-
monium, 2a; design? Sandycombe, 2.

3. *ib.*, 66a; J.L., no 64. This poem follows that satirizing Wilkie and
Bird, and thus contrasting the neglect of the true poet with the fame-
during-life of the mediocre artist.

4. *ib.*, 95, 94, 93a, 93, 92a, 64a. Bruce retired in dudgeon to his home
at Kinnaird; 1790 published *Travels to Discover the Source of the Nile*,
5 vols.; died 1794; autobiography in 1805 and 1813 editions, with a
biographical note by A. Murray. Explorations: see Akenside, *P. of I.*
(1st) i, 49.

"Columbus-like wishing for day to crown the long-sought . . .", 94;
"Could Rayligh linger out so many years In a dark prison . . .", 91a.
Of Bruce he writes: "feverish nights . . . To the weak Eylids that the
noon tide beam Has glared to nothingness their blood Throbbing
thoughts all in meandring more swift Quick rages thought on thought."

5. CXXXIX 17 (Watermark 1805). Farnley 105a, 47 (related to
Woodcock Shooting, signed 1813); hunting 48, 49; M. and Herse 20a–21
(?); *Hannibal* is mentioned 45.

Last word of poem may be "soon"; some words unsure, e.g. quicksets.
Lyric: CXXIX, 43a–44; it seems to say that the spring renews hope and
love despite everything.

6. CXXIX, 6a -7 (Dido); 1–2a (Phipps). Some special meaning seems
given to "practice". There was a Phipps who disliked T.'s pictures,
F., 135; Gen. Phipps, who entertained T. and others, belongs to a later
phase: F., 327, Th. ii, 44. For various uses of "practice" in eighteenth-

century art and literary criticism. "The term 'practice' was thus identified physiologically with health in terms of the bodily motions and in this sense the stirring of the animal spirits was, as Addison suggested, the physiological basis of aesthetic pleasure." Cohen, 213 f. One variant of the many epigrams has "to prove his skill". Note "Hannibal", CXXIX, 45.

7. *ib*., 122a.

8. CXXXV, 27a.

9. CXIII (watermark 1808), probably 1810. Brooch poem: J.L. (2), note "jealous care" and "prying air", and odd use of "enervate". Itinerary: J.L. (2), no. 50 1 and k. Note also ballad on love the deceiver, CVI, cover; J.L. (2), no. 48.

10. CXXXI, 131. "Still" is unsure. A dash after "far". In building up the concept of the *Fallacies of Hope*, T. may have been reacting against John Danby's elaborately treated *Ode of Hope* (in *Posthumous Glees*): six lines with ending couplet, "O'er life's rough Sea amid the Tempest's roar pilot my rolling bark and set me safe on shore." (Cf. Glee on p. 27). For a physiognomist's statement of the importance of Hope in Turner's character: RD 42.

11. Th. i, 173.,

12. Cited Th. ii, 196–7. T.'s dislike of criticizing his fellow artists has its roots in his fear, his feeling that by refraining from all criticisms he had the right to resent the attacks on himself. The verses satirizing Wilkie and Bird show his real feelings; but he would not have spoken out those feelings. For the comparison of Wilkie and Teniers, W. (2), 105, 145. There thus seems likelihood that T. did paint up two pictures to injure the effect of *The Blind Fiddler*, 1807: W. (2), 121; F., 135 f.; A. Cunningham i, 144; P. Cunningham; R. and S. Redgrave.

For linking of Bird and Wilkie: *Examiner*, 1811, 247; 1814, 206.

13. Full title: *Elements of Art A Poem; in Six Cantos, with Notes and a Preface; including Strictures on the State of the Arts, Criticism, Patronage, and Public Taste.* See TD for T.'s copy.

14. Shee, 28. Falk, 167, cites as in his possession a letter to A. B. Johns written *c.* 1813 (?1814) commenting on *Examiner* which showed "how the High-mightinesses of Art were treated in that hotbed of servility, *London*", where it might be supposed artists were all drones fattening in the Academic hive. That after a long life "not passed in inglorious sloth", any man's reputation should be immolated to enhance the value of a penny sheet of paper to 8½*d*. was no cheering prospect, and still more deplorable that the public should relish such treatment. Another sheet, the *Champion*, had broached a new doctrine, "Encouragement never made genius", and so was unnecessary. Genius would find its own path and poverty was its best guardian. T. comments by citing, "As one in darkness long immersed Peeps through a cranny hole and calls it Day". And suggests that in the light of this new doctrine, henceforth, like the Cornish curate and his congregation, all artists should start (without encouragement) *fair*.

Letters to Johns: F., 228 f., 231.

15. Shee, 31.

16. At the start of the book.

17. *ib.*, 37–39. A word I cannot read before "thought analytically considered".

18. *ib.*, 30.

19. *ib.*, 6, citing Collins on Music, *Ode to Passions*. He goes on to discuss unity of effect.

20. *ib.*, 7. Cf. 13, on difference between Judgment and Taste. Both are needed or Taste degenerates and "judgment sinks into systematic rules".

21. *ib.*, 11; see Ziff (2), 132, n. 27, for different readings.

22. *ib.*, 25; Ziff, 131, n. 26. See *ib.*, 8, for "plodding taste" (Shee). Cites as exponent of uninspired application Ryley, "a man certainly not dully deficient not in intellectual powers abstemious devoted to his art and the innumerable sketches left at his death prove how oft he corrected his design Nor past an idle day without a line generally dated each sketch and I have several books so dated that shew marks of improvement and prove how far common interlects can be cultivated by sheer industry and intense application, from fondness & choice he arduously pursued the art, but alas the sterile soil denied him bread and provokes the labourer's toils." For Ryley CXXIX,8 ("List of Drawings in different Portfolios": Rooker, Hamilton, Hoppner, Gilpin, nineteen Academy figures by Ryley, R.A.). He was a pupil of Mortimer.

See further his notes in Opie's Lectures, 1809 (TD): 14, on difficulty of term beauty; 21, impossibility of greatness in art by perseverance, without "interlectural perception of soul. No energetic power[s] of body avails the artist no speculated calculations of those that are to rise or fall no friendly patron or powerful relative . . ." Cf. 43, 55, and 58.

In the lectures he is careful to be less challenging: cf. 21, where he stresses the need not to attempt premature originality.

23. J. L. (2), 32 ff., discussing Cowper, Campbell, etc. One of the most amusing of the series is *The Pleasures of Affection, a Poem; as excited by remembered Acts of Benevolence and Friendship during the Christmas Holidays*, Charles Turner, 1817. Falk mentions *The Fallacies of Hope*, by C. C., 1832, but I cannot trace it.

24. *Examiner*, 1811, 380; Callcott's picture was no. 198. In 1816 Hazlitt thought T. might for once take a lesson from C.'s *Entrance to the Pool of London* (175); W. (2), 257. Callcott linked with T., 1822: W. (3), 28 f. Something of personal chagrin can also be detected in the way T. to some extent matched himself in the years after 1807 against Wilkie, attempting genre-pieces and writing verses that lampooned Wilkie and Bird as having had their wits turned by overpraise: Ziff (3), 207, 211 f.; J.L. (2), no 55.

25. See in general Constable, esp. 125–8, and App. 1 here, which draws much from him. Artists who furthered W.'s reputation: P. Sandby, J. I. Richards (personally associated with W.); then Turner, Lawrence, Westall, Bourgeois, Tassaert, Constable, etc., with amateurs like Dr Munro and Sir G. Beaumont, Oldfield Bowles and T. Wright. In general, see further, F. Haskell, *Patrons and Painters* (1963) and F. Davis, *Victorian Patronage of the Arts* (1963).

26. Th. i, 172. He adds, "His remarks on pictures were admirable: no beauty and no defect escaped him."

11. *Politics and Symbolism*

1. Cited on title-page of Sellon's book, see ch. 9, n. 13. For the sort of attention aroused: *Examiner*, 1811, 616, 627, 665, 676, 691.

2. XLII; F. failed to see what they were. The titles were *Sailor's Journal* and *The Token*.

3. J.L. (2), no. 43; CII, 1a and on; note Iceberg and stranded ship: CI, 18, cf. 14–17; F. (2), pl. xxiv, probably *c.* 1800. T.'s poem opens with a reminiscence of Thomson's *Summer*, 1004 f.: Gama "by bold ambition led, and bolder thirst of gold."

4. *ib.*, nos. 41–42; CII, 3 and 4a.

5. At start of book.

6. Pages 32–33; Ziff (2), 128, with different readings from mine. He reads "littleness" for "bitterness", etc.

7. MS. 12 (box 2), 27, 27a; Ziff (2), 128.

8. MS. 1 (box 2), 12. His respect for Reynolds lies in considering him "the Father of the English School", MS. 3 (box 1), 3–4, and 11 (box 1), 2–3; Ziff (2), 127.

9. CXXIII, 105a, 110a. Cf. passages on rope-twisting and timber in Jason poem: J.L. (2), 67.

10. *ib.*, 26, 28a, 35a. The mortal strife of "arts and the love of war" seems put back into feudal days – but see Akenside later in this chapter (on dissociation). See *Liberty* iv, 284, for leagued barons and T.'s lines, 26. See also n. 10 of ch. 1 here.

11. See ch. i, 19–20, for the Jason poem. Note the John Bull ballad twice recorded in the sketchbooks, once in full: CVI, 11–12; Th. i, 375.

12. Fawkes (1): *Speech of Walter Fawkes, Esq. Late Representative in Parliament for the County of York; on the Subject of Parliamentary Reform, delivered at the Anniversary Celebration of the Election of Sir Francis Burdett, Bart. at the Crown and Anchor Tavern, May 23rd 1812.* Reprinted 1813 with *The Letter, addressed by him to the Lord Viscount Milton, M.P. on the same subject* (first appeared in *Leeds Mercury* 7 November 1812).

Fawkes maintained his radical opinions, e.g. *The Englishman's Manual: or a Dialogue between a Tory and a Reformer*, 1817 – but the tone here is far less vehement. Dialogue IV is headed with the passage from *Henry IV* 2, 3, on danger. A passage that seems typical of his fiery but sensible character.

13. J. L. (2), 46.

14. *Examiner*, 1811, 739, 769.

15. Th. ii, 264 f.

16. Th. ii, 138; Livermore (1), 82. It would be of interest to compare T.'s use of symbols with those of Blake, Fuseli, and Palmer. Note Loutherbourg in Macklin's *Bible* did a headpiece for each book, in which Hebraic emblems were generally set amid rolling clouds; the volume of *Apocrypha*, published 1816 after his death, wholly illustrated by him, had preface explaining the symbolism: Boase (2), 167. Note further Ward and the vulgarization by Martin.

17. *Liberty* iv, 904, with note. T. adds, "Be no such horrid commerce, Britain, thine" – against all the facts.

18. CXX, Z, reverse. Hard to date, but certainly earlier than the paintings.

19. F., 335; J.L. (2), 61–62. The painting was probably in part suggested by plates in Burnet (3): II, fig. 4, Cuyp's *Embarcation of the Prince of Orange*, and VIII, fig. 1, West's *Landing of Charles II*. In West's work the main actors fill the whole picture (as in *Death of Wolfe*, etc.), while B. notes that in the Cuyp the two main actors are very small, but brought out by clothes of red and black and by their setting in the centre "against the most retiring part, and surrounded by light", 15. T. then paints a companion piece to the Cuyp, a political retort to West. (T. showed interest in Brixham and William in CXXXVII, inside cover.)

20. CCCLXIII, 43, penultimate page of his last book.

21. CXXXIII, 1: difficult to read, but main meaning sure. Orders poem: J. L. (2), no. 57. Ruskin: Th. ii, 154. Roberts: Th. ii, 45 f.

22. General Argument (2nd version).

23. P. of I. i, 349 ff.

24. Home: ii, 149. Genuine: iv, 125 (2nd). S. Palmer in sketchbook 1824–5 (see Palmer, 12; Grigson, 12, 25–28, 159 f.): "Note that when you go up to Dulwich it is not enough on coming home to make recollections in which shall be united the scattered parts about those sweet fields into a sentimental and Dulwich looking whole. No. But considering Dulwich as the gate into the world of vision one must try behind the hills to bring up a mystic glimmer like that which lights our dreams. And those same hills (hard task) should give us promise that the country beyond them is Paradise", 81. His designs in the Ashmolean Museum, 1825, have their start in this sketchbook. (In many of Turner's more topographical or romantic water-colour engravings we have the sentimental and Dulwich-looking abode; in his true idylls we have the gate into a world of vision, Paradise.)

25. Argument to II.

26. II, 23 f. He thinks of the medieval world as the primary source of the separations, but sees the struggle as carried on into his own world; they will be ended when freedom is fully achieved, and when Albion extends "to all the kindred powers of social bliss a common mansion, a paternal roof", 42 ff.

27. Opie, 58; F., 230; Gage, 76.

28. J. L. (2), no. 67, 70.

Note on symbols. The spire was for T. an emblem of aspiring hope. He links it with the ascending pillar or curve of smoke, e.g. London is veiled in murk of "commercial care and busy toil" "save where thy spires pierce the doubtful air, As gleams of hope amidst a world of care", *London*, 1809 (J.L., no. 5); "scarce seen thy numerous spires In honor reard & as the smoke aspires" (no. 41). "The high raised smoke no prototype of Rest, Thy dim seen spires rais'd to Religion fair Seen first at moments thro that World of Care" (no. 42); (white sails on blue sea) "as village spires Point as in foam where Hope aspires" (no. 50n.).

His interest in spires shows in the anecdote: "A church spire having been left out in a sketch of a town, 'Why did you not put that in?' 'I had not time.' 'Then you should take a subject more suited to your capacity.' "(Th. ii, 153.)

The use of a spire as a central point for a composition was old; it

had the further value of expressing the human centre of a landscape.
Thomson also links smoke and spire. "And villages embosomed soft in
trees, And spiry towns by surging columns marked Of household smoke,
your eye excursive roams – " And he goes on in a way that stresses this
aspect of human centrality, "Wide-stretching from the Hall in whose
kind haunt The hospitable Genius lingers still, To where the broken
landscape, by degrees Ascending, roughens into rigid hills" (*Springs*, 954
ff.). Note how the Picturesque intrudes as the human aspect gives way
to wild nature: broken, roughens, rigid.

Ruskin notes the use of a white column of smoke in *Ulysses deriding
Polyphemus* (taking from Pope a touch not in Homer). "Turner was,
however, so excessively fond of opposing a massive form with a light
wreath of smoke (perhaps almost the only proceeding which could be
said with him to have become a matter of recipe – see, for very marked
example, vignette of 'Gate of Theseus', in illustrations to Byron),
that I do not doubt we should have some smoke at any rate ..." (9),
376 f.

Smoke, representing the spire in dissolution, at the mercy of the elements, thus tends to represent man's fragility, the fallacies of his hope.
Note how Thomson anticipates: "till all the stretching landscape into
smoke decays", *Summer*, 1441.

The smoke symbol is thus linked with such images as the dissolution
of "the gaudy pile which airy Hope has rais'd", Jerningham in his poem,
Peace, Ignominy, and Destruction (1797), speaking of the French
Revolution.

Further note on Akenside. Probably Turner, in his Garrateer's Petition
had in mind Akenside's poem *The Poet: A Rhapsody*, where the poet
is "cursed with dire poverty" in "garret vile" (Ziff (3), 212). Ziff has a
valuable discussion of Akenside's influence on Turner. See (3), 203, for
the archetypal forms cited at the end of T.'s first lecture and the way
in which his following remarks are based on Akenside. We see how
thoroughly T. had assimilated A.'s main ideas. Twice T. cites *The
Pleasures* after analysing the light and colour of Poussin's *Deluge* (Ziff,
204 f.). T. shows that he is trying to grasp and express the multiplicity of
associations, impressions, ideas that are fused in the aesthetic image.

Thus he paraphrases Akenside, seeking to re-express his ideas in
terms that illuminate the art process. "And hence the rise in poetic
allusions so feelingly ascribed to the action of the mind, the pleasure of
imagination commensurating supposed space, or continuity of Time,
from the same ideal source. Ideal quality and comparative enquiry as
to form endeavour to modify conjecture into theory, to express harmoniously and represent practically. Thus Painting and Poetry, flowing
from the same fount mutually by vision, constantly comparing Poetic
allusions to natural forms in one and applying forms found in nature to
the other, meandering into streams by application, which reciprocally
improved, reflect, and heighten each other's beauties like ... mirrors."
(End of first lecture.)

He is attempting to set out a dialectical view of the interaction and
fusion of mind and nature in art. This interaction occurs in both poetry
and painting, though there is a different relation to space and time

in each expression. (This I take to be the meaning of the difficult first sentence). The realization of the ultimate unity of poetry and painting can help the development of both poet and artist.

In the notes on Opie and in the lectures Turner shows how long he had brooded on the relation of the two arts and on the valid forms of trans-position. See Ziff (3) and J.L. (2). He stresses "the contrariety of means" in two arts "drawn from the same source and both feeling the beauties of nature" (Opie, 61–72). "The painter's beauties are definable while the poet's are imaginary as they relate to his associations." The poet "seeks for the attributes of sentiments to illustrate what he has seen in nature". The painter must "adhere to the truth of nature" (CVIII, 53a, 52a, etc.). He discusses these points at some length. One interesting point is raised by a consideration of the poetic phrase "wavy air". In the poem "One word is sufficient to establish what is the greatest difficulty of the painter's art: to produce wavy air, as some call *the wind*". To define wind the painter "must give the cause as well as the effect ... with mechanical hints of the strength of nature perpetually trammelled with mechanical shackles." He can represent motion, but cannot "attach quality of motion" of the kind expressed by "the great poet of nature Thomson in his Summer, a time beyond delineation, yet most truly drawn". Thus "While from the bladed field the hare limps awkward And the wild deer gaze at early passenger Roused by the cock, the soon-clad shepherd leaves His peaceful cottage". (These are, in fact, a changed and com-pressed conflation of lines 57–60, 63–64; one of the examples showing that Turner knew large sections of Thomson by heart, in his own re-ordered way.) The painter succeeds, he says, when he represents motion; but the poet can imbue the same motion with connotation, giving it meaning and significance.

The problem is pursued in detail in the fourth perspective lecture: Ziff, 198–201; J.L. (2), 13–14.

12. *Gathering Strength*

1. F. 192. Devon paintings helped him in his release from topography etc.

2. Livermore (4); F., 212. Came to be near Reynolds's old house: Th. i, 167. Chantrey's rich wife lived at Twickenham before marriage. T. liked being near Brentford.

3. Havell drew it for Cooke's *Thames Scenery*, 1814. Bills: F., 192.

4. Gage, 80, pl. 33, 34; Elsam, pl. 6, 8; Dandy, pl. xv; A. Watts, p. xxvii, n; Fetcham: *J.R.A. Arts*, September 1963, 297. T. liked design-ing houses or parts of them, e.g. doorway for his house in Queen Anne Street; at Farnley, etc. Note letter to Holworthy, January 1826 (F., 293): "But consider the pleasure of being your own architect day by day its growing honors hour by hour increasing stroke by stroke..."

See F. (2), p. xxxv; CXX, R; CXXVII, 2–3, 7, 12a, 13a, 14a, 21a, 35; CXI, 2; CXIII, 13, inside cover; CXIV, 73a–74a, 77a–79, 86a, etc.

5. Livermore (4) on Soane's Fitzhanger Manor at Ealing.

6. XC, 21, 52a, 59; note Jason, 49a, and other historical sketches. The painting has four lines from Dryden's *Aeneid*, stressing sunrise.

7. Ruskin, (9), 372 f.; Th. i, 173 (Lybian horses).

8. R.A.: F., 193. (Pictures at own gallery, F., 190 f.)

9. Th. i, 167.

10. Th. i, 168. Trimmer says he had dined too, at Queen Anne Street, "where everything was of the same homely description. I should say he never altered his style of living from his first start in Maiden-lane." Frugal meals: "You were welcome to what he had, and if it was near dinner-time, he always pressed us to stay, and brought out cake and ale; the cake he would good-humouredly stuff into my pocket." He says William was "latterly his son's willing slave", stained and varnished his pictures, so T. used to say "his father began and finished his pictures for him". C. Turner once went into studio, found William on his knees colouring a canvas; T. came in, good-humouredly trundled him out, telling him he was on forbidden ground, 163. Blackbirds: Th. 88, 122; i, 166 f. Snaps a tendon, i, 178. Further for William at the Gallery; RD 11.

Tale of Mulready and Pye to a feast of "a bit of strong cheese and a pint of stale porter", Th. i, 166; Pye rebutted the insinuations, WP, 1549.

11. Th. i, 164 f.; F., 196 f.

12. Th. i, 173 f., Latin; 308 f., Greek. Note CLXIII, 3a: three Greek names, one incorrectly transliterated.

13. Th. i, 171.

14. *ib.*, 170 f. *Frosty Morning* hung over fireplace in gallery. Tale of Gilpin painting horses, *Hannibal*; T. denies: i, 170.

15. *Diary*, 8 April.

16. Clare, 80; C. Johnson; J. L. (2), 58, Faded: F., 196; W. (2), 211.

17. Dinner: F., 197.

18. CXXX-CXXXIV. Wolcot's Dodbrook house was "a picturesque place". Lord Bovingdon, later Earl of Morley, at Saltram. Demaria, at one time scene-painter, Opera House, London; later worked for Macready, with David Cox an assistant, at Birmingham Theatre. Catalina who sang at Festivals, Exeter and Truro, late August, was at Saltram. R. says that one of the R.A. "scarcely credited" that T. gave a picnic; he also stresses T.'s lack of stinginess. Water-colour, *Plymouth Dock from Mt Edgecombe* in *Southern Coast* has festive sailors in place of his own party. After the cramped inn night T. was up before six, to draw a bridge. He and R. also went to Cothele and "had a picnic on the romantic banks of the Plym".

19. Redding (1) (2) (3); F., 197–203. T. was often thought to look like a seafarer, e.g., Leslie (Th. ii, 321). For his respect for a real sea-captain: RD, 8, 11.

20. Th. i, 219–21. T. gave Johns an oil-sketch later, F., 202. f. Letters to Johns, see ch. 10, n. 14.

21. F. 431. Fawkes's pheasants: CLIV, Y; F., 228.

22. CXIII, 14a, 18, 24a, 61a, 15a, 17 (on moorcock).

23. F., 203f. Combe was Dr Syntax, one of whose quests was for the Picturesque. T.'s MS is lost. Finances: F., 204 f. Holdings in Funds, end of July 1813, £9,399 18s. 1d. (only some £2,000 increase in two years, but doubtless much spent on building).

24. *The New Monthly Mag.* statement that the second time he lost his MS must be a joke: W. (2), 22 f.

25. *Examiner*, 1814, 107 f.

26. F., 207–9. C. Turner as Assoc. Engraver: F., 209 f.

27. F., 215–17.

28. Hazlitt: F., 280 f. T.'s own gallery: F., 212 f. For Review poem: CXXXVI, 182, also refers to "destined prize".

29. F., 213 f.; W. (2), 229. Smirke: F., 229. T.'s summer, 214.

30. Praise by Uwins: Memoir i, 39. Dinner: F., 218. Fall of R.A. Chandelier: W. (2), 240 f. Sir David Murray and old Devonian who had held umbrella over T. while sketching for Brook. "To have been in that old man's place that afternoon." Falk, 129.

31. F., 220 f.; Farington, 5 June 1815. B. I. Exhibition: W. (2), 247.

32. Th. ii, 41 f.; Monkhouse ,90; F., 226 f. Dad is plagued with weeds.

33. The dog, I assume, represents the animal life of the girl. H. Thomson's *Crossing the Brook* of 1803: W. (2), 58 f.; engraving, J. Young. Note CXXXI, 68: tree by stream, tree trunk as footbridge,"Tree in shade" and "Girl crossing" – this as the link. The female on the bank in T.'s *Brook* may be the mother; note the dark tunnel-space behind her. Note also the symbolism of Zuccarelli's *The Spring Head* (engraved E. Brandard): two children play by the spring, a woman stands at their side, a man lounges across the stream.

34. F., 228 f.; Armstrong, 24. R.A.: F., 231. School: W. (2), 253, in rivalry with B.I. Dulwich gallery, *ib.*, 253.

35. Whitaker's History of Yorkshire, F., 242; expenses, 243. West and model, 242 f.

36. Mrs F.'s Diary, F., 243.

37. BML, no. 45; F., 244—31 July.

38. See n. 22 above; this one is 14a.

39. F., 244. Two more letters to H. about the arrangements. T. left on 15 September. Did he visit Belvoir? F., 224 f.

40. Beaumont and Knight were on the Committee.

41. Drafts: CXL, 3, 4, 7a, 8, 11, 11a in pencil. F., 248, points out that while R. Hunt criticized T.'s richness ("a profusionof showy habiliments", etc.) as well as the "miserable blotches" of the figures, in the same issue Leigh Hunt praised Keats and found in him as virtues what R. H. found as vices in T.

T. and Artists' Gen. Benevolent Inst.: F., 247. T. and R.A. records: W. (2), 227. Gas in R.A., *ib.*, 277.

42. CLIX-CLXII. Things lost: CLIX, 101. This book has guide-notes, ref. to a *Manual*, itinerary. "Did you see my baggage?" etc., 102.

43. CLVI-CLVII.

44. F., 249 f. Letter, BML, no. 49, *Mag. of Art*, 1900. Needless to say, F. cuts the reference to getting children.

Farnley material connected with Civil War: CLIV.

45. Constable and Dort: F., 252, also prices. Dawson Turner: F., 252. Chantrey and diploma: 254; W. (2), 291 f.

Waterloo: Clare, 82; Th. ii, 42; W. (2), 285. (The *Sun* saw, however, "a terrific representation of the effects of war".)

Sir J. Leicester and *Sun Rising* (cleaning): F., 255.

46. CLXV–CLVII, note in last (inside cover), 'Callcott's Edinburgh from Brede Hill'. Interest in work as usual, e.g. CLXVI, 50a–51.

47. Farington, 4 March 1818. F., 253.

48. Falk, 43. Thomas Sanders Dupuis: 5 November 1733 to 17 July 1796; member of R. Soc. of Musicians, December 1758; on death of Boyce, 1779, organist of Chapel Royal. Died of overdose of opium at his house, King's Row, Park Lane; buried 24 July 1796 in west cloisters, Westminster Abbey. *Gent. Mag.*, 1796, 621 f., says that though ill he attended the Chapel and so probably brought on his end: he "raised a very good fortune", as well as "indulging in a liberal spirit of hospitality". I can find no proof of a connexion between J. D. and the composer, but in view of Caroline's marriage to Nixon it is possible, since Sarah is shown to have kept moving in musical circles. J.D. might also have been a grandson. Charles Dupuis with a Park Lane address was married September 1796. See further p. 264 here.

49. Introduction to his book. Full title: "Journal of a Residence in Ashantee by Joseph Dupis, Esq. Late his Britannic Majesty's Envoy and Consul for that Kingdom. Comprising Notes and Researches Relative to the Gold Coast, and the Interior of Western Africa; chiefly Collected from Arabic MSS. and Information Communicated by the Moslems of Guinea: to which is prefixed an account of the Origin and Causes of the Present War." Dedicated to George IV; engravings by C. Williams after Dupuis.

50. CLII, inside cover; J.L. (2), no. 65.

51. F., 257. Fawkes's show: W. (2), 296; F., 258 f.; W. Carey (1). At R.A.: F., 259. Scott: F., 257. On Wednesday, 7 July, eleven of the Academy Club, including Turner, went up the Thames in the Ordnance Shallop (lent by Duke of Wellington) with ten rowers; river day with city barges and pleasure boats. To Barnes, ate a loaf and cheese in boat, then to Eel Pye House at Twickenham, soon after 3 p.m.; at four sat down to "excellent fare brought from the Freemasons Tavern under the management of a Clever Waiter. We dined in the open air at one table and removed to another to drink wine and eat fruit", Farington.

Italy: F., 160 f. Constable Associate in August. Rhine project: Ruskin, *Works* XXXV, 595; CLXIX, 7–8.

52. *Dido* was based on Claude's *Sea Port*. T. at first willed the pair to hang with the Claudes in National Gallery (later replaced the second by *Sun Rising*).

53. Led on to works like *Harbour of Dieppe*, 1825; *Cologne*, 1826. Monckton Milnes (Lord Houghton) in 1869: "When the steamer came in sight of Dort, I knew exactly what to expect, from Turner's picture at the Fawkes at Farnley; and the moment I got into the streets, there came Van der Heyden and Teniers all about one." J. Pope-Hennessy, *The Flight of Youth*, 1951, 214.

54. CLVIII, watermark 1814, but with 4 June Eton drawings datable as 1818. A. Cozens had been much interested in clouds (Oppe, 97) and composed a book of Skies, which seem to have been used in the New Method (reduced from 25 to 20): the method is to express form by variations in thickness and spacing of hatched lines, Oppe, 48–51; cf. Gilpin's poem. Studies of clouds also by Dahl and Blechen after the writings of Howard and Goethe: see Badt. Constable copied out Cozens's plates: Key 64. Turner comes closest to an interest in clouds for their own sakes.

Note Th. ii, 95: Rose of Jersey, "On one occasion I had the audacity to ask him if he painted his clouds from nature. One has heard of 'calling up a look'. The words had hardly passed my lips when I saw my *gaucherie*. I was afraid I had raised a thunderstorm; however, my lucky star predominated, for, having eyed me for a few moments with a slight frown, he growled out, 'How would you have me paint them?' Then seizing upon his fishing-rod, and turning upon his heel, he marched indignantly out . . .''

13. *Italian Light*

1. F., 261 f. John Soane, 15 November, goes on, "To the question how many *scudi* would be required for ransom money in case a pig was stopped on his way to this Paradise and 500 *scudi* being named, he grunted forth a grunt of 'a large sum'. On the journey, having occasion for a nap (Napoleon), he produced one which had been concealed in a purse that he had within an inner pocket. A king could not have been ushered into the world with more ceremony." See A. T. Bolton. In general: Eastlake (3) ii, ch. 4.

In 1819 the precocious Bird and the aged Wolcot died. J. Martin at the B.I. showed *Fall of Babylon*, a vulgarization of T.'s vortex-cataclysm. Tenant trouble: CLXIX, 27–28; resolution about picture removals at R.A., 24a; minutes, 39 f.

2. BML, no. 67. Water-colour of scene before the overturn was done for Fawkes.

3. F., 264.

4. BML, no 54; F., 266.

5. F., 266. House, 267–9. Marshalls, 275 f. Receipt, CXCVIII, last leaf. At R.A. proposes increase pensions, F., 265. For the Marshall property, lots were drawn; T. lost and got nos. 7–8, with £42: Falk, 116 f., receipt re repairs, 1843, facsimile opp. 116. Wapping figures a lot in songs of C. Dibdin, etc.

6. Legal proceedings about Queen Anne Street, F., 269 f. Perhaps about this time a pencilled note to Emma Wells, from Queen Anne Street (PTh. ix): "Dear Emma I am sorry to say that at present I am hard at work in the Gallery but will be happy to have a peep at you in the Parlour – whenever you please Yours truly JMW Turner."

7. F., 270; work done, 271; Christmas, 272 (Fairfax relics). Fawkes now owed him £960 15*s*. 1*d*. T. tried to buy Reynolds's sketchbook: W. (3), 14.

8. R. Hunt praised: F., 273 f.

9. F., 276 f.

10. *Morning Chronicle:* F., 210. Finberg's criticism: F. (2), 87.

11. F., 280, use of asphaltum.

12. *Sun*, 3 May 1823. Elmes and Soc. of British Artists: W. (3), 51.

13. Two works: F., 280. Rivers: 280 f. Trip: CCII–CCIII. 6 September 1823, letter to Wells about poultice, "My Daddy cannot find the recipe", F., 281 f.

14. F., 282 f. CCXI, 7. Auditor: CCV, CCXa.

15. F., 283; Th. ii, 133; i, 291. Cf. *Waterloo* and ch. 11, n. 19, above.

16. BML, no. 66; F., 283 f., who cuts the part he disapproves of.

17. Falk;, 197 F., 300. Perhaps the building obsession expressed a

wish for a new start in his system of living. Trimmer says that T. was once rather smittten by a sister of his mother, but gives no indication of date: Th. i, 180.

18. *Rossetti Papers*, 1903, 383; tale expanded fictionally by Frank Harris. 1824: CCXa – note CCXI, 28a, 28, 29a. 1834: CCXCI (c), Bedrooms: Petworth, Butlin (1), no. 15; CCXLIV, 69: F., 125. Venice: CCCXVII, 34. Poem: J.L. (2), no. 47; CVIII, 31–31a. Sexual imagery: see further Stokes 60–62, 64 (which I had not read when I made my own formulations).

Lecture 46 FFS 25 (38) ff. Goes on interestingly to the relations of lines to chiaroscuro and colour. bringing out his sense of the unity of them all. Notes rough, many additions, hasty spellings (foilage, raidance); "living" above "mellow raidance." *Peter Martyr* much affected him, cf. *ib.* 35, 6.

19. Cooke's show included *Smugglers of Folkestone fishing up smuggled Gin:* F., 284. Sketches along coast: CCIX, CCX. Cure for dry rot, etc., in second book. This year, 1824, Paris Salon had works by Lawrence, Constable, Copley Fielding, Harding, Prout, J. Varley – Constable's *Hay Wain* especially important in impact.

20. In 1825 Fawkes gave up his mansion, lived a few minutes' walk from T., who often dined with him and was at entertainment, after marriage of eldest F. son, when an infant prodigy played the harp. Soon F. was confined to bed. T. still dined with family, was there the day before he left England. Uwins on Fawkes: F., 292. T. often met eldest son in London: F., 294.

Formation of National Gallery, 1823–4: W. (3), 64, ff. T. dining with Wilkie for first time; W.'s sister "conceived the most rooted objection" to him "from his habit of tasting everything and leaving a good deal of everything upon his plate", *ib.*, 78 f.

21. F., 289 f.; Crabb Robinson, *Diary*, 7 May 1825; W. (3), 1, 86. R. Hunt, *Examiner*, wanted Cotman, etc., to return to Barret and de Wint. More troubles about *Trafalgar*, F., 290. Etty: Gilchrist ii, 216. W. Collins tried to defend his criticisms to Turner: "The interests of art are most essentially injured by attempts to praise eccentricity", etc.

22. F., 290, 382, 356 f.

23. A. Watts on J. O. Robinson: F., 290 f.

24. Th. ii, 130.

25. See n. 2 above T. stresses the height of H.'s place: "You talk of mountains as high as the moon and the creaking timber wain labouring up the steep", etc. More on Belvoir.

Allason must have cropped up somehow particularly between T. and H., cf. letter to H., 6 May 1826, F., 296 f. See also n. 6 above: F., 269 f.; and F. (7), 406, 444, 601.

26. F., 297 f.; CCXVI–VII. Diligence accident: CCXVI, 154: *ib.*, 19, "Callcott" on sky.

27. F., 298, early December. Goes on to say Phillips has a daughter; Munro is in town, does not blush so much. Maguilpe (megilp) or Gumtion: English varnish. Ostend: see p. 251 here.

28. Long abusive self-justifying letter from Cooke: Th., 186–8; F. (15), introduction; RD 25–6 25–6, 36–7.

29. F., 299 f.; W. (3), 127 f.

30. Tabley sale scared artists, as Parliament not sitting; feared prices would fall and tried to get postponement. But prices were high. T. bought back *Sun Rising* and *Blacksmith Shop*: F., 301 f.

31. Dido: CCXXVII (a), 15. CCXXVII, 11: "Cuyp – all one tone." CCXXVI 64: "Give my love to Miss Wickham. Hopes that windows are now fully squared, and seen through in perspective. JMWT."

32. F., 303 f.; facsimile, C. Home, between o ii and o iii. Marsh seems W. Marsh, his stockbroker; J. B. Quilly engraved *The Deluge* in mezzotint (pub. 1828); Broadhurst wanted *Cologne*. Petworth: Sam Rogers, F., 304. Letter to Cobb about letting a house: *ib.*, To Orde, 15 December 1827, F., 305.

33. F., 306.

34. To Eastlake, Paris: BML, no. 74. To Jones, 13 October: Th. i, 225–7, "Tell that fat fellow Chantrey, that I did think of him" at Carrara. To Chantrey: Th. i, 224 f.; F., 308 f. To Lawrence, on Sistine Chapel, and Signorelli: F., 309 f.

35. Th. i, 221: including account of how he painted on tempera; says T. never finished work till on walls of R.A. Hobhouse iii, 294, says the Romans were filled with pity and wonder.

36. Original in PTh., v. cf. Gotch, 279 f.: "He does not quite agree with Ugo, and Albina plays the piano wretchedly close to the bed-room, so that he is not very comfortable. We tried dining at home for a while, but they did not use us well, and now we go out – he is used to rough it." A friend of Leslie: "He made himself very social, and seemed to enjoy himself, too, amongst us", F., 317.

37. CCXXXVII, 8a–9.

38. Uwins, ii, 239–41; F., 312 (Severn). Sketchbook: CLXXVIII.

39. Incident in water-colour: F., 314.

40. Clare, 83; F., 314. Letter BML, 79, to Wells (26 June 1829) on clash of invitation (Chantrey) to Purfleet for turtle dinner.

41. BML, no. 76.

42. Mentions Eastlake's bad eyes; news of Johns, R. Westmacott, Wyatt: F., 316 f.

43. F., 329; five artists at first, then as many as funds allow.

44. RB, 36–40; Clare, 83.

45. *Forum Romanum*, 1823, shows a strong Poussin frontality.

46. CCLXIII. Related or similar works appear in other sets, but this is the major collection.

47. Thus, *Ramsgate*, 299, leads to the drawing engraved in *S. Coast*, or that in *Ports of England*, May 1827. Scenes: 323, study for *Golden Bough;* 344, Funeral of Lawrence in St Paul's, 1830.

48. Butlin (1), no. 30.

49. RB, no. 73. *What You Will*, 1822, seen as an imitation of Watteau, also as "scrap of spoilt canvas", W. (3), 29; in such works as this Stothard had much influence on the figures. C. R. Leslie (3) i, 200, 203, mentioning that T. was friendly with Flaxham and Stothard, says that S. was the only living painter he praised, also Th. ii, 35.

Venice: Bonnington had two Venetian subjects in B.I., 1828.

14. *The Fires of Colour*

1. BML, 96; F., 319.

2. Th. ii, 233 f.; F., 320. Goes on about Jones and yellow."Chantrey is as gay and good as ever." "The stormy brush of Tintoretto was only to make the Notte more visible."

3. Eastlake Academician, next General Meeting. Shee: W. (3), 185. (At this time Peel, Home Secretary, was considering the appointment of a "distinguished amateur" as President: W. (3), 186 f. Business letter, 17 June, F., 322. Tale of T.'s agent, "a clean, ruddy-faced, butcher's boy" (A. Watts) buying back *Venus and A.*, 1830, at auction: F., 425. Lawrence's collection of drawings: F. 324.

Letter of Westmacott in 1831 R.A. in PTh. vii, 319. The painter Newton goes mad: W. (3), 260.

4. CCXXXIX, 70. Clare, 106; M. Davies, 154, Colour scheme (blue, white, pink, gold) remains of water-colours on blue paper in early 1830s.

5. F., 322, dealing with Glover's departure to Australia: see W. (3), 195.

6. W. (3), 228, and Frith i, 126 f. The *Morning Chronicle*, however, at this time called T. "a tubby little man".

7. F., 325. Jones tells of Chantrey's joke, imitating Lord E.'s step and raps on T.'s door. C. R. Leslie (3) i, 102–7, 162–4, 200: "Plain spoken, often to a degree of bluntness, he never wasted words, nor would he let others waste words on him. After conferring the greatest favours, he was out of the room before there was time to thank him." T. at breakfast upset a cream-jug over the new lilac French merino gown of Mrs Haslar, E.'s granddaughter; he shuffled off and at lunch gave her a water-colour sketch of the episode with an apology, "So sorry" (Falk, 93).

8. Creevey, August 1828. W. (3), 342–4; F., 325 f. Story of T. arguing with E. about number of windows in a house: Th. ii, 156 f. Arnald: Autograph letter in PTh. ix.

9. F., 325; R.A. business. *Lord Percy:* see no. 349, TGRM.

10. Scotland: F., 327–9; W. (3), 246–8. Letter to Cobb.:F., 331. Gen. Phipps: F., 327. T. and palettes of Reynolds and Hogarth: W. (3), 324; F., 331. Callcott praised at T.'s expense: W. (3), 211. Attacks on R.A. and B.I., *ib.*, 206–8.

11. F., 330; Th. ii, appendix. Mortmain: 9 George II c. 36. Executors, Wells, Trimmer, Rogers, G. Jones, C. Turner. CCLXV: notes on legacy duty, etc. (also cholera medicine, 42).

12. F., 332 f.; Clare, 88.

13. T. to Lenox: F., 332 f.; T. visited Fingal's Cave over the rocks.

14. Th. ii, 96; F., 333. Note CCLXXV (?1831), 1a–2, "Engaged Catherine McInns to serve as cookmaid in the servant kitchin."

15. *The Times*, 2 January; F., 333 f.; *Examiner*, 8 January.

16. Jones and Nebuchadnesser: F., 335; Lenox and *Staffa*, 335 f. Funny: 337. Stanfield's *Wreckers:* W. (3), 244.

17. W. (3), sv. index, "Nat. Gallery"; F., 337; Clare, 88.

18. F., 338 f. Perhaps T. feared the publicity of a private Bill like that Soane was having introduced into the Commons.

19. C. Cavendish Fulke Greville, *Journal* ii, 337 (also, artist Lucas was there).

20. F., 339–41. Montro's sale: F., 342.

21. F., 343. Cites Fuseli: "T. is the only landscape-painter of genius in Europe." Use of old plates: F., 341. Letter to Maw, *ib.* For Maws: Amey. B.S.A. winter show, 345. No buyers: *Athenaeum;* W. (3), 253.

22. Falk, 193–8. For the same story told of Chelsea: Th. ii, 275 f.

23. The fact that in 1834 the Sibyl-theme in the Aeneas saga comes up again is perhaps significant. *Aeneas and the Sibyl* seems done while starting off with Sarah.

24. *Diary:* see WP, 1546.

25. Business letter, F., 350; S.B.A. show, 350 f. This year the musical nephew was in London. Panorama of country traversed by Liverpool and Manchester Railway: W.(3), 287 f.

26. F., 352. Reissue of Rogers' *Poems* in parts, 352; dinner with Tom Moore, 353 f.; letters, 355 f.

27. For smoke as a sort of elemental spire, also expressing human fragility: note at end of ch. 11. Staffa: C. R. Leslie (2) i, 205–7; Th. ii, 242 f.; Armstrong, 232; Ruskin, *Works* xxxv, 577; Wyllie, 90; Clare, 109; CCLXIII. Cf. *A Rough Sea:* RB, no. 96.

For the simplification of *Petworth Park*, cf. *Chichester Canal* and *A Ship Aground*.

28. RB, 51, for the titles of sea-works showing him turning back to Dutch Masters: this is the counterpart to works like *Staffa.* (T. paid direct tributes in his work to Raphael, 1820; Ruisdael, 1827, 1844; Rembrandt, 1827; Watteau, 1831; Caneletto, 1833; van Goyen, 1833; G. Bellini, 1841 – and in a way to Wilkie, 1842.)

29. Stothard: see ch. 13, n. 49. Jewish subjects show the turn to Rembrandt.

30. *Art Journal*, 1860, 100; W. (3), 293 f.

31. Th. ii, 131, 154. Uwins: W. (3), 283.

32. *What you Will, The Letter, Music at P.* (RB, no. 92); *Richmond Bridge – Play; Hero and Leander.*

For Fuseli: Antal (2), nos. 40a, 50, 52, 60a, 62. Also J. Brown: TGRM pl. 45 (pp. 328 f. for relation to Fuseli) and nos. 625–6.

33. Livermore (2).

34. Tale that he painted *Bridge of Sighs* in two or three days, hearing Stanfield was engaged on the subject: W. (3), 253.

35. CCLXXXIII, 1–9; pencil sketches, CCLXXXIV; CCCLXIV, 373 (water-colour); perhaps three oils. Swinburne, 252; Ruskin, *Works* iii, 423; Armstrong, 117, 120, 146, 236; Berenson, 86; Milliken, 47.

36. Ruskin (9), 379; *Mod. Painters*, 1860, v. See W. (3), 281 f. for tale of Sibyl figure cut from sketchbook and fixed on (cf. dog in Mortlake Terrace). Childe Harold: RB, 12; Swinburne, 246–9; Chignell, 119–21; Hamerton, 257–62; Ruskin further, *Works*, vii, 431; xiii, 140–5, 408, 445; xxi, 130. With quotation, canto iv, 26, "the garden of the world".

37. *A.R.*, 1834, 54, 94, 124, 153.

38. *Gent. Mag.*, 1834, 477–83; *A.R.*, 1934, 156. Note earthquake at Santa Martha and Cartagena, *A.R.*, 71, 152.

J. S. Davis's account brings out the painting on top of a sketch. Adds, "I understand he was cursedly annoyed – the fools kept peering into his colour box, and examining all his brushes and colours."

15. *The Sea of Blood*

1. F., 360–2. M. and Argus: 359.

2. F., 362 f.; in general Q. Bell.

3. F., 363 f. D. first knew T. by Rogers' *Italy;* then was left cold by R.A. pictures; was won over by works of 1836. MS.: 364. See also RP; 243. Attacks on Gainsborough in *Blackwood's*: W. (3), 311.

4. Regulus was a favourite of eighteenth-century history-painters. T. had turned to it at Rome, but had long had it in mind: Shee notes twenty-six references in 1811 poem (Thomson, *Winter*, 513). Wilson (Constable, no. 15b) and West (W. (1) i, 260) did Departures. For Salvator's *Death of R.: The Times*, 21 October 1958.

5. F., 364. Auditor and Visitor; gives Rigaud picture to R.A., 365.

6. BML, 105 and 108; F., 365 f.

7. WP, 1544.

8. The idea goes well back: CIII and LXXXI, 57; also CCCXLIV, 427 (pencil, with part of letter to Fawkes). T. is probably also thinking of Byron swimming the Hellespont.

Sea-piece in B.I.'s Old Masters show: F., 367.

9. F., 369; winter B.I., *ib.*

10. F., 371; Th. i, 335 f.; Falk, 146; T. Woolner; W. (3), 63; WP, 1545. In France T. sketched a flotilla of steam tugs escorting ships. The ship: Th. i, 340; Schetky, 1823, on Trafalgar ships, W. (3), 63. Also RD 12–8.

11. F., 37.

12. Ruskin, *Works*, xxxv, 576 f; RD 11.

13. Griffith, agent for his oils and water-colours; later published the set of big engravings issued by T. himself. Letter to him, 31 May, showing how he got dates wrong and appointments confused: F., 380 f. Ruskin adds about his praise of the Kenilworth drawings: "There were few things he hated more than hearing people gush about particular drawings. He knew it merely meant they did not see the others." More likely it linked with his discomfort at facing his works. "Anyhow, he stood silent; the general talk went on as if he had not been there." See RP ii 66–7.

Thackeray's abusive comments on *Slavers:* F., 378.

14. BML; F., 381. Plate for Griffith: F., 382.

15. Windus a coachmaker as buyer; also Chantrey and Bicknell: F., 383; letter on prices, *ib.*

16. Note to *Praeterita*, 6 July 1841; F., 384. Engravings: F., 384 f.

17. Jones, MSS. additions to *Recollections of Chantrey;* F., 385. Th. ii, 121 f. and 150; i, 177 f. (also grief over supposed death of Trimmer). Gives arm to Collins: Th. ii, 129.

18. See 101 a and b, RB.

19. Th. ii, 141, (T. about 60?). Cf. refusal to revisit Farnley.

20. Th. i, 342, and i, 207; F., 417.

21. RB, 60. Eastlake (2) ii, 281 f.; in (3) ii, 116, he says of himself;

"I think it would be easier for me to abandon the art than to be a *white* painter."

22. Boase (1), 342; Livermore (1), 80; Tinker, 149–52; Clare, 106; Armstrong, 150–3; Ruskin, many references, esp. *Works* iii, 571–3: vii, 187 f., xxxv, 318 f., xxxvi, 81 f. The fine passage about it (see J.L. (2), 25 f.) had a strong effect on William Morris at Oxford.

Note Typhon in Willoughby poem: J.L. (2), 19 ff., 50 f. Keats's shark, *ib.*, 18 f. (cf. usurer-shark in Orders poem). In youth T. planned an apocalyptic *Water Turn'd to Blood*.

23. J.L. (2), 24. Parodies of T.'s poem: J.L. (2), 53 f.; F., 408; Th. ii 194–6.

24. CI, 9; CX, 39a–40; J.L. (2), 24 f.; Th. ii, 218, 333; Ruskin (9). 393. Note Reynolds, 13th Discourse (*Works* ii, 70): "Like the history-painter, a painter of landscape in this style and with this conduct 'of selecting materials and elevating style,' 'sends the imagination back into antiquity; and, like the poet, he makes the elements sympathy with his subject.'" Ruskin invented the phrase, Pathetic Fallacy.

16. *The 'Forties*

1. Scheme: F., 386–8. Jersey: Th. ii, 97. Griffith: F., 389, Ruskin, *Works* xiii, 477–84.

2. Th. i, 334 f; i, 207; F., 390; Ruskin (9), 356; Finberg (2), 135. Bayliss 34. Probably a mere joke lies behind Thornbury's statement that the Dragon in the Hesperides was said to have been based on a paste-board dragon used in a London pantomime: ii, 343. Ruskin thought the dragon a remarkable prefiguring of what palaeontology was to discover; but it seems T. had repainted it: Ruskin, *Works* xiii, 118; F., 148 f. He may have redone it after studying the geologists.

Jones and T. talking about Wilkie's funeral: F., 390 f. Stanfield criticized the sails: T., "I only wish I had any colour to make them blacker."

3. Th. i, 177; ii, 50–52; F., 391; Falk, 189 (letter of Campbell). Note the similar tale told (and invented ?) by Trelawney.

4. BML ii, 125; F., 391.

5. F., 391 f. Companion: ? the E.H. and wife who went with him in 1840, or the Lady in Jersey who wrote, "Turner did not go with us or join us" in 1813. I have no doubt there were many trips in England and a few abroad that have escaped notice.

Whales: ILN, 13 November 1965. See also Butlin, no 31; CCCLIII; and *Sunrise with Sea Monster* (Tate, not shown). Boase (1), 344, for use of T. Beale's *Nat. Hist. of Sperm Whale*, 1835, with cuts by W. J. Linton. Letter to Bicknell, 31 June 1845. "Whale or two on the canvas."

6. F., 383, for more entries in Diary.

7. F., 394 f. Baudelaire has more insights into the relation of art and society, and the crisis of art in an industrial world. But R. has a far finer perception and sense of nature, seeks more thoroughly after basic principles, and comes out at last with a fuller grasp of the crucifixion of art and man in a fragmenting society. Thackeray in *Fraser's:* F., 409 f.

8. F., 397.

9. BML, 136; F., 398.

10. F., 399, 406 f., 414; visit of R., 399, second edition of his book; E.R. was a capable amateur aritst; R. and Munro, 400.

11. F., 400; RD 45–9. Bridge between Maidenhead and Taplow, completed 1839. Wellington went to see, turned away in disgust, "Ah, poetry." Falk, 184.

12. F., 401; Forster, *Life of Dickens* ii, 86; Th. ii, 151.

13. Th. ii, 231 f. For his own pun on his name as Mallard (Duck): Th. ii, 234; BML, 57 – with Jeremiah for Joseph; also pun on Souls (Soles). Indenture of Twickenham for the Charity, to escape Mortmain: F., 402.

14. F., 402 f.

15. F., 403; Ruskin, *Works* ii, 673 tries to explain T.'s lack of religious direction.

16. Th. ii, 117–21; F., 404 f. For Hammersley also see Appendix 4. Letter to Dawson T.: Falk, 185.

17. F., 405 f. McCracken: F., 405.

18. Ruskin dinner, F., 406, "sad news from Switzerland". Debate on R.A.'s privilege of eight pictures; T. supports, 407. Ruskin abroad, 411 f.

19. F., 407 f.; sales, 409.

20. F., 411. Thackeray noted Hall's likeness to Pecksniff.

21. Tale of Eu and the King, F., 410 f.; Redgrave ii, 96. Tries to dissuade R. not to oppose parents about going abroad, F. 411 f.; Works xxxv, 342. Hobbs, R.'s attendant, on T.'s treatment of Ticino Valley, "Well, he is a cunning old gentleman, to be sure; just like Mrs. Todgers, dodging among the tender pieces with a fork" (*Martin Chuzzlewit*).

22. F., 413; at R.'s birthday, 8 February. In B.I. had *Queen Mab's Cave*.

23. F., 413 f.; she saw in *Trafalgar* "the disposition of the figures unstudied apparently". Adds, "The old gentleman was great fun." For tale about *Walhalla*, 414 f.

24. F., 415 (will). Etty: Gilchrist ii, 215 f.; Etty finally packed up, June 1848, *ib.* 247 f. Chelsea: Communication, C. Edwards; Falk, 203 f. Chelsea rate-books show Mrs. Booth taking Davis Place in October 1846; in continuous possession till 29 September 1867. Vauxhall: Th. ii, 280 – note the fireworks in *Juliet*. We cannot trust L. Martin's account of a visit in 1839 which F. oddly takes seriously: F., 376 f. In 1849 J. Martin moved to Lindsey Row, not far off. He had been connected with T. in the fight against piracy of engravings: F., 415 f.: note to R., 3 December 1846.

In 1846 Davis Place was part of the Cremorne New Road, leading from Battersea Bridge to the Cremorne Estate; the present Cremorne Road has a different site. There were no numbers to the houses till 1870; between October 1876 and March 1877 the premises were renumbered 118–19 Cheyne Walk. Turner lived at 119.

25. F., 416 (1878); 437 (April 1872); Bartlett to R., 7 August 1857.

26. CCCLXIII, 29–28a, 29a–30; Livermore (3) mistakes. F. 417. Maclise's later visit to the Margate house: "Was he an artist?" "I don't know what trade he was, sir; but he lived very quiet and ate very simple

food; he know'd no one." S. Cooper ii, 15; F., 418. Ruskin said T.'s health and mind failed suddenly 1845.

27. F., 419. Venetian pictures at R.A., 419 f.

28. F., 422 f. Note to R., 420; Lenox, 420 f.; Reinagle affair, 421 f. He promised to be one of a group of artists at Roberts's studio, three o'clock, Friday, 2 June 1848 (Mulready, Cooper and ten more) – letter of R. to J. Knight: PTh. ix.

29. Th. ii, 246–9; F., 423. He contacted Williams, however, as a copyholder of the Duke's Manor of Isleworth Syon, Middlesex.

30. F., 423; Th. ii, 264. Farnley Christmas presents. The tales of drink come from this period, e.g. a fellow Academician complained of seeing two cabs, T. says, "That's all right, old fellow. Do as I do; get into the first one", Falk, 119, Th. ii, 168, on "wallowings" at Wapping. CCXCI 52: "Bread and Cheese. Bottle of ale. Dinner. 2 Small bottles of Stout. Glass of Gin and Water." Seems near end of 1834. "Tuesday 5 o'clock. Mr. Harpur", 66.

31. See n. 25 above; Th. ii, 265.

32. Falk, 204. In 1868 Mrs. B. removed to Haddenham Hall, Oxon, where she died: Wallbrook.

33. Pennells, 120, 228, 248: under Friday, 21 September 1906.

34. Puggy: Th. ii, 276, cf. 93. "There are two old boatmen still living at Sunbury, who well remember rowing out T. on his sketching excursions. It is still their unspeakable wonder how 'a man like that', who always took a bottle of gin out with him for inspiration, and never gave them any, could have been a great genius", Th. ii, 163.

35. Feret; Falk, 213.

36. Falk, 42; he notes Mrs. Danby, for whose benefit a musical drama *Rob Roy* or *Auld Lang Syne* was given at the Wisbech Theatre (first appearance of T. Robinson, future dramatist): 13 June 1834. But this can hardly be Sarah. F., 424 f., codicil, revokes 9 August 1846 codicil, gives £100 each to three daughters of Wells.

For Georgianna as preferred to Evelina: 1832 codicil (Th. ii, 414).

Wreck Buoy at R.A., 1849; earlier paintings at B.I.

37. F., 426.

38. F., 426 f. For business relations, e.g. Gillott of Birmingham: F., 409; Falk, 111 f. Interview: W. J. Stillman (Falk, 214 f.), with stress on his eye; T. says of his paintings (in connexion with *Staffa*, in U.S.A.), "I wish they were all put in a blunderbus and shot off."

39. RB, 64.

40. RB, 66; K. Clark (1), 112 f. The raised viewpoint links with the Old Masters.

41. C. Johnson, 42, 95, 105.

42. *Mod. Painters* (7th ed.), 1867, II ii, ch. i, par. 21. Note also, *ib.*, ch. ii, par. 13, no raw colour, "no warmth which has not grey in it, and no blue which has not warmth in it", the most inimitable tints, as with all great colourists, "his greys". Takes *Mercury and Argus* as example. "The pale and vaporous blue of the heated sky is broken with grey and pearly white, the gold colours of the light warming it more or less as it approaches or retires from the sun; but, throughout, there is not a grain of pure blue; all is subdued and warmed at the same time by the mingling grey and gold, up to the very zenith, where, breaking through

the flaky mist, the transparent and deep azure of the sky is expressed with a single crumbling touch; the key-note of the whole is given, and every part of it passes at once far into glowing and aerial space." But it is not a definition of a single moment; the past and future of the moment is subtly expressed by the actual movement and tension of colour.

Armstrong says, "T. feels, and makes us feel, the solidity beneath, on which he lays the successive vesture provided by the ages, with a delicacy and tenderness approached by no one else." Monkhouse comments on "his power of rendering atmospherical effect and the structure and growth of things. He not only knew how a tree looked, but he showed how it grew. Others may have drawn foliage with more habitual fidelity, but none ever drew trunks and branches with such knowledge of their inner life. Others have drawn the appearance of clouds, but T. knew how they formed", etc.

43. *ib*., ch. 2, par. 15 f.

44. See note on spires and smoke, end of ch. 11. G. Jones's picture of Wilkie's funeral is a close-up of the coffin being lowered, piously sentimental.

45. R. Melville, rightly suggesting that T. could not bear to carry such a work further. Th. i, 195; f., 49 f., 281; LS lvii; C. Baker, 106; Clare, 102; Clark (1), 117. Also in *Rivers of England*, 1824.

46. Formerly only *What you will* was square; the four Petworth panels were rather thin oblongs on account of space to be filled. See RB, 68 ff.

47. Uncertainty about corners at times, e.g. *Angel* with fish and flask protruding in right-hand lower corner.

48. See A. Stokes, 61, 70, 73, on the doll element, the Punch features, the disarticulated body ("part objects"). But we must grasp this obstinate inorganic element as expressing an inner resistance to his central purpose the definition of unitary process in all its dynamic symmetry-asymmetry. (Perhaps we should link the dumpy forms with his sense of personal ugliness and unattractiveness; we then see a struggle between this element and the sense of beauty – of harmony, rhythmic release, organic unity). Perhaps in a sort of desperation he produced his bubble-headed tadpole shapes, waving like weeds in the undercurrents of water. Stokes, 75, writes of the engulfed mariners of *Fire at Sea* as "having become, as if protectively, globular, saffron-coloured fish". Note the nose of the life-study here, illust. 5, cf. 3.

17. *The Theory of Colour*

1. In *Outline of Logic*, 1850, references to Plato, Pythagoras, Hippocrates, Bacon, Harvey, Newton, Kepler, Berkeley, Hume, Leibnitz. Akenside, *ib*., 400. Field lived 1777–1854. He appears as Field of Bristol in Farington. He was Girtin's friend: Th. ii, 36.

2. Th. ii, 42 f. The Rev. Syer Trimmer and Rev. H. Trimmer, both subscribers. Turner is described as of "Sandicombe Lodge", so F. must have been now out of touch with him. His connexion seems via the Trimmers. For the debt of the Pre-Raphaelites to Field: W. H. Hunt ii, 374 f., 455.

For Turner's sense of the limitation of Rules: "In these elevated branches of art Rules my young friends must languish." "The higher qualities of sentiment or application intellectual feeling, forming the poetic, historic, or descriptions gained from nature and her works, are far beyond dictation" (fourth lecture). After citing Milton on evening, he says, "Here then rules surely cease" in dealing with the phrase "Twilight grey"; for "how define dignify'd purity without producing monotony of color?" "Rules only exist by the mixture of black and white" (i.e. they can only be concerned with the production of a grey). Nor can rules "ever hope to define that tone which cautious Nature throws around her mantle, all evanescent twilight, where rules must ever tremulously stand. If they date to stipulate for hue, "tis here the highborn soul is told to seek nature and not pursue one humble quarry". (The artist must look at reality and seek to define its evanescent subtleties, not get tied-down in questing for a literal "grey"). See Ziff (3),201, 206; J.L. (2), 14.

3. Th. i, 194 f.

4. CVIII, 40a, incorrectly given by F.

5. F., 372, 348, 372. Ruskin, *Diary*, February 1844. *Castle of I.* xxvii; J.L. (2), 56 f.

Lecture 46 FFS 31–4 (44–7); also Gowing. Rough script, many additions. Stress on Genius, strong for the Lectures: "and here we are left by Theory, and where we ought to be left, for the works of Genius. . . .", "the utmost range of art. . . . The imagination of the artist dwells enthroned in his own Recess, incomprehensible as Darkness" (or "from Darkness", "cause" also seems inserted), "and ever words fall short of illustration and become illusory." Note imitation of Akenside's style; goes on to name him and further imitate: "High born soul – not to descend to any humble quarry – for amid the various forms which this fall would present Like rivals to his choice, what human breast E'er doubts, before the transient and Minute, To Prize the Vast, the Stable, the Sublime?"

Note also: "the compelling power of colors, used as a shade to Light: that wrought the Whole to Harmony", 37 (50). And opposition of cold and warm scales: "these tones upon the same principles of Nature, White being the Light of the Cold, yellow of the warm scale."

Note too his stress on the changing effects of nature: "Nature and our perception of her effects, th(r)o all the mutability of Time and Seasons they are out Materials and offered daily as our pattern of imitation, towards which we are assisted by each Class of Theory" (third last page).

6. Th. ii, 263 f.

7. Th. ii, 259–63. "I recollected putting aside a rather curious head of him in profile, and, you may be sure, on the following morning after the interview [at the R.S.] I lost no time in looking up the portrait, which, I regret to say, one of my assistants had without my orders effaced." He made at least four daguerrotypes of T., "for which he paid me; and some I rubbed out where we tried the effect of a sharp, narrow cross light, in which some parts of the face were left in strong shadow." Mayall thought his appearance much like that of Spence the naturalist. The lady he mentions must be Mrs. Booth.

8. Goethe, 165, 296 f., 245 f., 274 f., 326 f., 280 f. "Off again", 153;

"There lies the question", 287; "too general to make much of", 342 f.

9. R. D. Gray, 112 r., citing Goethe, pars. 284, 697. He further cites CXII 16, "Every body participates of the colour of the light . . ."

10. Goethe, 334 f., 350, 326, 352 (word I cannot read before "simbolis- ing"), 351, par. 901, 342.

11. See Gray, 114, who, however, takes the paintings solely as a criti- que of Goethe, 114–16; he, however, rightly points to the deep cleavage of G.'s and T.'s idea on Light-Darkness.

RB, 72, "The elliptical tendency of T.'s vision and his irridescent colour were ideally suited to illustrate the theory." Wolff, too, simply sees G.'s theory as "a theoretical foundation for paintings", 94 f.; also J. L. (2). Eastlake in his preface pointed out that Goethe's theory had more relevance to artists than Newton's. Note *The opening of the Wallhalla*, shown at R.A. with the Goethe pictures; the sunlight is identified with the return of peace, "science and the arts" – with Fallacious Hope as its opposite, linked with War. And *The Sun of Venice*, where the morning represents a delusive calm leading on to the sunset with its demon.

12. Note that Vulva (volva, volvere) and vortex (vertex, vertere) have both much the same meaning of "turning round and round". (We have here a glimpse of the birth-trauma element in T.'s image; but does not detract from its truth. Birth is a fundamental form of process).

13. Collingwood, 78. This identification of Angel and Artist (Turner) helps the similar identification with Moses.

Though Ruskin never consciously grasped the nature of T.'s imagery, perhaps there was an intuitive response of some kind, which linked *Modern Painters* with the later social criticisms. His breakdown in 1878 came on top of his preface to a Turner exhibition, in which, writing of T.'s early picture of Coniston Fells with those Fells in view, he described how T.'s "health, and with it in great degree his mind, failed suddenly with a snap of some vital chord" (Collingwood, 260). There seems, at one level, a self-identification with Turner.

Note T.'s earlier apocalyptic *Skeleton falling off a Horse in Mid-Air* (M. Davies (2), no. 5505; TGRM, 226), apparently suggested by West's *Death on a Pale Horse* (for which see Carey's long account). See also Bryan Robertson, *Spectator*, 18 March 1966).

18. Last Days

1. G. D. Leslie, 144; F., 428 f. Court acts on Eastlake's side: S. A. Hart, 29. Jones resigns as Keeper: F., 429. Roberts's dinner-party, 1850: Falk, 214: T. in good spirits, proposes health in hurried way, runs out of words and breath, drops into chair with hearty laugh, rises again, ends with a hip-hip-hurrah. Refuses to give address when helped into cab; says, "Tell him to drive to Oxford Street and then I'll direct him."

2. F., 430. He seems to have one of the Fairfax relics; comments on Vernon Coll.

3. F., 431. Day before, wrote that he was too ill for R.'s birthday- party, 8 February.

4. F., 432 f., "odd and jocose remarks" to Maclise.

5. P. Cunningham, p. xxx; F., 432. Rosse was President of Royal Society. Hart, 50: tale of taking him to re-formed R.A. Club (?7 May: F., 432 f.). Note to Griffith, 1 May, "I am yet unwell and unable to walk much." Letter, 19 May: F., 433 f.

6. 28 May, called on C. Turner, "the last Time I ever saw him". Palgrave, 434.

7. Th. ii, 273; F., 435. F., 435–7.

8. Falk, 220 ff.; negotiations with Gambart, 221; Th. ii, 275; also version from Eastlake to S. Rogers; Barlett's letter to R.; Fritt i, 139 f. Lady Eastlake (I) i 273.

9. Registry and Funeral: F., 438–40. The decision of the Court will be found in the Public Record office: C, 33, 1040.

10. RB, 76.

Hannah Danby. There are many accounts of Hannah and Queen Anne Street in its later days; but they add nothing new to the picture of grime and neglect. Here are some, briefly cited.

Caroline Fox, 22 May 1849, calls Hannah "a mysterious-looking old housekeeper, a bent and mantled figure who might have been yesterday released from a sarcophagus" (Falk, 214); Sidney Cooper in 1845 thought her like one of the ogres in pantomime before the transformation; W. Callow lets himself out (Falk, 180); Trimmer gives long account of the place (Th. ii, 278 ff.; cf. i, 178) and mentions Hannah setting palettes, cats gathering in the area, prints damp-spoiled (ii, 264); Rippingille (ii, 173), "an old tabby cat, lying upon a bit of ragged green baize on a table at the area window, and sometimes an old woman in a mob cap, who looked like a being of the last century, or the other world"; Dr Shaw (ii, 174–7) with a story of the visit to the Marshalls of Shelford Manor; the drawing room "peopled by filthy tailless cats" (ii, 177 f.); Mrs Ruskin (Millais) in J. G. Millais i, 156.

Some more comments on his character. Trimmer on his modesty: "I have heard him speak most enthusiastically in praise of Gainsborough's execution and Wilson's tone, and he plainly thought himself their inferior. My father had some admirable oil sketches of Gainsborough; by candlelight one evening Turner examined them so closely, that next morning he said he had hurt his eyes. We were once looking at a Vandervelde, and on some one observing, 'I think you could go beyond that,' he shook his head and said, 'I can't paint like him' " (Th. i, 176). Against puffing: F., 231.

David Roberts on his jollity among his brother painters (Th. i, 47); Leslie on his gay dinner-talk (ii, 136.) He locks a too-pertinacious arguer in an inner room; loves jokes (ii, 154 f.). Once we find him enjoying fame, saying tipsily, "Hawkey, I am the real lion . . ." (ii, 88).

Many tributes to his incessant zeal of work. Hannah's comment, "I have never known him idle", may stand for them all. Tributes to his character: lack of guile, kindliness (ii, 127). Clara Wheeler tells of impression made on Dr M'Culloch, geologist: "That man would have been great at any and everything he chose to take up; he has such a clear, intelligent, piercing intellect." For more personal accounts: Th. ii, 318 f.; 321 (Leslie); 93; (Rippingille) 322 f. For his umbrella and carpet-bag (which he would not let the ladies at Cowley Hall unpack), ii. 92 f.; he usually walked the fifteen miles from London to the Hall, plus bag.

Ostend Explosion, 1826. Turner's statement that the *Hull Advertiser* suggested he had been blown up is incorrect; nothing about him occurs in the September-November issues – or in the *Rockingham* of Hull. It seems that Fawkes had read of the explosion; knowing that Turner might be in the neighbourhood, he wrote to T. senior, who grew alarmed and gave a confused account to his son later. The *Advertiser* on 29 September gave a lurid account of the event: "The wounded are innumerable. Nearly every house in Ostend is more or less damaged. . . . Several poor fishermen were killed in the boats. . . . A ship, nine miles off at sea, felt the concussion like the shock of an earthquake. The Captain of one of the barges coming with passengers was so alarmed at the explosion, that he jumped overboard." Hence Fawkes' anxiety. (Information: R. F. Drewery.)

Appendices

1. *Opinions on Wilson*

1. J. H. Pott in 1782, discussing Historic Landscape, sees three types: where figures dominate, where landscape dominates, where both are equal. He thinks the first far the best, and criticized Wilson's *Niobe*, while praising Zuccarelli:

"One of the grandest scenes Mr. Wilson has painted, represents a land storm, in which is introduced the story of Niobe, from which it is impossible for the eye to escape, as it contains many figures, all in action, and a large Apollo in the middle of the sky. Mr Wilson's known and approved powers in landscape, would lead us to think, that he also meant these figures should be subordinate. Zucarelli has been more happy in placing the incantation of the witches before Macbeth in a land storm, in a celebrated picture painted by him, as the fury of the elements is so proper upon this occasion, and assists the effect of the storm so well. However, I believe the chief cause of the fine effect of this picture is, that the story is evidently principal in the composition, the proportion the figures bear to the landscape, and their situation in the front line indicate this. In another beautiful picture of Mr. Wilson's representing Cicero at his villa, the objections before mentioned do not take place; the figures there are highly proper, and give a wonderful meaning to the whole scene" (28–30). Reynolds, too, while admiring the storm in *Niobe*, felt that the figures make the effect grotesque

2. Wolcot (Peter Pindar), poet and amateur artist, wrote in the same year, that of Wilson's death, 1782, in his *Lyric Odes to the R. Academicians*:

> And *Loutherbourg*, when Heav'n so wills
>   To make Brass Skies, and Golden Hills,
> With Marble Bullocks in Glass Pastures grazing,
>   Thy reputation too will rise,
>   And people gaping with surprise,
> Cry, 'Monsieur *Loutherbourg* is most *amazing*!" ...
>   Till then, old red-nos'd *Wilson's* art
>   Will hold its empire o'er my heart,
> By Britain left in poverty to pine.

He was thus one of the pioneers in appreciating Wilson and fighting against the prevailing stereotypes. He it was who rescued Opie from the tin-mines.

3. By 1790 the tide was turning. *The European Magazine* cited *Observations on the Present State of the R.A.*, which criticized Reynolds's strictures on Wilson.

4. Flaxman told Farington, 12 December 1975, "the French artists in Rome held the character of Wilson, as an Artist, very high".

5. Wolcot in the supplement to the 1798 edition of Pilkington's *Dictionary* compared him several times with Claude. "Claude was rather the plain and minute historian of landscape; Wilson was the poet."

6. In 1799, when the Altieri Claudes were being admired, Robert Smirke pointed out "the absurdity of representing an ancient sacrifice in a *ruined* temple, of mixing a modern Italian building with ancient temples with circumstances which represented ancient times. The silly manner in which he tells his stories, all show that Claude wanted sense. Wilson is much his superior in conception, and exhibits more good sense by preserving propriety" (F., 60).

7. Fuseli, praising Wilson in 1801, remarked – surely with *Niobe* in mind:

"Though in effects of dewy freshness, and silent evening lights, few have equalled and fewer excelled him, his grandeur is oftener allied to terror, bustle, and convulsion than to calmness and tranquillity. He is now numbered with the classics of the art, though little more than a fifth part of a century has elapsed since death relieved him from the apathy of cognoscenti, the envy of rivals, and the neglect of a tasteless public." (Cunningham: probably from lecture of that year, though not in 1848 edition.).

Fuseli repeated his praises in the 1810 and 1815 editions of Pilkington, in which he was involved. He set him with Hogarth, Gainsborough, Reynolds: 1801, II Lecture, 129 (cf. *Analytical Rev.*, September 1789, unsigned, V, 40). In Lecture IV, 1805, 217 f.:

"The landscape of Titian, of Mola, of Salvator, of the Poussins, Claude, Rubens, Elzheimer, Rembrandt and Wilson, spurns all relation with this kind of map-work (topography). To them, nature disclosed her bosom in the varied light of rising, meridian, setting suns; in twilight, night and dawn. Height, depth, solitude, strike, terrify, absorb, bewilder in their scenery. We tread on classic or romantic ground, or wander through the characteristic groups of rich congenial objects." He goes on to belittle the transcripts of the Dutch school. We have seen from Turner's exchange with Britton, 1811, how aware he was of·Fuseli's criticisms on this point; and he probably therefore took all the more care in the Backgrounds Lecture to say little of the Dutch, though he was also thinking of Reynolds, and, as partisan of landscape, wanted to remove it from the artforms which Reynolds was liable to stigmatize as vulgar or too imitative of nature; for the same reason, perhaps, he did not mention the side of Wilson concerned with the particular aspects of English landscape (Leslie (2), 101).

8. Shee in *Rhymes on Art*, 1805, said that Wilson united Claude's composition with Poussin's execution, "avoiding the minuteness of the one, and rivalling the spirit of the other". Now at last "the authentick productions of his hand are purchased at all fashionable sales, with an avidity that procures for the picture-dealer the affluence that was denied to the Painter".

9. Dayes in his *Works*, 1805, called him "this giant of the English school", whose compositions were not "encumbered with a multitude of parts, a fault frequently observed in Claude." Cf. Carey, *Letter to L. . . A.*, 1808.

10. Hoppner, 1 June 1806, with Farington, "considering the qualities of Claude & Wilson as He shd. those of two fine Women, He should acknowledge the beauties of Claude, but say Wilson was a piece of more relish".

11. A few days later Farington recorded that Ozias Humphrey, seeing a View of Rome, cried, 'It is as simple as possible & grand as it can be; it is as if Michael Angelo had taken it up. Compared with Claude the largeness and dignity of Wilson's mind is most striking" (Constable letter, 9 May 1823).

12. Hoppner again: in two review articles in *Quarterly Review*, 1807, defended Reynolds, but gave strong praise of Wilson, attacking the patrons and connoisseurs for their neglect, refers to his growing fame and denies the charge (cited by Edwards in his *Anecdotes*, 1808) that his paintings were incomplete. "Every touch of his pencil was directed by a principle that required the subserviency of particular parts to the full establishment of the whole." Wilson looked on nature "with the enthusiastic eye of a poet. We recollect no painter, who with so much originality of manner, united such truth and grandeur of expression."

13. Hazlitt, representing the backward-looking attitudes, in 1814 attacked the elevation of Wilson at Claude's expense. He agreed that his local colour had harmony and depth, and he owned a fine feeling for proportion and for light and shade, but called him deficient in accuracy of outline and even in perspective and actual relief. His trees seem pasted on like botanical specimens. "In fine, I cannot subscribe the opinion of those who assert that Wilson was superior to Claude as a man of genius; nor can I discern any other grounds for this opinion than what would lead to the general conclusion that the more slovenly the work the finer the picture . . ." (W. (2), 229).

2. *Akenside, Thomson, and the Earthly Paradise*

Akenside has a strong sense of the interconnexion of all things; and he seeks to grasp the process by which the imagination works in seizing on resemblances or correspondences. In part he uses the associative principle, but he looks beyond this to explain the dynamic force and the unity of the process. "One movement governs the consenting throng" – with a dominant delight or sadness. He uses the notion of magnetism to explain the strong links. "Such is the secret union, which we feel A song, a flower, a name at once restore Those long-connected scenes . . . with all the band Of painted forms, of passions and designs Attendant: whence, if pleasing in itself, The prospect from that sweet accession gains Redoubled influence o'er the listening mind." Memory plays a key-part in using "these mysterious ties" to preserve her "ideal train . . . intire". But there are also certain inherent factors, an "early tincture", "one homebred colour" which persists indelibly. (Turner knew these passages from the Third book well, since he cites three compressed pieces from them in the lectures.)

It follows, then, that in imaginative acts a sudden kindling occurs in which the mysterious ties act on "the ideal train" of Memory to beget a new unity, a single governing movement, in which the "homebred colour" plays its dynamic part. And further, if the "secret union" operates successfully, earthly life is transformed. The prospect by the sweet accession gains "redoubled influence". The action of memory-imagination is then occurring at a moment of harmonious development in which the self and nature are happily united. The earth becomes hesperidean, a 'visionary landscape' (ii, 666). The finer organs of the mind are attuned by nature's hand "to certain species of external things", as when the Memnonian image gave out music to the ray of sunrise. "So the glad impulse of congenial powers, Or of sweet sound, or fair proportion'd form, The grace of motion, or the bloom of light, Thrills through imagination's tender frame, From nerve to nerve: all naked and alive They catch the spreading rays." The soul, then, responsive "to that harmonious movement from without", discloses every "tuneful spring" (source of joy and harmony). "Then the inexpressive strain Diffuses its enchantment: fancy dreams Of sacred fountains and Elysian groves, And vales of bliss"

Thus for Akenside (and for Turner) the image of an idyllic or paradisaic earth is not a random or wilful fancy; it is a necessary image of imaginative harmony, of actual experience.

The problem, then, is what breaks the continuity of this harmony. For Akenside, part of the answer lies in the "early tincture" which can set up compulsions of folly or disaster. And these compulsions are, in some unexplained way, linked with the corruptions of society.

Thomson's *Spring* has a picture of the Golden Age of "uncorrupted man" when "harmonious Nature too looked smiling on", and 'winds and waters flowed in consonance". Now man has lost "that concord of harmonious powers", so that "all is off the poise within". There is "endless storm" arising from "ever-varying views of good and ill", so that man becomes the foe of man; the social feelings are extinct. Nature "disturbed is deemed, vindictive to have changed her course". Hence the Deluge. This disaster is described, and Thomson goes on to lament the ending of a vegetarian way of life (*Spring* 234 ff.).

In *Autumn* (220) he speaks of Arcadian song from the days when man was free to follow nature. In *Winter* (834 ff.) he praises the Lapps, who despise the trade of war and escape "the restless ever-tortured maze of pleasure and ambition," by asking "no more than simple Nature gives".

These ideas sank deep into Turner and must always be taken into consideration when dealing with his paradisaic scenes and his scenes of retributive disaster. (Note also the passage in Young's Fourth Night, beginning, "How changed the Face of Nature, how improved?")

How strongly the paradisaic image had become identified with the Claudean landscape is shown by Reynolds's phrase for the latter: "the tranquillity of Arcadian scenes and fairy-land" (ii, 70). Claude was felt to give the clues to the Golden Age, as Poussin to the Heroic. For the English Garden as paradisaic: *Lines written in a Window at Lord Radnor's at Twickenham*, 1748, "Elysium all without, within the same, As high as Art can reach or Fancy frame. The poet's pencil and the sculptor's art, Shine through the whole and brighten every part." Mason, *The English Garden*, "A gleam of happiness primaeval . . ." (ii, 204); landscape-artists or Sons of Claude depict Arcadias (iii, 325) – Poussin, Claude, Salvator are the painters invoked.

Havens notes the contradiction in Thomson between his ideas of progress and of pastoral simplicity (primitivism), but sees it only as a "cleavage in his life", not in his culture. This cleavage has a number of linked inner conflicts, one of the chief of which is the contradiction between the attempt to achieve the concrete colour-image and the intellectual elevation of Newtonian mechanism, which sees the concrete and the coloured as merely subjective, comparatively unreal beside the abstractions of mechanics.

3. *Turner and the Industrial Scene*

Despite his extreme interest in men at work and their tools, Turner did not deal with the factory system directly to any extent. Still, he did not ignore it.

Some examples of his eye for labour process from the sketchbooks: "For washing the Dye the wool is packed in the Basket of Frame work", CCXIV, 165a, in Holland; "Ferry Horse ridden Sideways," *ib.*, 214a; Sawyers, "Float of Unbarked Timber Trees – lash't", CCXVI, 28, on Meuse; "Cargo covered with Mats as Clothing", CCXLVIII, 17a. Interior of foundry, XX, 21a, 22; watermills and windmills, CXLVI, 3, Yorks; men mending bridge near Durham, CLVII, 19a–21; "Barges unloading coals" at lock gates, CLV, 2; "Carpenters at work mending the sluice", *ib.*, 17; a stone quarry at Pevensey, CXXXVIII, 15; "Bargemen hanging up clouts &c on the shrouds – good incident to avoid the long line of shrouds", XCVII, 67a; iron bridge (?railway on Thames at Richmond), CXLIII, 1; donkey by mineshaft, LXX, 1; gravel-pit, XXXIII, E; iron foundry, *ib.*, B. Endless details about ships and ship-work.

Where he treated the large-scale industrial scene, it was mainly for the effects of the smoking chimneys, e.g. *Leeds*, 1816 (Mellon Collection); or to add his own poetic alchemy, e.g. *Newcastle*, 1823, for *Rivers of England*.

It was through the steamship that he most fully and deeply treated the advent of industrialism. After his early wrecks, it is the steamship that we see battling with the elements, e.g. *Staffa* and *Snow Storm*, or supplanting sail, e.g. *Téméraire*. And he kept up other aspects of sea-life, e.g. *Life-boat and Manby apparatus going off to a stranded vessel making signal (blue lights) of distress*, 1831. C. Manby's apparatus for firing a rope by a mortar was first used in 1808; his *Essay on the Preservation of Shipwrecked Persons* came in 1812.

The first steam passenger boat crossed the Channel, Brighton to Havre, in 1816, in 1820 the first iron steamship sailed London-Paris. In 1819 the *Savannah*, built as a wooden sailing ship but fitted with steam-power, crossed the Atlantic, but mostly by using sails. In 1835 there was a genuine sea-passage from Canada to England. In 1835 the *Forfarshire* was launched for the Dundee, Perth and London Shipping Co, and greeted with much enthusiasm – "airy, commodious and elegant", with saloon panels painted by Horatio McCulloch, whose landscapes were liked in Scottish baronial homes. It left Hull on 5 September 1838; the boiler sprang a leak; but the captain, anxious for the ship's prestige, carried on. The ship was driven on to a rock on the Farne Islands – with Grace

Darling, daughter of the Longstone lighthouse-keeper, helping in the rescue of the survivors. (This caused a demand for portraits of her and paintings of the wreck; a panorama and a play were produced).

Dalyell in 1812 says, "In a country such as Britain, where every individual is either immediately or remotely connected with the fortune of the sea, the casualties attendant on the mariner must be viewed with peculiar interest." He adds, "Perhaps not less than 5,000 natives of these islands yearly perish at sea." In the first census, of 1801, the total population numbered ten and a half million. Shipping in its various forms was thus the most important industry, the most dangerous, and right in the forefront of technological progress; it was also the form of work which linked Britain directly with her Empire, the colonial peoples, the rest of the world in general. Hence it was well based for the symbolic use that Turner made of it. See in general, Boase (1).

4. Turner and his Fellow Artists

As part of his feeling of the R.A. as a maternal protective body Turner wanted to maintain friendly and easy relations with his fellows there, and to see the organisation itself as effective and as internally harmonious as possible. Lupton noted, "Turner was a great observer of all that occurred in his profession; of reserved manners generally, but never coarse (as has been said); though blunt and straightforward, he had a great respect for his profession, and always felt and expressed regret if any member of it appeared to waste or neglect his profession" (Th. ii, 36). He wanted a happy family in the R.A. He "was ever anxious to allay anger and bitter controversy; often I have heard him, in subdued tones, try to persaude the excited to moderation; he would do this by going behind the speaker, and by a touch or word soothe an acrimonious tone by his gentleness. He was unable to speak, but would by his attempt to express himself delay a question until it had received more serious and calm consideration" (an Academician, Th. ii, 108). He worked hard on the Benevolent Association (ii, 267–71; F., 247, 253, 280, 284, 329) and had his own large charity scheme.

In a letter to Hammersley's father (4 December 1848) he warned him of the need for a young artist to have some means of support during his first years in a "profession which requires more care, assiduity, and perseverance than any person can guarantee" (ii, 115 f.).

His care not to disparage other artists is stressed, and compared with Constable's ways (ii, 35, 45). Many artists paid tributes to his kindliness and helpfulness: D. Roberts (ii, 46 f.). He fought on the

Hanging Committee to get in the work of Bird, then unknown; and
finally removed one of his own pictures and hung one of Bird's
(ii, 111 f.). He moved one of his pictures to give a work by Jones a
better place (ii, 112). Hearing Lord E. express regret of Jones's
absense at Petworth, he wrote urgently to J. and got him down, a
few weeks before E. died (ii, 124; F., 368). He painted-in a cat to
help Howard in difficulties (ii, 37 f.; i, 172). He encouraged Frith
as a young painter (Frith i, 126 f.); also W. S. Witherington;
R. C. Leslie (2), 57, "I see – a gull – I like your colour." He helped
Reinagle to get a gratuity of £50 in January 1837 – and next year
was on the Committee which found R. guilty of showing as his
own a picture by a poor artist, Yarnold. Even Haydon said that
Turner had done him justice.

He liked professional jokes, e.g. the exchange of puns about
Painters (ii, 140, 266 f.; F., 301); Mulready's joke about a cow by
T. as a dough-pig (ii, 139 f.). He liked merry-making among artists,
e.g. F., 259 f., 270–2, and clubs such as that of the R.A. or the
Conversatione Society (Th. 316n). He liked puns, etc., thus, an
oyster stall is "The Bivalve Courtship', CCXXIX(a), 7.

Occasionally we find him beaten in exchanges, e.g. with Fuseli
(ii, 161); but had his own way of parrying comments he didn't like
or questions he didn't want to answer, e.g. "You have beaten me in
frames" (Thomson), i, 195. For a conflict with Constable: Roberts
(Th. ii, 44–45); with Reinagle: Frith i, 129 f.

Roberts says he liked to take part in R.A. debates, "but such was
the peculiar habit of his thoughts, or his expressing them (the same
aerial perspective that pervades most of his works pervaded his
speeches), that when he had concluded and sat down it would
often have puzzled his best friend to decide which side he had taken"
(ii, 46), cf. i, 178. C. R. Leslie (3) i, 205: "His voice was deep and
musical, but he was the most confused and tedious speaker I ever
heard. In careless conversation he often expressed himself happily;
and he was very playful; at dinner talk nobody more joyous."

Frith gives us an example of his speechifying. "The stammering,
the long pauses, the bewildering mystery of it, required to be
witnessed for any adequate idea to be formed. In writing I fear it is
impossible to convey it. It was not unlike the most incomprehensible
of the later pictures, mixed up with the "Fallacies of Hope". After
looking earnestly at the guests before him, he spoke:

" 'Gentlemen, I see some – ' (pause and another look round)
' new faces at this – table – Well – do you – do any of you – I mean
– Roman History – ' (a pause). 'There is no doubt, at least I hope
not, that you are acquainted – no, unacquainted – that is to say
– of course, why not ? – you must know something of the old –
ancient – Romans.' (Loud applause). 'Well, sirs, those old people –
the Romans I allude to – were a warlike set of people – yes, *they*

were – because they came over here, you know, and had to do a good deal of fighting before they arrived, and after too. Ah! they did; and they always fought in a phalanx – know what that is?' ('Hear, hear,' said some one.) 'Do YOU know sir,? Well, if you don't, I will tell you. They stood shoulder to shoulder, and won everything.' (Great cheering). 'Now, then I have done with the Romans, and I come to the old man and the bundle of sticks – Aesop, ain't he? – fables, you know – all right – yes, to be sure. Well, when the old man was dying, he called his sons – I forget how many there were of 'em – a good lot, seven or eight perhaps – and he sent one of them out for a bundle of sticks. "Now", says the old man, "tie up those sticks, tight", and it was done so. Then he says, says he, "Look here, young fellows, you stick to one another like those sticks; work all together", he says, "then you are formidable. But if you separate, and one go one way, and one another, you may just get broke one after another. Now mind what I say," he says – ' (a very long pause, filled by intermittent cheering). 'Now', resumed the speaker, 'you are wondering what I'm driving at' (indeed we were). 'I will tell you. Some of you young fellows will one day take our places, and become members of this Academy. Well, you are a lot of sticks' (loud laughter). 'What on earth are you all laughing at? Don't like to be called sticks? – wait a bit. Well, then, what do you say to being called Ancient Romans? What I want you to understand is just this – never mind what anybody calls you. When you become members of this institution you must fight in a phalanx – no splits – no quarrelling – one mind – one object – the good of the Arts and the Royal Academy' '' (Frith, i, 137–9).

This speech brings out clearly how Turner had made the Arts and the Royal Academy the repository of his family and social emotions.

5. *Varnishing Days*

The emotions which Turner felt towards the R.A. and his fellows overflowed in particular at the Varnishing Days. Frith says (i, 129) in his early days they "extended generally to nearly a week, luncheon being served daily in the Council-room". Ruskin says "Turner was always the first at the Academy". He even arrived as early as 4 a.m., never later than 6, and was last to leave. "He might be seen standing all day before his pictures; and, though he worked so long, he appeared to be doing little or nothing. His touches were almost imperceptible. yet his pictures were seen, in the end, to have advanced wonderfully. He acquired such a mastery in early life that he painted with a certainty that was almost miraculous."

He did not walk about, "but kept hard at work, nose to the canvas, sure of his effects" (Th. ii, 167).

He had his seaman's deal chest with colours in powder form, or prepared in vials, with his collection of worn brushes; a steel pallette knife. We hear of him playfully taking a bit of paint from someone's else palette; he took some orange vermilion or ultra-marine tempered with copal from the brothers Redgrave. Stanfield told F. P. Seguier, "I saw Turner apply water-colours with his fingers as a finishing-glaze to certain of his oils." To test this sort of story, Chantrey made a × over a ship's sail in an oil of his and took away inches of wet glazing; Turner grinned. (Falk, 160–3; Th. ii, 257.) Constable disliked the Varnishing Days and would have liked them abolished. Turner said to C. R. Leslie, "That will do away with the only social meetings we have, when we all come together in an easy, unrestrained manner. When we have no Varnishing Days, we shall not know one another." Leslie adds, "I believe had Varnishing Days been abolished while Turner lived, it would almost have broken his heart" ((3) i, 201 f.). See further RD 2, 4, 6, 7.

There is no need to record the large number of tales about his behaviour on these days. Many of them deal with his attempts to knock out someone else's painting with stronger and brighter colours, and are often heightened in order to show him as a ruthless competitor. No doubt at times he did do his best to outshine some other painting, but often the whole thing was part of a game, an expression of the high spirits he felt on these occasions; and often, too, he sought to help others. Thus, he smeared lampblack over the sky of his *Cologne*, so as not to injure the effect of two portraits by Lawrence (ii, 113 f.; F., 296). He swept in a circle on the wall in Hart's *Milton visiting Galileo*, and improved the work (Hart, 94). He advised Maclise about his *Sacrifice of Noah after the Deluge*, and added some touches, including "a rainbow, or reflected rainbow" (F., 416). When Stanfield had told S. Cooper to lower the tone of some ground where sheep lay; Turner came up, "Put it out – it destroys the breadth!" He laid some colour over the part where Cooper was working and walked off. Stanfield said, "Don't touch it again – he has done in a moment all that it wanted." When C. thanked T., he grunted and said nothing. Straight after, in the Café de l'Europe, Gillott among the dealers bought the work for £300 without seeing it (Cooper ii, 2 f.). Thornbury (ii, 188 f.) has a story of his once helping Constable; helps Callcott, F., 178 f.

For tales of conflict: with Geddes over *Téméraire* (Th. ii, 344); with D. Roberts over *Masaniello* (Frith i, 131 f.); with G. Jones over *Bridge of Sighs* (with T., beaten in the game); Jones MSS., Th. ii, 241 f.; with Constable, Th. ii, 187 f., and C. R. Leslie (3) i, 202; over Rembrandt's *Daughter*, ii, 165; Wilkie, F., 295 f.

6. *Turner and his Art*

A few more details. There are many tales of his hate of being watched; yet he enjoyed the Varnishing Days, when he worked with a maximum publicity. W. L. Leitch once saw him painting four water-colours at once. Once he saw an old water-colour at a friend's house, looked at it a long time, pulled a box of colours from his pocket, and set to work on it "like a tiger" for some hours. "When people came to see him, he would sometimes come down quite dizzy 'with work'. But I fear that latterly he drank sherry constantly while he painted" (Th. ii, 151). If so, it was after 1846. In the Jura a friend saw his name in the inn's book and asked what sort of man he was. "A rough clumsy man," was the reply; "and you may know him by his always have a pencil in his hand" (i, 198).

Mrs. Austin said, "I find, Mr. Turner, that in copying one of your works, touches of blue, red, and yellow appear all through the work." He answered, "Well, don't you see that yourself in nature, because if you don't, heaven help you" (Th. ii, 139). Jones wrote *splendide mendax* on the frame of *Bay of Baiae;* T. smiled and said it was all there, and that all poets were liars; he left the words on the frame (Th. i, 228 f.). He told a friend of one work, "I put in that effect because it was necessary."

He hated imitators of his work (i, 177; ii, 256). Complaints were made about his dislike of giving sketches away by persons who did not understand he needed them for work (Th. i, 179; ii, 185). But he disliked anyone trying to get anything of his for nothing; tale of printseller for whom he made a rough sketch to show him what engraving he wanted (Th. ii,, 148). Complaints were made at times that he hadn't produced what the person commissioning wanted (ii, 133).

He is said to have begun a Carthaginian picture while staying with Munro at Novar, with the servants posing for him in the open, the ghillies holding off young people who wanted to come too near (Falk, 112). This, however, does not sound like his way of working.

T. tells Trimmer he painted a picture on a tablecloth (Th. i, 174). Trimmer on body-colour and "cobalt is good enough for me", 174 f. A black cow against the sun: "It is purple, not black, as it is painted. He said Yellow was his favourite colour. On walks he would point to a piece of moss or a weed growing from a wall and observe, 'That is pretty', in a low voice" (176 – more on method, i, 233, 229–33; F., 110). More remarks and jokes about yellow: Th. ii, 141, 233 f.; i, 176, 227; Falk, 130, 161. Ruskin commented on his dislike of fresh green. He told Miss Fawkes, of a water-colour of hers, "Put in a jug of water"; later she realized he was advising her to soak the paper. He liked to spit in his paint-powder: Th. i,

223. T. as the Ochre man: W. (3), 253. He laughed at Eastlake for his "fastidiousness" in working so slowly: Eastlake (3) ii, 134.

Eastlake said that as a Visitor in the Life School he infused new ideas into the practice of the students, having larger views than most. He placed the model upon a white sheet, to make them see in a new way. In his quest for new patterns he did not scorn any line of approach. He encouraged three small children, who had dipped their fingers in red, blue, yellow, to dabble their fingers in the foreground of a drawing where the sky was finished. He said once that he could do anything with the pencil. C. Stokes, stock-broker, wagered he could not make a picture out of straight lines; he produced *Farmyard with Cock* (LS, no. 17, pt. iv).

Frith was present when a salad was offered to him at a dinner. Turner observed to his neighbour, "Nice cool green that lettuce, isn't it? and the beetroot pretty red – not quite strong enough; and the mixture, delicate tint of yellow that. Add some mustard, and then you have one of my pictures' (i, 130 f.).

7. *Engravings*

When he got his first commission to draw for engravers, he was 18 (1793); he was paid 2 guineas a plate, plus a small expense account. Each drawing, made on the spot, was feebly engraved by J. Walker for the *Copper Plate Magazine*. The great problem of engravers was to find methods that enabled as many pulls as possible to be made. Mezzotints, in their heyday in the later eighteenth century, provided only a few prints. In the years 1799–1811 (save for 1809) T. drew for the Oxford Almanack – the copper plates engraved by the capable James Basire (see Wedmore in D.N.B. on the three James). In 1805 C. Turner did the mezzotint of *The Shipwreck*. John Pye did *Pope's Villa* for Britton's *Fine Arts in England*. Older men used cross-hatching for clouds and the like; Pye used a change in the direction of lines for light-effects. T. is said to have been delighted with his work: "You can see the light." (He got Pye to take over the *Oxford High Street*, and Pye did also *Oxford from the Abingdon Road*, 1818.) Britton did much to develop line-engraving in the early nineteenth century, especially through his *Architectural Antiquities* (1st vol., 1807), in which we see the whole style of landscape-engraving change.

In 1809 T. began his *Liber Studiorum* (continued till 1819, seventy-one of the intended 100 prints appearing). The venture failed through lack of support and T.'s attempts to run the advertising and publishing all on his own; he tried to cut trade discounts and wanted cash down: 14 guineas a set – though when the Society of Artists of Clipstone Street wanted a copy, he asked the full sum, but sent them a guinea as gift to their funds. He was so exacting and paid his engravers so badly, he lost man after man.

He made the drawings in sepia wash or bistre, and sought to gain atmosphere by patterns of light and shade. He first thought of mezzotint, then turned to aquatint (Sandys and Girtin had used it; and Turner consulted Girtin's brother John). Unfortunately, in 1808 a flow of showily tinted aquatints (e.g. Ackermann's periodical *Microcosm of London*) began.

The first engraver was F. C. Lewis, who was to carry on after T. etched the outline, at £5 a plate. Then T. wanted him to do the aquatinting first. Lewis made technical objections. T. asked him to do both etching and aquatinting without increased fee, while he himself gave finishing touches. Lewis completed only one plate, which was issued later. (He was being paid 15 to 40 guineas for each of the Claude drawings in the royal collection, which he engraved.) T. then decided to get the engraver to lay the ground and trace out the subject; he himself then was to use the etching tool and engraver to do the biting, with T. supervising and correcting. C. Turner was the second man called in. He did the first twenty plates with a mezzotint finish; then asked for 10, not 8, guineas a plate. (Pye says T. declared prints had been stolen; he had seen them in a shop. It turned out the woman who stitched the prints together had been given proofs instead of money, and had sold them to buy bread.)

The break with C. Turner lasted nineteen years, then was healed. C. T. published three more engravings and worked on two that were never finished. After the breach. T. took charge; at least eleven plates were all his own work. He also repaired plates as they were worn out. (Only some thirty prints of high quality were obtainable.)

Other engravers who worked for him and claimed that they lost as a result were G. Clint and T. Lupton: working respectively for 6 and 5 guineas a plate. When in 1848 Pye tried to get proofs from them, they had none. Lupton said: "The pounds, shillings and pence of the affair ran thus. Copper plate, 7s. 6d.; mezzotint ground, 15s. My own labour seven or eight weeks. As to provings innumerable, resulting from the difficulty of obtaining an agreeable colour as nearly approaching to that of the drawings as possible; consequently the proving was not only difficult but expensive, even to the amount of two or three shillings a time. N.B. I forgot the beginning. The engraver had also to lay the etching ground and trace the subject on the plate for the painter to etch, which was his uniform practice."

Turner used to disregard the system used by his engravers to distinguish proof and print. The capital letters (denoting the class of the subject) were given in mere outline in proofs; they were black or tinted in prints. When repairing plates, T. skilfully changed worn patches, cleared off the marginal notes of numbers pulled, and reissued prints from the worked-over plates at higher prices. And he did this again and again, with no indication of states or distinction between proof and print.

Plates were thus altered to a considerable extent without any system of classification, and prints were indiscriminately issued, with varying quality. Strange actions for a man who in other ways was so passionately concerned with the quality of his products.

No collector managed by 1851 to built up a set of first-rate impressions of all plates in differing states. (Lahee, printing proofs for many years, had a unique set of fine pulls.) Till 1840 dealers did not keep the *Liber* in stock. Then with the new rise of his reputation a demand began; and at his death a keen competition set in. Charles Turner had a large set of proofs made at T.'s orders. When they quarrelled, T. refused to pay them; C.T. set them aside as a total loss, even gave some to servants to light fires with. Now he told Pye "he little thought at that time of the robbery he was committing on his children." Soon after T.'s death he sold his set (minus one, "of a wreck") to Colnaghi for £900; the print put aside sold a few days later at 20 guineas. Griffith the dealer had also made a good collection; he told Pye he bought them at an obscure Soho shop at 2*s*. or 2*s*. 6*d*. each. When in 1873–4 the Court of Chancery ordered the sale of all the prints and plates that had been in T.'s possession, many unknown or fine impressions fetched up to £50 each; twenty complete sets of the *Liber* sold from 270 to 850 guineas apiece.

To return to other engravings. In 1812 Wyatt of Oxford comissioned a drawing of the High Street. Pye engraved under T.'s scrutiny. (He did some more plates, and would have done yet more but for T.'s low rate of payment). From now on T. did large numbers of drawings for use as book illustrations. The *Liber* drawings were monochrome, following Claude. But otherwise he kept to the custom of his youth, when engravers worked from coloured drawings – which had the advantage of being able to be sold afterwards. In the 'twenties and 'thirties the water-colours provided were rich in colour and deep in tone, body-colour being used on tinted papers – though in later life he tried sepia drawings.

1811–27 was much taken up with *Views of the Southern Coast of England*. Cooke, himself an engraver, commissioned forty drawings at 10*s*. each. T. kept on pressing for a raised fee, after pushing it up to 10 guineas. He asked for an extra 2½ guineas (to apply also to the work already done), plus twenty-five India-paper proofs of each. But the book's price had been based on the original fee and T. had been offered a share of profits. Angry letters were exchanged till T. broke with Cooke. (Note letter in PTh. viii, opp. p. 402: to Cooke, "There is something in the manner of your note received yesterday, being so extraordinary and differing so materially from the conversation of Wednesday last that I must request you to reconsider the following" – rest lost, save for signature). Problems of printing were created by a plate like *Kirkstall Abbey*, first indicated by etching on soft ground, with fine ground laid over this (? mezzotint or aquatint) – on top, much that is clearly mezzotint – the whole reinforced by drypoint. Such a plate could produce only a few good prints.

A conflict was going on all the while between what the public wanted (topographical detail) and T.'s interest in effect of light and air. The earliest extant proof of the series, *Lulworth Cove* (March 1814), is dominated by white chalk – though *Weymouth*, much the same date, is altered much in black lead to strengthen the shapes of boats and the rigging. Cf. *Lyme Regis*, November 1814, to stress the stratification of the cliffs, "to counteract the sweeping lines of all the hills". He adds, "The lights I want had better be reserved until the next proof." That proof has a note by W. B. Cooke: "On receiving this proof, Turner expressed himself highly gratified – he took a piece of *white chalk* and a piece of *black*, giving me the option as to which he should touch it with. I chose the white; he then threw the black chalk to some distance from him. When done, I requested he would touch another proof in *black*. 'No,' he said, 'you have had your choice and must abide it.' How much the comparison would have gratified the admirers of the genius of this great and extraordinary artist!"

The system of first correcting by pencil (e.g. architectural detail), then on a second proof by sweeping lines of white chalk to subdue the detail in terms of aerial perspective, seems adopted (cf. the proofs of frontispiece of *Antiquities of Pola*, 1818). On *Gledhow* (engraved *c*. 1815) the paper is deeply scored by the knife and hatched all over with white chalk; the marginal notes bid the engraver "make the lights produced by the scrape very brilliant", the chalk "being more for general tones". At the same time he wants detail correct and clear; there is a marginal sketch of a roof outline.

In 1818 came the first part of the lavish *History of Richmondshire* (scenery of N. Riding), a project never completed; it did well, but the costs, round £10,000, were only just met. T. had been commissioned to make 120 drawings, but in fact, made twenty at 25 guineas each. They were simpler than the *Views*, finer in colour.

About 1820 the advent of soft steel plates had a drastic effect; many hundreds of impressions could be made, but the engraver had a much harder job and his tools were soon blunted. T. feared a fall in artistic values, but by 1830 he, too, used steel for smaller engravings and even tried it for etching and mezzotint. (Tale of Lawrence and bucket-engravings in Th. is incorrect: Bell, E, xxii). Steel allowed delicate light-effects in line, but impeded free handling.

The Rivers of England was engraved in mezzotint on steel. By

1826 T. gave up mezzotint; he made experiments on copper and steel (eleven of the plates found after his death). He wrote to G. Cooke on *Hythe* (November 1824): "I shall be in town in the course of the week, so let me see another proof, because of the sky – which I have not touched upon because I want you to say if it can be burnished – lighter in tone – *with safety*, thus [diagram showing sky growing lighter as it nears the sun behind the mass of dark foliage on right]." In the PS. he adds: "in general *very good*, secondly the Figures and Barracks excellent; but I think you have cut the Bank called Shorne Cliff too much with the graver by Lines [diagram] which are equal in strength and width and length, that give a coarseness." They "do not look like my touches or give work-like look to the good part over which they are put – The Marsh is all a swamp. I want flickering lights upon it up to the sea, and altho I have darkened the sea in part yet you must not consider it to want strength . . . Get it into one tone, flat, by dots, or some means, and let the sea and water only appear different by their present lines."

Rivers sought to combine the breadth and mezzotint-softness of *LS* with the fullness of detail in *S. Coast;* but the attempt fell down on technical difficulties. (Of the six men employed, four had shown their mettle in *L.S*) C. Turner was to start the series (1 January 1824) with a modified repetition of the *Norham Castle* theme; but the problem of details and atmospherics was too much for mezzotint on steel. Three plates broke down during printing. The compromise of copper was tried. Again T. asked too much.

1827 saw the start of his most ambitious work, *The Picturesque Views of England and Wales*, originated by Charles Heath: 120 engravings to be issued in serial form. The drawings show his mature control of air, light, weather effects. The engravers were mostly men he had tried out, and he supervised as usual. Heath was ruined. Three more firms tried to carry on; the venture collapsed in 1838. Next year T. bought up the plates and stock for £3,000 at auction. He said to Bohn, "So sir, you were going to buy my England and Wales, to sell cheap I suppose – make umbrella prints of them, eh? – but I have taken care of that. No more of my plates shall be worn to shadows.' Bohn replied that he wanted the prints, not the plates; and T. told him to come along next day. Bohn then offered £2,500 but T. demanded £3,000 and the deal fell through.

The Art Union in April 1839 attributed the failure to the general use of steel plates which produced "a cheaper class of publications". We may add that the hardening of style tended to obscure the differences of the drawings used, so that T.'s work was less distinguishable from its imitations. By 1830 there was a flood of cheap topographical and scenery engravings. Books with portraits of high ladies began to drive out the Picturesque Landscapes. Also, lithography (strangely never used by T.) was growing popular, exploited by the new Victorian sentimental school with artists like Edwin Landseer. T. had gone on retouching the proofs with indefatigable care and patience, and he kept the same attention for the larger plates issued. (Notes: "I must ask you to take out particularly every appearance of the Rings at the upper part." On foreground object: "I mean it for a bough shiver'd off.") He still insisted on graduations such as undermined the staying powers of the *England and Wales* plates. (For an effort to get cheaper printing in Scotland, 1842: F., 387 f.)

In 1830 he had been commissioned to do vignettes for Rogers' *Poems*, which were carried out in steel; T. lent them out for £5 each. He made drawings on blue paper with use of body-colour for *The Rivers of France* (3 vols.); and in 1832-7 drew for many books. Murray's *Life and Works of Byron*, Finden's *Illustrations of the Bible*, Moxon's *Milton*, Campbell's *Poems*, etc. (For the Fall of the Rebel Angels, *Paradise Lost* VI, he told E. Goodall to add hosts of figures to the plate himself.) He next concentrated on large line-engravings of his oils (F., 386 f.). Half of these were made on copper, despite the dominance of steel. Even on copper a plate took some two years of steady work; on steel (in a plate 24 by 17 inches) the work was too hard.

As an example of T.'s criticism of a plate in his later years we may take some of his words to Miller on the large *Modern Italy* in October 1841. Miller has written to say that if he were sure the sky was right he could go more confidently on. T. told him not to touch "the sky for the present, but work the rest up to it". He declared, "The question of a perpendicular line to the water – pray do not think of it until after the very last touched proof, for it has a beautiful quality of silvery softness, which is only checked by the rock" – at the waterside in the centre – "which is the most unfortunate in the whole plate. How to advise you I know not, but think fine work would blend the scene with the reflection of it with the water." He wanted the foreground more spirited and bold. "The figure in front would be better with the white cloth over the face by one line only; and perhaps a child wrapped up in swaddling-clothes before her would increase the interest of the whole." Miller then inserted the swaddled child. T. wrote, "I have gone through the distance and Town down to the Chalk line very carefully and tho it appears not much at first sight yet in filling in and fine close lines you will find all your making out work kept to advantage . . . I wish you would indulge me in dotting in close the piece of sand chalked (hieroglyph) and then made lighter in tone altogether. I have left the sky because I want to know if you can burnish in a few light thin clouds, as looking rather dark, and might save more trouble if you can do so." He added, "Thank you for the child – make the Head rather larger. Don't be alarm'd about the Foreground. I see you are afraid about the left corner, Grapes and foliage, but when you have done the middle part, say the Town – I'll soon beat them out, there being plenty of good work. The wall is the part I like the least.'' (Three more long letters of instructions in Rawlinson (1) ii, 340 f.)

The directions given by T. to his engravers are very useful in helping us to grasp how he looked at a picture.

Finally we may claim that he did much to raise the whole standard of British engravings (and so of the appreciation of art in general), and that the engravings popularized his work – or at least certain aspects of it. But he was struggling against the current. It might indeed be said that in many engravings, and in the drawings done for them, we see his link with the worse aspects of the glibly and superficially romanticising trends, yet in the general development of his art the sheer fire of his vision of process burns out the impurities.

8. *Turner and Money*

Turner's attitudes to money were complex and at times show a neurotic obsessional element; but that does not mean that the legend of him as a miser holds water. He had a genuine frugality; he refused to carry on the usual social round of entertainments, partly because of his wish to keep a maximum of energy for his work, partly because he realized that he lacked the manners of the conventional host, partly because he disliked the waste of money. Other people, especially artists, who envied or merely could not understand him, took the obvious line of considering him a miser. This interpretation was furthered by the dealers, whom in later life he often took pleasure in tormenting.

See Lupton on his way of raising prices (Th. ii, 37; cf. 131–3); the tale of a dealer really believing he was a Jew (i, 407); his anger at Windus reselling at profit after pestering him to sell (Falk, 190). See also Frith i, 141–3; Th. ii, 151.

There were many tales, some obviously fabricated or twisted, of his meanness: Thomson and the lunch invitation (Th. ii, 143); demands payment for a coach fare (ii, 145; cf. 132, 323); half a crown to a gardener (ii, 151 f.); wants back money left under pillow (ii, 96); does not pay for his father's tablet (ii, 145 f.); actually paid a companion's toll over Waterloo Bridge (ii, 155); bought cloth for R.A. seats (twisted, ii, 142); was mean over little things (sherry-bottle with broken cork for decanter), etc.: ii, 172); argues with bus conductor (ii, 155); leaves someone else to pay bills (plain lies, i, 227 f.). Where he does show up badly is in his treatment of engravers for the *Liber*, etc.; his meanness here is surprising.

On the other hand, there is no doubt that he could be extremely generous: his behaviour to the Fawkeses after Walter's death (in exaggerated form, Th. ii, 130); his saying to a friend, "Don't wish for money; you will not be happier, and you know you can have any money of me you want"; his thrusting-out of a begging woman, then rushing to give her a five-pound note: he lends money to a friend's widow, then refuses to let her pay him back, tells her to send her children to school (ii, 131; cf. 157 f.); Jones says that the many tales of his parsimony and covetousness were "generally untrue", *ib.;* refusal to allow distraint on tenants two years in arrears (houses in Harley Street, ii, 132 f.); taking a large bill for artists dining at Blackwall from Chantrey and paying it (ii, 135) and C. R. Leslie (3) i, 203; release of Goodall, engraver, from a ruinous contract, at a loss of £500 to himself (Falk, 109; cf. Th. ii, 150).

An important story is that (i, 396) told by Heath, who, one day with Turner, noted that he was ignoring a bill for £200, due that very day. Here we see his attitude to money coinciding with that towards his pictures, which he ardently hoarded, yet badly neglected.

9. *Letter of Evelina Dupuis (to Jabez Tepper, solicitor to the Turner cousins)*

18, Great Ormond Street, W.C.
Novr. 24th, 1865.

If, as a late Revd. friend stated to me from your own words to him, I owe principally to yourself that arrangement on the conclusion of the Suit in Chancery, "Trimmer versus Danby", which secured for my enjoyment the Legacy mentioned in my father's "Will", this, as a plea for addressing you, may avail also in the Appeal I am advised by my friends to make to your sympathy under circumstances of a Mortgage, the result of disappointment and grievous pressure. Yet neither is for the object of alluding to the past, so fraught with adverse destiny, that I would invoke consideration now, or seek to move a feeling in this behalf whose avowal by yourself conferred consolation, and strengthened hope, in former years, when it also entered your thoughts to advantage me by the change of my annuity to property in the Funds.

But it is simply to bring under the same favourable notice what is inseparable from the present time that I venture on this step, so to convey to you the knowledge that my actual position, being that of extremely narrowed circumstances, is very far from happy or secure, and the kind intent which moved you in the case of the annuity has so far failed in result, that, through inforseen, if not undue charges, in addition to others partly unavoidable from the necessity of a grown-up family, which have entailed, besides Legacy duty, Insurance, Mortgage, etc. involved that income, I am not really in the receipt of much more than one third of the original Grant, a sum therefore inadequate to my support, and wholly so for the attainment of those comforts at my time of life, which I am sure you wished me to enjoy.

But without dwelling further on the recital of griefs & vicissitudes calculated to awaken sympathy, & without indulging hope in any way that may not be agreeable to your own feelings & interests, I venture to submit these unhappy circumstances as they stand, and beg leave to ask if, through your influence something could be done to relieve my annuity from its present incumberances which amount to £325, and thus alleviate the sorrows which oppress the last lineal descendant of the race of Turner, the surviving daughter of an artist of such repute.

Thus afflicted,
(Signed) E. Dupuis

The Chancery decision of 19 March 1856 laid down that "Evelina Dupuis is entitled after the expiration of five years from the death of the said Testator to the Annuity of £100 for her life given her by the first Codicil to the said Testator's Will, after paying or providing for the Legacy duty payable in respect thereof and that the first half yearly payment thereof is to be made as hereinafter directed."

Later the plaintiffs (the executors) are directed: "on or before the 14th day of November next [to] transfer £3,333 6. 8. Bank Consolidated £3 per cent Annuities part of the Testator's estate into the name and with the privity of the said Account General in trust to the said first third and fourth above mentioned Causes [of the 5th, 15th, 17th March; dealing with Hannah's claims] to an account to be entitled "The Annuity Account of Evelina Dupuis subject to duty'. And the said Accountant General is to declare the trust thereof accordingly subject to the further order of the Court. And it is Ordered that the interest to accrue due to the said Bank £3 per cent Annuities when so transferred be from time to time and when the same shall accrue due paid to the said Evelina Dupuis the wife of Joseph Dupuis during her life or until the further order of the Court for her separate use . . ."

The rights of Evelina in the £3,333 6s. 8d. are also cited in relation to Mrs. Booth's claims. Lady Eastlake (1) i 273, who was in a good position to know the facts, recognizes Evelina's parentage: "To his own daughter he left not a penny, though his housekeeper gets 150 l. a year."

Falk, 239, f., cites Evelina's letter to Tepper, whose mother, Mary Tepper, was a first cousin to Turner; he acted efficiently in the suit for the various relations. Falk says this letter is in TD, but Mr. Turner has been unable to find it for me.

Joseph Dupuis can hardly have been the son or grandson of the composer, who seems to have had only three sons: Thomas Skelton, 1766–1795 (said to have died without issue, J. Foster, *Alumni Oxoniensis* 1715–1886 i), George who died in infancy, Charles, 1770–1824, who had a son Charles Saunders Skelton, *c*. 1798–1874. It is, however, possible that Joseph belonged to some branch of the same family. He did not however go to Oxford as seems to have been the family habit.

Joseph had been Vice-Consul at Mogador, 1811–16. Then after being Consul at Ashanti and Member of the Council at Cape Coast Castle 1817–22, he became Vice-Consul at Tripoli 1825–34, and at Sfax, 1836–42. He died on 14 February 1874. Presumably Evelina went abroad with him, which would explain much of Turner's failure of interest in her.

Two more Dupuis appear in the Foreign Office List (1904): Hanmer Lewis Dupuis who began his career as Clerk to the Mission at Tangier in January 1863 and ended as Consul for the Ionian Islands, March 1896, retiring on a pension in 1899 and dying at Corfu May 1911. And Joseph Hutton Dupuis, beginning as Vice-Consul at Naples, 1857 and ending as Consul for the Canary Islands 1882, retiring 1890 and dying 1903. These may well have been sons of Joseph and Evelina. (Information from C. L. Robertson).

W. E. F. Ward is editing a reprint of Dupuis *Journal* (1966).

Bibliography

Abbreviations: BMag, *Burlington Magazine;* Conn., *Connoisseur;* JWCI, *Journal of the Warburg and Courtauld Institute;* WS, Walpole Society.

Ackermann, *Repository of Arts* ix, 1813; Aikin, J., *The Seasons,* 1792 (*Essay on the Plan and Character of T.'s Seasons,* first pub. 1778); Aldridge, A. D., *J. of Hist. of Ideas* v, 1944, 292–314 (Akenside's sources); Allston, Washington, *The Sylphs of the Seasons and Other Poems* 1813; Alston, J. W., *Treatise on Painting,* 1804; Anderson, J., *The Unknown Turner,* 1926 [a work of much delusion]; Anderton, Extended R.A. Catalogue at Burlington House; Anon, (1) *A Catalogue Raisonne of the Pictures now Exhibiting at the British Institution* (June 1815), (2) ditto, *in Pall Mall* (1816), (3) *A Practical Treatise on Painting in Oil Colours,* 1795; Antal, F., (1) *BMag,* 1940 (Reflections on Classicism and Romanticism), (2) *Fuseli Studies,* 1956 ,(3) *Hogarth,* 1962; Armstrong, W., *Turner,* 1902; Arnoult, L., *Turner, Wagner, Corot,* 1930; Ashby, T., (1) *T.'s Vision of Rome,* 1928, (2) *BMag* xxiv, 1914, 218, (3) *ib.* xxv, 1914, 98, (4) *ib.* xxv, 1914, 241–7 (Tivoli); Athenaeum, 1879, ii, 406, 349, 470, 501, 600, 636 (Farnley); Avison, C., *An Essay on Musical Expression,* 1753 (1st ed., 1752).

Badt, K., *John Constable's Clouds,* 1950; Baker, Collins, *Gaz. des B.A.* xxxiii, 1948; Ballantyne, J., *Life of David Roberts,* 1866; Barbier, C. P., (1) *W. Gilpin,* 1933, (2) *S. Rogers and W. Gilpin,* 1959; Barry, James, *Works,* 1809; Bayes, W., *Turner,* 1931; Bayliss, Wyke, *Olives,* 1906; Beach, J. W., *The Concept of Nature in Nineteenth Century English Poetry,* 1936; Beckett, R. B., *Conn.* cxx, 1947, 10–15; Beechey, H. W., Memoirs of Reynolds in *Lit. Works,* 1885; Bega, *The Turner Spell;* Bell, C. (surgeon), *Essay on the Anatomy of Expression in Painting,* 1806; Bell, C. F., (1) *Exhibited Works of JMWT,* 1901, (2) Intro. to Cat. of J. R. Cozens's Drawings, WS (with T. Girtin) xxiii, 1934–5 (3) WS v, 1915–17, 77 f., (4) *Studio T. Vol.* (T. and Engravers), (5) WS, 1917 (James Moore); Bell, JWCI xxii, 1959, 347–58; Berenson, *Seeing and Knowing,* 1953; Binyon, L., (1) *T. Girtin,* 1900 (2) *English Water Colours,* 1933; Black, Ladbroke, *Some Queer People;* Boase, T. S. R., (1) JWCI xxii,

1959, 337–44 (shipwreck), (2), *ib*. xxvi, 1963, 148–77 (Macklin, Bowyer), (3) *ib*. x, 1948 (Boydell), (4) *English Art 1800–70*, 1959, (5) JWCI xix, 1956; Bolton, A. T., *Portrait of Sir J. Soane R.A.*, 1927; Borenius, T., *Cat. of Pictures and Drawings at Harewood House*, 1936; Bos, Du, *Reflexions critiques sur la Poésie et la Peinture*, 1719; Britton, J., (1) *Fine Arts of the English School*, 1812, (2) *British Press*, 9 May 1803, (3) *Autobiography*, 1849; Broughton, Lord (John Cam Hobhouse), *Recollections of a Long Life;* Burgh, W., see W. Mason (2); Burke, F., *Philosophical Enquiry into our Ideas of the Sublime and the Beautiful* (1756); Burnet, J., (1) *Turner and his Works*, 1852, with mem. by P. Cunningham, (2) 2nd ed., 1859, *A Practical Treatise on Painting*, 1828, (3) *Critical Remarks*, etc.; Bury A., *Richard Wilson R.A., The Grand Classic* (1947); Butlin, M., (1) *T.'s Watercolours*, 1962, (2) see Rothenstein (2), (3) *The Later Works of JMWT*, 1965.

Carey, W. P., (1) *Some Memoirs of the Patronage and Progress of the Fine Arts*, 1826, (2) *Observations on the Probable Decline . . . of Brit. Hist. Painting*, 1825, (3) *Cursory Thoughts*, 1810, (4) *Desultory Exposition*, 1819, (5) *Observations on . . . the British Inst.*, 1829 (6) *Critical Dissertation . . . of Death on a Pale Horse*, 1817, (7) *Brief Remarks*, 1831; Cecil, L., *Printseller*, 1903 (Morland); Ceste, C., *La Revolution française et les Poètes anglais*, 1906; Chignell, R., *JWMT*, 1902; Clare, C., *JWMT* 1951; Clark, H. F., *The English Landscape Garden*, 1948; Clark, J. H., *Practical Illustrations of Gilpin's Day*, 1811; Clark, K., (1) *Landscape into Art*, 1956, Penguin, (2) Lecture, Cat. Arts Council Exhib., *JMWT*, 1952, (3) *Looking at Art*, 1960, (4) *Ambassador* viii, 1949, 75–90 (Petworth), (5) *Leonardo da Vinci*; Cohen, R., *The Art of Discrimination*, 1964; Collingwood, W. G., *Life of Ruskin*, 1911; Collins, Baker, C. H., *Cat. of Petworth Coll.*, 1920; Constable, W. G., *R. Wilson*, 1953; Cook, D., *Art in England*, 1869; Cook, E. T., (1) *Hidden Treasures of the Nat. Gallery*, 1905, (2) *Life of J. Ruskin*, 1911; Cooper, D., *BMag* xc, April 1948 (Iconog. of Wilson); Cooper, T. S., *My Life*, 1904; Creevey, T., *Creevey Papers*, ed. H. Maxwell, 1904; Croft-Murray, E., (1) *BMag* xc, 1948, 106–9, (2) *BM Quarterly* x, 2, 49–52 (Monro School, shipping at Dover); Cummings, F., *BMag*, April 1962 (Poussin, Haydon); Cunningham, A., (1) *Life of Wilkie*, 1843, (2) *The Lives of the Painters*, 1829; Cunningham, C. C., *Art Q.* xv (Detroit), 1952, 323–30 (T.'s Van Tromp Paintings); Cunningham, P., *Mem.* attached to Burnet (1), 1852; Cust, L., *BMag*, May 1912.

Dalton, J., *Countrymen*, Winter 1964, 381–6 (Girtin); Davies, M., (1) *The British School*, 1959, (2) *ib.*, 1946; Davies, R., *T. Girtin's Water-Colours*, 1926; Dayes, E., (1) *Works*, ed. E. W. Brayley, 1805, (2) Work Diary, V and A, Box 111, 8622; Desenfans, Noel,

Plan . . . to preserve among us, and to transmit to posterity, the portraits of the most distinguished characters, 1799; Dillon, E., *Art J.*, 1902, 329, 362 (T.'s last Swiss drawings); Dodgson, Campbell, 6 *Aquarelle von JMWT*, 1937; Donaldson, J., *The Elements of Beauty*, 1780; Dyer, G., *Poetics*, 1812.

Eastlake, C. L., (1) *Contributions to the History of the Fine Arts* i, 1848, ii, 1870, (2) *Materials for a History of Oil Paintings* i, 1847, ii, 1869, (3) see Goethe; Lady Eastlake, (1) *Journals and Correspondence*, ed. C. E. Smith, 1895, (2) *Mem.* to Eastlake (I) ii, Eaton, F., *The R.A. and its Members*; Edwards, E., *Anecdotes of Painting*, 1801; Eitner, L., *Art. Bull*, 1955, xxxvii (The Open Window and the Storm-tossed Boat); Elsam, R., *An Essay on Rural Architecture*, 1803.

Falk, B., *Turner the Painter*, 1938; Farington, J., (1) *Diary*, ed. J. Grieg, 1922–8, (2) MS. in Royal Lib., Windsor, 1793–1821, (3) *Mem. of Sir J. Reynolds;* Fawkes, H., *Mag. of Art*, 1881; Fawkes, W. R., (1) MS. Diary at Farnley Hall, (2) *Speech*, 1812, (3) 2nd ed. with *Letter*, (4) *The Englishman's Manual*, 1817; Feret, C. J., *Isle of Thanet Gazette*, 23 September 1916 (Sherrell); Field, G., (1) *The Analogy of Logic, and Logic of Analogy* 1850, (2) *Outlines of Analogical Philosophy*, (3) *Chromatics*, 1817, (4) *A Grammar of Colouring*, ed. E. A. Davidson, 1877, (5) *Chromatography*, 1835, (5a) 2nd ed., 1841, (6) *Aesthetics*, (7) *The Analogy of the Physical Sciences*, (8) *Tritogeneia*, (9) 3rd ed., 1846, (10) *Chromatography*, revised T. W. Salter, 1869, (11) modernized J. S. Taylor, 1885, (12) *Dianoia*, (13) *Ethics*, (14) *Rudiments of the Painter's Art*, 1850, (15) revised R. Mallet, 1870, (16) E. A. Davidson, 1875; Finberg, A. J., (1) with Rawlinson, *Watercolours of JMWT*, 1908, (2) *T'.s Sketches and Drawings*, 1910, (3) *The History of T.'s LS*, 1924, (4) *In Venice with T.*, 1930, (5) *Life of JMWT*, 1939, (6) 2nd ed., 1961, (7) *Complete Inventory of Drawings of T. Bequest*, 1909, (8) *T.'s Water-Colours at Farnley Hall*, 1912, (9) *Early English Water-Colour Drawings*, 1919, (10) *BMag* ix, 1906, 191–5, (11) WSi, 1911–12, 85–89 (IOW), (12) WS ii, 1912–13, 127–32 (doubtful drawings), (13) WS iii, 1913–14, 87–97 (S. Wales), (14) WS vi, 1917–18, 95–103 (S.W.), (15) *Apollo* i, 1925, 38–42 (Geneva), (16) *Conn.* xcvi, 1935, 184–7 (Yorks), (17) Intro. to T.'s *Southern Coast*; Finberg, H. F., (1) *BMag* |xcix, 1957, 48–51 (1797), (2) *ib.* xciii, 1951, 383–6 (T. Gallery, 1810); Finer, A., and Savage, G., *Selected Letters of Josiah Wedgwood*, 1965; Foss, K., *The Double Life of JMWT*, 1928; Freiberg, S., *Alte und Neue Kunst* iv, 1955, 133–9; Frith, W. P., *My Autobiography*, 1887; Fuseli, H., (1) Transl. of Wincklemann's *Reflections on the Paintings and Sculptures of the Greeks*, 1765, (2) *Lectures on Paintings*, 1801, (3) *Lectures*, 1820, (4) *Lectures*, ed.

Knowles, 1830, (5) Translation of Lavater's *Aphorisms*, 1788, (6) *Aphorisms* in Knowles, 1831.

Gage, J., (1) *BMag*, January 1965, (2) *ib.*, February (T. and Picturesque), (3) *Apollo*, July 1964 (Magilphs and Mysteries); Galt, J., *Life, Studies, and Works of B. West*, 1816–20; Gandy J., *Rural Architecture*, 1801; Gilchrist, A., *Life of W. Etty*, 1855; Gill, F. T., *Turner*; Gilpin, W., (1) *Observations, relative chiefly to Picturesque Beauty, made in the year 1776* (2nd ed., 1792), (2) *Observations on the Western Parts of England . . . Isle of Wight*, 1798, (3) *Remarks on Forest Scenery* i, 1791, (4) *Observations on the River Wye* (3rd ed.), 1792, (5), *Three Essays on Picturesque Beauty* (2nd ed.), 1794; Girtin, T., (1) *Water-colours* (Studio), 1924, (2) *Doctor with Two Aunts*, (3) with D. Loshak, *The Art of T. Girtin*, 1954; Goethe, *Theory of Colour*, trans. Eastlake, 1840; Gombrich, E., *BMag*. lxxx-lxxxi, 1942 (Reynolds's Theory and Practice of Imitation); Goodall, F., *Reminiscences*, 1904; Gotch, S. B., *Maria Lady Callcott*, 1937; Grant, J., *Mem. Manchester Society* i, 1805 (reverie); Grant, M. H., *Old English Landscape Painters;* Graves, A., and Cronin, W. V., *A History of the Works of Sir J. Reynolds*, 1899; Gray, R. D., *German Studies Presented to W. H. Burford* (T. and Goethe's Colour Theory), 1962; Green, T., *The Diary of a Lover of Literature* (anon, Ipswich,), 1810; Greenshields, M., *Museums J.*, lvii, 1957–8, 288 f.; Greville, C. C. F., *Memoirs*, ed. H. Reeve, 1888; Grigson, S. *Palmer*, 1947; Guillemard, F. H. H., *Conn.* lxiii, 1922 (Francia club), Add: Gowing. L., *Intro.* T. Exhib., Mus. Mod. Art, NY, 1966.

Hagstrum, J. H., *The Sister Arts*, 1958; Hamerton, P. G., *Life of JMWT*, 1879; Hamilton, H. E., MLN lxii, 1947 (Hagley Hall), 194–7; *Hansard Parl. Reports*, (1) House of Lords, 19 March 1857, (2) 27 June 1861, (3) 11 and 15 July 1861; Hardie, M., *Conn.*, August 1904; Hart, S. A., *Reminiscences*, ed. A. Brodie (privately), 1882; Hassell, J., *Aqua Picture*, 1818; Havens, R. D., *SP*, 1932, 41 (Primitivism and Idea of Progress); Hayes, J., (1) *Apollo*, November 1962, (2) *ib.*, August 1963, (3) *ib.*, July 1964 (Gainsborough's landscapes); Heath, V., *Recollections*, 1892; Hemmelmann, H. A., *Country Life Annual* (Loutherbourg), 1956, 152; Henderson, B. L. K., *Morland and Ibbetson*, 1923; Hermann, L., *JMWT*, 1963; Hetzer, T., *Wiener J. f. Kunstgesch*. xiv, 1950 (Goya und die Krise der Kunst um 1800); Hilles, F. W., and Bloom, H., *From Sensibility to Romanticism*, 1965; Hind, C. L., *Turner;* Hipple, W. J., *The Beautiful, the Sublime, and the Picturesque in British Eighteenth-Century Theory*, 1957; Hogarth, W., *Analysis of Beauty*, ed. J. Burke, 1955; Holme, C. J., (1) *Genius of JMWT* (ed) *Studio*, 1903, (2) *BMag*. xiii, 1908 (Girtin and Rembrandt), 375–81,

(3) *The R.A. from Reynolds to Millais* 1904; Hoppner, *Oriental Tales*, 1805; Houpt, C. T. *Mark Akenside*, 1944; Hoyland, F., *Listener*, 13 May 1965 (Gainsborough, Cornard Wood); Hughes, C. E. *Early English Water-Colours*, 1913; Hunt, W. H. *Pre-Raphaelitism and the P.-R. Brotherhood*, 1905; Hurdis, J., *Lectures showing the Several Sources of that Pleasure which the Human Mind receives from Poetry*, 1797; Hussey, C., *The Picturesque*, 1927.

Imison, J., *Elements of Science and Art*, 1803; Ingersolls-Smouse, J. *Vernet*, 1926.

Jerningham, (1) *The Shakespearean Gallery*, 1791, (2) *Peace, Ignominy, and Destruction*, 1797; Johnson, C., *The Language of Painting*, 1949; Jones, G., (1) *Recollections of Sir F. Chantrey*, 1849, (2) Reminiscences MS., in Ashmolean; Justi, C., *Winckelmann und seine Zeitgenossen*, 1866–72.

Kay, H. I., AWS, 1926 (Cotman at T.'s lectures); Key, S., *J. Constable*, 1948; Kirby, J., *Dr Brook Taylor's Method of Perspective made easy* (3rd ed.), 1768; Kitson, M., (1) *JMW Turner*, 1964 (2) with A. Wedgwood, *English Painting*, 1964, (3) *Listener*, 12 August 1965; Kitson, S. D., *Life of J. S. Cotman*, 1937; Klingender, F. D., (1) *Hogarth and English Caricature*, 1944, (2) *Art and the Industrial Revolution*, 1947; Knight, Payne, (1) *An Analytical Inquiry into the Principles of Taste*, 1805, (2) *The Landscape* (2nd ed.), 1795; Knowles, J., *Life and Writings of H. Fuseli*, 1831.

Laing, D., *Etchings by Sir D. Wilkie*, 1875; Lairesse, G., *The Art of Painting* (trans. Fritsch), 1738; Landseer, J., (1) *Rev. of Publications of Art*, 1808, (2) *Lectures on the Art of Engravings*, 1807; Laver, J., *Drama: its Costume and Décor*, 1951; Lavery, J., *Listener* (letter), 12 August 1965; Leach, F. D., *Ohio Univ Rev.* ii, 1960, 5–20 (Hogarth's Distressed Poet); Leslie, G. D., *Inner Life of the R.A.*; Leslie, C. R., (1) *Memoirs of the Life of J. Constable* (2nd ed.), 1845, (2) *ib.*, 1951, (3) *Autobiographical Recollections*, ed. T. Taylor, 1860, (4) *Handbook for Young Painters*, 1855; Leslie, R. C., (1) *Letter*, app. in Ruskin's *Praeterita*, (2) *Waterbiography*, 1894; LFA: *Library of the Fine Arts* iii and iv, 1832; Lindsay, J., (1) *Life and Letters*, August 1947, (2) *The Sunset Ship*, 1965, (3) *The Death of the Hero*, 1960, (4) *Arena* vi-vii (Coleridge), 1951; Liebreich, R., *Turner and Mulready*, 1888; Livermore, Ann, (1) *Conn. Year Book*, 1957, 78–86, (2) *Music and Letters* xxxviii, 1957, 170–9, (3) *Country Life* (T. and Children), 25 December 1958, (4) *ib.* (S. Lodge), 6 July 1951; Longton, *Proc. Wedgwood Soc.* ii (Empress Catharine).

MacColl, D. S., (1) *Nineteenth Century Art*, 1902, (2) *Artwork* v,

1929, 91–94, (3) *BMag* xii, 1907, 345, (4) *Cat. Turner Coll.*, 1920; Macfall, H., *The Modern Genius*, 1911; Mack, Maynard, in Hilles and Bloom (A Poet in his Landscape: Pope at Twickenham); McKillop, A. D., *The Background of Thomson's Seasons*, 1942, (2) in Hilles and Bloom (Local attraction and cosmopolitanism); Maggs Bros., Cat. of Autographs; Manwaring, E., *Italian Landscape in Eighteenth-Century England*; Mason, E., *The Mind of H. Fuseli* 1951; Mason, W., (1) *The English Garden*, 1772–9, (2) *ib.*, "corrected, to which are added a Commentary and Notes by W. Burgh Esq; LL.D.", 1783; Mauclair, C., (1) *Turner*, 1938, (2) Trans. E. B. Shaw, 1939; Maurice, T., *Hagley, A Descriptive Poem*, 1776; Mayne, J., *T. Girtin*, 1949; Melville, R., *New Statesman* (rev. RB), 21 November 1964; Merchant, W. M., *Shakespeare and the Artist*, 1959; Millais, J. G., *Life and Letters of Sir J. E. Millais*, 1899; Miller, H., *First Impressions of England and its People*, 1845; Miller, T., *Turner and Girtin's Picturesque Views*, 1854; Milliken, W. A. *Cleveland Mus. of Art*, 1958; Mitchell, C., *BMag* lxxx–lxxxi (Reynolds), 1942; Mitford, J., B.M., Add. MS. 32570, f. 279; Monkhouse, W. C., (1) *Turner*, 1879, (2) *Scribners Mag.* (portraits), July 1879; Moore, T., *Memoirs, J. and Corr.*, ed. J. Russell, 1853–6.

Neilson, W. A., *Essentials of Poetry*, 1912; Nettleship, J. T., *G. Morland*, 1898; Nichols, J. B., *Illustrations of the Lit. Hist: of Eighteenth Century*, 1817–58; Nicholson, B. (1) *BMag* xcvi, 1954, 243 (2) *Wright of Derby*, 1966; Nicholson, F., *The Practice of drawing and painting Landscape from Nature, in Water Colours* (2nd ed.), 1823; Nicholson, N. H., *Newton Demands the Muse*, 1946; Norris, F., *Annual Vol. of Old Water-Colour Club* ii; Northcote, *Memoirs of Sir J. Reynolds*.

Opie, *Lectures*, 1807; Oppé, A. P., (1) *Alexander and J. R. Cozens*, 1952, (2) *The Water-Colours of Turner, Cox and de Wint*, 1925, (3) *BMag* xcviii, 1955, 393.

Palmer, A. H., *Life and Letters of S. Palmer*, 1892; Partington, W., *The Private Letterbook of Sir W. Scott*, 1930; Paul, L., *The Mariner's Mirror*, lv, 1914, 266–74; Pendered, M. L., *J. Martin, Painter*, 1923; Pennell, E. R. and J., *The Whistler Journal*, 1921; Platt, J., Thornbury 1862 interleaved and broken into 13 vols., in B. M.; Pope, A. (Girtin) in Anderton (W. (2), 44 f.); Portal, P. P. F. de, *Des Couleurs Symboliques*, 1837; Pott, J. H., *Essay on Landscape Painting*, 1872; Pouilly, L. de, *The Theory of Agreeable Sensations*, 1749; Price, Uyedale (1) *Essays*, 1819, (2) *Essay on the Picturesque*, 1794, (3) *Dialogue on the Distinct Character of the Picturesque and the Beautiful*, 1801; Pye, J., *Patronage of British Art*, 1845; Pyne, W. H., *Somerset House Gazette*, 1824.

Quarterly Review, April 1862.

Rawlinson, W. G., (1) *Engraved Work of JMWT*, 1908, 1913, (2) LS, (3) see Finberg (1); Redding, C., (1) *Frazers Mag.*, February 1852, (2) *Fifty years Recollections*, 1858, (3) *Past Celebrities whom I have known*, 1856; Redford, G., *Art Sales*; Redgrave, R., (1) with S. Redgrave, *A Century of British Painters*, 1866, (2) *Mem. compiled from his Diary*, by F. M. Redgrave, 1891, (3) with S. R., *Dict. of Artists of the English School*, 1878; Reynolds, Sir J., (1) *Lit. Works*, 1885, (2) *Discourses*, ed. R. W. Wark, 1959; Rigaud, S., MS. Mem. of his father; Ritchie, L., *Liber Fluviorum*, 1853; Roberts, J., *Introductory Lessons in Water Colours*, 1800; Robertson, J. L., *Poetical Works of J. Thomson*, 1908; Robinson, H. Crabb, *Reminiscences and Corr.*, ed. T. Sadler, 1869; Rogers, J. S., *Opie and his Works*, 1818; Roget, J. L., *A Hist. of the Old Water-Colour Soc.*, 1891; *Rossetti Papers, The*, 1903; Rothenstein, J., (1) *Turner*, 1962, (2) *Turner*, with Butlin, 1964, (3) *Intro. to English Painting*, 1965; Röthlisberger, M., *C. Lorraine*, i, 1963; Royal Academy of Arts, MS. Minutes of Council Meetings; Ruskin, J., (1) *Modern Painters*, 1843–60, (2) *ib.* in *Works*, 1903–12, (3) *Pre-Raphaelitism*, 1851, cited from Everyman ed., (4) *Cat. of T. Sketches in Nat. Gallery*, 1857, (5) *Drawing by the late JMWT presented to the Fitzwilliam Mus.*, 1861, (6) *Cat. of Sketches and Drawings . . . Marlborough House 1857–8*, 1857, (7) *Notes on the Drawings of the late JMWT*, 1878, (8) *Drawings and Sketches by JMWT . . . in the Nat. Gallery*, 1881, (9) *Notes on the Turner Gallery 1856–7* as in (3) above, (10) *Lectures on Architecture and Painting delivered 1853*, as in (3) above; Russell, R., *Listener* (T. and W. Country), 23 August 1962; Rutter, F., *Wilson and Farington*, 1923.

Sandby, W., *History of the R.A.*, 1862; Schetky, Miss, *J. C. Schetky by his Daughter*, 1877; Scott, J., (1) *Critical Essays*, 1785, (2) *A Letter to the Critical Reviewers*, 1782; Shee, M. A., (1) *Rhymes on Art*, 1805, (2) *Elements of Art*, 1809; Shipp, H., *Apollo Miscellany* (T., the Background of Aesthetic Theory), 1951; Shirley, A., *The published Mezzotints of D. Lucas after J. Constable*, 1930; Skene, J., *Memories of Sir W. Scott*, ed. B. Thomson, 1909; Smith, J. T., (1) *Nollekens and his Times*, ed. Gosse, 1895, (2) *A Book for a Rainy Day*, (3) *Remarks on Rural Scenery*, 1797; Solly, N., *Mem. of the Life of D. Cox*, 1873; Stokes, A., *Painting and the Inner World*, 1963; Stokes, H., *Girtin and Bonnington*, 1922; Street, J., *Listener* (Poets and Garden), 19 September 1963; Swinburne, C. A., *Life and Works of JMWT*, 1902.

Taylor, B., *Animal Painting in England*, 1955; Thompson, A. H., *Camb. Hist. Eng. Lit.* (Thomson) x, 1913; Thornbury, (1) *Life of*

JMWT, 1862, (2) 2nd ed., 1877, (3) see Platt; Timbs, J., *Anecdotal Biography*, (1) 4th s., 1863, (2) 2nd s., 1860; Tinker, C. B., *Painter and Poet*, 1938; Townsend, H., *JMWT*, 1923; Todd, R., *Tracks in the Snow*, 1946; Twining, T., trans. of Aristotle's *Treatise on Poetry* with essay, 1789.

Upcott, W., *A Bibliographical Account of the Chief Works Relative to English Topography*, i, 1818; Uwins, T., *Memoir*.

Vittoria, Duchess of Sermoneta, *The Locks of Norbury*, 1940; Vollmer, H., in Thieme-Becker, *Allgemeines Lexikon der Bildenden Kunstler* xxxiii, 1939, 493–6.

Waagen, G. F., (1) *Works of Art and Artists in England*, 1838, (2) *Treasures of Art in GB*, 1854, (3) *Handbook of Painting* (Eastlake), enlarged, etc, by Dr Waagen, 1860; Walbrook, H. M., *Daily Telegraph*, 22 June 1924; Waterhouse, E., (1) *Painting in Britain 1530–1790*, 1953, (2) Poussin et l'Angleterre jusqu'en 1744, *Actes du Colloques N. Poussin* i, 1960, (3) *Gainsborough*, 1958; Watts, Alaric, Biog. Sketch in L. Ritchie; Wedmore, F., (1) *T. and Ruskin*, 1900, (2) *Studies in English Art*, 1876; West, B., *Discourse delivered to the Students of the R.A. etc.*, 1793; Whalley, Dr. *Parish of Whalley* (4th ed.), 1876; Whitley, W. T., (1) *Artists and their Friends in England 1700–99*, 1928, (2) *Art in England 1800–20*, 1928, (3) *ib.* 1821–37, 1930, (4) *T. Gainsborough*, 1915, (5) *BMag* xxii, 1913 (T. Lectures), 205–8, (6) *Conn.* lxix, 1924, 13–20; Williams, D. E., *Life and Corr. of Sir T. Lawrence*, 1831; Williams, I. A., *Early English Watercolours*, 1952; Wind, E., (1) *Vortrage d. Bibliothek Warburg*, 1930–1: Humanitatisdee und heroisertes Portrat in des Engl. Kultur d. 18 Jahrhunderts, (2) *JWCI* ii, 2, 1938–8: Hist. Painting; Wolff, E. B., *German Life and Letters* vi, 1952–3 (Goethe's reputation as scientist in nineteenth-century England); Woodall, M., *Cat. of R. Wilson and his Circle* (Tate), 1949; Woolner, T. *His Life and Letters;* Wornum, R. N., *The T. Gallery*, 1875; Wroot, H. E., *Miscellanies of Thoresby Soc.* xxvi (T. in Yorks), 1924; Wyllie, W. L., *Life of JMWT*, 1905.

Young, J., *A Cat. of Pictures by British Artists in the Possession of Sir J. Flemming Leicester, Bart.*, 1825.

Ziff, Jerrold, (1) *BMag* cv, 1963, 315–21 (T. and Poussin), (2) *JWCI* xxvi, 1963 (Backgrounds Lecture), 124–47, (3) *Studies in Romanticism* iii, Summer 1964, 193–215.

Index

Aeneas, 91–2, 114, 131, 154, 166–7, 192, 264

Akenside, M., 72, 98, 108, 136, 158–9, 172, 186–9, 272, 319, 324–5, 339, 348

Allston, 82

Angelo, H., 107

Angerstein, 53

Arnald, 227

Barker, H. A., 87, 88

Barry, J., 107, 202

Baudelaire, 315, 336

Beaumont, Sir G., 40, 66, 105–6, 136, 151, 169, 194, 198–200, 322

Beckford, 53, 92, 117, 308

Beechey, 102–3, 110, 118, 272

Beech-trees, 55, 299–300

Bell, E., 13, 30–32

Bird, 163, 320–2, 330, 352

Blake, W., 59, 82, 106, 187, 274, 300

Bloomfield, 137

Boaden, J., 124, 127

Bonomi, 95

Booth, Mrs. C., 92, 230–31, 242–3, 260, 285–6, 337, 364

Bourgeois, Sir F., 45, 93, 103–4, 111, 308, 322

Bowyer, 85

Boydell, 83–5, 127, 304

Brentford, 13, 27, 28, 291

Brewster, 273

British Institution, 115, 127, 132, 171, 198–201, 231, 236, 240, 333

Britton, J., 121, 152, 318

Brooking, C., 64

Brown, Capability, 61

Bruce, J., 163–4

Burnet, J., 116, 324

Byron, 48, 181–4, 235, 335, 361

Cadell, R., 31, 227

Calcott, A. W., 46, 87, 127, 147–8, 151, 153, 173–4, 194, 198–200, 217, 225, 241, 258, 272, 313, 322, 328, 354

Calcott, J. W., 47, 148, 298

Campbell, T., 158, 172, 189, 232, 249, 254, 319, 322, 361

Canaletto, 40, 58, 235

Carew, 247

Carlisle, Sir A., 241, 313

Carlyle, 250, 265

Cézanne, 109, 142, 176, 288, 309, 314

Chantrey, Sir F., 20, 244, 310, 332–3, 363

Chelsea, 231, 260–64, 286, 337

Children, 16–22, 90, 130, 292

Claude, 40, 50, 52, 53, 57, 66–8, 71, 73, 76, 93, 101, 127–9, 154, 157, 198, 205–6, 240, 246, 255, 300, 302, 307, 312, 318–19, 346–9

Clevely, 51

Cloud-studies, 206, 329
Cobb, G., 244
Coleridge, S. T., 106, 136, 182, 187, 250
Collins (poet), 322
Collins, W. (artist), 215, 331
Combe, W., 197, 327
Constable, J., 58, 61, 93, 105, 128, 131, 195, 206, 219, 273, 304, 308, 322, 331, 347, 352–4
Cook (artist), 31
Cooke, W. B., 145, 151, 197, 209–10, 214, 217, 220, 225, 358
Cooper, S., 284, 342, 354
Cotman, J. S., 87, 331
Covent Garden, 11–15, 25–8, 46, 53, 121, 194
Cowper, 59, 87, 322
Cozens, A., 82, 106–8, 329
Cozens, J. R., 40, 60, 93, 117, 155, 209, 295, 299
Crabb Robinson, 153, 213
Cuyp, 66, 71, 93, 127, 307, 324

Danby, Evelina (Mrs Dupuis), 147, 149, 195, 199, 220, 243, 263–4, 287, 316, 363–5
Danby, Georgianna, 124, 147, 200, 220, 243, 263, 316
Danby, H., 24, 148, 220, 258–60, 286–7, 295, 342
Danby, John, 46, 94, 148, 287, 297, 321
Danby, Sarah, 46–9, 56, 93–5, 119–20, 124, 143, 147, 148, 168, 212, 220, 230, 243, 338, Her daughters by John: 48, 124
Dance, G., 29, 91, 153

Daniell, W., 127, 132, 311
Dart, Ann, 35–8
David, 114
Davis, J. S., 335
Dayes, E., 26, 28, 37, 54, 59–60, 63, 88, 111, 294, 299, 305, 309
Delacroix, 229
Demaria, J., 88, 195, 305
Denman, Maria, 213
Dibdin, C., 177
Dibdin, T., 315
Dickens, C., 257
Dodsley, 152, 318
Ducros, 60
Dupuis, J., 147, 264, 329, 364
Duroveray, 27
Dyer, 79

Eagles, Rev. J., 240, 243
Eastlake, C. L., 196, 219–20, 248, 259, 272, 283, 332, 335, 341–2
Eastlake, Lady, 256, 259, 286, 364
Egremont, Lord, 201, 226–7, 241, 244, 247, 333, 352
Elgin, Lord, 52, 298
Etty, W., 215, 226, 255, 260, 272

Falconer, 41
Farington, J., 12, 28, 32, 40–2, 46, 52–5, 67, 92, 98–9, 104, 110, 132, 146, 150, 153, 175, 194, 198, 296, 299, 307–11, 329, 346
Farnley, see Fawkes
Fawkes, F. H., 22, 153, 257, 283
Fawkes, Miss, 355
Fawkes, W. R., 22, 146, 153, 179–82, 192, 197–205, 208–9,

214–7, 305, 316, 323, 329–31, 363

Field, G., 144, 271–2, 315, 339

Finberg, A. J., 109, 210, 222, 253, 306

Flaxman, 153, 332, 346

Francia, L., 86–8

Frith, W. P., 125, 226, 295, 352–6

Fuseli, 53, 62, 82, 84, 105, 152, 156, 235, 304, 346, 352

Gainsborough, 14, 16, 40, 57, 65–6, 81, 84, 174, 198, 209, 237, 335, 342

Gandy, 191

Gardens, 61, 71, 300

Gilpin, S., 45, 53

Gilpin, W., 51, 55, 61, 62, 90, 141, 293, 298

Giorgione, 232

Girtin, T., 16, 28–9, 32, 40, 42, 46, 52, 54, 59, 86, 88, 93, 98, 102, 209, 294–8, 305, 308, 339

Glover, J., 209, 310, 333

Goethe, 144, 270, 278–81, 340

Goldsmith, O., 84, 154

Goyen, van, 235

Gray, 76, 84, 138, 156

Greaves, 263

Greene, T., 41, 50

Griffith, T., 243, 287, 335, 342, 358

Grosley, 58

Hall, 259

Hamerton, 47, 253

Hamilton, W., 84, 322

Hammersley, J. A., 258, 351

Hammersmith, 129–31, 191

Hardwick, T., 27

Harley St., 55, 87, 130, 146, 363

Harris, Jack, 29

Harris, Moses, 275

Havell, W., 127

Haydon, 118–9, 122, 226, 352

Hazlitt, 125, 142, 198, 201, 210, 269, 322, 347

Hearne, T., 40, 294, 300

Heath, C., 217, 220, 360, 363

Helmholtz, 275

Henderson, J., 40–2, 294

Hoare, Sir R., 53

Hobbema, 65, 307

Hogarth, 63, 81, 145, 159, 174, 176, 198, 255, 333

Holland, R., 241

Holworthy, J., 199–202, 207, 211–12, 216–17, 239

Hoppner, J., 42, 46, 53, 87, 92, 106, 117, 124, 232, 296, 308–9

Howard, H., 153, 175, 194, 352

Humphrey, O., 12, 103, 347

Hunt, Leigh, 125

Hunt, R., 132, 173–4, 209, 328, 331

Hurdis, 79–80

Ibbetson, J. C., 57, 64, 300

Impressionists, 176

Islington, 11, 191

Jaubert, Roch, 94–5

Jeremiah, 94, 306, 337

Jermingham, 84, 85, 325

Jones, G., 120, 134, 184, 210, 219, 224–5, 244, 335, 336, 341, 352, 363

Johns, A., 196, 321, 327

Johnson, Dr., 62, 332
Judkins, 121 315,

Kauffmann, A., 84, 196, 303
Keats, 136, 187, 328
Kingsley, W., 261–2
Kirby, J., 141
Klee, 109
Knight, Payne, 60, 82, 133, 199, 299

Landseer, Sir E., 226, 241, 272, 284, 361
Landseer, J., 85, 132, 149
Langthorne, 52, 72, 76
Laporte, J., 32, 40
Lawrence, Sir T., 82, 118, 195, 224, 245, 287, 331, 332
Leslie, C. R., 118, 155, 283, 310, 342, 354
Leslie, R. C., 20, 34, 243, 352
Lessing, 84, 305
Liebreich, 125, 310
Lock of Norbury, 141
Lockhard, 256
Loutherbourg, P. J. de., 32, 57, 63, 64, 85, 117, 131, 156, 210, 294, 298, 307, 323
Lowe, M., 28

Macklin, 63, 83, 84–5, 306, 323
Maclise, 118, 234, 342, 354
Mallet, 52, 72, 75, 80, 84, 123, 136
Malton, T., 27, 42, 293, 294, 316
Mannerism, 44, 54, 55, 299
Margate, 33, 34, 121, 131, 210, 229–30, 242, 257, 292
Marsh, W., 146
Marshall Family, 11–12, 27, 209, 330, 342

Martin, J., 156, 209, 323, 330
Mason, 61, 73, 79, 141, 156, 158, 349
Maw, J., 241, 334
Mayall, 115, 275–8
Merry, R., 172
Milman, 122
Milton, John, 52, 72, 76, 84, 112
Monro, Dr., 28, 32, 40, 61, 107, 294, 295, 297, 322, 334
Moore, J., 296
More, J., 72
Morland, 57, 300
Morland, G., 16, 29, 40, 57, 64, 300, 309
Mulready, 272, 352
Munro, H. A. J., 114, 214, 239, 284, 310, 331, 355

Napoleon, 94, 154, 186, 201
Narraway, J., 29, 35–9
Nelson, Lord H., 53, 118
Newton (artist), 241
Newton, Sir Isaac, 81, 144, 245, 273–4, 278, 339
Nixon, H. C., 310
Nixon, H. G., 48, 124, 310
Nixon, R., 28, 42–4
Northcote, J., 82, 105, 110
Norton, St., 94, 147, 163

Opie, 53, 84, 105, 178, 190, 308, 322, 326, 346
Ossian, 72, 87, 98

Palgrave, F. T., 284
Palice, 27
Palmer, S., 107, 308, 323
Pantheon, 29–30
Pantomime, 253–4, 336

Pasquin (Williams), 33, 41
Pether, 306
Petworth, 20, 134–5, 136, 218, 219, 226–7, 235, 241, 244–5, 247, 352
Phillips, T., 153, 225, 331
Picturesque, 32, 44–5, 62–4, 71, 138, 141, 190, 191, 294, 301, 308, 312, 313, 314, 316, 327, 360
Pocock, N., 51
Pope, 166–7
Porden, W., 294
Porter, R. K., 86–7, 88, 89, 310
Pott, J. H., 59, 90, 299–300, 345
Pouilly, L. de, 144
Poussin, G., 58, 301
Poussin, N., 17, 44, 66–71, 73, 76–7, 98, 100–101, 112, 127, 157, 198, 206, 246, 307, 309, 325, 332
Pre-Raphaelites, 128, 285, 339
Price, Dr D., 230, 286
Price, Uvedale, 55, 62, 141
Provis, M. A., 297
Pye, J., 42, 152, 183, 286, 358
Pyne, J. B., 107, 272, 310

Queen Ann Street West, 146, 151, 208, 259, 261, 285, 286, 287, 330

Raimbach, A., 44, 100
Raphael, 156, 208, 307
Redding, C., 195–6, 254
Redgrave, R., 287
Reeve, Lovell, 31
Reinagle, 44, 199, 272, 338, 352
Rembrandt, 40, 67, 93, 133, 176, 218, 233, 235, 307
Reynolds, Sir J., 14, 16, 28–9, 54, 65, 84, 150, 209, 275, 287, 323, 330, 333, 336, 346, 349
Reynolds, S. W., 127
Rippingille, 234, 236, 342
Rigaud, J. F., 28, 84
Rigaud, S., 42, 43, 44
Roberts, D., 186, 285, 341, 351
Rogers, S., 172, 218, 225, 227, 229, 334, 361
Romney, 12
Rosa, Salvator, 44, 64, 73, 76, 303, 335
Rose of Jersey, 135
Rossetti, W. M., 212
Rossi, 46, 103, 104, 110, 150
Rowlandson, 58
Rubens, 65, 67, 296
Ruisdael, 61, 65, 71, 218, 307
Ruskin, 14, 35, 169, 186, 192, 212, 234, 237, 239, 240, 243, 251, 252, 253, 254–7, 259, 260, 282, 288, 308, 309, 325, 334, 335, 336, 337, 340, 341
Ryley, 322

Sandy, P., 27, 40, 55, 58, 60, 294, 322
Sandycombe Lodge, 191, 192, 199, 339
Scott, S., 64, 300
Scott, W., 227–8
Serres, D., 56, 64
Serres, J. T., 55–6, 98, 300
Shee, Sir M., 46, 73, 153, 169, 171, 225, 259, 283, 317
Shenstone, W., 61, 85, 301
Sherell, F., 263
Smirke, R., 52, 64, 104, 110, 153, 199, 304, 318
Smith, J. R., 29

Soane, Sir J., 103, 118, 135, 150,
    303, 333;
    his son, 207, 330
Spencer, H., 310
Sporting pictures, 301
Stockdale, P., 79
Stothard, T., 27, 45, 84, 118,
    225, 233, 317, 332

Taylor, J., 125, 150
Teniers, 117, 321
Thackeray, 125, 255, 313, 335
Theatre, 63, 262, 302–4
Thomson of Duddington, 273,
    362
Thomson, H., 131, 199, 328
Thomson, J., 51, 61, 67, 71–82,
    85, 91, 123, 136, 137, 139,
    144, 154–8, 177, 181–5, 189,
    249–50, 255, 274, 301–4, 313,
    318, 325–6, 348–9
Titian, 100, 140, 178, 214, 232,
    307
Thornbury, G. W., 15, 24, 33,
    34, 90, 118, 120, 121, 125,
    153, 183–4, 213, 234, 242,
    257, 272, 294–5, 336
Tresham, H., 102, 111, 242, 317
Trimmer, H. S., 13, 15, 22–4,
    73, 90, 102, 119, 130, 169,
    175, 192–4, 199, 220, 272,
    293–5, 327, 331, 339, 342, 355
Turner, C., 117, 129, 231, 245,
    284
Turner Family, 11, 23–4, 95–7,
    143, 151, 287
Turner, G., 89
Turner, J. M. W., 'art-children,'
    38, 119–22; blood-sports,
    196–7, 201, 320; colour theory
    and practice, 100–101, 150,
    221–3, 232–3, 235–6, 265–7,
    269–82, 288–9, 338–41; colour
    structures, 221–3; engravings,
    18, 30, 197, 215, 228, 231,
    252, 332, 356–62; fishing,
    18–22, 134–5, 151, 161, 193;
    gallery, 110, 116, 118, 130–32,
    193, 198, 200, 258, 260;
    Liber Studiorum, 128, 130,
    132, 356, 358, 363; lectures,
    65–6, 69–70, 134, 149–50,
    201, 205, 209, 210, 214, 231,
    240, 242, 274–5, 317, 325–6,
    331, 340; madness, 124–6;
    money, 21, 43–4, 111, 137,
    146–7, 362–5; music, 35, 48,
    93, 101, 143–5, 235, 297–8,
    313, 315–6; politics, 77–8,
    154–5, 178–86, 237–8, 239,
    242, 246–7; smoke, 140, 324–
    5; tours, 30–33, 42, 53–4, 94,
    98–102, 130–33, 151, 167,
    195–7, 199–204, 207–9, 214–
    20, 225–8, 231, 244, 246,
    254, 257–9; verse, 17, 70, 93,
    136–8, 154–5, 161–8, 171–2,
    177–9, 190, 201, 205, 212–13,
    219–20, 225–6, 237–8, 248,
    259–60, 281, 299, 317, 320–21,
    341; will, 220, 227, 259–60,
    263–4, 287–8, 337, 338; works:
    Abingdon, 140, Aeneas and the
    Sibyl, 91, 192, 237, Angel in
    the Sun, 251, 259, 270, 282,
    339, Apollo and Daphne, 241,
    Apullia, 197–8, 205, Army of
    Medes, 94, 319, Bacchus and
    Ariadne, 135, 270, Banks of
    the Loire, 220, Battle of Fort
    Rock, 154, 199, Battle of Nile,
    50, 75, 88–90, 112, Bay of

Baiae, 92, 192, 210, 221, 237, 241, 355, *Bligh Sands*, 199–200, *Boats carrying out anchors*, 112, 125, 223, *Boccaccio*, 112, 125, 223, *Bridge of Sighs*, 229, 334, *Burning of the Houses*, 234–8, 239, 270, *Buttermere*, 44, *Calais Pier*, 51, 105, 112–13, 116, 205, 232, *Calais Sands*, 225, 232, *Caligula's Palace*, 227, *Campo Santo*, 50, *Carnarvon Castle*, 50, 76, 315, *Childe Harold*, 221, 228, 236, 237, 246, *Cicero*, 221, *Cologne*, 329, 354, *Conflagration, Lausanne*, 236, *Cottage destroyed by Avalanche*, 138–9, *Country Blacksmith*, 130, 332, *Crossing the Brook*, 142, 149, 199–200, 206, 213, *Dawn of Christianity* 270, *Decline of Carthaginian Empire*, 201, 206, *Deluge*, 112, 195, 205, 309, *Destruction of Sodom*, 112, *Dido and Aeneas*, 198, 210, 237, *Dido Building*, 142, 199, 205, 234, *Dido Directing*, 218, *Doldabern Castle*, 76, 95, *Dort*, 202, 206, 298, *Dunstanburgh Castle*, 73, *Dutch Boats in Gale*, 93, *Entrance of Meuse*, 205, *Ehrenbreitstein*, 246, *Eruption of Souffrier Mountains*, 205, *Evening Star*, 225, 232, *Fates and Golden Bough*, 92, 231, 237, *Festival at Macon*, 105, 216, *Field of Waterloo*, 202, 205, *Fifth Plague*, 91, 98, 112, *Fighting Téméraire*, 242–3, 246–7, 267, 350, *Five at*

Fennings Wharf, 236, *Fire at Sea*, 213, 236, 339, *Fishermen at Sea*, 32, 157, 298, *Fishermen upon a Lee-shore*, 98, 112, 210, *Fishing upon the Blyth Sand*, 140, *Fishmarket on the Sands*, 225, *Fountain of Indolence*, 231, *Frosty Morning*, 140, 195, 206, 210, *Garreteer's Petition*, 136, *Goddess of Discord . . Hesperides*, 127, 309, *Golden Bough*, see *Fates*, *Hannibal*, 51–2, 139, 153–9, 173, 177, 179–80, 182, 192, 260, 266, *Harbour of Dieppe*, 215, 329, *Heidelberg*, 270, *Hero of a Hundred Fights*, 270, *Hero and Leander*, 241, *Holy Family*, 105, 309, *Homer Reciting*, 184, *Jason*, 132, 200, *Jessica*, 225, *Juliet and Nurse*, 239–40, 245, *Kilgarran Castle*, 50, 213, *Lake Nemi*, 192, *Leeds*, 350, *Letter*, 235, *Lifeboat*, 227, 350, *Light and Colour*, 270, 280–82, *London*, 324, *Lord Percy*, 227, *Loretto Necklace*, 220, *Medea*, see *Vision*, *Mercury and Argus*, 215, 221, 239, 318, 320, *Morning*, 76, *Mortlake Terrace*, 218, *Mouth of Seine*, 232–3, *Music at Petworth*, 235, *Narcissus and Echo*, 127, 309, *Nebuchadnezzar*, 228, *Neapolitan Fishergirls*, 243, *Norham Castle*, 269, *Orvieto*, 219, 225, *Palestrina*, 156, 221, 225, *Peace*, 223, 252, 268, *Petworth Dewy Morning*, 140, *Petworth Park*, 232, *Phryne*, 242,

Turner, J. M. W. – *contd.*
246, 248, 270, *Pilate*, 223,
225, 234–5, 246, *Plymouth
Dock*, 145, *Pope's Villa*, 167,
Prince of Orange, 184–5, 228,
247, 324, *Rain, Steam and
Speed*, 257, 267–8, 336, *Ramsgate*, 332, *Regulus*, 219, 240,
319, 335, *Rembrandt's Daughter*, 218, 223, *Rheinfelden*,
267, *Richmond Hill*, 205, 206,
Rise of Carthage, 193, 260,
Rockets, 243, 265, *Rome from
Mt. Aventine*, 239, *Rome from
the Vatican*, 208, *Rosenau*,
243, *Sandbank with Gypsies*,
138, *Schaffhausen*, 125, 311,
Shade and Darkness, 281–2,
Shipwreck, 51, 116–17, 205,
Sketch of Cowes, 138, *Slavers*,
213, 223, 234, 243, 248, 265,
Snow Storm, 223, 252, 350,
Snow Storm, Avalanche etc.,
245, *Somer Hill*, 140, *Spithead*,
131, 136, *Staffa*, 228, 232,
248, 338, 350, *Sun of Venice*,
256, *Sun rising through Vapour*,
130, 332, *Temple of Jupiter
Panellenius (two)*, 184, 200,
206, 309, *Tenth Plague*, 98,
Thomson's Aeolian Harp, 136,
Tivoli, 202, *Transept of Ewenny Priory*, 42, *Ulysses deriding
Polyphemus*, 219, 223, 246–7,
315, 325, *Unpaid Bill*, 133,
Venus and Adonis, 333, *Vision
of Medea*, 219, 227, *Visit to
the Tomb*, 270, *Walhalla*, 256,
341, *War*, 251–2, 268, 270,
Warkworth Castle, 75, 91,
Watteau Study, 141, 227,
What you Will, 332, *Windsor
Castle*, 139, *Woman Reclining*,
232, *Wreck Buoy*, 338, *Wreckers*, 231, 239, 248, *Wreck of
Minotaur (Transport)*, 139,
205, *Yacht approaching Coast*,
265

Turner Mary, 11, 24, 38, 41, 45,
92–6, 111, 121–2, 291

Turner, Mary Ann, 13

Turner, William, 11, 23–7,
29, 45, 53, 94, 119, 151, 193,
199, 216–20, 225, 247, 291,
318, 330

Twickenham, 14, 203, 221, 262,
see also S. Lodge

Uwins, 219

Van der Velde, Adrian, 15, 51,
66

Van de Velde, Willem, 64, 93

Van Dyck, 232

Venice, 232, 235, 245, 256, 266,
332

Vernet, 64, 66, 307, 312

Waagen, Dr. G. F., 215

Walpole, H., 58

Walton, H., 12

Walton, I., 73

Wapping, 209, 330, 338

Ward, J., 82, 301, 323

Ward, W., 57

Warton, T., 78

Watteau, 65, 227, 233, 332

Watts, A., 27, 118

Wedgwood, J., 54, 58, 61

Wells, Clara, 21, 34, 38–9, 119,
128, 220, 224, 240, 254, 256,
342

Wells, W. F., 38–9, 55, 92, 115, 129, 240, 247

West, B., 52, 55, 93, 102–3, 110, 117, 118, 130, 132, 153, 195, 197, 201, 296, 299, 308, 324

Westall, R., 82, 130, 304, 317

Westmacott, R., 125, 241, 332

Whales, 254, 259, 265, 336

Wheatley, F., 12, 44, 84, 304

Wickliffe, 183

Wilkie, 117, 125, 131, 163, 209, 225, 244, 268, 272, 320–22

Williams, T., 147, 262, 338

Wilson, 40, 44, 50, 57, 66–8, 76, 83, 93, 98, 101, 112, 116, 140, 176, 198, 209, 296, 298, 302, 309, 342–6

Winckelmann, 84, 178

Wolcot, Dr., 195, 330, 345

Woodforde, 55

Woollett, W., 83, 209

Woolner, 242

Wright, J., 90, 93, 309

Wyatt, 103–4, 110, 118, 129, 309, 332

Yarnold, 352

Young, E., 73, 84, 349

Zoffany, 198

Zuccarelli, 57, 66, 195, 328